The rough guide to
MOROCCO

W9-DFI-641

=The=
rough
guides

Other Rough Guides available include:
TUNISIA, FRANCE, SPAIN, PORTUGAL, GREECE, PERU, MEXICO, AMSTERDAM & HOLLAND and **YUGOSLAVIA.**

Forthcoming
KENYA, ITALY, EASTERN EUROPE, CHINA, PARIS and **NEW YORK**

Series Editor

MARK ELLINGHAM

Thanks

    – above all – to Nat, who read, edited and endured, even travelled, through most of these pages. Also for writing, informing, encouraging and otherwise achieving this book to: Jutta Bornholdt, Jill Denton, Donald Duff, Esteban y Pilar, John Fisher, Peggy and Clifford Jansz, Michelle de Larrabeiti, Lucinda Montefiore, Peter Morris, Dan Richardson, Nick Stone, Ursula Stone, Jeremy Wright; to my mother, Barbara Ellingham, who helped sit this one out in all sorts of ways; and to the countless Moroccan friends and acquaintances who took time to share their interest.

    We would like in particular to express gratitude to Mr Hajouji of the Moroccan Tourist Board in London for considerably smoothing the way.

Acknowledgments

We are grateful to Peter Owen for permission to reprint Part X of *Points in Time* by Paul Bowles, © Paul Bowles; to Marion Boyars for 'The unseen' from Elias Canetti's *The Voices of Marrakesh*, translation © Marion Boyars; and to John Hatt for the extract from Walter Harris's *Morocco that Was*.

First published in 1985
Reprinted with updatings 1986, 1987
by Routledge & Kegan Paul plc
11 New Fetter Lane
London EC4P 4EE

Published in the USA by
Routledge & Kegan Paul Inc
in association with Methuen Inc
29 West 35th Street, New York, NY 10001

© 1985, 1986.

Set in Linotron Helvetica and Sabon
by Input Typesetting Ltd, London
and printed in Great Britain
by Cox & Wyman Ltd,
Reading, Berkshire

© Mark Ellingham, 1985

Library of Congress Cataloging in Publication Data

Ellingham, Mark
  The rough guide to Morocco.
  (The Rough guides)
  Includes index.
  1. Morocco—Description and travel—Guide-books.
I. McVeigh, Shaun. II. Title. III. Series.
DT304.E44 1985   916.4'045   85–1940

ISBN 0–7102–0153–2

The rough guide to
MOROCCO

Written and researched by
MARK ELLINGHAM AND SHAUN McVEIGH

With additional accounts by
Jill Denton, Dan Richardson, Peter Morris and
Jutta Bornholdt

Maps by
Mark Coates

Edited by
MARK ELLINGHAM

Routledge & Kegan Paul
London and New York

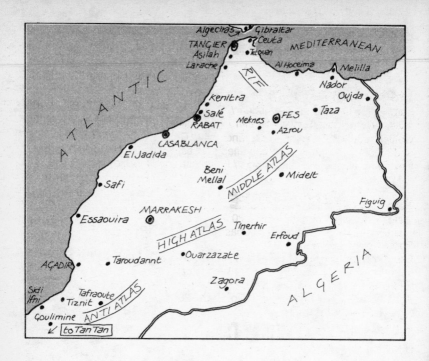

CONTENTS

You tell me you are going to Fes.
Now, if you say you are going to Fes,
That means you are not going.
But I happen to know that you are going to Fes.
Why have you lied to me, you who are my friend?

– MOROCCAN SAYING
(quoted in Paul Bowles's
The Spider's House).

Part one
BASICS

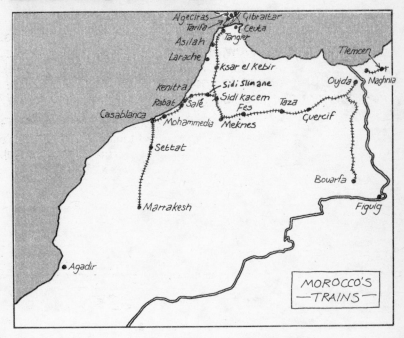

MOROCCO'S
—TRAINS—

MOROCCO: WHERE TO GO – AND WHEN

Just an hour by ferry from Spain and Western Europe, Morocco is a Mediterranean and Atlantic country, increasingly industrialised and urban-based. It was until 1956 a French and Spanish Protectorate; French is still widely spoken and Casablanca, its principal city, looks like nowhere so much as Marseilles. Yet, coming here for the first time, you are likely to be struck most by its differences, and what appears, at least on the surface, a totally unfamiliar society. For Morocco is above all an Arab and Islamic nation – a kingdom whose rulers once controlled an empire stretching from Senegal to Northern Spain, and from the C16 to the present maintained an almost total isolation from the West. And it is too, a part of Africa and the developing Third World. In the mountains that make up over a third of its land mass, it is possible to draw up tribal maps of the Berber populations; in the south the last range, the Anti-Atlas, gives way to the pre-Sahara.

Coming to terms with this – and **adapting** to the different concepts of time and of purpose – is important. Tourism is long established in Morocco but it remains an ambivalent experience: what is interesting and picturesque is all too often someone else's misery. And there is also the initially startling realisation that Morocco has definite attitudes towards *you*. The northern cities, and to a lesser extent the south, all have their share of hustlers, often highly sophisticated in their psychological technique – 'Are you a racist?', they will fire at Western sensibilities if you decline their services. Universal too, are the tales of adoption by 'students', eager to practise their English and show you around town: a process which may take a day, may be thoroughly amicable in tone, but may also end with you lost in some back alley and paying to be shown the way home. It isn't an attractive notion to feel yourself outside, or at best irrelevant, to local life; for a while, however, you have to adopt it. Over half the Moroccan population is unemployed, nearly two-thirds live below the poverty line, and pride has become a flexible virtue. Likewise, if anyone needs reminding that it's still a man's world, Morocco provides the proof. There is absolutely no tradition of a woman's personal autonomy: independent means available and, reinforced by 'liberated' Western images, harassment can be virtually constant. For this reason, many women choose to travel with at least one man (see p. 23).

These matters stated, however, you can begin seeing the country as more than a succession of struggles – which, of course, it is. Perhaps most surprising is the intensity of life, quite at odds with Western preconceptions of Orientalism. A week in Morocco feels like a month, a month like three, and, outsider though you are, it is difficult to go for long without meeting, talking and coming upon real and incredibly open hospitality. Don't get stuck into branding all Moroccans who approach as hustlers either – too many travellers do, and end up just as isolated from the people as the coach-shuttled and air-conditioned package tourists. And be prepared to try some of the more unusual routes, described in the guide but not part of the standard 'tourist circuits'. In the Atlas mountains, especially, you can have a great time, and travel here still feels a little like exploration.

Physically, the country divides into four basic zones: the **coast**; the great **cities** of the plains; the **Rif** and **Atlas** mountains; and the oases and desert of the **pre-Sahara**. With two or three weeks – even two or three months – you can't expect to cover all of this, though it is quite easy (and strongly recommended) to take in something of each aspect. The mountains, at all events, you are unlikely to miss. The three ranges of the Atlas, with the Rif a kind of extension in the north, cut right across the interior – physical and historical barriers, and inhabited for the most part by the indigenous Moroccan **Berbers**. Contrary to most preconceptions, it is actually the Berbers who make up the bulk of the population: only around 10 per cent of Moroccans are 'pure' Arabs, although with the shift to the industrialised cities such distinctions are becoming less and less relevant.

The attractions of each of the individual regions are discussed in the chapter introductions. Broadly, though, **the coast** is best enjoyed in the north at either **Tangier**, **Larache** or **Saidia**, in the south at **El Jadida** or **Essaouira**. If you're flying to Morocco, you're quite likely to arrive at **Agadir**, centre of the Moroccan tourist industry: this is perfectly functional but you'll probably want to move fairly swiftly out. **Inland** – where the real interest of Morocco is concentrated – the outstanding cities are **Fes** and **Marrakesh**. The main Imperial Capitals of the country's various dynasties, these are almost unique in the Arab world for the chance to witness a city-life still in large part medieval. Fes, in terms of monuments, is the highlight, though Marrakesh, the beginning of the south, has the most enduring excitement. In the **High Atlas**, the most beautiful and the most easily accessible of the mountain ranges, hiking is becoming increasingly popular. The area around **Mount Toubkal**, the highest peak in North Africa, is the centre – and well worth considering even if you've never previously done any mountain walking (you don't need to climb). More adventurously, you might take to some of the **piste** roads, dramatic and switchbacking mountain tracks – either by car or by relying on the local Berber transit-trucks. In the **pre-Sahara**, too, there's an obvious excitement in the routes, although these are mostly covered by standard local buses and collective (*grand*) taxis. The **oases** here, beautiful in themselves, share with parts of the Atlas a bizarre and fabulous mud (or *pisé*) architecture: the **kasbahs** and **ksour**, whose turrets and multi-patterned walls, built like Gothic castles, are now slowly crumbling back into the earth.

As far as **climate** goes, spring and winter are the traditional 'seasons' for Moroccan travel, though there's nothing to stop you travelling anywhere in the country even in July or August. Ideally, however, you'll want to visit the south – or at least the desert routes – outside **midsummer**: most of the day it's far too hot there for casual exploration, and although buses leave early (around 4–5 a.m.) you're inevitably handicapped unless you have a car. **Winter** is perfect for Marrakesh and for the desert, but is also correspondingly popular – drawing richer, older and mainly French tourists. **Spring**, which comes late (April–May) by European standards, is probably the best overall time, with a summer-like climate in the south and in the mountains, and water warm enough for swimming on both Mediterranean and Atlantic coasts. If you plan to explore the **mountains** the only practicable time is really April–October: through the winter, the High Atlas and Rif are usually snow-covered and accessible only for skiers or serious expeditions.

For details of **festivals** – and why the month of **Ramadan** is such a good time to travel – see p. 19.

AVERAGE TEMPERATURES

	JAN	FEB	MAR	APR	MAY	JUN	JUL	AUG	SEP	OCT	NOV	DEC
AGADIR	69	70	72	75	76	78	80	79	79	78	76	69
AL HOCEIMA	61	62	65	67	72	78	83	85	81	74	69	63
CASABLANCA	63	63	66	68	72	75	81	81	80	77	68	64
ESSAOUIRA	64	64	64	66	68	68	72	70	70	70	68	66
FES	61	63	66	72	79	88	97	97	90	81	66	61
MARRAKESH	66	66	73	79	84	91	102	101	91	82	70	66
MEKNES	59	61	64	70	74	84	93	93	86	79	66	61
OUARZAZATE	63	67	73	80	86	96	102	100	91	80	70	62
RABAT	63	64	66	70	73	77	82	82	81	77	68	64
TANGIER	59	61	62	66	72	77	80	82	79	73	64	61
TAROUDANNT	72	73	79	81	86	90	99	100	95	90	77	72
ZAGORA	69	73	78	86	93	102	108	106	97	86	78	70

Note that these are all very much average temperatures: Zagora often hits 120° at midday in midsummer, whilst in the Rif and High Atlas mountains winters can be literally freezing.

GETTING THERE

Flights from Britain

Flying, the fastest way of getting out to Morocco, is rapidly becoming the cheapest too, if you're prepared to accept the time limits imposed by **charter deals**. **From London**, you have two main options: either to fly direct to Morocco (usually Agadir or Tangier) or to go to Spain (ideally, Malaga or Almeria) or Gibraltar and then on by ferry from there. Out of season, you may find return flights to **Tangier** or **Agadir** falling as low as £90–100; in midsummer, however, or at Christmas or Easter, they're sparse on the ground and you might have to pay 50 per cent more than this – if you can get a ticket. Flights to Spain, and **Malaga** particularly, are usually easier to come by, and booking at the last minute can come down to £70–80 – sometimes even less. **Gibraltar**, with low season flights at around £85 (summer and Christmas about £125) return, is also a good standby. For all these flights, the widest listings are to be found in the classified travel sections of the London weekly magazines *Time Out* and *LAM* or, nationally, in the *Sunday Times*, *Observer* and *Private Eye*. *Gibraltar Travel Ltd* (24 New Broadway, London W5; 01 579 0307) are a reliable source of Gibraltar flights. *STA* (74 Old Brompton Rd, London SW7; 01 581 1022) *USIT* (52 Grosvenor Gdns, London SW1; 01 730 6525) and *WST* (37 Store St, London WC1; 01 580 7733) are reliable **student/youth** orientated agents who may be able to offer special discounts on certain flights.

For greater flexibility, and longer period returns, a **scheduled flight** can sometimes be worth the extra money. *Royal Air Maroc*, the national airline of Morocco, offer reasonably competitive fares to Tangier, Casablanca, Marrakesh and Agadir: though for their reductions you need to book 14 days in advance and specify a date of return. For prices (Tangier from around £145; Marrakesh from £185) contact their office at 174 Regent St, London W1 (01 439 8854), or talk to any travel agent – they can all arrange scheduled deals.

Lastly, you might want to consider taking an all-in **package deal**, with a 1/2 week return flight and hotel accommodation. Numerous operators cover Tangier and Agadir, and a few (mainly more upmarket) also offer Fes, Rabat and Marrakesh. Local travel agents can again advise on these, and sometimes offer knock-down holidays (or flights only) if they still have space 2-3 weeks before departure, or you can get a full list of operators from the *Moroccan National Tourist Board* (in Britain at 174 Regent St, London W1, 01 437 0073: but see p. 11 for other addresses). Most of the major holiday operators (*Thomas Cook, Thomson, Sovereign*, etc.) have flights leaving from both London and **Manchester**. *Joe Walsh Tours* (01 760991) specialise in flights from **Dublin**.

If you have the money, two Moroccan **specialists** who can arrange flights and accommodation around particular needs are *Creative Leisure* (Suite 25–30, 12/13 Henrietta St, London WC2; 01 836 2916) and *Morocco Bound* (35/36 Great Marlborough St, London W1: 01 734 0019).

Flights from North America

From the US and Canada it usually works out cheaper to fly to **London** – or **Madrid** and **Malaga** – rather than going directly to Morocco. *Royal Air Maroc*, however, fly **from New York** to Tangier, Rabat and Casablanca, and they sometimes have promotional fares which include coupons for use either on domestic flights within Morocco or for links between New York and various American or Canadian cities. These can make the standard Apex fares of around $580 low season, $680 high, considerably more attractive. For details, contact any of the *RAM* offices: in New York at 666 Fifth Ave. (212 974-3845), in Chicago at 8 South Michigan Av., Suite 700 (312 782-7956), or in Montreal at 1000 Sherbrooke, Suite 1907 (285-1687).

Students can get a 20 per cent discount on RAM fares by booking direct through one of these offices rather than through an agent.

Overland

By train, coach or car it's a minimum three-day journey from London to Morocco. However, if you're interested in taking in something of France or Spain en route, or even coming the other way via Italy, Tunisia and Algeria, there are obvious attractions. Costs, unless you're hitching, aren't often among them – though for anyone under 26 there are the usual train reductions on Inter-Rail and Transalpino/Eurotrain.

By train

Transalpino/Eurotrain tickets are about 35 per cent below standard rail prices, and are available from London (or any British or European city) to Tangier, Rabat and Casablanca. Current costs for the trip from London to Tangier, inclusive of the ferry across from Algeciras, are £62 single, £122 return. The ticket is valid on most European trains (though some Express services have a surcharge) and allows any number of stopovers along your specified route. With a Moroccan destination, the ticket is valid for six months (as opposed to the usual two). You can book through most student travel agencies or through any of Transalpino or Eurotrain's *regional offices* (personally or by post). Addresses include; TRANSALPINO: London (71/75 Buckingham Palace Rd, SW1; 01 834 9656), Liverpool (3 Myrtle Parade, Myrtle St; 708 9462), Glasgow (150 West George St; 333 9177), Belfast (24 Lombard St; 248 823) and Dublin (24 Talbot St; 723 825); EUROTRAIN: London (52 Grosvenor Gdns, SW1; 01 730 8111) and Oxford (13 High St; 242067) and others.

Inter-Rail is a similar system to Transalpino and covers the same countries (Morocco and all of Europe). Its great advantage is cost (currently £122) and flexibility: an *Inter-Rail card* is valid for one month, during which time you have unlimited free rail travel and half-price reductions on most ferries (including those from Spain to Morocco). Although the Moroccan rail system is not very extensive (see the map at the front of this section), this will still allow you a satisfying fortnight's circuit, taking in Tangier, Rabat, Fes, Meknes and Marrakesh. If you're adventurous, and into concerted travel, it will also set you well on the way to completing the '**Maghreb loop**': coming down to Morocco through Spain, and then paying for trains through Algeria and Tunisia before regaining Inter-Rail territory in Italy. The practicalities of this route are outlined on p. 338. Inter-Rail cards are again available through most travel agents and all of Transalpino's offices, as well as major British Rail 'travel centres'. Hidden costs are occasional supplements, and 50 per cent of the fares between the British station you set out at/return to and the channel ports.

North Americans are not officially valid for Inter-Rail – though it's often possible to buy a pass all the same – and have a separate system called **Eurail**. The *Eurail Youth Pass*, which is the under-26 equivalent of Inter-Rail, is slightly more expensive and it doesn't include trains in Morocco (though it does get you down there through Spain). Cost for one month is currently $225, for two months $285. The pass can be bought from American travel agents before coming to Europe, or in London, among other outlets, from *STA* (74 Old Brompton Rd, SW7; 01 581 7733).

Standard rail tickets to Moroccan destinations can be bought from London's Victoria railway station (which is where Spain/Morocco-bound trains leave), or from *Thomas Cook* and other major travel agents.

By coach

On **coaches** there are no age restrictions. The journey to **Algeciras**, however, which is as far as you can go direct from London, is something of an endurance test – 46 hrs at the inside with a handful of stops at service stations along the way.

There are joint British and Spanish operators – *Euroways* and *Iberbus* – and these run two coaches a week out of season, rising to four a week from April to September. They are not, however, especially cheap; with a standard single from London-Algeciras running at about £80 (10 per cent reduction for students/under 26. For details contact *Euroways* London office (01 730 8235) or any large travel agent, either in Britain or Spain (where *Iberbus* are sometimes known as *Linebus*).

By coach too, or rather by converted double decker bus, the London based company *Top Deck* run **tours** down to and through Morocco. These are well established, and not a bad way to travel if you're happy with a group trip – young and often Australian dominated. For details on their two main itineraries – five weeks through Spain, Portugal and Morocco, or seven weeks taking in the

Algerian Sahara, Tunisia and Italy – they can be contacted at 64-65 Kenway Rd, London SW5 (01 373 5095), or you can book through *STA* and other youth/student travel firms.

Driving and hitching

If you plan to **drive** down to Morocco through Spain and France, you'll probably want to set aside at least 4-5 days for travel at either end: the 46hr coaches, detailed above, are virtually non-stop with two alternating drivers. Deciding on the best **route** is difficult. Most people seem to use the regular *Sealink* ferries over from Dover or Folkestone to Calais or Boulogne, and then head south **via Paris**. With Spain and Morocco as your main aim, though, you might do better by avoiding Paris altogether and following the coast road down to San Sebastian **via Nantes** and Bordeaux. This latter route is easier joined by using the slightly longer, more expensive ferries over from Portsmouth to Cherbourg or St Malo, or Plymouth to Roscoff. Or, at slightly greater expense, you can miss out France altogether by taking the **car and passenger ferry** from **Plymouth** to **Santander:** this runs twice weekly most of the year (except January); for details and prices phone *Brittany Ferries* in Plymouth (0752 21321). There is also a weekly **ferry** direct from **Sète** in France to **Tangier** (14hrs), but if you want to get on this you'll have to book several months in advance. Details from *Comanav*, SNCM, 12 Rue Godot de Mauroy, Paris (Tel. 1 2666 6019).

Hitching, you'll do well to buy a coach and ferry ticket to the furthest point south you can afford. Getting from London to **Rouen**, say, or **Tours**, doesn't cost a lot more than you'd have to spend on the ferry across from any of the channel ports, and will save a lot of potential time (and money) stuck outside Paris or Boulogne. Hitching in France *is* notoriously bad, though not quite so desperate as people sometimes make out. In Spain, lifts generally improve but for women hitchers (alone or together) risks, and harassment generally, are more overt. From the north virtually all roads converge on Madrid: from there on you have two main choices of **routes** to the Algeciras ferries: **via Merida**, **Sevilla** and **Cadiz**, or across La Mancha to **Jaen**, **Granada** and **Malaga**. There's

not a lot to choose between these in hitching terms, though for me the chance to stop off at Granada (and the Alhambra palace) wins out. In fact if you've time and inclination, there are few better ways to approach Morocco than after completing a circuit of the three great Moorish cities of southern Spain – Granada, Cordoba and Sevilla.

Hitching **back from Morocco**, starting at the car ferry in **Ceuta** is by far your best bet. It's quite possible you'll get a lift the whole way back to Britain from there. Other useful points to ask around are the campsites at **Fes** and **Martil** (near Tetouan), both traditional last stops.

The Spain-Morocco ferries

Virtually all overland travellers take one of the ferries over **from Algeciras:** either to Tangier (2½hrs) or to Ceuta (1½hrs). **Tangier** is on the whole a better idea if you're travelling by local transport. For one, it's actually in Morocco – Ceuta is a Spanish enclave – and it is also on the train line with connections to Fes, Meknes and Rabat. In summer there are three or four crossings daily (dropping to one or two in winter); fare for deck class (*turista B*) is around £8 one way, for an average sized car £26, a motorbike £8. To **Ceuta** there are much more regular crossings (twelve a day in season, eight out), an advantage if you're taking a car since you might have to wait a while for a place to Tangier. By car, too, Ceuta (see p. 53) is in easy reach of the Moroccan border and, beyond, of Tetouan and Chaouen; on foot all this takes time and effort, with local buses and taxis, while Tetouan itself (see p. 54) can be a slightly daunting place to start out in Morocco. You might well, however, want to use this crossing coming back to Spain – in reverse it works a lot smoother. Costs to Ceuta are approximately £5 one way *turista*, £18 for a car, £4 for a motorbike. **Tickets** for either crossing can be bought from any of the agents in Algeciras (there are dozens along the front – and the road from Malaga) or from the ferry terminal building.

In summer, a useful alternative to the Algeciras ferries are the **hydrofoils to Tangier:** three times daily from **Tarifa** (½hr), and once each from **Algeciras** (1hr) and **Gibraltar** (1hr). These are considerably more straightforward than the ferries – which always seem to leave an hour late and lose the best part of another in embarkation and customs. Tarifa is 40 minutes by bus from Algeciras (buses leaving regularly, up until around 7pm, from the main station, back from the seafront by the Hotel Octavio), and a pleasant little town to stay the night en route (try the *Hostal Villanueva*, or the unnamed *pension* by the church). All the hydrofoils are operated by a company called *Transtour* and **tickets** can be bought either at points of embarkation or in advance from agents in Algeciras (a good idea in midseason). One-way fares are around £8 from Tarifa or Algeciras, £12 from Gibraltar; passengers only. The hydrofoils don't run in rough weather, nor on Sundays.

There is also an ordinary **ferry** from **Gibraltar to Tangier** – the *Mons Calpe* operated by *Bland Line* (Cloister Building, Gibraltar; Tel. 79 200). This currently runs on Wednesdays and Fridays only (leaving Gibraltar at 6pm, and arriving in Tangier at 8pm) though services may increase with the opening of the Spain-Gibraltar border. Fares are around £16 a passenger, £30 for a car and £16 for a motorbike.

Melilla (see p. 80), the other Spanish enclave in Morocco, is a third possible arrival point: there are ferries over from **Malaga** and **Almeria**, and once there you're well poised for Taza and Fes – or for Algeria. Both ferries are year-round though there's a slight reduction in services from 1 October to 19 December. Normally, departures are daily from Malaga (usually at 11.30am, arriving Melilla at 8pm), daily except Sundays from Almeria (leaving 11.30pm, arriving Melilla 8am). Both ferries are operated by *Transmediterranea* and **tickets** available at travel agents or embarkation points: approximate fares for either crossing are £9 one way for a seat (*Butaca* class), £32 for a car, £7 for a motorbike.

RED TAPE AND VISAS

If you have a **British, North American, Australian, New Zealand** or any **Scandinavian** passport, you need no visa to enter Morocco for up to 90 days. **Dutch** or **Belgian** citizens, however, do need a visa due to new restrictions placed on Moroccans entering Holland. This cannot be obtained at the frontier and must be applied for at a Moroccan consulate – it normally takes 48hrs to process and remains valid for one month. Moroccan **consulates** include:

Amsterdam: Oranje Nassaulaan 1-1075 (736 215).

London: 40 Queens Gate Gdns, SW7 (01 584 8827).

Malaga: Av. de Andalucia 63 (329 962).

A few additional points. **Temporary passports**, including British Visitors' Passes, are not valid for entry – nor for getting a visa. Official Moroccan policy, too, forbids entry to anyone with an **Israeli** or **South African stamp** – if you have one it's worth getting a new passport, though you could just chance your luck. Less tangibly, the Moroccans also have a policy of discouraging **hippies**: if you think you look like one, try not to – and if you're turned back, borrow some clothes, hide your hair and try again when a new official comes on duty. At times of tension, too, the description '**journalist**' in your passport may lead to you being refused entry – even routinely some frontier officials pay close attention to this. If you think you may have trouble, Tangier is usually the best entry point – certainly not Ceuta or Melilla, which are occasionally closed completely.

Renewing a visa, or extending your 90 days, you have to go to the *gendarmerie* headquarters in the nearest large town to where you're staying. This should be fairly routine, though you will need to produce evidence that you can support yourself without working – so keep any bank exchange slips.

COSTS, MONEY AND BANKS

Despite recent inflation, one of Morocco's more prosaic attractions lies in its cheapness – in fact, if the Moroccan currency (the *Dirham*) wasn't artificially fixed everything would be absurdly cheap. As it is, **accommo-**

dation runs from around a £1 a night in a basic unclassified hotel, and £12 buys a double poolside room in a 4-star palace. The price of a **meal** can vary enormously, but the basic Moroccan staple of soup (usually the bean-based *harira*), *brochettes* (kebabs) and dates can be as little as 50-60p. More substantial Moroccan meals can be had for £1 and European-style meals in restaurants from around £3. **Drink** is really the only thing that compares unfavourably with Southern European prices: a bottle of Moroccan wine costs upwards of £2.50 and a small glass of beer at least 60p – considerably more in the smarter hotels which can sometimes be the only places serving alcohol. Beyond this, your only major outlay will be **transport** – expensive if you're hiring a car (£120 a week plus petrol) but quite reasonable by local means. The 475km trek from Fes to Marrakesh, for instance, costs around £5 by bus, or perhaps £8 if you use the faster, collective taxis.

To some extent, all of these things are affected by **where you are and when**. Inevitably, the big **cities** and **tourist regions** (Agadir especially) are going to be more expensive, and bottom-line hotel prices here can drift up to around £3 a night for a double. In more **remote parts** of the country, too, where all goods have to be brought in from some distance and where transport (often only trucks or landrovers) needs to be bargained, prices can be even more inflated; this goes particularly for the popular hiking region of Mount Toubkal. All in all, though, if you stay in the cheaper hotels (or camp), if you eat local food, and if you're sharing costs and rooms with another person, £35 a week would be enough to survive. On £50-60 you could actually be living quite well, and with £150 a week between two you'd be into near luxury.

Hidden costs in Morocco are that you'll almost certainly end up buying a few things – rugs, blankets, leather and jewellery are all outstanding – and that you'll be confronting real poverty. As a tourist, you're not going to solve any great problems, but with labourers' wages at around £2 a day, and less than half the population in permanent employment, even a small tip to a guide can make a lot of difference to individual family life. For Moroccans, giving money and goods is a natural function – and

a requirement of Islam. For tourists, by definition rich, begging demands at least some response.

Morocco's basic unit of **currency** is the **dirham** (*Dhm*), which is divided into *centimes* (100). Confusingly though, outside the cities money is frequently expressed in terms of *francs* (100 francs = 1 dirham) or even *pesetas* or *reales* (also usually 100 to the dirham). It is possible to buy a small amount of dirhams at the bank exchange desks in the Algeciras ferry terminal, but the currency is basically not exchangable outside Morocco, and there are in any case regulations against taking dirhams out of the country. When you're nearing the end of your stay it's best to get down to as little Moroccan money as possible.

Contrary to popular myths about Arab banking systems, Morocco's **banks** are efficient, and well distributed around the country. All charge the same commission and exchange rates, and there is little difference in services offered. If you're using a chequebook and **Eurocheque** card, however, you'll find the *SGMB* (*Société Générale Marocaine de Banques*) in the large cities the most likely to deal with them; with **Visa** or **Access** cards always look for the *Banque Crédit du Maroc*; **American Express** are represented by the *Voyages Schwarz* agency in Tangier, Casablanca, Rabat, Marrakesh and Agadir. In the **south**, beyond Marrakesh, you will often find the only bank is the *Banque Populaire*, who are generally limited to changing cash or travellers' cheques. **Banking hours** are normally Mon-Fri 8.30-11.30am & 3-5.30pm, though in the month of Ramadan (see p.19) they open only from 8.30-2pm. Outside these hours, you can usually exchange cash or travellers' cheques at the larger hotels and at travel agents or shops aimed at tourists (who will themselves accept almost any form of payment for goods – paper, plastic money . . . what do you have?). There is nothing to be gained by changing money on the street – or in shops – unless you really need to.

As to how to bring your money in, some **cash** (pounds, pesetas or dollars) and **travellers' cheques** are useful. Also worth considering are post office **International Giro Cheques**, which work in a similar way to ordinary bank cheques except that you cash them through post offices. In Morocco there are many more post offices than banks. Access to an **emergency source** of money – whether a credit card, or an arrangement with your bank or family to send money out if phoned – is also valuable. Despite the number of travellers' stories, very few people lose (or are conned out of) all their money in Morocco – but it does of course happen. In the last resort, your **consulate** are dutybound to repatriate you, however much they may say they can't help, but they will never lend you money to continue a holiday. Ever.

HEALTH

No **inoculations** are officially required for Morocco but it's wise to come at least with up-to-date typhoid-cholera, tetanus and polio. Anti-malarial pills, too, are often advised, and a good precaution if you're travelling to the south; these can be taken either daily or weekly – the former, though more of a nuisance, are less easy to forget completely. It is also possible to have gamma-globulin injections against hepatitis, though this is worth discussing with your doctor. If you are travelling for some time they may even make you more vulnerable, since the serum remains active only for three to four weeks.

Whatever, a general **travel insurance** scheme is well worth the money – in Britain you can take them out at almost any bank or travel agent for around £12 a month and this covers your money and baggage too. If you need to claim, you'll have to present all bills, including receipts from the *pharmacie*, and including a letter from the local police if you report anything as being stolen. Addresses of English-speaking (or, more often, French-speaking) **doctors** can be obtained from tourist offices, large hotels or your consulate. For most minor complaints, though, you can just go along to a **pharmacie**. Moroccan pharmacists are well trained and dispense a wide range of drugs, including many normally on prescription in Britain or North America. If they feel you need a full diagnosis, they can usually recommend a doctor – sometimes working on the premises. Medicines in Morocco, however, are expensive – most are imported from France – and it's a good idea to bring out a few **basics** with you. Some kind of pills for diarrhoea head most people's list – at some stage you're almost bound to get an attack. Mosquitoes can be a problem too, especially if you're camping, though personally I've never been bitten outside of Tangier.

One particular hazard in the south is **bilharzia**, which is said to infest most of the river valleys and oases. Nobody agrees on how widespread it is, but avoidance of all contact with oasis water is probably a wise precaution. Ordinary **tapwater** is also slightly suspect in parts of the south and it's better generally to stick to bottled mineral waters; in the northern cities tap water is quite drinkable, if a little unpleasant.

INFORMATION, LOCAL GUIDES AND MAPS

This book apart, the most ready (and obvious) source of information on Morocco are the country's **tourist board** (the *ONMT*), their offices and *Syndicats d'Initiatives* throughout Morocco, and local, often self-appointed **guides**.

The **ONMT** maintain general information offices in most major capitals, where you can pick up various pamphlets and lists. Most useful of these – indeed the one thing really worth calling in for – is their complete **list of officially graded hotels**, along with an up-to-date sheet detailing 'maximum hotel rates'. We've included numerous small hotels in this book that aren't classified in the ONMT book, and many more that are, but there may be times you'll find it useful to check out facilities or phone numbers. Pick up, too, the ONMT's series of **pamphlets** on **Tangier, Rabat-Salé, Casablanca, Fes, Marrakesh** and **Agadir**. Each of these have large and colourful maps printed on the reverse: the ones we've printed are generally more functional but these, being bigger and often covering a wider area, are useful complements. ONMT **addresses abroad** include:

London: 174 Regent St, W1 (01 437 0013/0074).

New York: 597 Fifth Av, NY 10017 (212 421 5771/5772).

Chicago: 6 South Michigan Av, C.I. 60603 (312 782 3413).

Montreal: 114 place Bonaventure, Post Box 751 (878 9536/9537).

Amsterdam: Leidsestraat 59 (25 1683).

Stockholm: 54 Sturegatan (62 3272).

In Morocco itself there's either a **Syndicat** or **ONMT** office in all towns of any size and interest – often both; addresses are detailed in the relevant sections of the guide. Occasionally they can supply you with particular local maps and they can of course try to help you out with specific queries. Their main use, though, is in fixing you up with an officially recognised guide.

Official guides, whom you pay on a fixed rate for a half or full day, can provide an interesting and sometimes very entertaining introduction to a city – particularly useful with the huge and initially confusing Medinas (or 'old towns') of Fes and Marrakesh. Their advantage over unofficial guides or 'students', who offer (or more often, force) their services in the street, is that they won't rip you off. If you are short on time or confidence, they ensure you get to see all the sights that you intended, and at the end of a tour take you back to your hotel or any arranged point and accept the standard rate – at present 25dhs for a half day, 45dhs for a full one, split between as many people as you want. Even in Fes, however, a guide of any kind is far from essential. If you don't mind getting lost, you can work your way round the maze of the old towns (in Fes's case, three distinct Medinas) and *souks* (market/craft quarters) . . . in time.

Unofficial guides – or '**students**' or '**friends**' – are much warned against in Morocco, and many are undoubtedly straight hustlers, at best out to gain commission from you buying goods (something *all* guides are into, to some

extent), at worst out for a straight piece of banditry (see p. 3). Just as many, however, are exactly what they claim to be – if possibly a little desperate in looking for a way to live – and, as they point out, will often undercut official guides and show you more interesting things. Whether you take someone on, and very young kids can be good if elder brothers don't materialise, is something you just have to develop a feel for. Never, at any rate, allow yourself to be bullied into accepting someone as a guide whom you don't feel easy with – there's no shortage of people. If you're unsure, a good way to make up your mind is to suggest drinking a mint tea together: 'take your time' is a favourite Moroccan phrase, and there's no reason why you shouldn't use it. Official Moroccan guides, incidentally, can identify themselves by a large brass-coloured 'sherrif's badge'.

Maps of Moroccan **cities**, beyond those we've printed and the ones you can get for free from the ONMT, are not particularly worthwhile. The most authoritative series, the **Plan-Guides** published by *Editions Gauthey*, look impressive but are next to no use once you're trying to find your way around the lanes of a Medina. What you will probably want, though, is a good **roadmap** of Morocco. The most accurate, when it's not out of print, is the *Michelin* (sheet 169); otherwise settle for the widely available *Kummerley & Frey*; both are 1:1,000,000. If you plan to do any hiking, or serious *piste*-driving, you might also want to get hold of one or more of the **Moroccan Survey sheets**, printed with names in French (rather than Arabic) and generally 1:50,000 or 1:100,000. The most interesting of these, covering all the main hiking areas of the Middle and High Atlas, can be obtained in Britain from either *West Col Productions* (Goring, Reading, Berks) or from the London map shop *McCarta* (122 Kings Cross Rd, WC1; 01 278 8278).

GETTING AROUND

Buses
The basic method of getting around Morocco is by **bus**, and with a little patience you can reach 95 per cent of the towns, villages and sites mentioned in

this guide on standard routes. There is a slight confusion, however, in the variety of different coach lines and companies. What you find, in every town of any size, is a *CTM* service (the national company) and a number of other lines, privately owned and operated. The **CTM** coaches are always the most comfortable and reliable, running to a fixed schedule and generally leaving on time; they are also, on average, 10-15 per cent more expensive. **Private lines** range between big companies like *SATAS* (who operate widely in the south and are usually up to CTM standards) and tiny one-bus outfits who leave at no specified times, waiting until there are enough passengers on board to justify a trip. In many of the larger cities – Rabat and Marrakesh, for example – the CTM and private lines share a single **terminal**, and you can find out the most useful departure and routes by wandering around the various windows. At others there may be two or more separate terminals (you will find these detailed in the main section of the guide), or there may be no choice anyway. On the more popular routes, like Fes to Marrakesh, or some in the south, try to buy **tickets** in advance; this may not always be possible and there may be a small charge, but it is always worth asking. Sometimes, at **small towns** along major routes, buses arrive and leave full, and you may find it difficult to get on at all; this can seem a big problem at the time but it's usually possible to get round it by taking a local bus or taxi another stage, or waiting for a bus which actually starts from the town. Approximate times of bus (and train) journeys are given in the *Travel Details* at the end of each chapter.

As a complement to buses, you'll probably want at times to use **grands taxis** – big Peugeots or Mercedes which carry six passengers (four in the back, two in the front) along specific routes. These work out 20-40 per cent more expensive than standard bus fares but they have two great advantages: the first is speed (they're often twice as fast), the second, frequency. On the most popular routes, there are *grands taxis* leaving more or less continuously through the day, so you don't have to worry about timetables. You just turn up at the terminal (these again are detailed, city by city) and ask for a *place* to a specific destination: as soon as six (or if you're willing to pay extra, four or five) people are gathered, it leaves. On the whole you don't have to bargain over the **price** – this is fixed for all passengers – though

you have to be sure that you're not paying for *une course*, the whole taxi. If you want to do a specific route or excursion, it is of course possible to hire a *grand taxi* individually (or for a group) but you'll have to haggle hard before getting down to a realistic level.

Petits taxis – usually Fiats or Simcas – are limited to journeys within cities, and to taking three passengers. Officially, all of these have meters, but in practice you're unlikely to find one that works (at least for tourists) outside the capital, Rabat. It is then a matter of bargaining a price – either before you get in (wise to start off with) or by simply presenting the right sum when you get out. *Petit taxi* **fares** range enormously. In Marrakesh and Agadir they can often be excessive – a standard 10dhs for what are really 5-6dh journeys – though everywhere it depends to a large extent on what you look like, how you act and where you're going. Don't be afraid to use them, nor to argue if you feel you're being unreasonably overcharged.

The Moroccan **train system** is limited, but it is comfortable, efficient and fairly fast. For possible **routes** see the map at the beginning of this section (they are all marked); for **times** see the *Travel Details*, or get hold of one of the timetables printed by *ONCF*, the national company. **Costs** for a second-class ticket are comparable to CTM buses – sometimes slightly cheaper; on third, *economique*, class they're well below. Most of the **stations** are positioned quite close to the modern centre of a town, in the French-built Ville Nouvelle quarter.

Hitching and trucks

Hitching is not very big in Morocco. Most people, if they own any form of transport at all, have mopeds – which are actually said to outnumber cars by something like five *hundred* to one. However, it is often quite simple to get lifts from other **tourists**, particularly if you ask around at the campsites, and for **women travellers** this can be an effective and positive option. You won't want to spend all your time driving round in tourist cars, but they can be a useful respite from the generally male preserves of buses and *grands taxis*.

Out on the road, it's inevitably a different matter – though as a man I've never had any problems inside a car. One thing you do often come across, though, is being asked to **pay for a lift**. Sometimes this is just opportunism, and you've a right to feel you're being ripped off and refuse to pay. Usually it isn't. In the countryside, where buses may be sporadic or even non-existent, it is standard practice for **vans** and **trucks** (*camions*) to charge passengers. You may be asked to pay a little more than the locals, and you may be expected to bargain on this price – but it's straightforward enough. In parts of the Atlas, the Berbers actually run **transit-truck** services, generally to coincide with the pattern of local souks. If you plan any of the more ambitious Atlas *pistes*, you'll probably be dependent on these or on walking. For some general guidelines – above all pay at the end – see Dan Richardson's account on p. 267.

Driving and car hire

To **drive** in Morocco, you'll need an *International Driving Licence* and *Green Card* – both of which are available from the AA and similar motoring organisations. By law, you must also be over 21.

Roads – at least over the main routes – are generally good, well contoured and tarmac-coated. There are, though, a few **local difficulties**: an element of banditry in the hashish-growing areas of the Rif mountains (see p. 67), maniac lorry drivers along the narrow southern routes, over-enthusiastic roadside rock and mineral sellers, and one or two nerve-racking mountain passes. On the positive side, there are relatively few cars, and city driving is no worse than anywhere in Europe – except that few people obey the **traffic laws**, which include driving on the *right-hand side* and giving preference to people coming onto roundabouts.

On the **pistes**, rough unsurfaced tracks in the mountains or desert, there are special problems. Here you do need a good deal of driving and mechanical confidence – and if you don't feel your car's up to it, don't drive a route. Moroccan **mechanics** are usually excellent, and all medium-sized towns have garages (most with extensive parts for Renaults and other French cars), but if you break down miles from anywhere you'll probably end up paying a fortune to get a lorry to tow you out. There is, too, the problem of having to re-export any car that you bring into the country.

You can't just write off a car: you'll have to take it out of Morocco with you.

Car hire is expensive at upwards of £115 a week, and car-driving anyway has disadvantages in sealing you off from the country. However, it can be worth while if you're pushed for time – especially in the **south**, where getting around and getting to see anything can turn out quite an effort relying on local buses. Details and addresses of car hire **firms** are given in the text, under the city listings: the cheapest places are mostly in Casablanca and Agadir. One company that is generally recommended, and which allows you to pick up a car in one city and return it at no extra charge to another, is *Leasing Cars;* they have offices in Casablanca (100 Blvd Zerktouni; 265 331), Agadir, Marrakesh and Tangier.

Whether you hire a car or drive your own, always make sure you're carrying a **spare tyre** in good condition (and a jack and tools). Punctures are very frequent, and even on quite major roads you can find yourself in for a long wait until someone drives along with a possible replacement.

Motorbikes – and above all trail bikes – are ideal transport in Morocco; good for most pistes, they're also a source of curiosity and keep you very open to local people. **Mopeds** or **bikes** are practical too – you can take them around on trains and even some buses or lorries.

Expedition routes and hiking

Morocco is still a country where expeditions are valid – and where you don't have to go far off a main road to find a very different land to the standard tourist circuits. The two main possibilities for adventurous travel are hiking or piste-driving. **Hiking** is best in the High Atlas – and most popular around Mount Toubkal (see p. 221 for details and practicalities). **Piste-driving** can take you across the Atlas ranges or along some of the desert tracks between outlying oases in the pre-Sahara. To an extent we've covered, or at least made suggestions for, all of these options. If you're thinking of doing some serious hiking, though, you'll find the **Guide Collomb:** *Atlas Mountains* invaluable (it's available from specialist bookshops or by post from West Col Productions, Goring, Reading, Berks), and might want to consult some of the *Expedition Reports* at the **Royal**

Geographical Society (1 Kensington Gore, London SW7). The RGS's **Expeditionary Advisory Centre** (01 581 2057) will help locate relevant material, maps and reports.

There are also an increasing number of small, **specialist companies** who offer expedition-tours to Morocco. Perhaps the most experienced are *Guerba Expeditions* (Westfield House, Westbury, Wiltshire; 0380 830476), who run converted trucks across the Saharan pistes, and also trekking in the High Atlas. Also active in High Atlas treks are *Exodus Expeditions* (100 Wandsworth High St, London SW18; 01 870 0151); who hike the Djebel Saghro in winter, *Sherpa Expeditions* (131a Heston Rd, Hounslow, Middlesex; 01 577 2717) and *Explore Worldwide* (7 High St, Aldershot, Hants; 0252 319448).

Flights

Royal Air Maroc operate **internal flights** between all the major cities, though many are only connected via the airport at Casablanca. If you're very tight on time, you may want to use the service between **Tangier** and **Marrakesh** (via Casa); this would cost around £25, well above bus and train fares, but, at 2hrs, as opposed to nearly 13hrs, saving considerable effort. Details of other *RAM* flights, and addresses of local offices, are given in the main part of the guide. Remember that you must always reconfirm flights at a *RAM* office 24-48hrs before departure.

Student and under-26 youth **discounts** of 25 per cent are available on all *RAM* domestic flights, but only if the ticket is bought in advance from one of their own offices.

SLEEPING

Hotels in Morocco are cheap, excellent value, and usually quite easy to find. The only times you may have problems getting a room are at peak season (mainly August, but also Christmas/Easter), and then only in a handful of main cities and resorts – Fes, Agadir, Tangier and sometimes Tetouan.

There is a basic distinction in Morocco between *classified hotels* (which are given star-ratings by the tourist board, and start at around £2.50 a double) and *'Medina hotels'* (un-starred, un-listed by the ONMT, and from £1.40 or so for a double). **'Medina hotels'**, found in the old, Arab-built part of a town – the Medina – are obviously the cheapest options, and have the advantage of being at the heart of things, where you'll want to spend most of your time, and where all the sights and markets are concentrated. Points against them are that the Medinas can at first be daunting – with their mazes of narrow lanes and blind alleys – and that the hotels themselves can at worst be dirty, flea-ridden pits with tiny windowless cells and half-washed sheets. At best they're far different – and can be really beautiful with whitewashed rooms grouped about a central patio – though there is nearly always some problem with water. The Medinas remain substantially unmodernised, hot showers are a rarity, and the squat toilets sometimes pretty disgusting. None the less, a lot of them are fine, and we've included numerous Medina recommendations in the guide.

Classified hotels are almost always in the Ville Nouvelle – the 'new' or administrative quarters, originally built by the French and usually set slightly apart from the Medina. The star-ratings are self-explanatory: starting at the bottom with 1*B, 1*A, 2*B, etc., and going up to 4*B, 4*A, and finally 5*Luxury. Prices are extremely reasonable for all except the 5* categories (which can – and do – set their own rates). At the lower end, there's little difference between 1*B and 1*A places, either of which will get you a basic double room with a washbasin for £2.50-£3.00, with a private shower for another £1. Going up to 2* and 3* there's a definite progression in comfort, and you can find a few elegant, old hotels in these categories which used once to be extremely grand but have since slipped in competition with the new purpose-built tourist complexes. However, if you're going for a slice of luxury, the dominant feature is likely to be finding a room with access to a **swimming pool** – which means, on the whole, four stars. This will set you back around £10-15 for a double, but at the upper end of this scale you're moving into real style, with rooms looking out onto palm-shaded pools and gardens, sometimes converted from old palace residences.

Ideally, the best course is to alternate between the two extremes, spending most of your time in basic Medina hotels but going for the occasional blast of grandeur. Don't at all events limit yourself to the middle categories – these are mostly dull, and staying wholly in the Ville Nouvelle cuts you off from the most interesting flow of traditional Moroccan life.

On the lower price levels – though often no cheaper than a shared room in the Medina – there are also six **youth hostels**, or *Auberges de Jeunesse*. One, at Asni in the High Atlas, is a hiking base – useful and recommended. The others are all in major cities. Those in Rabat and Casablanca are excellent, central options; Fes and Marrakesh are good fall-backs, close to the train stations; Meknes is all right but a little far from everything. Addresses and details are given for all of these in the relevant sections of the guide. One general attraction is their use for meeting other travellers, including Moroccans on holiday who sometimes visit them for just this purpose.

Campsites, too, are good meeting grounds, and even if you're staying elsewhere they can be worth calling in at to fix up a lift or find people to share petrol costs. Most are extremely cheap, at around 30p a person and 30p for a tent, but there are also a few more flashy 'International' places with major facilities and prices to match. Details and addresses are again given in the guide. Campsites don't give total **security**, and you should never leave valuables unattended. Camping outside official sites, this applies even more; though if you're hiking in the Atlas it is usually possible to set up a camp and find someone to act as *guardien*. In the Atlas, too, there are **Refuge Huts**, run by the French Alpine Club, *CAF*; for details of these, see p. 221.

Two **general points**. First, in **peak season** Medina places can raise their prices well above normal, and you can often get a cheaper room by sticking to the fixed-price 1*Bs and 1*As. Second, in the Medina hotels don't be too put off by the uncertain presence of showers. Throughout all Moroccan Medinas you'll find local **hammams** – steambaths, where you can go and sweat for as long as you like, get scrubbed down, and douse yourself with endless buckets of hot and cold water. Some of these places we've detailed in the text, but the best way of finding one is always to ask at the hotel you're staying – you will sometimes need to be led there, since they are often unmarked and very hard to spot. *Hammams*, as part of the Islamic tradition of cleanliness and ablutions, sometimes have a religious element, and you may not be welcome (or allowed in) to those built alongside mosques, particularly on the Thursday night before the main (Friday) service of the week. On the whole, though, there are no restrictions against 'Nazarenes' (Christians). In some towns, you will find separate *hammams* for women and men; at others they are designated with different hours for either sex (usually 9am-7pm for women, 7pm-1am and sometimes 5am-9am for men. Women seem particularly welcoming (see p. 23). For men, there's a strange element of modesty: you undress facing the wall, and bathe in pants or swimming trunks. An alternative to *hammams* are *bain douches* (individual showers).

FOOD AND DRINK

Like accommodation, food in Morocco falls into the two basic camps: with ordinary Moroccan meals served in the **Medina cafes** (or bought from stalls), and **tourist menus**, French-influenced and usually rather bland, in most of the hotels and Ville Nouvelle restaurants. There are of course exceptions – you find cheap local cafes in the new towns and occasional 'palace' style places in the Medina – but in general this holds good. Once again, you'll do best by sticking largely to the cheap Medina places (most of them cleaner than they look) with an occasional blow-out, if you can afford it, in the best restaurants around.

Starting with the **basics**, the simplest Moroccan meals usually centre on a thick, very filling soup – most often the spicy, bean-based *harira* (which is a meal in itself, and eaten as such to break the Ramadan fast). To this you might add a plateful of kebabs (either *brochettes* – shish kebabs, or *kefta* – made from mince) and perhaps a salad (which is often very finely chopped, and halfway to becoming the Spanish gazpacho), and dates bought from a market stall. Or you can go for a *tajine* – essentially a stew, cooked slowly in an earthenware pot over a charcoal fire, mopped up with bread and often unbelievably delicious. Either alternative will set you back about £1 for a fulsome meal if eaten at one of the hole-in-the-wall, two or three table places in the Medina; you are not expected to bargain for cooked food, but prices can be lower if you ask before you start eating. **Vegetarians** can get by quite happily on most of the soups (though some use lamb for stock) and usually on the *tajines* (which you can anyway ask to be served without meat). In the north, too, you can get shops to prepare you a *pain beurré* – buttered hunks of French bread, filled with cheese or whatever else is going.

Slightly more expensive dishes, available in some of the Medina cafes as well as the more expensive **restaurants**, include fish on the coast, and chicken (*poulet*), either spit roasted (*roti*) or with lemon and olives (*poulet limon*). You will sometimes find *pastilla*, too, a delicious pigeon-pie, prepared with millefeuille pastry coated with sugar and cinnamon, and a particular speciality of Fes. And, of course, there is *couscous* – the most famous Moroccan dish, based on a huge bowl of steamed semolina-rice, and piled high with vegetables and mutton, chicken or occasionally fish. Couscous, however, tends to be disappointing. There is no real tradition of 'eating out' publicly in Morocco, and this above all is a dish that's prepared at home – often for a special occasion (Friday, the holy day, in richer households; perhaps a festival in poorer ones).

Basics

Pain, l-*hobs*	Bread	Sel, l-me*lha*	Salt
Oeufs, be*da*	Eggs	Sauce, l-merga	Sauce
Poissons, l-*hout*	Fish	Sucre, a*zouka*r	Sugar
Viande, l-*hem*	Meat	Legumes, l-khou*dra*	Vegetables
Huile, zit	Oil		
Poivre, leb*zar*	Pepper	Vinaigre, l-khel	Vinegar
Salade, chal*ada*	Salad		

Soups, salads and vegetables

Ha*n*ra	Spicy, bean soup	Frites, l'batata	Potatoes
Potage	Thick soup	Tomates, ma*t*echa	Tomatoes
Bouillon	Thin soup	Epinards, salk	Spinach
Salade Marocaine	Mixed salad	Oignons, l-bas*la*	Onions

Main dishes

Tajine de viande/l-*hem*	Meat stew
Tajine des poissons/l-hout	Fish stew
Couscous (aux sept legumes)	Couscous (with seven vegetables)
Poulet aux olives et citron	Chicken with olives and lemon
Djaja mahamara	Chicken stuffed with almonds, semolina and raisins
Boulettes de viande, *ke*fta	Meatballs
Biftek, l-habra	Beefsteak
Mechoui	Roast lamb
Pastilla/B'stilla	Pigeon pie

Meats, poultry and fish

Poulet, djaj	Chicken	Sardines, sardile	Sardines
Pigeon, le*h*mama	Pigeon	Merlan, l-mirla	Whiting
Lapin, qniya	Rabbit	Crevettes	Prawns
Mouton, l-*h*ouli	Mutton	Langouste	Lobster

At **festivals**, which are always the best time for interesting food, and at the most expensive tourist restaurants, you may also come upon the traditional *mechoui* – a whole sheep roasted on a spit. To supplement these Moroccan standards, most tourist restaurants add a few **French dishes** – steaks, liver, various fish and fowl, etc. – and the ubiquitous *Salade Marocaine*, actually very different from the Moroccan idea of salad, based as it is on a few tomatoes, cucumbers and greens. With a sweet of fruit or pastry, these meals usually come to around £3 or so a head.

Sweets, too, are available in some Moroccan cafes, though more often at cakeshops or street stalls. They can be excellent. The most common are *cornes de gazelles*, sugar-coated pastries filled with a kind of almond paste, but there are infinite variations. Yoghourt (*yaourt*)

is also delicious, and Morocco is surprisingly rich in seasonal **fruits**. In addition to the various dates – sold year-round but at their best fresh from the October harvests – there are grapes, melons, strawberries, peaches and figs; all advisably washed before eaten. Or for a real thirst quencher (and a good cure for bad stomachs), you can have quantities of prickly pears, or cactus-fruits, peeled in the street for a couple of dirhams. Names of fruits are detailed in the lists below.

As an Islamic nation, Morocco gives **drinking** a low profile. It is in fact not generally possible to buy any alcohol at all in the Medinas and for beer or wine you always have to go to a tourist restaurant or hotel, or a bar in the Ville Nouvelle. Moroccan **wines**, however, can often be very good, if a little heavy for drinking without a meal. Among

---

Sweets and fruits

Cornes de gazelles, kab l-ghzal	Sweet pastries	Kermus d'ensarrah (or Takanareete)	Cactus fruit
Fromage, formage	Cheese	Pêches, l-khoukh	Peaches
Dattes, *tmer*	Dates	Oranges, limoune	Oranges
Figues, chr*ih*a	Figs	Melon, l-battikh	Melon
Amandes, louze	Almonds	Pasteque, dell*ah*	Watermelon
Bananes, banane	Bananas	Raisin, lazneb	Grapes
Fraises, l-fraise	Strawberries		

Drinks

Eau, agua, l-*ma*	Water	Thé, atay	Tea
(Minerale, maz*d*ini)	(Mineral)	(à la menthe, dial neznaz)	(Mint)
Bierre, birra	Beer	Café, qahwa	Coffee
Vin, sh-*rab*	Wine	(au lait, bi la*h*lib)	(with milk)

Some Arabic phrases

What do you have . . .	*Ash*noo kane...
. . . to eat?	. . . f'l-*mak*la?
. . . to drink?	. . . f'l-mush*a*roubat?
What is this?	Shnoo *ha*da?
Can you give me . . .	A*tee*nee . . .
. . . a knife/fork/spoon	. . . moos/for*she*ta/*mal*ka
. . . a plate/glass/napkin	. . . t'b-sil/*kess*/l-*fo*ta
Less/without sugar	Shwee*ya*/ble a*zou*kar
This is not what I asked for!	*He*dee mus*hee heea lit* lubt!
This is not fresh/clean!	*He*dee mus*hee treea*/n'*keea*
This is good!	*He*dee mus*hee* muz*yena*
The bill, please	L'h'*seb* minfa*d*lik
Please write it down	Minfa*d*lik, k'*tib*'h

NOTE that where foods/dishes are commonly available in all kinds of restaurants both **French** and **Arabic** words are given; where possible it is always good to try and use some Arabic – the letters printed in *italics* should be stressed. For further relevant phrases, see p. 340.

brands worth trying are the strong reds, *Cabernet* and *Gris de Boulaoune;* rosés are tasty too, though the whites are all a bit insipid. Those Moroccans who drink in **bars** – a growing number in the industrial cities – tend to stick to **beer**, usually the local *Stork, Flag Pils,* or, preferably, *Flag Special.*

On a non-alcoholic front, the national drink is *thé à la menthe* – green **tea**, flavoured with sprigs of mint and a minimum of four cubes of sugar per cup. This tastes a little sickly at first but it's worth getting used to it: perfect in the summer heat, the drinking of mint tea is also a ritual if you're invited into anyone's house (you leave after the third glass) or if you're doing any serious bargaining in a shop. In cafes, it is usually cheaper to ask for a pot (*une théière*) between two or three people. You could also try

asking for red or amber tea – more expensive and very rarely available, but delicious when it is. So too, though this time very widespread at cafes or street-stalls, are fresh-squeezed *jus d'orange,* and *jus d'amande, jus des bananes* and *jus de pomme* – the last three all milk based and served chilled. Other **soft drinks** include, inevitably, Coca Cola, along with Fanta and other fizzy lemon-ades – all quite cheap and served in larger than usual bottles. **Mineral water,** which is a worthwhile investment throughout the country, is usually referred to by brand name, ubiquitously *Sidi Harazem* or *Sidi Ali,* or the naturally sparkling *Oulmes.* **Coffee** (*café*) is best in French-style cafes – either black (*noir*), *cassé* (with a drop of milk), or *au lait.*

COMMUNICATIONS: POST, PHONES AND MEDIA

Letters between Western Europe or the USA and Morocco are totally unpredict-able: they arrive, but whether this takes three days or three weeks is very much up to chance. Similarly, receiving letters **poste restante** has an air of lottery about it. The main problem here is that Moroccan post office workers don't always file letters under the name you might expect. It is always a good idea to ask for all your initials to be checked (including M for Ms, etc.), and if you're half-expecting anything, to suggest other letters too. To collect you need your passport. To have mail sent, it should be addressed (preferably with your surname in italics) to *Poste Restante* at the *PTT Centrale* of any major town – Marrakesh is notoriously inefficient. **Post office hours** are normally 8.30-2pm. Alternatives to sending *poste restante* to post offices are to pick a big **hotel** (anything with three or more stars should be reliable) or to have things sent c/o **American Express** – represented in Morocco at Tangier, Fes, Rabat, Casablanca, Agadir and Marrakesh. For addresses of the Amex agents check the relevant cities in the guide: and, unless you've a car, avoid the one at Rabat, which is an expensive taxi ride out at the Hilton.

The public **phone system** is usually housed in a city's main Post Office (*PTT*), though it often has a separate entrance

and stays open longer hours – some-times 24hrs a day. Unfortunately, it can be almost as chaotic as the post, with calls (even to London) taking up to two hours to connect. In Rabat and Casa-blanca, however, you can now make international calls direct (after some queueing), and this is hopefully going to apply to other cities within a couple of years. In the meantime, you can get round delays to some extent by phoning through a hotel: most, even quite small places, will do this for you, though you should make sure you agree on the rate in advance – currently it's 8dhs a minute to Britain and Western Europe, 28dhs to Canada and the US. Local calls, from phone-boxes, are quite straightforward. Each city has its own code (displayed in the box); and the phones accept 10, 20 and 50 centime or 1 dirham coins.

As for other means of staying in touch, British **newspapers** (and the appalling *International Herald Tribune*) are avail-able in all the main cities, and there are two French-language Moroccan dailies if you're interested in the country's official line. You can, too, pick up the **BBC World Service,** broadcast on various frequencies through the day between 6am and midnight, local time. The most consistent evening reception is gener-ally on 9.41 and 5.975mhz (31.88 and 50.21m), but full times and programme listings are available from the BBC or from the British Council in Rabat.

MOSQUES AND MONUMENTS

Without a doubt, the major disappointment of travelling around Morocco is not being allowed into its **mosques**: all non-Muslims are excluded, as too from the 'monastic' **zaoulas**, and the rule is strictly observed. The only mosque that you *can* visit is the Almohad ruin of Tin Mal, in the High Atlas; though you are also allowed to enter the courtyard of the Sanctuary-mosque of Moulay Ismail at Meknes, and that of the Bou Inania medressa in Fes. Elsewhere you have to be content with an occasional glimpse through open doors, and even in this you should be sensitive: people don't seem to mind tourists peering into the Kaira-ouine at Fes (the country's most important religious building) but in the country you should never approach a shrine too closely, including the numerous domed and whitewashed **koubbas** – the tombs of *marabouts*, or local saints.

As some compensation, many of the most beautiful and architecturally interesting of Morocco's monuments are either open to public view – the Imperial gateways, or **babs**, of the main cities for example, and of course the **minarets** (towers from which the call to prayer is made) attached to the mosques – or can be visited. Among the latter, highlights include the **Berber kasbahs** (fortified castle residences) of the south; a series of city **palaces** and **mansions**, often converted to use as **craft museums;**

and the intricate **medressas** of Fes, Meknes, Salé and Marrakesh. The medressas, many of them dating from the C13-14, are perhaps the most startling – and certainly the most 'monumental' – of Moroccan buildings, each displaying elaborate decoration and designs in stucco (gypsum, or plaster), cedarwood, and tile-mosaics (known in Morocco as *zellij*). Originally religious universities, or student residences for a neighbouring mosque-school, they had largely fallen into decay and disuse by the present century and are now almost all secularised. Their role is discussed in the chapter on **Fes**, which has the richest and most varied examples: see p. 148–9.

Unlike Tunisia and Algeria, Morocco never saw extensive **Roman** colonisation – and indeed the south of the country was unconquered by any outside force until the French invasion of the 1920s. What ancient sites there are, therefore, are limited. The most interesting, and really the only one to go out of your way to visit, is **Volubilis**, close to Meknes (see p. 130). **Prehistoric sites**, with extraordinarily preserved **rock-paintings**, do exist in the south of the country, though most are extremely difficult of access – including the most significant, at Foum-el Hassan. Probably the most rewarding that you can get to without much difficulty are those at **Oukaimeden**, near Marrakesh.

FESTIVALS

If Islam's popular image is rather puritanical and ascetic, Morocco's **festivals** – *Moussems* and *Amouggars* – do their best to break it. The country abounds in holidays and festivals of all kinds, both national and local, and stumbling upon one can be the most interesting and enjoyable experience of any travel in Morocco. So too, perhaps surprisingly, can coinciding with one of the major **Islamic celebrations** – and above all the month of *Ramadan*, when all Muslims (which in effect means all Moroccans) observe a total fast from sunrise to sunset.

Ramadan, in a sense, parallels the Christian Lent: the ninth month of the

Islamic calendar, it commemorates the time in which the Koran was revealed to Muhammad. In contrast to the Christian West, though, the Muslim world observes the fast extremely rigorously – indeed Moroccans are forbidden by law from 'public disrespect' and a few each year are jailed. What the fast involves is abstention from food, drink, smoking and sex during daylight hours. This sounds a disastrous time to travel – local cafes and restaurants often close, and people can get on edge towards the month's end – but it is actually the best of all. At sunset, signalled by a siren and the lighting of lamps on minarets, an amazing calm and wellbeing falls on the streets, as everyone drinks a bowl of *harira* and, in the cities at least, gets down to a night of celebration and **entertainment**. If you can spend some time at Marrakesh during the month, you'll find the Djemaa el Fna square there at its most active, with troupes of musicians, dancers and acrobats coming into the city just for the occasion; in Rabat and Fes there seems to be a continual promenade, with cafes and stalls all open through to 3am; and in the southern towns and Berber villages, you will often come upon the ritualised *ahouaches* and *haidus*, circular, trance-like dances often involving whole communities.

As a non-Muslim outsider, you are not expected to observe Ramadan but you ought to be sensitive about breaking the fast (and particularly smoking) in public. In fact, the best way to experience Ramadan – and to benefit from its naturally purifying rhythms – is to enter into it. You may not be able to last without an occasional glass of water, and you'll probably breakfast slightly later than sunrise, but it is still worth the attempt.

At the end of Ramadan comes the feast of the **Aid es Seghir**, a climax to the festivities in Marrakesh, though observed more privately in the villages. Also extremely important to the Muslim year is the **Aid el Kebir**, which celebrates the willingness of Abraham to obey God and sacrifice his son Isaac. It coincides, too, with the beginning of the Islamic year, and is a traditional family gathering – every household that can afford it slaughtering a sheep (which can be seen tethered all over the place for weeks before the event, and being cured on the streets for days afterwards). To Western eyes this is a little gruesome, though it is really no different to Christmas. The third main religious holiday is the **Mouloud**, the Prophet's birthday, but although this is widely observed and moussems timed to take place in the weeks around it, it is really much less significant.

Islamic religious holidays are calculated on the **lunar calendar**, so their times (and those of Ramadan) rotate throughout the seasons. Exact dates in the lunar calendar are impossible to predict – they are set by the Islamic authorities in Fes – but approximate dates for the next three years are:

	1985	1986	1987
Beginning of			
Ramadan	21 May	11 May	1 May
Aid es Seghir	20 June	10 June	31 May
Aid el Kebir	27 Aug	17 Aug	7 Aug
Mouloud	25 Nov	15 Nov	5 Nov

In addition, there are five main **secular holidays**, all celebrated to some extent. These are tied to Western calendar dates:

New Year's Day	1 January
Feast of the Throne	3 March
Labour Day	1 May
Green March (see p. 316)	6 November
Independence Day	18 November

On all Moroccan public holidays **banks, post offices** and most **shops** will be closed; **transport** may be reduced but never stops completely.

Moussems – and, less elaborately, *Amouggars* – are held in honour of saints or *marabouts*, and are basically local affairs. Outside the *Aid es Seghir* and *Aid el Kebir*, however, they make up the main religious and social celebrations of the year for most Moroccans and above all for the country Berbers. Most amount to little more than an elaborate market day with religious overtones but some have developed into more substantial occasions – a sort of cross between a religious pilgrimage and a Spanish fiesta – and a few have taken on national significance. Most of the principal events are detailed in the main section of the guide, but below are some of the most important or spectacular, all worth considerable effort to

Asni	June	Moussem of Moulay Ibrahim.
Goulimine	June	Asrir moussem.
Chaouen	August	Moussem of Sidi Allal el Hadj.
Setti Fatma	August	Moussem of Setti Fatma.
Imilchil	September	Marriage moussem of the Ait Haddidou.
Moulay Idriss	September	Moussem of Moulay Idriss I.
Fes	September	Moussem of Moulay Idriss II.
Salé	Mouloud	Moussem of Sidi Abdullah ben Hassan.

see, and to try to establish exactly when they're happening – dates, fixed at the last minute by local *caids*, are often very fluid, though the great majority take place in the summer.

Lastly, there is a huge **Folklore Festival** at Marrakesh in the first and second weeks of June. This is essentially a tourist event, with groups of dancers, musicians and entertainers brought in from all over the country, but apart from the artificiality of the setting it's all very

authentic – and always draws large crowds of Moroccans. And there are also a handful of regional festivals held to celebrate the end of a particular **harvest**. These include almonds at Tafraoute (late February), roses at El Kelaa des Mgouna (end of May), cherries at Sefrou (June) and dates throughout the southern oases (end of October/beginning of November). Again the more interesting or important are detailed in the main section of the guide.

SOUKS

Souks – markets – are a major feature of Moroccan life, and one of its great attractions. They are to be found everywhere: each **town** has a quarter, large **cities** like Fes and Marrakesh have labyrinths of individual souks (each filling a street or square and devoted to one particular craft), and in the countryside there is a movable network, shifting between the various **villages** of a region. The villages, in fact, are often named from the **day of their market** – they may hardly exist at other times – so it's easy to see when they're on. *Souk el Had* is the Sunday (literally 'first') market; *el Haine* – Monday; *el Tleta* – Tuesday; *el Arba* – Wednesday; *el Khemis* – Thursday; and *es Sebt* -Saturday. There are no village markets on **Fridays** (*el Djemaa* – the 'assembly', when the main prayers are held at the mosques), and even in the cities *souks* are largely closed on Friday mornings and subdued for the rest of the day.

Moroccan **crafts**, or *artesania*, traditions are still highly active, and even goods mass-produced for tourism are surprisingly untacky. To find pieces of real quality, however, is not that easy – some have become dulled by the centuries of repetition, others corrupted by modern techniques and chemical dyes. In general, if you're buying it is always worth getting as close to the source of goods as possible, and to steer clear of the main tourist centres. **Fes** may have the richest traditions but you can often find better work at much cheaper prices elsewhere, and **Tangier** and **Agadir**, neither of which have imaginative workshops of their own, are certainly best avoided. As stressed throughout the guide, the best way of getting an eye for standards and quality

is to visit the various Traditional Crafts museums spread around the country: there are good ones in Fes, Meknes, Tangier, Rabat and Marrakesh.

Two crafts which have survived into this century with considerable originality are **carpet-making** and **wood marquetry**. Moroccan **carpets** are not cheap – you can pay £1000 and more for Arab designs in Fes or Rabat – but it is possible to find **rugs** at quite reasonable prices, from £20 to £30, for a strong, well-designed weave. Most of these will be Berber and the most interesting usually from the High and Middle Atlas; if you're looking seriously, try to get to the town souk at **Midelt**, or the weekly markets in **Azrou** and in the villages around **Marrakesh**. On a simpler and cheaper level, **Berber blankets** (*foutahs*, or *couvertures*) are good, too – often very striking with bands of reds and blacks; for these, **Tetouan** and **Chaouen**, on the edge of the Rif, are promising. **Marquetry** is one of the few crafts where you'll see genuinely old pieces – inlaid tables and shelves – though the most easily exportable objects are inlaid boxes and chess sets, beautifully made from thuya and cedar wood in **Essaouira**. **Pottery** on the whole is disappointing but, tourist-produce though it is, I personally like the blue and white designs of **Fes** and multicoloured pots of **Chaouen**. 'Silver' **jewellery** went into decline with the loss to Israel of Morocco's Jewish population, the country's traditional metalsmiths and general artesans; in the **south** however, you can pick up some fabulous Berber necklaces and bracelets, always very chunky with bold combinations of semi-precious (and sometimes plastic) stones and beads.

There are, too, **Moroccan clothes**. Westerners – men at least – who try to imitate Moroccan cool by wearing the cotton or wool *djellaba*, or cloak, tend to look a little silly. But there are brilliant cloths around, and walking down the dyers' souks is an inspiration. **Leather** is also excellent, and here you can buy and wear goods with confidence. The classic Moroccan shoes are *babouches*, open at the heel, immensely comfortable and produced in yellow (the usual colour), white, tan and occasionally grey; a good pair – and quality varies enormously – goes for around £9.

Whatever you buy, though, and wherever you buy it, you will want and be expected to **bargain**. There are no hard and fast rules on this – it is really a question of paying how much something is worth to you – but there are a few general points to keep in mind. First, bargaining is entirely natural in Morocco: if you ask the price in a market, the answer, as likely as not, will come in one breath – 'Twenty, how much will you pay?' Second, don't pay any attention to initial prices, these are simply a device to test out the limits of a particular deal or situation: you don't think in terms of paying one third of the asking price (as some guides suggest), it might well turn out to be a tenth or even a twentieth. Third, don't ever let a figure pass your lips that you won't be prepared to pay – nor start bargaining for something you have *absolutely* no intention of buying, there's no better way to create bad feeling. Fourth, don't be afraid of starting too low, nor of being laughed at or insulted – this is part of the ritual; your part is to be agreeable, slightly disinterested (leaving, or having a friend try to get you to leave speeds things up), and to take your time – if the deal is a serious one (for a rug, say) you'll probably sit down over tea with the seller, and for two cups talk about anything but the rug and the price. And last, most golden rule of them all, never go shopping with a **guide** or hustler, even 'just to look' – the pressures are either too heavy or too boring, depending on how long you've been in the country and learned to cope with them.

In the main city souks – and particularly in Marrakesh – you may find **exchanging goods** more satisfying than bargaining a price. This way you know the value of what you're offering better than your partner (though he'll have a pretty good idea too), and in a sense you're giving a fairer exchange. Items particularly sought after are training shoes – even well worn in, T-shirts with designs (Bob Marley has the biggest currency of all), brand-name jeans, basic medicines (in country areas) and *Marks & Spencer* (!) clothes.

An approximate idea of what you should be paying for craft goods can be gained from checking the **fixed prices** in the state-run *Centres Artisanal*. Even here though, there is sometimes scope for bargaining and prices at all events are higher than you should pay elsewhere.

KIF (HASHISH)

Drug-taking – almost exclusively of **Kif** (hashish, *chocolaté*, cannabis) – has for a long time been a regular pastime of Moroccans and tourists alike. Indeed, in the 1960s and 1970s, even in the 1930s, its ready accessibility, good quality and cheapness were a major tourist attraction. It is, however, **illegal**, or as the ONMT puts it:

Tourists coming to Morocco are warned that the first article in the Dahir of April 24th 1954 prohibits the POSSESSION, the OFFER, the DISTRIBUTION, the PURCHASE, the SALE and the TRANSPORTATION as well as the EXPORTATION of CANNABIS IN WHATEVER FORM. The Dahir states a three months to five years IMPRISONMENT penalty and a fine of 2,400 to 240,000 dirhams or one of these only. Moreover the law court may ordain the SEIZURE of the means of transport and the things used to cover up the smuggling as well as the toxic products seized.

What this means in practice is slightly different. There is no real effort to stop Moroccans from smoking or dealing, but as a tourist you are peculiarly vulnerable. Not so much from the **police**, who are on the whole happy to regulate the trade, as from the **dealers**. Apart from the obvious tricks – selling camel dung, etc. – many of the dealers have developed meaner, more aggressive tactics. They sell people hash (or occasionally even plant it) and then return, or send friends, to threaten to turn you in to the police; or they simply do tell the police, collect their hash back and perhaps split whatever you've been willing to pay for your freedom. Either way it can all become pretty paranoid and unpleasant.

What can you do to avoid all this? Most obviously, keep well clear – above all in the kif-growing areas of the **Rif mountains**, and the drug's centre at **Ketama** – and always reply to hustlers by saying you don't smoke (you prefer drinking, you have bad lungs . . .). Or if you are coming to Morocco to indulge, don't buy anything in the first few days (not in Tangier and Tetouan), and only smoke* where you feel thoroughly confident and in control. Above all, **do not try to take any out** by air (*Midnight Express* could

equally have been about Morocco) and don't even think of taking any into Algeria or over to Spain. Penalties in **Algeria** are amazingly harsh (theoretically a life sentence is possible), and there's nearly always a prison sentence in **Spain**, too. Apart from which, if you take kif over to Spain you're unlikely to save much money: in Malaga and along the Costa del Sol prices are low, and Spanish law actually allows you to buy (though not sell) small quantities for personal use.

If you do find yourself in trouble there are **consulates** for most nationalities in Rabat, and to a lesser extent in Tangier (see their respective listings for addresses). Consulates are not notoriously sympathetic to drug offenders – the British one in Rabat has an old French poster on the wall, '*Le kif detruit l'esprit*' – but they can help with technical problems and find you legal representation.

* Kif in Morocco is not necessarily smoked – a traditional speciality is *majoun*, a kind of fudge made with the pounded flowers and seeds of the plant. As James Jackson wrote, in *An Account of the Empire of Morocco, 1814*, 'a piece of this as big as a walnut will for a time entirely deprive a man of all reason and intellect'. It is also reputed to be a good stomach-settler.

SEXUAL HARASSMENT

As an Islamic and Arab country, and a Mediterranean one too, Morocco can be a difficult country to travel – and its *machismo* all too predictable. Below are two accounts, the first by Jill Denton who travelled with a man, the second by Jutta Bornholdt (who didn't).

● Morocco is a completely male world to travel: the streets and cafes are male territory (and harassment our condition of entry), and even contact with women rarely occurs without a male intermediary.

The most publicly assertive women you will see are undoubtedly the Berber peasants, who descend on the towns to trade their produce at the weekly souk. In consequence they enjoy a measure of economic independence, and their exuberant dress – candy-stripe, sparkling shawls, fluorescent socks and bold jewellery – seems to testify to this greater freedom. Other women, by comparison, are inconspicuous – both in manner and dress. This is most obvious in the small towns and countryside, but in the cities

things aren't far different and the moves towards Westernisation have often made matters worse. Within the traditional extended family, women and children formed an almost separatist (though male-imposed) community over which older women and the mother with many sons wielded considerable power. But adoption of a 'nuclear family' lifestyle and improved living standards (for example a private bathroom, rather than the local *hammam*) are fast eroding the basis of this power. Married women face increasing isolation within the home, whilst at the same time the education and incentives to escape marriage or motherhood are denied them. Small wonder, then, that Moroccans are often suspicious of our values and way of life.

I did once hear a whisper of subversion in the steambaths – the *hammam* – where I wallowed one day in the luxury of endless hot water and exclusively female company. I sat amongst women with henna in their hair and reluctant kids wedged between their knees, and we weighed each other up for a while before beginning to chat in French. I was recommended kids: 'Fun!', and warned off marriage: 'Like another big kid!'. Everyone laughed a lot, but then in Morocco single motherhood is still a big joke. The *hammam* is definitely worth a visit.

Elsewhere, out in the male world, I felt that Moroccan men wanted the best of both worlds – to benefit from Western Woman's 'moral laxity' and to retain their strict control over Muslim women. Of the male egos I bumped into, not one could understand that freedom from a husband's watchful eye means also the freedom to say 'no'. I was, however, awarded the status of honorary man. I drank, ate, smoked and slept in one room with three men (one, my travel friend). In the next room our host's 18yr-old-sister prepared our meals, washed our dishes. For a month she had not left the house: 'It's the school holidays – where could I go?' Had she merely dined with us, in the presence of her brother's male friends, there would have been dishonour. Predictably, her brother resented the time I spent with her in the kitchen. So too, I think, did her mother. Older women are less likely than their daughters to understand French, but it was really my behaviour which put a barrier between us – male-imposed definitions of dividing women into either 'decent' or 'whore' complicate and restrict any contact.

With the exception of the steambath, in fact, I always met women through men – and I wouldn't have stayed in men's homes had I not been with a man in the first place. It *is* a man's world in Morocco, and even something as apparently simple and casual as a five-minute conversation in a cafe can be totally misinterpreted. I wouldn't want to put women off visiting Morocco – I had fun there despite the hassles – but don't feel you can act as normal. It doesn't work.

● When Karim and I arrived in Casablanca we expected harassment, we expected limitations and prejudices against Western women, we didn't, however, expect that these problems would make us cut short our stay from six to three weeks.

Sexual harassment in Morocco seemed different to the sort we'd experienced in southern Spain or Italy, it was stronger and more pervasive. Imagine spending the whole day surrounded by men for whom a look is an invitation and whose gaze is impossible to avoid. If you turn away you'll find another – at no point can you relax or show an interest. Travelling cheaply, using buses and local cafes, made this even more intense. Often the only refuge was our hotel room. It's not that anything dangerous or dramatic happened to us – no horror stories to create or confirm – it's just that after two or three weeks we found that the only way to cope was to close up emotionally and once you've done that travelling becomes like visiting a zoo.

We liked Morocco in some ways, it's beautiful and can be a good experience, but the steady disregard of Moroccan men became too big a barrier.

Some books
Fatima Mernissi: *Beyond the Veil: The Sexual Ideology of Women* (Schenkman, US; 1975) Ten years old now, but still an enlightening study by the foremost Moroccan sociologist – and a figurehead of the country's tiny feminist movement.
Nancy Phelan: *Morocco is a Lion* (Quartet, 1982) In some ways this is a rather ordinary, lightweight travel book – but it's well observed, and it is by a woman writer who met and stayed and talked with women in Morocco.
Elizabeth Fernea: *A Street in Marrakesh*
Vanessa Maher: *Women and Property in Morocco* (Cambridge University Press, 1974).

OTHER THINGS

ADDRESSES Arabic names – *Derb, Zankat,* etc. – are gradually replacing French ones. The main street or square of any town, though, is still invariably *Avenue* or *Place* Hassan II (the present king) or Mohammed V (his father).

Addresses are written in the normal French/British way, and street signs usually in French and Arabic lettering.
BRING . . . If you want to bargain for craft goods, bring things to exchange (see p.22); if you're going hiking in the Atlas,

presents are helpful and appreciated, and salt-tablets, insect repellent and aspirin useful (see p.222). An alarm clock is needed for early morning – sometimes 5am – buses. Camera films are available but expensive in Morocco.

CONSULATES AND EMBASSIES are mostly listed under their respective cities – essentially Rabat, but also to an extent Tangier and Casablanca.

CONTRACEPTIVES Durex are available from most *pharmacies*, so too is the pill (officially on prescription but this isn't essential). If you're suffering from diarrhoea the pill (or any other drug) may not be in your system long enough to be absorbed, and consequently may become ineffective.

CUSTOMS You're allowed to bring a litre of spirits into Morocco, which is well worth doing.

GAY ATTITUDES Homosexuality is widespread in Morocco, although in certain parts of the country (the Rif, for example) it is virtually taboo. The days of Tangier – and to a lesser extent, Marrakesh – as gay resorts are largely over, the Moroccan government having instituted a major clean-up (and whole-sale closure of brothels) after Independence. Gay sex is of course still available, and men travelling alone or together will certainly be propositioned – but attitudes are increasingly hustling and exploitative on all sides. There are no laws governing homosexuality in Morocco.

HOSPITAL EMERGENCIES Dial 15 for an ambulance.

LAUNDRIES in the larger towns will take in clothes and wash them overnight, but you'll usually find it easier to ask at hotels – most will have them done for you (even the really basic places).

LEFT LUGGAGE is usually safe at railway station *consignes* and at CTM terminals – there's a small charge.

ODD ESSENTIALS Above all, toilet paper.

POLICE There are two main types: the *Gendarmerie* (who run security, and are the police you meet at checkpoints in the South and in the Rif) and the *Sûreté*.

To report any kind of crime, or for help, the *Sûreté* are distinctly preferable. Police emergency number is 19.

SHAVING A very cheap and rather wonderful luxury for male travellers – Moroccan cut-throat barbers are entirely reliable.

SKIING The main centre is at Oukaim-eden, near Marrakesh (Dec-April); other smaller resorts are at Mischliffen (nr Azrou) and Ketama in the Rif. Details from the Moroccan Tourist Board, or in Morocco from the *Fed. Royale Maro-caine de Ski, Haut Commissariat a la Jeunesse et aux Sports*, Blvd Mohammed V, Rabat.

STUDENT CARDS won't help you much in Morocco – and they're no longer any help with Algerian border rules (see p. 85) either.

SWIMMING POOLS Towns of any size tend to have a municipal pool – they're always very cheap and addresses are given in the guide. In the south, you'll be dependent on campsite pools or on those at the luxury hotels (who often allow outsiders to swim, either for a charge or for drinks or a meal). On the Atlantic **beaches** always take care – currents and undertows can be very strong.

TAMPAX are available at general stores, not *pharmacies*, in most Moroccan towns. Don't expect to find them in country or mountain areas.

TIME Moroccan time is GMT +1hr. This normally makes it 1hr behind Spain, but the same as British Summertime.

WORK Your only chance is teaching English. The *Centre for British Teachers Ltd* (Quality House, Quality Court, Chancery Lane, London WC2; 01 242 2982) regularly advertise posts. Or you can contact the *British Council* (in Rabat at 6 Av. Moulay Youssef; or in London), the *American Language Center* (13 Rue Abou Faris el Marini, Rabat; also in Tangier, Fes and Marrakesh) or *American School* (Rue Al Amir Abdelkader, Agdal, Rabat; also in Casablanca and Tangier). Reasonable spoken French is normally required by all of these, though not necessarily TEFL qualifications.

MOROCCAN TERMS: A GLOSSARY

AGADIR fortified granary.
AGDAL garden.
AGUELMANE lake; also **DAYET**.

AIN spring.
AIT tribe (literally 'sons of'); also **BENI**.
ALAOUITE ruling Moroccan dynasty –

from the C17 to the present king, Hassan II.

ALMOHAD the greatest of the medieval dynasties, ruled Morocco (and much of Spain) from c.1147 until the rise to power of the Merenids c.1224.

ALMORAVIDS dynasty which preceded the Almohads, from c.1060-c.1147.

ANDALOUS Muslim Spain.

BAB gate.

BARBARY European term for North Africa in the C16-19.

BARAKA sanctity, charismatic blessing.

BERBERS native inhabitants of Morocco, and still the majority of the population.

BORDJ fort.

CAID district administrator: **CADI** is an Islamic judge.

CHLEUH southern Berber from the High or Anti Atlas.

COL mountain pass (French).

DAR house.

DJEBEL mountain; hence **DJEBALI**, someone from the mountains.

DJEDID, JDID old.

DJEMAA, JAMAA mosque, or Friday (the main day of worship).

DJINN nature spirits (genies).

FAKIR, FKIH Koranic schoolteacher or lawyer, or just an educated man.

FASSI inhabitant of Fes.

FILALI alternative name for the Alaouite dynasty – from the southern Tafilalt region.

FONDOUK inn and storehouse, known as a caravanserai in the eastern part of the Arab world.

GNAOUA Moroccan negro, originally from Guinea; also a sect, or confraternity, who play drum trance music.

HADJ pilgrimage to Mecca.

HAMMAM Turkish-style steambath.

IDRISSID first Arab dynasty of Morocco – named after its founder Moulay Idriss.

IMAM Prayer leader and elder of mosque.

JOUTIA flea market.

KASBAH palace-centre and/or fortress of an Arab town; also a feudal family castle in the south. Like the Spanish 'Alcazar'.

KIF hashish, cannabis.

KOUBBA dome, used of small *marabout* tombs.

KSAR, KSOUR (pl.) village or tribal stronghold in the south.

LALLA female saint.

MAGHREB 'West' in Arabic, used of Morocco and the North African countries.

MAKHZEN government.

MARABOUT holy man, and by extension his place of burial. These tombs, usually whitewashed domes, play an important (and unorthodox) role in the religion of country Berber areas.

MECHOUAR assembly place, court of judgment.

MEDINA literally 'city', now used of the original Arab part of any Moroccan town. The kasbah is usually a quarter of the Medina.

MELLAH Jewish quarter.

MEDRESSA student residence, and in part a teaching annexe, for the old mosque-universities.

MIHRAB niche indicating the direction of Mecca (and of prayer).

MINARET tower attached to mosque.

MOULAY decendant of the Prophet Mohammed, a claim and title adopted by most Moroccan sultans.

MOULOUD anniversary and festival of the birth of the Prophet.

MOUSSEM pilgrimage-festival.

MUEZZIN singer who gives call to prayer.

NAZARENE, NSRANI Christian.

OUED river; also **ASRIR**.

PISE mud and rubble building material; also **TABIA**.

PISTE rough track.

QAHOUAJI cafe patron.

RAMADAN month of fasting.

RAS source: **RAS EL MA**, water source.

RIBAT monastic fortress.

SIDI, SI respectful title – 'my lord' – used of saints, rulers, elders or the boss.

SOUK market, or market quarter.

TIGHREMT similar to an agadir – fortified Berber home and storage place.

TOUAREG nomadic tribesmen of the disputed Western Sahara, fancifully known as 'Blue Men' after the blue dye of their cloaks (which gives a slight tinge to their skin).

TIZI mountain pass; **COL** in French.

ZAOUIA cult-centre based around a marabout or his tomb.

Part two
THE GUIDE

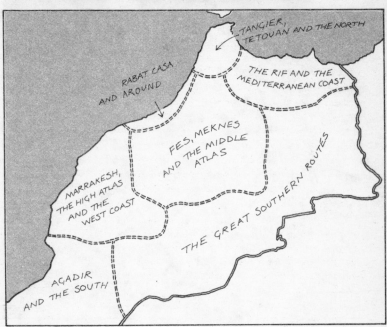

TANGIER, TETOUAN AND THE NORTH

THE RIF AND THE MEDITERRANEAN COAST

RABAT CASA AND AROUND

FES, MEKNES AND THE MIDDLE ATLAS

MARRAKESH, THE HIGH ATLAS AND THE WEST COAST

THE GREAT SOUTHERN ROUTES

AGADIR AND THE SOUTH

Chapter one
TANGIER, TETOUAN AND THE NORTH

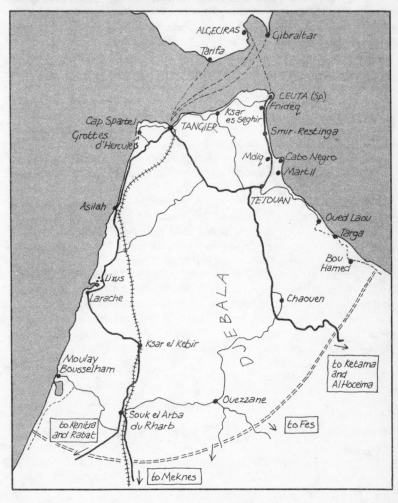

Most travellers arrive in Morocco at **Tangier** or **Tetouan** – but a good many take the option of going straight through. By general agreement these are the country's most frenetic and problematic towns, packed hard with *guides* and *hustlers* whose persistence and sophistication is, to say the least, unrivalled: Nowhere are the classic hustling scenarios (see p.3) so relentlessly performed, and nowhere with such effect, cashing in on every last dirham of first-time paranoia. On the ferry over you'll have already heard the worst stories, and knowing where you want to stay will avoid the most obvious pitfalls. But this accepted, either town can seem a daunting introduction to North Africa. Returning after even a week's travel they feel different places entirely: Tangier, seedy and hybrid from its long European contact, like a kind of Moroccan Brighton, Tetouan full of architectural interest in the outgrown elegance of its C17 Andalusian foundation.

Onward travel from Tangier is simplest by rail, trains leaving from right beside the port for **Rabat** (5hrs), **Meknes** (5hrs10) and **Fes** (6hrs). Alternatively – and covered in this chapter – you can break the journey along the coast at **Asilah**, or (by bus only) at **Larache**, each small-scale and easy-going resorts. Beyond Tetouan the natural target is **Chaouen** (1½hrs by bus), high in the mountains at the edge of the Rif and immensely laid back; little more than a large Berber village, it is also startlingly beautiful – walled, cobbled and brilliantly colour-washed.

Since almost everyone arriving in Morocco makes for either Rabat or Fes, this chapter has been arranged around the **routes** down – from Tangier along the coast, and from Ceuta through Tetouan and Chaouen; an alternative, quite straightforward, is to go from Tangier to Tetouan, and from there into the Rif and along the Mediterranean coast. Although the crossing from **Algeciras to Ceuta** is slightly cheaper than to Tangier, bear in mind that Ceuta is Spanish territory and you will spend time on local buses and at the Fnideq border before entering Morocco proper and getting to Tetouan.

TANGIER AND THE COAST

TANGIER (TANJA, TANGIERS)

For the first five decades of this century **TANGIER** was one of the most stylish resorts of the Mediterranean – an 'International City' with its own laws and administration and a bizarre floating community of exiles, expatriates and refugees. It was the home for varying periods of William Burroughs, Brion Gysin and the 1950s Beat writers, of Spanish and Central European refugees, Moroccan Nationalists, and – drawn by loose tax laws and Free Port status – of over seventy banks and four thousand companies, most of them dealing in currency exchanges illegal in the countries concerned. It was also, and to a very small degree remains, the world's first and most famous gay centre.

These days there's a definite air of decline about the town, most evident in the older hotels and bars. For with Moroccan Independence in 1956 Tangier's special status was removed and almost overnight the finance and banking businesses shifted their operations to Spain and Switzerland. The expatriate colony dwindled, too, as the new national government imposed bureaucratic controls and instituted a 'clean-up' of the city. Brothels – of which there were once nearly a hundred – were banned, and in the early 1960s 'The Great Scandal' erupted, sparked by a handful of paedophile convictions and escalating into a wholesale closure of the once outrageous gay bars. What remains is a slightly uneasy identity, halfway towards becoming a mainstream tourist resort – and an increasingly popular one with Moroccans on holiday – but still hinting at its more seedy reputation amid the shambling 1930s architecture and style. It is, as stressed, a tricky place for first arrivals – and hustler stories here should not be underestimated – but once you've got the feel of it, can still be a lively and very likeable town, shadow-bound by lapsing eras and with an enduring capacity for slight craziness.

Arriving

Arriving by ferry at Tangier, particularly for women, is something of an ordeal. You pass through customs into the terminal building and to a chaos of guides, unofficial guides and straight hustlers. The first words you will hear are the ominous 'Hello, my friend . . .', and if you don't respond you'll hear them repeated in French, Spanish, German, even Dutch and Swedish. You will also hear outrageous lies – that the hotels are all full, that the trains are on strike (this whilst standing with locals for tickets!), that Europeans and Americans are actually obliged to have guides . . . Whatever anyone says hold out. The only reason you might want to use an initial guide in Tangier is to take you to a particular hotel, but even this will probably work out more expensive than taking a taxi – which you can usually pick up at the exit of the port compound, about 400 metres walk.

In the **ferry terminal building** itself there's a *bureau de change* which sells dirhams at normal rates for most currencies and travellers cheques, but not on credit cards (see THINGS, p. 43, for these addresses). Also within the building is a *ONCF Office* for train tickets, worth queueing at immediately if you're going straight on to Asilah, Rabat, Meknes or

Fes. The **Port Railway Station** is almost directly below the terminal: you can't miss it as you emerge, and with persistence you should be able to find a seat, too. The most functional train for ferry arrivals is the afternoon *TC* for Rabat and Casablanca: this currently leaves Tangier port at 15.35, with a connection at Sidi Kacem for Meknes and Fes. There is also a night train, leaving at 21.20 (see p. 66).

Hydrofoils dock close to the ferry terminal, usually amid less pressure of guides as they tend to be dominated by groups of day trippers from the Costa del Sol, their trade already mapped out and monopolised. Arriving this way, if you want to change money and have cash to hand there's no need to subject yourself to the terminal *bureau* – the travel agents along the seafront will take dollars, pesetas and pounds, so will most hotels.

Tangier's **airport** is some 15km outside the town. There's an hourly connecting bus – to and from the Grand Socco – but be warned that it doesn't hang about; departures from the airport are on the hour from around 9.00-19.00. Taxis are comparatively expensive at around 40dh, though this is for the whole car and you can split costs between up to six passengers.

Like most Moroccan towns, Tangier has a **CTM bus station** and a number of privately operated terminals. The CTM is just outside the port compound, others are mostly gathered around. Wherever you're going ask times at the CTM first, if they don't have a bus you'll be directed across the road to one of six other companies. Alternatively, if you're heading for Tetouan (or even Larache, Ouezzane or further afield) it's possible to get a place in a **grand taxi**. The rank is right opposite the CTM station – ask any of the drivers and you'll be loaded into one of the cars. Make sure that you are not paying for a whole taxi, *une course*. The Tangier-Tetouan taxi run is completely routine, around 3dh more than the bus, but much quicker and more comfortable.

Orientation and finding a place to stay

After the initial confusion of an unfamiliar, Arab-looking city, Tangier is surprisingly easy to find your way around. As with all the larger Moroccan towns it is made up of two parts: the **Medina** – the original town, and the **Villa Nouvelle** built by its European colonisers. Within the Medina, a classic web of alleys and stepped passages, is the old fortified quarter of the **Kasbah**, a former Sultanate palace at its centre, smart residential houses scattered around.

With the **beach** and seafront **Avenue d'Espagne** there are three easy reference points in the city's main squares – the *Grand Socco*, *Petit Socco* and *Place de France*. The **Place de France** is a conventional French-style square at the heart of the new town, flanked by elegant cafes and a seaward-looking terrace-belvedere. From here the main city street, **Boul-**

evard Pasteur, leads off towards the Post Office, an *ONMT* Tourist Office
a couple of blocks along. In the other direction **Rue de la Liberté** runs
down to the **Grand Socco**, a rather amorphous open space separating off
the **Medina**. Access to this is through two horseshoe arches: the one on
the right opens onto the main Medina street, **Rue es Siaghin**, which
culminates in the **Petit Socco** – a tiny square of old cafes and cheap
hotels.

If you want **to stay** in the **Medina**, head on arrival for the Grand Socco
and make your way to the Petit Socco from there; the quicker route up
the steps to the Grand Mosque and Rue des Postes can be extremely
intimidating. Staying along or just off **the seafront** you can walk up
virtually any side street to the Boulevard Pasteur or its continuation,
Boulevard Mohammed V.

Tangier has dozens of **hotels and pensions** and finding a room is never
much of a problem. The town does, however, get crowded through July
and August, with some of the unclassified places doubling their prices. If
you want a cheap bed at this time of year you'll often do best by going
for one of the officially starred hotels. All hotels listed below are keyed
on one or other map and are to some extent recommended. As ever there
is a choice between staying in the Medina and in the new town/along the
seafront. The latter have a virtual monopoly on comfort (and running
water), and for women travelling together or alone have an easier feel.

SEAFRONT AND NEW TOWN HOTELS

All the following are along the **Avenue d'Espagne**, unless stated; all are
relatively cheap and have good or reasonable rooms.

Hôtel Valencia (1*A). Recently renovated and very well placed – almost
opposite the port, CTM and town railway station.

Hôtel Bretagne (1*B), *Hôtel Cecil* (1*B). Once grand, now heavily in
decay, but 1*B status keeps prices low and fairly standard.

Hôtel El Djenina (2*A). Dull, though well maintained (hot baths in all
rooms, etc.); just off the Avenue one block up Rue Grotius.

Hôtel El Muniria (1*A), Rue Magellan. Friendly, excellent value and with
a late night bar that comes highly recommended. Burroughs, Kerouac and
Ginsberg all stayed here when they first came to Tangier. (Rue Magellan
zigzags up from the seafront behind the crumbling Hôtel Biarritz).

Hôtel Ibn Batouta (1*A), Rue Magellan. No bar, no Burroughs, but
clean and right opposite the Muniria if you find it's full.

Hôtel Miramar (2*B). Much the best cheapish place on the seafront, very
1930s, very Brighton, and big rooms with hot showers.

Hôtel Lutetia (2*A) and *Hôtel Maroc*. Both in Rue Goya, just below
Boulevard Pasteur. Maroc is literally falling apart but a nice place in its
own way; Lutetia is fair for its category.

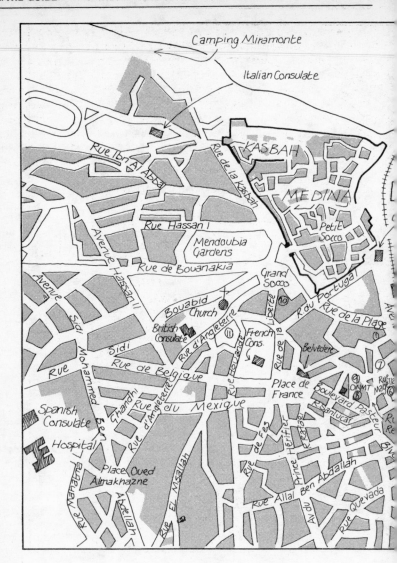

Camping Miramonte

Italian Consulate

KASBAH

MEDINA

Rue Ibn Al Abbas

Rue de la Kasbah

Rue Hassan I

Mendoubia Gardens

Petit Socco

Avenue Hassan II

Rue de Bouanakia

Grand Socco

Bouabid Church

British Consulate

Rue d'Angleterre

Avenue Sidi

Rue Sidi Mohammed Ben

Rue de Belgique

Rue de la Liberté

R du Portugal

Rue de la Plage

French Cons.

Belvedere

Place de France

Boulevard Pasteur

ONMT

Rue Magile

Rue Ghandi

Rue d'Angleterre

Rue du Mexique

Rue Bouarrad

Rue de Fes

Risanlucar

Spanish Consulate

Hospital

Rue Allal ben Abdellah

Place Oued Almakhazne

Rue El Msallah

Rue Abdellan

Rue Prince Héritier

Rue Prince

Av du

Rue Allal Ben Abdallah

Rue Quevada

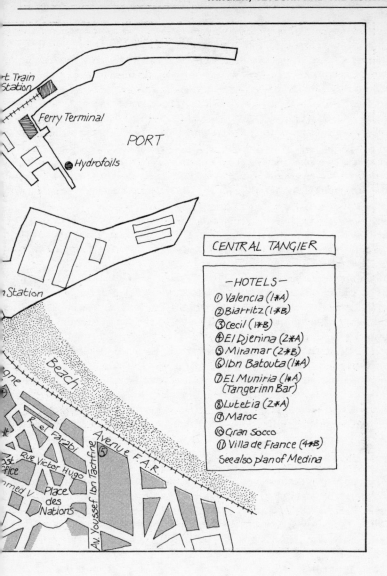

t Train
Station

Ferry Terminal

PORT

Hydrofoils

Station

Beach

CENTRAL TANGIER

— HOTELS —
① Valencia (1＊A)
② Biarritz (1＊B)
③ Cecil (1＊B)
④ El Djenina (2＊A)
⑤ Miramar (2＊B)
⑥ Ibn Batouta (1＊A)
⑦ El Muniria (1＊A)
　(Tanger inn Bar)
⑧ Lutetia (2＊A)
⑨ Maroc
⑩ Gran Socco
⑪ Villa de France (4＊B)
See also plan of Medina

R. el Farabi

Rue Victor Hugo

Avenue F.A.R.

Av. Youssef Ibn Tachfine

Place
des
Nations

Grand Hôtel Villa de France (4*A). This is one of the most elegant hotels in the country, with gardens, swimming pool and lively bar; it isn't, however, stacked with lifts and luxury fittings so remains moderately priced – around £10 for two. Worth booking in midsummer: 143 Rue de Hollande, Tel. 330 82.

MEDINA HOTELS

With the exception of the *Continental* and *Mamora* these listings are unstarred and fairly basic: safe enough, though, and with distinct character. See the Medina plan (p. 38) for a key.

Hôtel Gran Socco, Grand Socco. Very central and extremely easy to find, with some rooms looking out over the square. Good deals on big rooms for three to five people.

Hôtel Fuentes, Hôtel Mauretania, Pension Becerra, all in the Petit Socco – right at the heart of the Medina. Fuentes, with a terrace cafe above the square, is the friendliest, and also the oldest – numbering Camille Saint-Saens amongst Victorian guests.

Pension Palace, Hôtel Mamora (2*B), *Pension Marhaba*, Rue des Postes. Best of a rather bad bunch in a real hustler-dive of a street; the Palace is quite attractive, though, and Mamora a safe refuge. Marhaba, with good views of town and sea, is in an alley to the left before the Grand Mosque.

Hôtel Continental (1*A), Rue Dar el Baroud. Founded in 1888 and once the most fashionable hotel in Tangier, this is still in a world of its own – a grand piano in the hall, huge parrot cage and beautiful terrace above the port. It's just been renovated, but since most mainstream tourists don't want to stay deep in the Medina, prices remain low. To get there either take a taxi from the port, or walk up to the Petit Socco and take the Rue de la Marine to the left of Rue des Postes. Follow this round past the Grand Mosque and a terrace, and you'll come to the imposing old hotel gates.

There are also a number of pensions along **Rue de la Plage**, the street which runs up from the railway station to the Grand Socco, most of which charge outrageous prices to new arrivals ferreted along by port hustlers. Pensions *Miami* and *Talavera* are probably the best bets.

And lastly, Tangier has two **CAMPSITES**, each some way from the town. *Camping Miramonte* is the closest and most popular – 3km from the centre to the west of the Kasbah; to get there take local bus no. 2, 21 or preferably 1 from the Grand Socco. Just back from the 'Atlantic Beach', it's quite a pleasant site – cheap and with a reasonable restaurant, though none too safe for leaving anything around. The other, *Camping-Caravaning Tingis*, is some 6km east, out on the road to Malabata (bus 15 from the Grand Socco), and as its name suggests is an upmarket overpriced complex – complete with tennis court, swimming pool and mosquitos a-plenty.

The Town, Medina and Kasbah

Tangier's interest – and its attraction – is essentially in the town itself:
its cafe-life, excellent beach, and the tumbling streets of the Medina. The
few specific 'Monuments', with the exception (if it's open) of the Dar el
Makhzen palace, are best seen as adding direction to your wanderings.
The markets, though novel and bright enough, are not great sources of
bargains; Moroccan dealers tend to look on Tangier as a place to sell
whatever they can't elsewhere.

It was **the beach** and Tangier's mild climate which drew in the first
expatriates, the Victorian British, who used to amuse themselves in afternoon rides along the sands and weekends of pig-sticking in the wooded
hills behind. Today's pleasures come a little more packaged, with tourist
camel rides and a string of semi-club-like beach bars – each with their
own regulars, scene and exclusive compound. The *Ibn Battouta* is one of
the most relaxed, and a safe place to leave your clothes: if you stick to
the beach don't leave anything around.

Rambling about the town, the **Grand Socco** seems a natural place to
start – its name, like so many in Tangier a French-Spanish hybrid, stating
its origins as the principal market square. This it no longer remains, stalls
and entertainers having been cleared to make way for a local bus station.
It is still though something of an assembly place – everyone wandering
through in a Mediterranean evening *paseo*, and its cafes an interesting
place to sit and watch. So too those in the **Place de France**, which is
where half the people in the Socco are heading. The *Café de France*, here,
was a legendary hang-out throughout the years of the International Zone
– above all during the last war, when it was the centre of deals and
intrigue between agents from Britain and America, and Germany, Italy
and Japan. Later the emphasis shifted to Morocco's own politics: the
first Nationalist paper, *La Voix du Maroc*, surfaced here, and Allal el
Fassi, exiled from the French-occupied zone, set up his Istiqlal headquarters nearby.

The old **markets** of the Grand Socco have been moved partly into the
Rue de Portugal (running down to the port), partly onto cramped terraces
to either side of the Rue d'Angleterre. Most interesting of these is a small
terrace to the left, near the walls of the Villa de France hotel, where
Berber women from the villages sell their red, black and white striped
foutahs – rough-weave blankets worn sometimes four to a body as skirts,
shawl and head covering. Quality and prices for these are usually better
in Tetouan but the designs are much the same.

On the opposite side of the Rue d'Angleterre, a little way before the
threatened British Consulate, is a surprising **Anglican church** – still very
active and only slightly bizarre in its fusion of Moorish decoration and
English country churchyard. Here, among the laments of early deaths
from malaria, you come upon the tomb of **Walter Harris** (see p. 325),

most brilliant of the chroniclers of 'Old Morocco' in the closing decades
of the nineteenth century and the first of this.

From the Grand Socco you can reach the *KASBAH* in two ways: most
easily by following the Rue d'Italie/Rue de la Kasbah outside the walls

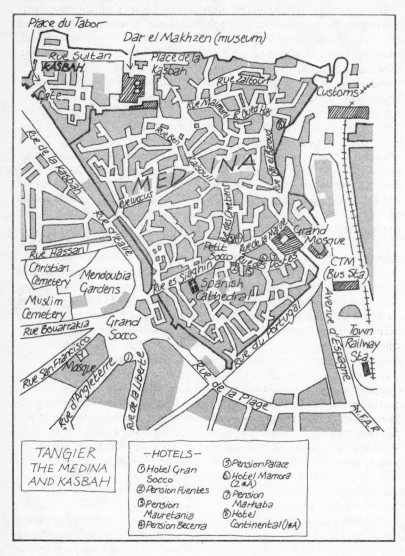

TANGIER
THE MEDINA
AND KASBAH

— HOTELS —

① Hotel Gran Socco
② Pension Fuentes
③ Pension Mauretania
④ Pension Becerra
⑤ Pension Palace
⑥ Hotel Mamora (2*A)
⑦ Pension Marhaba
⑧ Hotel Continental (1*A)

of the Medina to its main external gate. If you want to go this way take the horseshoe arch at the left end of the Grand Socco; the arch to the right opens onto the Rue es Siaghin and leads through the *MEDINA*, a more circuitous but more interesting approach.

Rue es Siaghin – *Silversmiths' Street* – was Tangier's main street into the 1930s, and remains an active thoroughfare, a series of fruit, grain and cloth markets opening off to its sides. Halfway up, locked and decaying, is the old Spanish Cathedral and Mission: to the right, just before this, was the *Mellah*, or Jewish quarter, centred on the Rue des Synagogues. Moroccan Jews traditionally controlled the silver and jewellery trade – hence *Siaghin* – but few remain in Tangier, having left on Independence for Gibraltar, France and Israel. Siaghin itself, well before that, had been taken over by tourist stalls: needless to say, it's a bad place to buy anything.

The **Petit Socco**, or Little Market, seems too small ever to have served such a purpose. Old photographs in fact show it almost twice the present size and it was only at the turn of the century that the Spanish hotels and cafes here were built. These, however, give the place its atmosphere – seedy, slightly conspiratorial, and the location for many of the Moroccan stories translated by Paul Bowles (see p. 327). In the heyday of the International City, with easily exploited Arab and Spanish sexuality a major pull, it was in the alleys behind the Socco that the straight and boy brothels were concentrated. William Burroughs used to hang out around the square in old suits bought from Moroccans which had been sent over to them by American charities. 'I get averages of ten very attractive propositions a day', he wrote to Allen Ginsberg, '. . . no stasis horrors here.' The Socco cafes lost much of their allure at Independence, when the sale of alcohol was banned in the Medina, but they remain a good place to sit around, talk and get some measure of the town.

It is beyond the Petit Socco that the Medina proper seems to start, 'its topography', to quote Paul Bowles, 'rich in prototypal dream scenes: covered streets like corridors with doors opening into rooms on either side, hidden terraces high above the sea, streets consisting only of steps, dark impasses, small squares built on sloping terrain so that they looked like ballet sets designed in false perspective, with alleys leading off in several directions; as well as the classical dream equipment of tunnels, ramparts, ruins, dungeons and cliffs.' Walking up from the square you can follow **Rue des Chrétiens/Rue Ben Raisouli** through much of this and emerge – with luck – around the lower gate to the Kasbah. Heading past the Socco towards the sea walls are two small streets straddled by the Grand Mosque. If you want to get out and down to the beach follow the **Rue des Postes** and you'll hit a flight of steps. If you feel like wandering take the other one, **Rue de la Marine**, which curls into **Rue Dar el Baroud** and the entrance to the old *Hôtel Continental* – another excellent place to sit about and drink tea. From here it's relatively simple to find your way across to the square below the Kasbah Gate.

The **Grand Mosque** itself, though it spreads across a whole block, is completely screened from public view – and, as throughout Morocco, entrance is strictly forbidden to non-Muslims. Enlarged in the early C19, the mosque was originally constructed by the great Moulay Ismail in celebration of the return of Tangier to Moroccan control in 1685. Prior to this the town had seen some two centuries of European rule: it was first conquered by the Portuguese in the aftermath of the Moors' expulsion from Andalusia and the Algarve, and in 1663 passed to the British as part of the dowry of Catherine of Braganza – bride to Charles II.

It was the British – in occupation for just twenty-two years – who destroyed the city's medieval fortifications, including a great upper castle which covered the entire site of the *kasbah*. Under virtually constant siege, they found it an expensive and unrewarding possession: 'an excrescence of the earth', according to Samuel Pepys, 'and a nest of papacy where Irish troops and Romish bastards could disport themselves unchecked.' Pepys, who oversaw the garrison's withdrawal, seems in fact to have had a miserable time, shocked at the women of the town ('generally whores'), at the governor ('with his whores at the little bathing house which he has furnished with jade a-purpose for that use'), and dining alone with the chaplain – with whom he had 'a great deal of discourse upon the viciousness of this place and its being time for God Almighty to destroy it'.

The **KASBAH,** walled off from the Medina on the highest rise of the coast, has been the palace and administrative quarter since Roman times. It is a strange, rather sparse area of walled compounds, occasional colonnades and a number of luxurious villas built in the 1920s when this became one of the Mediterranean's most chic residential sites. Richard Hughes, author of *A High Wind in Jamaica* (and of a book of Moroccan tales), was the first European to take a house – his address fabulously titled 'Numero Zero, Le Kasbah, Tangier'. Among those who followed was the eccentric Woolworth-heiress Barbara Hutton, whose parties included a ball where thirty Reguibat camel drivers and racing camels were brought a thousand miles from the Sahara to form a guard of honour.

Local guides point with some pride to these bizarre locations, but the main point of interest here is the former **Sultanate Palace,** or **Dar el Makhzen** – now converted to an excellent museum of crafts and antiquities. It stands near the main gateway from the Medina, the *Bab el Assa*, preceded by a formal court, or *mechouar*, where the town's pashas held public audience and gave judgment well into the present century. The entrance to the palace, a modest-looking porch, is in the left-hand corner of the court as you enter from the Medina – scores of children will probably drag you towards it.

The Palace – again built by Moulay Ismail in the C17 – last saw royal use as recently as 1912, with the residence of the Sultan Moulay Hafid, exiled to Tangier after his forced abdication by the French. The extraordinary negotiations which then took place are brilliantly chronicled in Walter Harris's *Morocco That Was*. According to Harris the ex-Sultan found it 'an uncomfortable, out-of-date, and out-of-repair old castle, and it formed by no means a satisfactory place of residence, for it was not easy to install 168 people within its crumbling walls with any comfort or pleasure'. Most of the 168 seem to have been members of the Royal Harem and well able to defend their limited privileges. Moulay Hafid, Harris reported, ended up with 'only a couple of very shabby rooms over the entrance' where he apologetically received visitors and played bridge with a little circle of Americans and Europeans.

Out of date and uncomfortable though the palace may have been, it is a by no means poor example of Moroccan craftsmanship and architecture. The design is classically centred on two interior courtyards, each with rich Arabesques, painted wooden ceilings and marble fountains; some of the flanking columns are of Roman origin, particularly well suited to the small display of *mosaics and finds from Volubilis* (see p. 130). The main part of the **museum**, however, is devoted to *Moroccan arts*, laid out according to region and including an exceptional collection of ceramics from Meknes and Fes. There is also a room, not always open, with some of Eugène Delacroix's sketches of Tangier – archetypal images of C19 Western Orientalism.

At the entrance to the main part of the palace is the *Bit el Mal*, the old Treasury, and adjoining this a small private *mosque*, near which there is entrance to the herb and shrub lined *gardens*. If you leave this way, you will emerge into a 'Moorish-style' cafe, the **Café-Restaurant Detroit** set up in the early 1960s by the Beat writer Brion Gysin. Gysin created the place partly as a venue for the *Trance Musicians of Jajouka*, drummers and pipe players from a village close to Tangier who achieved cult fame through an LP recorded by Rolling Stone Brian Jones. The cafe is now a straight tourist spot, but a particularly tasteful one and beautifully positioned: it looks expensive, although for mint tea and wonderful Moroccan pastries prices are no higher than normal.

Officially, the Dar el Makhzen *is supposed to open daily except Thursdays from around 9.30-12.00 and again from 15.00-18.00, but for the last year or so a quirk in the caretaker's character has meant it remaining closed. The* Cafe-Restaurant Detroit *has its own separate entrance on Rue Riad Sultan, the street running alongside the outer walls of the kasbah to the main gate and Rue de la Kasbah/Rue d'Italie.*

Eating and drinking

Cheapest places to eat in Tangier are mostly in the **Medina** – in and around the Rue des Chrétiens and Rue des Postes, off the Petit Socco. The hole-in-the-wall cafes on Rue des Chrétiens and Rue de Commerce (first alley to the left off Rue de la Marine) are all good for lamb or rabbit *brochettes, harira* or *tajine. Restaurant Ahlen* (8 Rue des Postes) has a few more tables and a little more variety.

In the **New Town** there are some inexpensive Spanish-style *fish restaurants* on Rue Sanlucar and its continuation Rue Mexique, a block back from the Place de France; or, slightly more pricey, down Rue de la Plage towards the sea. These apart you'll do as well as anywhere on the seafront itself – where the *Hôtel Biarritz* and numerous other restaurants offer reasonable set price meals.

If you're happy to pay **upwards of 30-35dhs** a head, Tangier also has some really good restaurants – most of them with solid French menus. The *Grenouille* (Rue Rembrandt, just off Blvd Pasteur), *Chez Larbi* (18 Rue Pepys, 1st left off Rue de Fes) and *Le Grillon* (52 Blvd Mohammed V) are all worth while. Somewhat kitsch – but quite interesting – are the various folkoric places, with musicians and occasional acrobats performing: *Mamounia Palace* (Rue es Siaghin), the *Detroit* (see above) and *Hammadi's* (Rue d'Italie), the latter also serving some of the best Moroccan food in the city.

Most of the old **clubs and bars** have either closed or degenerated. *Dean's Bar*, legendary through the 1950s and early 1960s with people like Noel Coward, Francis Bacon and Tennessee Williams passing through, is a good case in point – now extremely shifty; if you're curious it's just off the Grand Socco at 2 Rue Amérique du Sud. Much more congenial, and with very cheap drinks by Moroccan standards, is the *Tangerinn* (open 9pm-2am), below the Hotel Muniria on Rue Magellan. *The Parade.* (35 Av. Prince Héritier, off the Place de France; from 8pm) used to be Tangier's most elegant bar and still tries to keep up pretensions. Young Moroccans have recently taken up the *Caid's Bar* at the Grand Hôtel Villa de France (see main plan key).

For a little more action you're dependent on a bunch of fairly mediocre **discos** around Rue Mexique and Rue Sanlucar – parallel to Boulevard Pasteur. *Scott's*, halfway a gay disco, is probably the most lively.

Things

One general point: Tangier **streetsigns** are even more confusing than most, with the old French and Spanish colonial names still in use alongside their Arabised successors. *Rue de la Plage*, for example, is officially *Rue Salah Eddine el Ayoubi; Rue Rembrandt* is also known as *Rue el Jaba el Quatania,* and *Rue Goya* as *Rue Prince Moulay al Abdallah.* In addition *Rue* and *Calle* are both gradually being replaced by *Zankat.*

AIRLINES *Gib-Air/British Airways*, who sell the cheapest flights from Tangier to London (via Gibraltar), have an office at 83 Rue de La Liberté; flights are more or less daily in season – if you want to save a few pounds buy a Gibraltar-London ticket only and use the ordinary ferry across to Gib. *Royal Air Maroc* are on the Place de France, *Air France* at 20 Blvd Pasteur, and *Iberia* lower down at no. 35.

AIRPORT Tangier Airport is 15km out from the town. There are hourly *buses* to/from the Grand Socco, or you can share a *grand taxi* (around 45dhs for up to six passengers).

AMERICAN EXPRESS Operated by *Voyages Schwarz*, 54 Blvd Pasteur. Open Mon-Fri 9.00-12.30 and 3-7; Sat 9.00-12.30 only.

BANKS Most are grouped along Blvd Pasteur/Blvd Mohammed V. The *SGM Banque* (opposite the post office on Mohammed V) take cheques backed by credit and Euro cards. *Crédit du Maroc* (Blvd Pasteur) handle VISA transactions.

BOOKS AND NEWSPAPERS *Librairie des Colonnes* (54 Blvd Pasteur) stock English books, including some of Paul Bowles's Moroccan translations. Newspapers are sold outside the Post Office and at various shops along Blvd Pasteur, also by sellers around the *Café de France*.

BUSES Local ones from the Grand Socco, others leave down by the port – see ARRIVING (p. 31).

BUYING THINGS Tangier generally isn't a good place to buy – with prices and quality heavily geared to day-trippers from the Costa del Sol. There are a few things around, though: excellent Berber-inspired leather boots in the Petit Socco, and a tremendous selection of old postcards (and some fine carpet-pillows) at *Bazaar Tindouf*, 64 Rue de la Liberté.

CAR HIRE Most of the big companies have offices along Blvd Pasteur/Blvd Mohammed V – *Avis* at 54, *Hertz* at 36, *InterRent* at 87, among them. Cheaper and quite reliable are *Leasing Cars* (24 Rue Henri Regnault, and at the airport).

CAR REPAIRS AND INFORMATION Garages can be recommended by the *Royal Automobile Club de Maroc* at 8 Av. Prince Héritier. For Renaults try *Tanjah-Auto* (2 Av. de Rabat), Citroens at 33 Rue Victor Hugo (one block behind the post office).

CHEMISTS/PHARMACIES Several along Blvd Pasteur speak English.

CONSULATES *Britain* (52 Rue d'Angleterre; 358-95), *USA* (29 Rue el Achouak Chemin des Amoureux; 359-04), *Netherlands* (47 Av. Hassan II; 312-45), *Sweden* (3 Rue Henri Regnault: 358-72), *Denmark* (2 Rue Ibn Albanna; 385-02).

HOSPITAL Emergency number is 342-42; or for the Spanish Hospital (*Hôpital Espagnol*) 310-18.

POST, PHONES, POSTE RESTANTE All at the main *PTT*, 33 Blvd Mohammed V; open Monday-Saturday 8.30am-12 noon; phone section 24 hrs.

TAXIS Small, green-roofed *petit taxis* should be very cheap, charging around 1dh a person for short rides within the town; ranks by the port entrance and in the Grand Socco. See ARRIVING for details of *grands taxis* to Tetouan, etc.

TOURIST OFFICE English-speaking and helpful; ask for their free maps of Fes, Rabat-Salé and Marrakesh, each useful supplements to the ones we've printed. The office is at 29 Blvd Pasteur, just down from the Place de France and open Mon-Sat 8am-2pm

TRAINS Except for the 'town'-only morning train to Fes and Oujda, departures are from both *port* and *ville* stations; tickets are best bought in advance. See p. 66 for an approximate timetable.

Ferries

There are regular daily **ferries** from Tangier to Algeciras, two or three a week to Gibraltar and at least one boat a week to Sète in France. In addition *Transtour* operate **hydrofoils** daily in season to Tarifa, Algeciras and Gibraltar.

Two companies run the **Tangier-Algeciras ferries** – *Transmediterranea* (31 Rue Quevedo, off Blvd Pasteur) and *Limadet* (13 Rue Goya/Av. Prince Moulay Abdallah), and between them there are usually four boats a day in spring and summer, down to two in the winter. You can buy tickets for these ferries direct from the companies or (without commission) from any travel agent along the Boulevard Pasteur or seafront; there is also a ticket office at the entrance to the port. Although boats invariably depart an hour or so late, you *must* check in at the port at least one hour before the official departure time. Here, at the Ferry Terminal, you have to get an embarkation card and departure card from the 'Depart' desk of the ferry companies. Take this, along with your passport, to the police 'Visa de passeport' desk on the same floor (opposite the bar) where you then need to have your passport stamped before going through customs to the boat. Arrive later than an hour before official departure time and you will probably find the visa police have knocked off – which means you have to wait for the next ferry.

Similar procedures should be observed for the **Gibraltar** ferry, 'Mons Calpe', operated by *Bland Line* (*Gibmar Travel*, 22 Av. Mohammed V; 396-33); and for *Comanav's* liner to Sète (times and tickets from *Voyages Comanav*, 149 Av. Mohammed V; 304-57).

Hydrofoils to Spain and Gibraltar are slightly more expensive than the ferries and don't run in bad weather – but they are considerably quicker and more efficient. Spring and summer departures are three times daily to Tarifa (30 minutes), once each to Algeciras (1hr) and Gibraltar (1hr). Again you can buy tickets direct from the operator (*Transtour*, 54 Boulevard Pasteur; 340-04) or from most travel agents. Departures are from a separate quay, just in front of the ferry terminal building, where there's an individual 'visa de passeport' office – normally open half an hour before the official (and more often than not, actual) departure time. *NB. There are no hydrofoils on Sundays.*

AROUND TANGIER: CAPES, CAVES AND KSAR ES SEGHIR

West – the Caves of Hercules and the 'Atlantic Beach'
If the Tourist Board pushes one image of Tangier it must be the **Caves of Hercules**, whose strange sea window, shaped like a map of Africa, lurks glossily from the cover of the official leaflet. The name, like Hercules' legendary founding of Tangier, is purely fanciful but, 18km outside the town and above the 'Atlantic Beach', they make an attractive excursion; a good base, too, if you feel like camping for a few days by the sea – even in the middle of August only a straggle of visitors share the long surf beaches. Take care though, the currents here can be very dangerous quite close to the shore.

Heading for the caves you're dependent on *grand taxis* (who charge around 100dhs for the 34km round trip, and can be persuaded to drop you in the morning and pick you up late afternoon) or on irregular buses and a 6-7km walk. If you go for the latter, take the hourly **airport bus** from the Grand Socco and ask to be put down at the turning for 'Les Grottes' (5km before the airport). As you approach the coast a small track leads off left to the ruins of Cotta, for which see below; the caves themselves are signposted a kilometre or so beyond.

By taxi or with your own transport there's a more interesting route – around and above the coast via *La Montagne* and *Cap Spartel;* from the Place de France take Rue Belgique to the beginning of the Rue de la Montagne. 'The Mountain', less imposing than its name suggests, was a rebel base against British and Portuguese occupation of Tangier but is now thoroughly tamed – its cork and pine woods shielding the town's most exclusive villas. Among them are two vast royal palaces, the first built by Moulay Hafid and now one of King Hassan's growing roster, the other, heavily guarded, among the numerous Arab retreats of the sheikhs of Saud. At 11km you reach a short turning to the lighthouse at **Cape Spartel** – a dramatic and fertile point, known to the Greeks and Romans as the 'Cape of the Vines' – beyond which begins the vast and wild **'Atlantic Beach'**, broken by a rocky spit and then rambling off for as far as you can see. There's a *campsite* on each side of the spit, both near reasonably-priced *café-restaurants;* two hotels also – the pricey 3* A *Hôtel Grottes* and, beyond the caves themselves, the cheaper *Hôtel Robinson* (2*A).

The **Caves of Hercules** are natural formations, occupied in prehistoric times, but most striking for a man-made appearance: thousands of disc-shaped erosions created by centuries of quarrying for mill stones. There were still Moors cutting stones here for a living into the 1920s but by this time their place was beginning to be taken by professional guides and discreet sex hustlers. It must have made an exotic brothel. Today there's a standard admission charge (daily, 9am-sunset), though you're unlikely to get away without a guide, too, whose descriptive abilities tend to be somewhat crushed by the utter obviousness of all there is to see ('wet cave', 'dark cave', 'sea', etc).

Ten minutes' walk past the caves the road turns inland from the beach and a rough farm track leads in 200 metres to the ruins of **Ancient Cotta**, a small C2-3 Roman town based around the production of *garum* – a kind of anchovy paste. Parts of the factory, and of a temple and baths-complex, can be made out, but it's not a very inspiring or significant site.

East – Cape Malabata and Ksar es Seghir

There are few quicker contrasts than the bay east of Tangier. As you approach **Cape Malabata** it's almost a different world to the town – based exclusively on a *Club Méditerranée* and a handful of huge modern hotel complexes. But round the cape, and there is virtually no more development the whole way downcoast to Ceuta, just a beautiful road, winding above some tremendous stretches of beach which if you're happy to camp – for free, there are no organised sites – must be among the best in the north. The only problem is a shortage of **buses**. Tangier and the Ceuta border point at FNIDEQ have no connecting service, and the only buses to KSAR ES SEGHIR leave and return early in the morning.

Once you've tracked down the bus – which usually leaves from outside the Hotel Rif along the seafront – **KSAR ES SEGHIR** is as relaxed and picturesque a base as could be imagined, still largely enclosed by 20ft-high Portuguese walls. A small fishing port, it attracts a fair number of Moroccan summer campers, but few Europeans. There's a friendly *café-restaurant* on a terrace above the sea, occasional *rooms* to let if you ask around, and, as long as you watch possessions, infinite scope for camping.

ASILAH

The first town beyond Tangier – and first stop on the railway – **ASILAH** is a very much a resort. Too much so in many ways, with local attitudes shaped by a British *Camp Africa* package complex along the beach. If you're reasonably young everyone assumes that this is where you're from, and that you'll laugh with tourist novelty every time they yell out 'Hey, Fish and Chips'. If you've spent any amount of time in Morocco this can seem somewhat tedious.

On the positive side, the town is small, quite lively and very easy to manage – hustlers limiting themselves to souvenir selling and enthusiastic attendance at the tourist discos. And Asilah is one of the most elegant of the old Portuguese Atlantic ports, its square stone ramparts flanked by palms and its beach outstanding – an immense sweep of sand stretching halfway to Tangier. There are four large organised **campsites** to the north of the town, off the road to Tangier. The nearest, about 2km walk, is *Camping International*, popular, cheap and with good facilities; *Camp Africa* and the others are 2-3km further along the beach, beyond the **railway station**.

Arriving by **bus** (1hr from Tangier) you're dropped in a square just on the edge of the Medina, about 100 metres north of the ramparts. On the left of the square – facing ramparts and sea – is the *Hôtel Nasr*, a pretty basic place but pleasantly run and with the cheapest **rooms** around. Walking down to the ramparts you come to the slightly more expensive and crazily decorated *Hôtel Marhaba* and, to its left opposite a small town gate, the 1*B *Hôtel Asilah* – probably the most attractive cheap option with some rooms on a terrace above town and walls. One of these places should have space: if not, there are straw-hut-rooms on the roof at *Pension al-Karam* (by the beach, just behind the up-market 2*A *Hôtel Oued el Makhasine*) and the rather luxurious *Hôtel Oasis* (2*B) in a square to the right (facing the sea) of the bus station.

Asilah's **beach** is inevitably the main focus of life – by night too, with its *La Estrella* disco. The **town** itself was just a small fishing port before the tourists came, quietly stagnating after the indifference of Spanish colonial administration. Whitewashed and cleaned up, it has now quite a prosperous air – the town mosque, for example, is being rebuilt and doubled in size – and its towers and ramparts make quite a pleasant place to wander around. There's a Djebali villagers' **market** held most days around the ramparts, and a small **hammam**, where, unusually, the keeper charges for a group and gives you the place to yourselves: ask directions, it's in an alley off the second long street inside the Medina walls. Also, though it doesn't always open without persuasion, there is the town's **palace**, built in 1909 with forced tribal labour by the local brigand Er-Raisuli.

Raisuli was one of the strangest figures to emerge from what was an almost routinely bizarre period of Moroccan government. He began his career as a cattle-thief, achieved notoriety with a series of kidnaps and ransomings (including the British writer and *Times* journalist, Walter Harris), and was eventually appointed governor over practically all the tribes of north-west Morocco. Harris described his captivity in *Morocco that Was* – an 'anxious time', made the more so by confinement in a small room with a headless corpse. Despite this they seem to have formed a real friendship, Harris finding Raisuli a 'mysterious personage, half-saint, half-blackguard' and often entertained him later in Tangier.

Another British travel writer, Rosita Forbes, visited Raisuli at his Asilah palace in 1924. The rooms, which are now mostly bare, were hung with rugs 'of violent colours, embroidered with tinsel', their walls lined with cushions stuffed with small potatoes. It seems logical enough decoration – the palace today still looks more of a Hollywood glitterbug mock-up than anything created for real. The great reception room, a long glass terrace above the sea, even has dialogue to match. Raisuli told Forbes that he made murderers walk to their death from its windows – a 90ft drop to the rocks. One man, he said, had turned back to him, saying 'Thy justice is great, Sidi, but these stones are more merciful.'

The *Palais de Raisuli*, as it is known, overhangs the sea-ramparts towards the far end of the Medina (away from the beach). It is used in August for an 'International Festival'.

LARACHE

Much less visited than Asilah, **LARACHE** is one of the best towns in the north to spend a few days by the sea – a relaxed, easy-going place where it's mostly Moroccans who come to holiday. Falling into their pattern presents few problems. The local beach is a good one, football there an obsession and fish restaurants plentiful. Nearby, too, are the scattered ruins of *Ancient Lixus*, legendary site of the Gardens of the Hesperides.

The town itself is attractive, if not spectacularly so: a kind of half-hearted amalgam of Tangier and Tetouan. It was the main port of the northern Spanish zone and – though the central Plaza de España has switched to become the Place de la Libération – still bears much of their stamp. There are faded old Spanish hotels, Spanish-run restaurants and Spanish bars, even an active Spanish cathedral for the small colony who still work at the docks. Yet for all this it seems a very Moroccan, and rather a dignified, sort of place.

Before the Spanish colonisation in 1911, Larache was a small trading port, its activities limited by dangerous offshore sand bars. Without these it might have rivalled Tangier, for it is better positioned as a trade route to Fes. Instead it provided a small living in the construction of pirate-ships, built with the wood of the nearby Forest of Mamora for the 'Barbary Corsairs' of Salé and Rabat. It was also Spanish for a period in the C17 and fortified by them before being reclaimed and repopulated by Moulay Ismail. The **Chateau de la Cigogne** ('Storks Castle'), a hulking three-sided fortress-compound which you pass on the way into town, owes its origin to this first occupation.

From the second, the most striking piece of Spanish architecture is the town's main square, the circular **Place de la Libération** – just back from the sea and a straightforward 200m walk from the (combined) *bus station* and *grand taxi* rank. There are two good cheap **hotels** in the *place* – the once-grand, still elegant *Hôtel Espana* (1*B), and slightly more expensive, sea-view *Cervantes*. If these are both full, which is unlikely, there are also three pensions on the street from bus station to place (Rue Mohammed Ben Abdellah), along with the luxuriant pool-and-gardens *Hôtel Riad* (3*A).

A high Mauresque arch at the centre of the Place gives onto the **Medina**, a surprisingly small wedge of alleys and stairways leading down towards the port. It is now the poorest area of Larache – better-off families have moved out to the new parts of town, leaving their houses here to the elderly – but doesn't seem so bad, artfully shaded and airy in its design. The colonnaded market square, just inside the arch, was built by the seventeenth-century Spanish, a fairly lively focus, whilst to your left, past the dingy *Hôtel Watan* there are some reasonable hole-in-the-wall eateries. If you want to stay in the Medina, the *Pension Atlas* is just right of the square, as you go in, and should be the cheapest place in town.

The shore below Larache is wild and rocky, but cross its estuary and there are miles of fine sandy beach – sheltered by trees and flanked by a handful of cafe-restaurants. You can go there by bus (no. 4 from the port, every 20 minutes: sometimes starting from the *place*), a roundabout 7km route, or you can get straight over from the port – a dirham each in small fishing boats. From the *place*, the quickest route down to **the port** is along a sea-front path, past the crumbling **Fort Kebibat** ('Little Domes'), built by Portuguese merchants in the C16.

Eating, except in the Medina cafes, or the sardine-grills down at the port, is still resolutely Spanish. The best place is the *Restaurant-Bar El Pozo*, opposite the Hotel Espana: a little more expensive than the rest but worth the difference. El Pozo also serves *raciones* at the bar; otherwise steer for the cheapest cafes in the square around the entrance-arch to the Medina.

Ancient Lixus

Founded by Phoenician colonists around 1000BC, **LIXUS** is thought to have been the first trading post of North Africa and was probably its earliest permanent settlement. It became an important Carthaginian and later Roman city and was deserted only after the break-up of the Empire in the C5AD. As an archaeological site it is significant, and the legendary associations make rich ground for imaginings, but it has to be said that the actual excavated ruins are not especially impressive. In fact, with the single exception of Volubilis (near Meknes), the best surviving monuments of Roman Africa are all to be found in Tunisia and Algeria.

This acknowledged, if you're spending any amount of time at Larache, or passing through by car, the Lixus ruins are well worth an hour or two's exploration. They lie below and upon the summit of a low hill on the far side of the estuary from the town: at the crossroads of the main

Larache-Tangier road and the lane to Larache beach. It's a 4-5km walk from either the beach or town, or you can use the bus which runs between the two. The site is not effectively enclosed, so there are no real opening hours.

The **Lower Town**, right beside the main road, consists largely of factories for the production of salt – still panned roundabout – and, as at Cotta, of anchovy-paste *garum*. They seem to have been developed in the early years of the first century by the Carthaginians, and they remained in operation until the Roman withdrawal.

A track, 200 yards down the road to Tangier, leads up to the Acropolis, or **Upper Town**, passing on its way a dozen or so rows of the Roman **Theatre and Amphitheatre**, unusually combined into a single structure. Its deep circular arena was adapted for circus games and the gladiatorial slaughter of animals. Morocco, which Herodotus knew as 'the wild beast country', was the major source for these Roman *venationes* and local colonists must have grown rich from the trade. Amid **baths** built into the side of the theatre, a small mosaic remains in situ, depicting *Neptune and the oceans*.

Climbing above the baths and theatre you pass through ramparts to the principal enceinte of the **Acropolis**, a rather confused network of walls and foundations – of **temple sanctuaries**, an early **Christian basilica**, and a number of **pre-Roman buildings**. The most considerable of the sanctuaries, with their underground cisterns and porticoed priests' quarters, were apparently rebuilt in the C1 AD but even then retained Phoenician elements in their design.

The **legendary associations** of Lixus – and the site's mystique – centre on the Labours of Hercules. For here, on an island in the estuary, Pliny and Strabo record reports of the Palace of the 'Libyan' (by which they mean African) King Antaeus. Behind stretched the *Garden of the Hesperides*, to which Hercules, as his penultimate labour, was despatched. In his quest – the Golden Apples – it is not difficult to imagine the tangerines of northern Morocco, raised to mythic status by travellers' tales. And indeed the site itself seems to offer reinforcement to conjectures of a mythic pre-Phoenicien past. Megalithic stones have been found on the Acropolis, and some early form of sun worship seems still to be echoed in the local name – *shamush*, 'the sun-burnt'.

KSAR EL KEBIR, SOUK EL ARBA AND MOULAY BOUSSELHAM

Heading south from LARACHE, the main road and most of the buses by-pass **KSAR EL KEBIR** – and unless it's a Sunday, when the town has one of the region's largest markets, it seems as well to accept the fact. However, as its name – literally 'the Great Enclosure' – suggests, this was once a place of some importance. Founded in the C11, it became an early Arab power-base, enlarged and endowed by both Almohads and Merenids and coveted by the Spanish and Portuguese of Asilah and Larache. Here in 1578 the Portuguese fought the most disastrous battle in their nation's history – a Crusading expedition which saw the death or capture of virtually the entire nobility – and the Moroccans saw the fortuitous accession of Ahmed el Mansour, the greatest of all Merenids Sultans, who went on to conquer Timbuctou.

Ksar el Kebir fell into decline in the C17 after a local chief incurred the wrath of Moulay Ismail, causing him to destroy the walls; neglect followed, although its fortunes revived to some extent under the Spanish protectorate. If you stop off here a while, the **Sunday markets** are held right by the bus and *grand taxi* terminals – and on any morning of the week there are quite lively **souks** around the main *kissaria* of the old town; this is in the quarter known as *Bab el Oued* (the Gate of the River).

Beyond Ksar el Kebir, a decaying customs post at ARBAOUA marks the old colonial frontier between Spanish and French zones. **SOUK EL ARBA DU RHARB**, a sprawling roadside town where there are *grill-cafés* (and hotels if you get stuck), is the first village of any size, though it is little more than its name specifies, 'the Wednesday market of the Gharb plain'. However, if you're making for either OUEZZANE or MOULAY BOUSSELHAM, this is the place to come. To Ouezzane there are infrequent buses but quite routine (and very much quicker) *grand taxis*; Moulay Bousselham is well served by both – and it is also, if you are happy to be a more or less lone European, a very attractive resort.

Having pledged that buses are prolific to **MOULAY BOUSSELHAM** it's perhaps worth adding that just because there's one around doesn't mean it's about to leave. *The Bousselham bus* – at least when I took it – was one of those classically timeless Moroccan exercises. It arrived out of nowhere, quarter full and engine revving with urgency, a flurry of action as everyone piled on, then slammed doors and 50 metres down the road. There we all stopped, trying to persuade a handful of country women to get on – or if not, to at least consider the idea. Five eventually did, meanwhile four other passengers had decided to stay in Souk el Arba; and so it all continued, up and down the road to try and fill the bus before an eventual and furious altercation set everything smoothly in motion.

Even after this kind of a morning, though, Moulay Bousselham seems a worthwhile place to arrive. A smallish village-resort, it's little more than a single street, crowded with cafe-grills and sloping down to the sea at the side of a broad lagoon. Rare along the Atlantic, the **beach** here is sheltered by cliffs. It has a sudden drop-down shelf, too, creating a continual thrash of breakers – all a lot of fun, and strictly patrolled. For more realistic swimming you can wander round to the lagoon, which is where most people stay, at a really beautifully-positioned **campsite**. If you're *not* camping, alternatives are distinctly limited: you might get a room above one of the cafes, but otherwise there's just one small **hotel**, the 3*A *Le Lagon* (Tel. 28). The hotel, incidentally, has the only bar in the place – along with a surprisingly good cinema and somewhat ritzy nightclub.

OUEZZANE (WAZZAN)

Midway from the coast to CHAOUEN, **OUEZZANE** lopes down around an outreach of the Djebala mountains – the edge of the Rif and the old traditional border of the *Bled es-Makhzen* and the *Bled es-Siba*, the governed territories and those of the lawless tribes. As such, it became an important power base through the last two centuries and its sheikhs were among the most powerful in Morocco.

The sheikhs – the *Ouezzani* – were also the spiritual leaders of the influential **Tabiya brotherhood**. They were *shereefs* (descendants of the Prophet) and came of a direct line from the Idrissids, the first and founding dynasty of Morocco. This however seems to have given them little significance until the C18, when Moulay Abdallah es-Shereef established a *zaouia* at Ouezzane. It acquired a huge following, becoming one of the great points of pilgrimage and an inviolable sanctuary for all Muslims. Unlike Chaouen, the town which grew about was not itself sacred – but until the turn of this century Jews and Christians were allowed to take only temporary accommodation in one of the *fondouks* set aside for the purpose. Walter Harris, who became a close friend of the Ouezzani shereefs* of his time, found the town 'the most fanatical that Europeans may visit' and the zaouia a virtually autonomous religious court.

The **Zaouia**, distinguished by an unusual octagonal minaret, is the most striking building in the town and though the Tabiya brotherhood now maintain their main base elsewhere it continues to function and is the site of a lively spring *moussem*. (As throughout Morocco, however, entrance to the zaouia precinct is forbidden to non-Muslims). The older quarters of Ouezzane – many of their buildings tiles, gabled and elaborately doored – enclose and rise above the building, newer suburbs sprawling into the hills on each side. It's an attractive enough place, and if of little specific interest, has a definite grandeur in its site. Few tourists

---

*Two of these *shereefs* became quite mad – one shooting pilgrims at random from a balcony of the zaouia, with a soldier positioned below to warn them! As ever Harris gives a tragi-comic account in *Morocco That Was*.

stay since it is only a couple of hours on to Chaouen, but there are worse places to be stranded. The bus and *grand taxi* terminal is about 50m below the main square – the **Place du Souks**, where you'll find three reasonable, basic **hotels**. The main **souks** climb up from an arch here, behind the *Grand Hôtel*. Ouezzane has a local reputation for its woollen rugs – most evident in the weavers' souk, around the Place Rouida near the top end of the town.

There are a fair number of **buses** to both Meknes and Fes but if you're stopping or staying buy onward tickets well in advance; it's not unusual for them to arrive and leave full. Getting to CHAOUEN, though, is rarely a problem.

CEUTA, TETOUAN AND CHAOUEN

CEUTA (SEBTA)

A Spanish enclave since the C16. **CEUTA** (or *SEBTA* in Arabic) is a curious political anomaly. It was retained by Spain after Moroccan Independence in 1956 but today functions only as a military base, its economy bolstered through limited duty-free status. On a clear day you can almost see Gibraltar, which, in the absence of anything else of interest, seems somehow symbolic.

Since the Algeciras ferries take an hour less than to Tangier, however, this is a popular **point of entry**. Coming over on a first visit to Morocco try to arrive early in the day so you have plenty of time to move on to Tetouan – and possibly beyond. There is no customs/passport check at the port since you don't officially enter Morocco until the border at FNIDEQ; 3km out of town, reached by local bus from the seafront. As you come off the ferry turn left – the bus stop is about 100 metres down, in the second main square, Plaza del General Galera. Once across the frontier the easiest transport on is a shared *grand taxi* to Tetouan (split six ways, currently 10dhs each); buses are infrequent though a couple of dirhams cheaper. There are **exchange facilities** on each side of the frontier.

In Ceuta itself there isn't a great deal to do. There is no real beach to speak of – locals go by bus to *Playa Benzou*, some way out of town – and by London discount prices the 'duty-free' cameras and radios are expensive. Most of the town, which is surprisingly large, is modern, functional and provincial in the dullest Spanish manner. There is a

Cathedral, *Our Lady of Africa*, in the main **Plaza de Africa** opposite the ferry quay, and an oldish quarter rambling up from the end of the long main street, **Calle Jose Antonio**. Beyond this you can walk out and around the peninsula in little over an hour.

Three to a dozen blocks in width, the town occupies a long wedge to the west of the port. As its buildings give out the land swells into a rounded pine-covered slope: a geographical echo of the Rock of Gibraltar, with which it forms the so-called *Pillars of Hercules*, gateway to the Classical World. This part of Ceuta, **Monte Acho**, is occupied more or less exclusively by the military. Walking the circuit, signs direct you to the **Ermida de San Antonio**, an old convent completely rebuilt in the 1960s and dominated by a monument to Franco, whose Nationalist forces sailed from the port to begin the Spanish Civil War. Unlike most mainland Spanish towns, which have been to some extent de-politicised, Ceuta's streetnames still read like a roll-call of France's *Falange*.

If you **plan to stay** overnight be warned that it isn't easy to find a room – and not cheap when you do; with its large garrison and cheap consumer goods Ceuta has a constant flow of Spanish families. Much the best bet, if you've a card, is the **youth hostel** (*posada de juventud*) at Plaza Viejo 27, with dormitory beds and low-priced rooms for 2-6 people. To get there turn left as you come off the ferry and walk along the seafront to the start of c/Jose Antonio, the main street; just at the beginning of this, by a sign for *Tonyo's Hifi*, stairs lead off right to the Plaza. Besides the hostel, there are a dozen or so *hotels, hostals* and *pensions*, most of them along c/Jose Antonio or its continuations. A complete list and a map of town are available at the **Oficina de Turismo** by the ferry dock, and displayed in its window if it's closed. Cheaper pensions – and some good **bars** with food – are mostly grouped right at the far end of c/Jose Antonio, by which time it has become c/Falange Española.

TETOUAN

For anyone coming from CEUTA, TETOUAN is the first experience of a Moroccan town: a disadvantage you're quickly made aware of. The Medina here can seem huge and totally unfamiliar, and the hustlers, with large quantities of kif to offload have the worst reputation anywhere in Morocco.

It is, however, an unusually striking town, poised above the slope of a tremendous valley and backed against a dark mass of rock. It's name, pronounced *Tet-tá-wan*, means in Berber 'Open Your Eyes', possibly a reference to the town's hasty construction by Andalusian refugees in the C15. The refugees, both Muslims and Jews, brought with them the most refined sophistication of Moorish Andalusia – an aristocratic tradition that is still reflected in the architecture of the Medina. Their houses, full of extravagant detail, are quite unlike those of other Moroccan towns: indeed, with their tiled lintels and wrought iron balconies, they seem much more akin to the old Arab quarters of Cordoba and Sevilla.

Arriving and finding a room

Arriving by bus or *grand taxi* you'll find yourself on the edge of the new town – slightly left of centre near the bottom of our townplan. If you're moving straight on, there are regular **buses** from the station here to Chaouen, Meknes, Fes and Tangier; ask around at the various windows before buying a ticket as both CTM and private companies operate on each of these routes.

Staying in Tetouan, try to ignore all offers and head for one of the **hotels or pensions** listed below and keyed on the plan. You're likely to do best at the first five – all officially classified – since other pensions including those we've listed raise summer prices well above the basic rate. This is partly because newly arrived tourists pay whatever they're asked, but also a reflection of demand. With its excellent local beaches, Tetouan is a popular Moroccan resort and rooms in July/August can take a while to find.

Hôtel Trebol (1*A), 3 Yacoub el Mansour. Right behind the bus station, safe, a little damp, but more or less adequate.
Hôtel Principe (1*A), 20 Youssef Tachfine. Much better in all respects. Halfway up from the bus station to the main *place* of the New Town.
Hôtel Nacional (2*B), 8 Rue Mohamed Torres. Reasonable, if dull; sometimes insists on full pension in midsummer.
Hôtel Regina (1*B), 8 Rue Sidi Mandri. Thoroughly recommended though often full. Three blocks up from the bus station.
Hôtel Dersa (3*B), 8 Boulevard General Franco. Expensive, if marginally the best in town. Opposite the Regina.

Pension Riojana, Pension Florida, Pension Bienvenito, Pension Iberia. All of these are in – or just off – the central Place Moulay el Mehdi. Iberia, above the B.M.C.E. bank, is very small but a definite first choice.
Pension Esperanza, Pension Fes. Best of many overpriced places along the Boulevard Mohammed V.
Pension Cosmopolita, 5 Boulevard General Franco. Slightly pricey but very clean. Opposite the Regina.
Pension Camas, Pension Suiza, Rue Luneta. Both very basic – on a narrow street at the edge of the Medina, reached from the corner of Place Hassan II.

There are some thirty or so **other pensions**, a few of them within the Medina itself – most around its periphery. The highest concentration is in the circular **Place Hassan II**, which separates the new and old towns.

These, the favoured choice of bus station hustlers are positively worth avoiding: if a guide brings you here he'll have virtual access to your room as long as you stay, and he's *not* going to believe that you don't want to buy kif, or anything else on offer. This goes, too, for a good many 'students' and 'guides' who lay claim to you in the streets: a tedious and at times aggressive exercise. But despite this, and first impressions around the bus station, it is not too difficult to get **some bearings** and to find your own way about.

The **NEW TOWN**, built by the Spanish as the capital of their colonial zone, follows a fairly straightforward grid. At its centre is the **Place Moulay el Mehdi**, with the PTT (post/phones office) and main banks. From here the grid stretches east towards the **MEDINA**, still partially walled, and entered from the **Place Hassan II**. This square, sprawling with cafe tables, is the real heart of the town – a gathering place through the evening, when hash-smokers fill out its upper-storey dens and half the town strolls through.

By day, at least, the Medina is good just to wander. It's not as large as it appears and you won't get lost for long without hitting on an outer wall and gate, beyond which you can loop round back to the New Town. Specific points of interest are detailed in the following section, or for an easier introduction official guides can be arranged at the **Tourist Office**, a few yards down Blvd Mohammed V from the Place el Mehdi. The office (open Mon-Fri 8am-2pm & 3-6pm; Sat & sometimes Sun 8am-2pm) will also **change money** when the banks are closed.

The town and Medina

Tetouan has been occupied twice by the Spanish. It was seized, briefly, as a supposed threat to Ceuta, from 1859-1862: a period which saw the Medina converted to a town of almost European appearance, complete with street lighting. The second occupation began in 1913 and stretched over five decades of this century. Tetouan served first as a military garrison for the subjugation of the Rif, later as the capital of the **Spanish Protectorate Zone**, and as such almost doubled in size to handle the region's trade and administration. 'Native tradition' was respected to the extent of leaving the Medina intact, and even restoring its finer mansions, but in social terms there was more or less negative progress: Spanish administration retained a purely military character and only a handful of schools were opened throughout the entire zone – a legacy which had effects well beyond Independence in 1956. The town adapted with difficulty to the new French-Moroccan-dominated nation and continues in a slightly uneasy relationship with central government. This came again to the surface with the 1984 riots.

Looking around Tetouan, you inevitably seem to gravitate towards the **Place Hassan II** – the old assembly-place and market square, still domi-

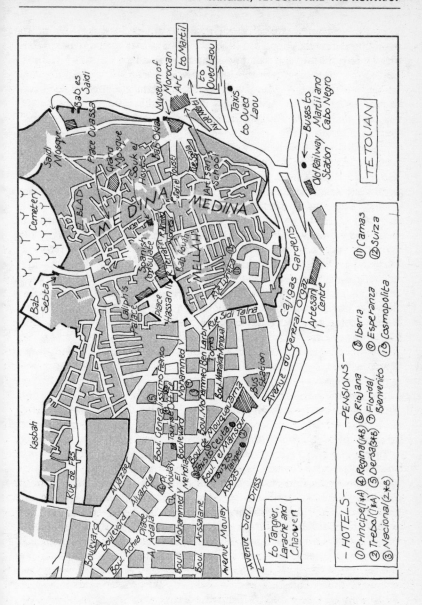

Bab es Saïdi
Saïdi Mosque
Place Ouassa Saïdi
Grand Mosque
Museum of Moroccan Art
to Martil
to Oued Laou
Taxis to Oued Laou
Buses to Martil and Cabo Negro
Old Railway Station
TETOUAN

Cemetery
EL BLAD
Souk el Houts
Bab Okla
Sidi Ali ben Reyaïs
Derb en Nakhla
Artisan School
MEDINA
MEDINA
Spanish Consulate
L'Terrada Prince
Bab Rouah
MELLAH
Retiro

Bab Sebta
Cajigas Gardens
Callipus Palace
Place Hassan II
Rue Sidi Talha
Artesan Centre
Kasbah
Rue de Fès
Alcazar
Alvarca
Al Adala
Boul. General Orozco
Mohammed V
P. Moudy Tourist Office
Boul. Mohammed Ben Larb
Boul. Mohammed El Mehdia
Boul. de Ceuta
Boul. Youquouama
Boul. Y. el Mansour
Tangier
Alcazar
Bus Station
Avenue au General Orgaz
Boul. Achla plage
Boul. Arsalane
Avenue Moulay Abbas
Avenue Sidi Driss
to Tangier, Larache and Chaouen

— HOTELS —
① Principe (1*A) ④ Regina (H8) ⑥ Riojana
② Trebol (1*A) ⑤ Dersa (3*B) ⑦ Florida
③ Nacional (2*B) ⑧ Bienvenito

— PENSIONS —
ⓐ Iberia ⓓ Camas
ⓑ Esperanza ⓔ Suiza
ⓒ Cosmopolita

nated by the Spanish Consulate. The usual approach to the Medina is through the arch beside it, the **Bab el Rouah** (Gate of the Winds). The next lane to the right of this opens onto the main street of the **Mellah**, built as late as 1807 when the Jews were moved from an area around the Grand Mosque. Few of them remain today, although if you ask around someone will probably point out the old synagogues.

Entering the MEDINA proper at **Bab el Rouah** you find yourself on the **Rue Terrafin** – a relatively wide lane which (with its continuations) cuts straight across to the East Gate, Bab el Oqla. To the left of the street a series of alleys give access to most of the town's food and craft souks. The **Souk el Houts**, a small shaded square directly behind the grounds of the Spanish Consulate, is one of the most active – devoted to fish in the mornings, meat in the afternoons, and with an all-day smattering of local pottery stalls. At its top end, two lanes wind up through a mass of alleys, souks and passageways towards the Bab Sebta. Following the one on the left for about 20 metres you'll see an opening (on the right) to another small square. This is the **Guersa el Kebira**, essentially a cloth and textile souk, where a number of stalls sell the town's exceptional *foutahs* – strong and brilliantly striped lengths of rug-like cotton, worn as cloak and skirt by the Djebali Berber women.

Leaving the Guersa at its top right-hand corner you should emerge more or less on the **Place de l'Oussa**, another really beautiful little square – easily recognised by an ornate tiled fountain and trellis of vines. Along one of its sides is an imposing C19 *fondouk*, or caravanserai; on another, a 'Moorish Cafe' – elegantly tiled and with good views over the quarter from its roof. Beyond the square, still heading up towards the Sebta (Ceuta) gate, are most of the specific **craft souks** – among them copper and brass workers, long-reputed *babouche* makers, and carpenters specialising in elaborately carved and painted wood. Most of the shops along the central lane here – **Rue el Jarrazin** – are focused on the tourist trade, but this goes much less for the souks themselves.

So too with the souks around the **Rue de Fes**, off to the left: and easiest reached by following the lane up the side of the Caliph's Palace in Place Hassan II. This is the main throughfare of a much more mundane area of ordinary workaday goods and an occasional villagers' flea market or *joutia*. At its main intersection – just to the right as you emerge on the lane up from Place Hassan II – is the **Souk el Foki**, once the town's main business sector though little more than a wide alleyway. Following this past a small perfume souk and two sizeable mosques you meet up with the Rue el Jarrazin about 15 metres below the **Bab Sebta**. Walk out this way, passing (on your left) the superb portal of the *Derkaoua zaouia*, and you enter a huge and very ancient **cemetery** – in use since at least the C15 and containing unusually elaborate Andalusian tombs. Fridays excluded, non-Muslims are tolerated in most Moroccan cemeteries, and walking here you get illuminating views over the Medina and across the valley to the beginning of the Rif.

Had you proceeded along the main drag of Rue Terrafin/Rue Ahmed Torres/Rue Sidi el Yousti you would have reached the eastern edge of the Medina at **Bab Okla**. The quarter to the north of here, below the Grand Mosque, was the Medina's most exclusive residential area and contains some of its finest mansions. Walking towards the Bab you will see signs for one of the best of them, a *Palais* now converted into a (highly touristic) carpet and artesania warehouse. Considerably more authentic, and an interesting comparison of real quality, is the **Museum of Moroccan Arts** (*Musée d'Art Marocain*). whose entrance is just on the outside of the Bab Okla. A former arms bastion, this has one of the more impressive collections around of traditional crafts and ethnographic objects. Take a look particularly at the zellij – enamelled tile mosaics – and then cross the road to the **Artesan School** (*Ecole de Métiers*) where you can see craftsmen working at new designs in the old ways, essentially unmodified since the C14. Perhaps owing to its Andalusian heritage, Tetouan actually has a slightly different zellij technique to other Moroccan cities – the tiles being cut before rather than after being fired. A slightly easier process, this is frowned upon by the craftsmen of Fes – whose own pieces are more brittle but brighter in colour and closer fitting. Both school and museum are open 9-12noon & 2.30-5.30pm daily, except Tues & Sun; the school additionally closes down for most of August.

Outside the Medina there is little of interest. The **Caliphal Palace**, built during the reign of Moulay Ismail, was heavily restored for use by King Hassan's father and predecessor Mohammed V, and, as with all of Morocco's royal palaces, is no longer open to visitors. There is another **Artesan Centre** on the main road below the town, but a distinctly unimpressive one, of interest only if you're buying in the souks and want to check out prices and quality first. And, lastly, there is a pleasant if unmemorable **Archaeological Museum** (same hours as above). This was assembled during the Spanish Protectorate so features exhibits from throughout their zone – prehistoric stones from the Western Sahara among them. Highlights, as so often in North Africa, are the Roman mosaics, mostly gathered from Lixus and the ever-plundered Volubilis.

Some details
BEACHES Martil, Cabo Negro, Mdiq and even Oued Laou are all quite easy day-trips (see the following section). Buses to the first three leave frequently through the day from behind a ramshackle green and white building on the road to Ceuta. For Oued Laou there are 2 buses daily from the *main* station (8am/5pm) or you can share a *grand taxi* (from the Oued Laou road junction).

CAMPING Nearest official site is 11km out at Martil (see the following section.

EATING Cheapest in the Medina, particularly in the stalls inside Bab el Rouah and along Rue Luneta in the Mellah. For more variety or confidence try one of the many places on or around Blvd Mohammed V/Blvd Mohammed Torres. *Restaurant Moderne*, on Pasaje Acharc, is one of the best of these: to get there go through the arcades opposite Cinema Espanol on Place Hassan II.

GETTING TO CEUTA Much easier than vice versa. Both buses (from the main bus station; 8dhs) and *grands taxis* (from the next block along; 10dhs) leave quite regularly for the border at Fnideq. Once across you can pick up a local Spanish bus for the 3km into town. NB that baggage checks are often carried out both at the Mdiq border and again on arrival at Algeciras.

POLICE Opposite the *Hôtel Dersa* on the other side of Blvd General Franco.

THE TETOUAN BEACHES: FROM MDIQ TO OUED LAOU

Despite the numbers of tourists passing through Tetouan is above all a resort for Moroccans: a character very much in evidence at most of the beaches around. Through the summer, and particularly after Ramadan, whole villages of family tents appear at **Martil, Mdiq** and further down the coast around **Restinga Smir**. At **Oued Laou**, getting on for 40km to the east of town, there's a younger and slightly alternative feel – something which is attracting small but growing groups of German, French and to a lesser extent British travellers.

West: Martil, Cabo Negro and Mdiq

MARTIL, essentially Tetouan's town beach, was its port too until the river between the two silted up. Through the Middle Ages it maintained an active corsair fleet, twice prompting Spanish raids to block the harbour. Today it is a small but quite lively fishing town, slightly knock-together in appearance, with its rows of holiday shacks along the seafront. The beach, which stretches all the way round to the upmarket villas of Cabo Negro, is excellent: good fine-yellow sand and uncrowded for all its summer popularity. *Camping Martil*, the official site, is just back from the beach, by the river on the east side of town – friendly and cheap, though not a place to leave bags unattended. Almost opposite, on Rue Miramar, is the *Hôtel Nuzha*, unclassified but charging roughly 1*A prices for standard pension rooms. If this is full they will probably find you a room nearby, or there are two cheapish pensions by the bus station: the *Hôtel Rabat* and clean, preferable *Pension Rif*.

Most of the Martil buses go on to **CABO NEGRO**, an attractive alternative for lying about on the sands but without casual places to stay other than the 3*A *Hôtel Petit Merou* (tel. 8110). To get to MDIQ, or the sprawling complexes and campsites of SMIR-RESTINGA, you leave from the same point in Tetouan (see above) but on a separate local bus. **MDIQ**, for most tastes, is overcrowded and overdeveloped with a large *campsite* and several holiday clubs – though in Moroccan terms this in itself is a novelty; if you want a room here the one cheap option is *Hôtel Playa* (1*B). **RESTINGA-SMIR** is more a collective name for a length of beach than for an actual place or village: an attractive strip of the Mediterranean but without great appeal unless you happen to be staying at the *Club Méditerranée* or one of the other big hotels staked amidst the pines.

East: in the shadow of the Rif

East of Tetouan the coastline is almost immediately distinct. For a few kilometres the road follows the sea, still more or less continuous beach and dotted with communities of tents, but very soon it begins to climb into the foothills of the Rif, a first taste of the manically switchbacking Moroccan mountain roads. When you finally emerge at **OUED LAOU**, irrespective of its beach or appeal, you're likely to want to stay!

This, at least, is a positive option. Oued Laou is not an especially pretty place – Riffian villages tend to look sprawling and centre-less – but it has a terrific, near-deserted beach spreading for miles to each side. You can **camp** here, down by the river, or there's a small and very relaxed **hotel** right by the sea, the *Hôtel-Café Oued Laou*, If it is full, or if you want to pay less than their one-star prices, they'll find you rooms else-where – Oued Laou is a very no-problem easy-going sort of place. It is also one of the most accessible parts of the Rif, and good ground to meet and talk: hustlers have nothing to hustle except kif and rooms, and aren't too bothered about either. Having come out here, off the tourist route, it is assumed that you're not completely stupid or innocent. There's a Saturday **market** which draws villagers from all over the Laou valley and neighbouring hills.

If you have transport a very poor track heads inland from over Laou to CHAOUEN and another, pot-holed and for the most part *piste*, continues to TARGA (again a good beach, with two or three basic provisions shops and a few campers) and eventually EL JEBHA (see p. 73). No buses serve either of these routes.

CHAOUEN (CHECHAOUEN, CHEFCHAOUEN, XAOUEN)

Shut in by a fold of mountains, **CHAOUEN** becomes visible only once you have arrived: a dramatic approach to a town which, up until the arrival of Spanish troops in 1920, had been visited by just four Europeans. Charles de Foucauld, the French missionary explorer, was among them, entering in the disguise of a Jewish rabbi. Another, inevitably, was Walter Harris, whose main impulse, described in his book *Land of an African Sultan*, was 'the very fact that there existed within thirty hours' ride of Tangier a city in which it was considered an utter impossibility for a Christian to enter'.

The impossibility – and Harris very nearly lost his life when the town was alerted to the presence of 'a Christian dog' – went right back to Chaouen's foundation in 1471. The whole region hereabouts is sacred to Muslims through the presence of the tomb of *Moulay Abdessalam ben Mchich*, patron saint of the Djebali tribesmen and one of the 'four poles of Islam', and Chaouen was itself established by one of his Shereefian followers, Moulay Rachid, as a secret base to attack the Portuguese of Ceuta and Ksar es Seghir. Over the following century its population grew increasingly anti-European with the arrival of refugees from Moorish Spain, and it became a considerable centre of marabouts and pilgrimage. But beyond this the town was extraordinarily isolated. When the Spanish troops began their occupation they found Jews here speaking and in some cases writing, medieval Castilian – a language extinct in Spain for nearly four hundred years.

Chaouen is now well established on the excursion routes, though surprisingly little affected. There are the inevitable souks and stalls for coach-groups, and one real monster of a hotel has been allowed to disfigure the twin peaks (*ech-Chaoua:* the horns) from which it takes its name, but this is about all. Local attitudes towards tourists, and to the predominantly backpacking travellers who stop over, are relaxed; pensions among the friendliest and cheapest around, and to stay here a few days and walk in the hills is still one of the best possible introductions to Morroco.

Rooms and orientation

With a population of just 17,000 – a tenth that of Tetouan – Chaouen is more like a large village in size and feel: confusing only on arrival. **Buses** drop you at the marketplace, outside the walls of the town in a vague straggle of new buildings grouped about the Mosque of Moulay Rachid. To reach the **MEDINA** you walk up across the marketplace; its tiny arched entrance, the **Bab el Ain**, is just beyond the prominent Hôtel Magou. Through the gateway a clearly dominant lane winds up all the way through the town to the main square, **Place Outa el Hammam** (flanked by the gardens and ruined towers of the **Kasbah**), and beyond to a second smaller square, the **Place el Makhzen**. Either along or just off this main route are virtually all the **hotels and pensions** detailed below and keyed on the plan.

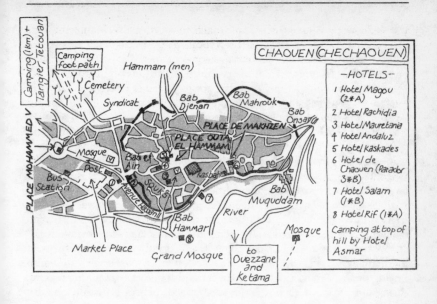

Hôtel Rachidia, Hôtel Mauretania, Hôtel Andaluz, Pension Castellana.
Unless you have an urge for luxury, these are the places to stay: half the
price of most pensions in Morocco, exceptionally clean, and each
converted from small, ordinary houses in the Medina. Rachidia is the
first you come upon, just inside the Medina walls to the right of the Bab
el Ain. Andaluz and Castellana are signposted up an alley to the left at
the near end of the main *place*; Mauretania down a brief network of
lanes to the right. If they have space, Castellana is the one to go for –
extremely easygoing but well run, with excellent communal evening meals
and a (male) *hammam* next door.

Hôtel Magou (2*A), *Hôtel Chaouen* (3*B). The upmarket choices.
Magou is well above average, but if you've money to spend make for the
Chaouen in the Place el Makhzen: this was the old Spanish luxury *parador*
and has its own swimming pool (10dhs to outsiders) and – rare in
Chaouen – bar.

Hôtel Salam (1*B), *Hôtel Rif* (1*A). Both on the lower road.

Camping Chaouen. Up on the hill above the town, by the big modern
Hotel Asma. To get there follow the signs to the Asma by road, or
(Fridays apart) walk up through the cemetery.

The town and river

Like Tetouan, Chaouen's architecture has a strong Andalusian character:
less elaborate (and less grand) perhaps, but often equally inventive. It is

a town of extraordinary light and colour – its whitewash tinted with blue and edged around the soft gold-stone walls – and it is a place which, for all its present popularity, still seems redolent of the years of isolation. The roofs of its houses, tiled and eaved, are an obvious physical assertion, in contrast to the flat tops found everywhere else in Morocco. But it is something you feel about the whole life here, even about the people themselves – inbred over many generations.

Since the **MEDINA** is so small, it is more than ever a place to walk at random: the things which draw your attention are not so much 'sights' as unexpected strands of detail. Make at some point, though, for the two main squares, and for the **souks** – just below the Place Outa el Hammam. There are basic town souks held twice weekly (Mons & Thurs) in the market square, so these are to some degree created, or at least geared, for the tourist industry. But both their quality and variety is surprising. When the Spanish arrived – just 60 years ago – Chaouen artesans were still working leather in the manner of C12 Cordoba, tanning with bark, and hammering silver to old Andalusian designs. And though you won't see any of this today, the town's carpet and weaving workshops remain active and many of their designs unchanged. Sellers are well used to students and travellers, and if you're staying for a few days prices can fall unmentionably low.

Place Outa el Hammam, the elongated main square, is where most of the evening life takes place, its cafes overhung by upper rooms – usually full of kif smoke, though when I was last here in May taken over by swarms of honey-bees. By day its focus is the **kasbah**, a quiet ruin shaded with gardens, built like so many of northern Morocco by Moulay Ismail. Off to the right in the first of its compounds are the old town prison cells, where Abd el Krim (see p.00) was imprisoned after his surrender in 1926. Five years earlier he had himself driven the Spanish from the town, a retreat which saw the loss of nearly 20,000 of their troops.

The *place* was once also the main market square, and off to its sides are a number of small **fondouks** – one of the more visible at the beginning of the lane opposite the kasbah (no. 34). Somewhat bizarrely, the local Djebala tribesmen, who form most of the town's population, have a particular tradition of homosexuality and there were *boy markets* held here until as recently as 1937, when they were officially banned by the Spanish administration. Djebali sexual preferences are just one of the characteristics which mark them apart from the notoriously *anti*-homosexual Riffians of the mountains beyond.

Place de Makhzen – the old 'government square' – is in some ways a continuation of the marketplace, an elegant clearing with an old fountain and pottery stalls strung out for the coach tours. If you leave the Medina at this point, it's possible to follow **the river** around the outside of the walls and up above the Bab Onsar. Here, you reach the **Ras el Ma**

('waterhead'), a small cascade in the mountainside with water so clear and cold that, in the local phrase, 'it knocks your teeth out to drink it'. Long a favoured spot – and to an extent a holy one through the nearby tomb of Sidi Abdallah Habti – there are a couple of cafes close by to while away the middle of the day, the further almost the exclusive preserve of Moroccan *kiyafs* ('kif-heads').

Buses and details

BUSES to Fes, and to a lesser degree, Meknes, are often full and you should really try to get tickets the day before – an exercise which may need some persistence. Current departure times to Fes are around 6.30am and 11.30am; to Meknes at noon. If you can't get on to any of these an alternative is to take a *grand taxi* or local bus to Ouezzane and another onwards from there. For Tetouan buses leave at least four times a day, much less of a problem.

EATING Outside the pensions which share food (the *Mauretania* and *Castellana*) there's a fairly small choice: a few places in the Place Outa el Hammam (*Restaurant Kasba* is probably the best of these), and the very reasonable *Restaurant Azhar* to the left of the Post Office.

HAMMAMS Chaouen, slightly unusually, has separate *hammams* (Turkish baths) for men and women. The male one is right next to the Pension Castellana, off Place Outa el Hammam; that for women, older and much more elaborate, is in the quarter of the souks – ask someone to show you the way, it totally defies written directions.

SWIMMING The *Hôtel Chaouen* has a pool, open to non-residents for a pricey 10dhs a day. Locals share a taxi to a *pool in the river*, a few kilometres downstream; an excellent alternative for which any of the pension people will give full instructions.

BANK *Banque Populaire* in the Place Mohammed V in the 'new town'.

FESTIVALS As the centre of so much *maraboutism*, Chaouen and its neighbouring villages have a particularly large number of *moussems*. The big events are those of Moulay Abdessalam ben Mchich (40km distant, usually in May) and of Sidi Allal el Hadj (9 August) but there are dozens of others, about which the town Syndicat may give out information; their office, not always open, is on Place Mohammed V.

THE SEA If you like the idea of a dizzying ride through the Rif, and a very small fishing village/beach at the end of it, you might consider going on to EL JEBHA (see p. 73). There are two buses a week, leaving around dawn.

TRAVEL DETAILS

Trains

Four trains a day currently leave Tangier: one to **Rabat and Casablanca**, the other three to **Meknes and Fes**. Each of them runs via **Asilah**, and each has a connection (at either **Sidi Kacem** or **Sidi Slimane**) if you want to switch to the other route. Times given below are likely to have changed slightly, though the pattern should be much the same.

1.**Tangier-Fes. Leaves Tangier** *town* **7.25**. Arrives Asilah (8.20), Sidi Kacem (11.05), Meknes (12.40), Fes (13.47). Change at Sidi Kacem for the 11.20 to Kenitra (12.34), Sale (13.12), Rabat (13.23) and Casablanca: Voyageurs (14.59).

2. **Tangier-Fes. Leaves 12.00**. Arrives Asilah (13.00), Sidi Kacem (15.26), Meknes (17.01), Fes (18.01). Change at Sidi Kacem for the 16.37 to Kenitra (17.51), Sale (18.25), Rabat (18.36) and Casablanca: Voyageurs (20.21).

3. **Tangier-Casablanca. Leaves 15.47**. Arrives Asilah (16.46), Sidi Slimane (19.23), Kenitra (20.19), Sale (20.44), Rabat (20.54) and Casablanca: Port (22.36). Change at Sidi Slimane for the 19.30 to Meknes (21.04) and Fes (21.59).
This is the best train to catch if you arrive by ferry and want to travel straight on the same day.

4. **Tangier-Fes. Leaves 21.20**. Arrives Asilah (22.21), Sidi Kacem (1.05), Meknes (2.49) and Fes (3.53). Change at Sidi Kacem for the *3.00am* to Kenitra (4.26), Sale (4.59), Rabat (5.10) and Casablanca:Voyageurs (7.13).

All trains except the early morning departure for Fes normally leave from both Tangier stations – *Port* and *Ville*.

Buses

From Tangier Asilah (7 daily; 1hr); Larache (6; 1hr40); Tetouan (12; 1½hrs); Rabat (2; 5hrs); Meknes (2; 7hrs); Fes (2; 8hrs).
From Asilah Larache (5 daily; 1hr).
From Larache Ksar el Kebir (3 daily; 40 mins); Souk el Arba (5; 1hr); Rabat (4; 3½hrs); Meknes (2; 5½hrs).
From Souk el Arba Moulay Bousselham (5 daily; 35mins); Ouezzane (3; 1½hrs).
From Ouezzane Meknes (2 daily; 4hrs); Fes (2; 5½hrs); Chaouen (4; 1hr20mins).
From Chaouen Ketama/Al Hoceima (2 daily; 5hrs/8hrs); Meknes (1; 5½hrs); Fes (2; 7hrs); El Jebha (2 a week; 7hrs).

Grand Taxis

From Tangier Regularly to Tetouan (1hr); less frequently to Larache, Rabat and occasionally Fes.
From Ouezzane Regularly to Souk el Arba (1hr) and Chaouen (1¼hrs).
From Tetouan Regularly to Tangier (1hr). Oued Laou and Fnideq (Ceuta border).
From Souk el Arba Regularly to Moulay Bousselham (½hr) and Larache (50min).

Ferries and hydrofoils

From Tangier: FERRIES to Algeciras (4 daily, 2½hrs), Gibraltar (3 a week, 2hrs) and Sete, France (weekly, 18hrs). HYDROFOILS in season to Tarifa (3 daily, ½hr), Algeciras (1 daily, 1hr) and Gibraltar (1 daily, 1hr). See p.7/8 for details.
From Ceuta: FERRY to Algeciras (12 daily, 1½hr).

Flights

From Tangier Daily flights to Casablanca (and thence to Marrakesh, etc.). International flights most days to London, Madrid, etc., and to Gibraltar (thence to London – quite cheaply – on *Gib Air*).
From Ceuta Most days to Malaga.

Chapter two
THE RIF AND THE MEDITERRANEAN COAST

Goldshot green of the Rif's slant fields here, vapor-blossoms resinous and summery . . . 'We've had a windfall of kif. Allah has smiled upon us'

Thomas Pynchon: *Gravity's Rainbow*

If anyone's heard of the Rif mountains at all, it is usually in connection with Ketama and the sale of **kif**, or hashish. There are towns enough in Morocco where you'll be offered kif for sale, but at Ketama it is simply assumed that this is why you are here. 'How many kilos?', they ask. Kif and Ketama are big business.

Talking about the Rif you have to state this first, for it dominates much of the region's character. Even where uncultivated, kif plants grow wild about the stony slopes – and where they are they seem to stretch forever. The cultivation itself is legal but 'standard' Moroccan rules forbid its sale, purchase and even possession. Don't be blinded by the local ways: police roadblocks are frequent, informers almost as thick as the smoke. An additional hazard are the industry's local mafias, cruising about the hills in their black Mercedes and not above a bit of traditional banditry. All through the year you hear stories of tourists driving along the road to Ketama to be stopped by a parked car or fallen tree. For them, 'how many kilos?' ceases to be a joke. If you're driving and reasonably cautious avoid the whole area around **Ketama**: bounded in the south by Had-Ikauen, to the east and west by Targuist and Bab Berred. If you're cautious and not driving, stay on the bus – it's a tremendous journey.

The **mountain range** itself is a vast limestone mass, over 300km long, up to 2,500 metres in height, and covered for the most part in dense upland forests. The whole impression is one of enormity, a grandiose place full of faintly outrageous views. You keep feeling it's far too hot for Alpine scenery and there are no healthy-horned cattle, just groups of workmen lying back on the pine-needles smoking kif. Travelling here, too, it's impossible to resist the feeling of nervous excitement – not just in that the roads seem designed to terrify, but in the very real sense of isolation, quite unlike the mere remoteness of the Atlas. The Rif is in fact

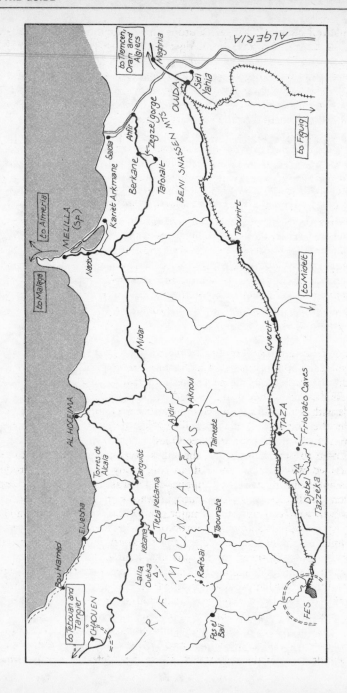

the natural boundary between Europe and Africa and with the Sahara it cuts off central Morocco from Algeria and the rest of the Maghreb. In the past this was a powerful barrier – it took the first European three months to travel from Al Hoceima to Melilla – and it is sustained today by the extraordinary sense of independence and traditional xenophobia among the tribes. There is no other part of Morocco where you feel so completely incidental to the ordinary local life.

Inevitably this applies much less to the towns – particularly to Taza and Oujda, important and historic posts on the 'corridor' into Algeria – and to those few points where the Rif gives way to the Mediterranean coast. Contrary to its daunting appearance from the great 'backbone' roads, the Rif does have beaches – albeit few and far between and virtually undeveloped beyond Tetouan. The only actual resort is Al Hoceima and even here the hotels give out after less than half a kilometre; elsewhere it's a question of a few sporadic campsites, the liveliest at Saidia on the border with Algeria. These attract quite a number of Moroccan families through July and August, and, while it falls in summer, at the end of Ramadan. Few tourists join them, though there's nothing to prevent you: unlike some of the Riffian mountain villages they are easy and out-going places, excellent ground for meeting people without the usual city/resort hustling.

Abd el Krim and the Republic of the Rif

Up until the establishment of the Spanish Protectorate in 1912 the tribes of the Rif existed outside government control – a northern heartland of the *Bled es-Siba*. They were subdued temporarily by *harkas*, the burning-raids with which sultans asserted their authority, and for a longer period under the Emperor Moulay Ismail; but for the most part bore out their own name of *Imazighen*, or 'Free Ones'.

Closed to outside influence, the tribes developed an isolated and self-contained way of life. The Riffian soil, stony and infertile, produced constant problems with food supplies and it was only through a complex system of alliances (*liffs*) that outright wars were avoided. Blood-feuds, however, were endemic, and a major contributor to maintaining a viably small population. Unique in Morocco, the Riffian villages are scattered communities, their houses hedged and set apart, and each family maintained a pillbox tower to spy out and fight off enemies. They were individual, too, in religion: the *Ulema*, five times daily prayer – and a central tenet of Islam was not observed; *djinns*, supernatural spirits from pagan nature cults, widely accredited; and great reliance placed on the intercession of local marabouts, or saints.

It was an unlikely ground for significant and organised rebellion, yet for over five years, between 1921 and 1927, the tribes forced the Spanish to withdraw from the mountains. Twice they defeated whole armies –

bringing down the Madrid monarchy in the process – and it was only through the added intervention of France, and nearly half a million troops, that the Europeans won eventual victory. In the intervening years the leaders of the revolt, the brothers Mohammed and M'hamid **Abd el Krim**, were able to declare a Republic of the Rif and to establish much of the apparatus of a modern state. Well-educated, and confident of the Rif's mineral reserves, they manipulated the *liff* system to forge an extraordinary unity among the tribes, negotiated mining rights in return for arms with Germany and South America, and even set up a Riffian State Bank. Still more impressive, they managed to impose a series of social reforms – including the destruction of family pillboxes, and the banning of kif – which allowed the operation of a fairly broad adminis-trative system. In their success, however, was the inevitability of defeat. It was the first nationalist movement in Colonial North Africa, and although the Spanish were ready to quit the zone in 1925, it was politi-cally impossible that the French would allow them to do so.

Defeat for the Riffians, and the exile of Abd el Krim, brought a virtual halt to social progress and reform. The Spanish took over the adminis-tration en bloc, governing through local caids, but although they exploited some mineral deposits there was no road-building programme or any of the other 'civilising benefits' introduced in the French zone. There were, however, two important changes: migration of labour (particularly to French Algeria) replaced the blood feud as a form of population control, and the Riffian warriors were recruited into Spain's own armies. This last had immense consequence, allowing General Franco to build up a power-base in Morocco. It was with Riffian troops that he invaded Andalusia in 1936, and it was probably their contribution which ensured fascist victory in the Civil War.

Abd el Krim was a powerful inspiration to later Nationalists and the Riffians themselves played an important guerilla role in the 1955-6 struggle for **independence**. When in April 1957 the Spanish finally surren-dered their protectorate, however, the Berber/Spanish speaking tribes found themselves largely excluded from government. Administrators were imposed upon them from Fes and Casablanca, and in October 1958 the Rif's most important tribe, the Beni Urriaguel, rose in open rebellion. The mutiny was soon put down, but necessitated the landing at Al Hoceima of then Crown Prince Hassan and some two-thirds of the Moroccan army.

A quarter of a century on, the Rif is still perhaps the most unstable part of Morocco – still conscious of under-representation in government, and still under-developed despite a substantial schools building programme, improved road communications and a large new agricultural project in the plains south of Nador and Al Hoceima. Labour emigration too remains high, Western Europe replacing Algeria as the main market, and (as throughout Morocco) there is widespread resentment at the difficulty of obtaining a passport for this outlet. With more sophisticated government systems, and a sizeable hierarchy of local administration, further tribal dissidence now seems unlikely. It is interesting to note, though, that it was in the Rif – above all in the towns of Nador, Al Hoceima and Tetouan – that the 1984 Riots began, and here that the most serious disturbances were reported.

ON TOP OF THE RIF: THE ROAD FROM CHAOUEN TO KETAMA AND AL HOCEIMA

There are very few journeys in Morocco as spectacular as that from CHAOUEN to AL HOCEIMA. The road quite literally and perversely follows along the backbone of the Western Rif, the highest peaks in the north of the country. You can look down on one side to the Mediterranean coast, on the other across the whole southern range: 'big mountains and more big mountains', as Paul Bowles put it, 'mountains covered with olive trees, with oak trees, with bushes, and finally with giant cedars.'

Even without the troubles of Ketama (see the introduction) this is not a route for inexperienced drivers. Though in good condition, it seems to be constructed entirely from switchbacks and hairpin bends. Beyond **BAB TAZA**, 23km out of Chaouen, you wind about the top of ridges, sheer drops on either side to deep and isolated valleys. Going by bus the Riffians sleep or talk it through – a fact that seems almost as remarkable as the scenery about.

One way or another **KETAMA** seems to have become a focal point of the Rif, though even more than usual in these mountains it's a scattered and sporadic sort of village. Arriving, even in transit, is an initiation, for absolutely everyone (passengers, conductor and all) are involved in *BUSINESS*. If you get off you will immediately be offered kif – immense, unbelievable quantities of it – and there is nobody who will believe that you are here for any other purpose.

This, really, is fair enough. Nobody does stay in Ketama unless they're doing business, and, anywhere in Morocco, if someone introduces themselves as 'from Ketama' there is no ambiguity about what they are offering. Dealers here are likely to try and get you to stay at their farms – something not recommended, even if you've an insatiable appetite and curiosity for kif production. I've met hardened travellers who have lost everything at knifepoint after taking up one of these offers. And, whilst horror stories will out, I also met an innocent Belgian camper-van driver who was stopped just outside the village and forced to buy a kilo of hash (for around £400).

Some of the tribes in the mountains have always smoked hashish, though it was the Spanish who really encouraged its cultivation – probably to keep them placid. This situation was apparently accepted when Mohammed V came to power, though the reasons for him doing so are obscure. There is a story, probably apocryphal, that when he visited Ketama in 1957 he accepted a bouquet of kif as a symbolic gift; the Riffis add that this was because he feared their power, though this seems to have been swiftly forgotten amid the following year's rebellion. Whatever, Ketama continued to supply the bulk of the country's kif, and in the early 1970s it became the centre of a significant drug industry, exporting to Europe and America. This sudden growth was accounted by a single factor: the introduction, supposedly by an American dealer, of techniques for producing hash-resin. Overnight the Riffians had an easily exportable product and, inevitably, big business was quick to follow. Large amounts of money are said to change hands between a whole network of officials, there is a brisk trade in informants and denunciations, and many of the large growers simply tell the police who they sell to.

The only **hotel** actually at Ketama is the old Spanish parador – the somewhat implausible 4-star *Hôtel Tidighine*, complete with its own golf course and swimming pool, used by wintering French tourists for the nearby ski-ing and boar hunting. The Chaouen-Al Hoceima buses stop right outside, a confusing terminus for, apart from the hustlers, there's virtually nothing else in sight. The main village, and the **cheap hotels**, are in fact at **TLETA KETAMA**, 8km down the road to Fes.

If you want to stay up in the mountains, but with rather less of the all-pervasive *business*, stop off either before Ketama at BAB BERRED or some way after at TARGUIST. **BAB BERRED**, a smallish market village and former Spanish administrative centre, is still very much in kif country – surrounded in fact by the plants – but it is less exclusively drug-orientated. There are two very basic **inns**. At **TARGUIST**, Abd el Krim's last stronghold and the site of his surrender to the French, you are actually outside the dope triangle. One of the larger villages of the Rif, with a couple of cafes and some **rooms** to let, Targuist attracts one of the biggest markets around – held every Saturday and drawing villagers from the dozens of tiny communities in the neighbouring hills. If you've got transport, time and the urge to see a remote Riffian market, there are also smaller gatherings nearby on Thursdays at ISAGEN, on Sundays at BENI BAR NSAR.

More relaxed, hardly less remote and an equal novelty, are the two **beaches** reached by tracks down from this road. **TORRES DE ALCALA** (also known as KALAH IRIS) is the easier to get to, with more or less daily buses from TARGUIST – and shortly, so it is rumoured, from AL HOCEIMA as well. A quiet fishing village, it was the main port for Fes in Saadian times but went into decline after the Turks established themselves on the offshore Islet of Ghomera, which they used into the nineteenth century as a base of piracy. As Al Hoceima continues to expand,

Torres de Alcala is likely to acquire tourist hotels, but for the moment there's just a seasonal **campsite**, a small unclassified **hotel** and some **cafe-rooms**. In a similar vein, though accessible by bus only twice a week (from CHAOUEN or KETAMA), is **EL JEBHA**, or the *Pointe des Pecheurs*. Scarcely more than a hamlet, with a little group of fishermen's cottages and a couple of **cafe-rooms**, this is reached by a crazily narrow and twisted track from EL KHEMIS, just outside Ketama. Few people get down there, which makes it all the more worthwhile – a good place to recuperate (or degenerate) as you gaze across the waters to Spain. Odd to think that exactly parallel across the straits are the resorts of Marbella and Torremolinos. If you can't wait for a bus out there are fairly regular fish lorries into the mountain markets around, and just occasionally someone drives down the outrageously potholed and plummeting track to OUED LAOU (see p. 61) and TETOUAN.

THE ROUTE DE L'UNITÉ: KETAMA TO FES

At the end of the Spanish Protectorate in 1957 there was no north–south route across the Rif, a marked symbol both of its isolation and of the separateness of the old French and Spanish zones. It was in order to counteract this – and to provide working contact between the Riffian tribes and the French-colonised Moroccans – that the great **Route de l'Unité** was planned.

The *Route*, completed in 1963, was built with volunteer labour from all over the country – Hassan II himself working at its outset. It was the brainchild of Mehdi Ben Barka, first President of the National Assembly and the most outstanding figure of the nationalist left before his exile and subsequent 'disappearance' in Paris in 1965. Barka's volunteers, 15,000 strong for much of the project, formed a kind of labour-university, working through the mornings and attending lectures in the afternoons.

Today the Route de l'Unité sees little traffic – travelling from Fes to Al Hoceima it's quicker to go via Taza, from Fes to Tetouan, via Ouez-zane. None the less it's an impressive road and a very beautiful one, certainly as dramatic an approach to Fes as you could hope for. Going by bus, the one village which might tempt you to stop off is **TAOUNATE**, the largest community along the way, set on a dark plateau above the valley of the Oued Sra – soon to be dammed to form a vast 35km-long lake. If you can coincide with the Friday market here, one of the most important in the Rif, you should be able to get a lift out to any number of villages. There's also a daily bus to FES EL BALI via **RAFSAI**, the last village of the Rif to be overrun by the Spanish and the site of a December *Olive Festival*. If you're into gratuitous scenic roads and have transport a 40km track extends beyond to the peak of Djebel Lalla Outka, reputed to offer the best view of the whole Rif range. **FES EL BALI** itself is a useful connecting point – with buses to the city of Fes and to Ouezzane – though of only passing interest. It takes its name, *el Bali* – 'the Old', from an C11 Almoravid fort, little of which remains. If you're stuck here there's a cheap basic hotel.

Going **east from Taounate** an attractive though less spectacular route heads through forests of cork and holm-oak towards the scattered and rather grim village of **AKNOUL**. From here you can pick up a bus or *grand taxi* down to TAZA, or sporadic buses over to NADOR or AL HOCEIMA.

TAZA AND THE DJEBEL TAZZEKA

TAZA was once a place of great importance – the capital of Morocco at the outset of the Almohad, Merenid and Alaouite dynasties, and controlling the only practicable pass to the east. This, the *Taza Gap*, forms a wide passage between the Rif and Middle Atlas. It was the route taken by Moulay Idriss and the first Moroccan Arabs, and the Almohads and Merenids both successfully invaded Fes from here. Each dynasty fortified and endowed the city but, as a defensive position, it was never in fact very effective: the local Zenatta tribe were always willing to join an attack and in the nineteenth century they managed to overrun it completely, central control only returning with the French occupation of 1914.

Modern Taza seems little haunted by this past, its monuments sparse and mostly inaccessible to non-Muslims. It is, however, a pleasant market town and its Medina saved from anonymity by a magnificent hilltop terrace site, flanked by crumbling Almohad walls. In addition there is considerable pull in the surrounding countryside – the national park of **Djebel Tazzeka** with its circuit of waterfalls, caves and scheist gorges. As a first stop in Morocco after arriving at Melilla or Oujda it's as good a choice as any, a friendly and easy-going place to get acclimatised.

The Town

Taza splits into two parts, the **Medina** and the French-built **Ville Nouvelle** – separated by nearly 3km of road and to all intents completely distinct. A shuttlebus runs between them, and another connects the new town with the bus and railway stations, both a fair walk below.

The **Ville Nouvelle** was an important military garrison in the Riffian war and retains much of the barrack-grid character. Its centre, the **Place de l'Indépendence**, actually serves for a population of 40,000 but it's so quiet you'd hardly know it. The two most functional **hotels** are both here. Best if you can afford it is the *Hôtel du Dauphine* (2*A), a rather stylish pre-war colonial building with an excellent cafe-bar downstairs; more or less opposite is a cheaper place, unnamed, unclassified but quite

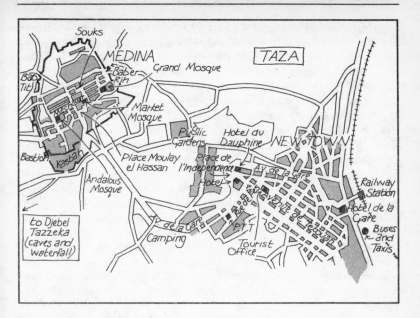

adequate. The *campsite*, uphill and to the left, is hardly more than scrub-land – semi-fenced and none too inspiring. Just beyond it, a concrete outpost in the middle of nowhere is the 3*A *Hôtel Friouato*, worth neither the walk nor the money. The cheap and basic *Hôtel de la Gare*, down by the train and bus station, is pretty drab too – but useful if you have to get the 4.30/5am bus to Nador. Most of the **restaurants**, and a small helpful **Syndicat**, are off the main *place* along the Avenue Tetouan.

Buses from the Place de l'Indépendence stop at the **MEDINA** in the Place Moulay Hassan, just below the **Mechouar** – the main street that runs through the middle of the quarter – a small and much modernised area, quite easy to find your way around. There are few particular sights, though if you enlist a guide it's possible to visit the former Merenid **medressa of Bou Abul Hassan**, off to the left of the Mechouar about twenty yards down from the (C12) Andalous Mosque. A rather inconspicuous building, usually kept closed, it has a particularly beautiful *mihrab*.

Largely ruined, and to the rear of the well-concealed Andalous Mosque, is an old house which was once the residence of the *Rogui* (Pretender) **Bou Hamra**. There is little to see today, but for some years at the turn of the century this was a powerbase controlling much of eastern Morocco. Like most protagonists of the period, Bou Hamra was an extraordinary figure – a sometime forger, conjuror and saint, he claimed to be the legitimate Shereefian heir and had himself proclaimed Sultan at Taza in 1902. The name *Bou Hamra* 'the man on the she-donkey' – recalled his bizarre means of travel around the countryside where he won followers through the performance of miracles. One of these involved talking to the dead, which he perfected by earlier burying a disciple, who would then communicate through a concealed straw; the pronouncements over, Bou Hamra stubbed out the straw (not presumably part of the original deal) and allowed the amazed villagers to dig up the by-then-dead witness. Captured by the Sultan Moulay Hafid, his own death was no less melo-dramatic. He was brought to Fes in a small cage on the back of a camel, fed to the court lions (who refused to eat him) and was eventually shot and burnt. Both Gavin Maxwell and Walter Harris give graphic accounts.

Taza's **souks** branch off to either side of the Mechouar, about halfway down between the Andalous and Grand Mosques. Since there are few and occasional tourists they are very much working and provision markets, free of the artificially produced 'craft' goods. In fact one of the most memorable is a *secondhand European clothes souk* – a frequent feature of country and provincial markets, the more fortunate dealers having gained access to the supplies of international charities! The *Granary* and the covered stalls of the *Kissaria* are also worth a look, in the shadow of the Djemaa es Souk or Market Mosque. The **Grand Mosque** stands at the end of the Mechouar, historically one of the most interesting buildings in the country – but, like that of the Andalous, so discreetly screened that it's difficult to gain any glimpse of the interior. Even the outside is elusive, shielded by a net of buildings, you have to walk up towards the Bab er-Rih for a reasonable impression of its plan. Founded by the Almohad sultan Abd el Moumen, it is probably the oldest Almohad structure in existence, predating even the partially ruined mosque at Tin Mal (see p. 231) which you *can* see and with which it shares most stylistic features.

Above the Medina at **Bab er-Rih** (*Gate of the Winds*) it is possible to get some feeling for Taza's historic and strategic significance. You can see up the valley towards the Taza Gap, Djebel Tazzeka and the Middle Atlas on one side, the reddish earth of the Rif behind on the other.

The actual gate now leads nowhere and looks somewhat lost below the road but it is Almohad in origin and design. So too are most of the circuit of walls, which you can follow round by way of a **bastion** (added by Moulay Ismail in Spanish style) back to the Place Moulay Hassan. Off to the left, below the kasbah, a road leads out towards the Djebel Tazzeka and to the town **swimming pool**.

The Djebel Tazzeka

A loop of some 123km around Taza, the **Djebel Tazzeka** is really a car driver's circuit, with views of the mountains to gaze at a while and carry on round. It does however have particular interest in the transition between Riffian and Middle Atlas scenery, and a specific 'sight' in the immense Friouato Caves. These are only 22km from Taza, a feasible hitch (stand at the turning, just below the Medina) or quite reasonable shared taxi ride (negotiate at the rank by the station).

The Tazzeka road curls around below the Medina and climbs to a narrow valley of almond and cherry orchards; around 10km out are the **Cascades de Ras El Oued**, a series of small waterfalls reduced to a trickle in the dry summer months. Beyond you loop up towards the first pass (at 1198m) and emerge beside the **Chiker lake**, again quite dry in midsummer and very strange in appearance. The **Friouato caves** lie near the far end of the depression, a short signposted ('*Gouffre*') turning to the right. Explored down to 180 metres, they are said to be the deepest in North Africa, their entrance (over 30 metres wide) must certainly be the most impressive. Although unlighted, the caves can be visited. There's a guardian about for most of the year who will steer you to some of the more spectacular caverns; you'll need a torch – if you don't have one wait and some other tourists may turn up.

For anyone with a car there are two interesting options beyond this point. Backtracking to the beginning of the Chiker you'll find a piste (said to be quite passable) which heads off left to MEGHRAOUA and TALZEMT, an adventurous approach through the Middle Atlas to MIDELT – eventually joining the P20 at ENJIL DES IKHATARN. Alternatively, and considerably easier, you can complete the Tazzeka circuit to rejoin the FES-TAZA road at SIDI ABDALLAH DES RHIATA. The last section of this route runs through the dark scheist gorges of the Oued Zireg, but the most dramatic and scenic point is undoubtedly the **ascent of the Djebel** itself. This is passable by car in dry weather but quite perilous: a very rough 7km track cuts up some 15km beyond Friouato, leading to a TV aerial near the summit. The view from the top, encased in forests of cedars, stretches to the Rif, to the mountains around Fes and to much of the eastern Middle Atlas.

Leaving Taza: the travel options

Whatever anyone may tell you about **buses** stopping at the Place de l'Indépendance you'll be best off at the main terminus beside the railway station: virtually everything leaves from there or calls in. Going **to Fes** you have the widest range of options. There are *grands taxis* leaving throughout the day, arriving at the Bab Ftouh (where you'll need to pick up a city-taxi or bus to get to the hotels at Bab Boujeloud or the New Town), and also four trains a day to the station in the New Town. In the other direction the trains run to OUJDA, much the easiest and simplest approach. You miss nothing by not stopping off at GUERCIF and TAOU-RIRT, both dull market towns along the monotonous eastern steppes.

Nearly all the **buses across the Rif** leave very early in the morning. There are currently two to NADOR (at 4.30 and 5am), one going via AKNOUL, the other over a new and more direct road across the Plain of Gareb. There is one and sometimes two early buses to AL HOCEIMA; this too goes via AKNOUL where you can catch sporadic local buses across the southern slopes of the Rif to TAOUNATE, a much less dramatic route than the Ketama pass.

AL HOCEIMA

If you're coming from the rather epic existence of the Rif, **AL HOCEIMA** can be a bit of a shock. It is not, in the tourist board's wildly optimistic claim, 'Morocco's most exclusive, international resort': but it is Mediterranean and developed enough to have little in common with the farming villages and tribal markets of the mountains. If you're travelling through the Rif you will probably want to stop here and rest up a couple of days – though you're unlikely to stay longer. In midsummer the town feels cramped, its beaches overcrowded and rooms are difficult to find. Nevertheless it does have a certain charm, and if you're deliberating between staying the night here or at Nador it's infinitely preferable.

The town divides fairly naturally into two parts. Around the **bay** – which saw the Spanish invasion in 1926 and Hassan's 32 years later – is a *Maroc-Tourist* complex with two 4-star hotels. Everything and everyone else is packed into the old Spanish fishing village of **Villa Sanjura** at the top of the hill. In midsummer this is a lively if rather characterless place, full of young Moroccans; the rest of the year it is almost empty save for a handful of old misplaced *Spaniolines* who for one reason or another couldn't leave with the rest in 1957.

The town centre is up here – the **Place du Rif**, enclosed by cafes and cheap places to eat. Most interesting of these is the *Café-Hôtel Florido*, a 1930s building decorated with the truncated Star of David (adopted by Abd el Krim in the Riffian flag) rather than the orthodox five-pointed star of Morocco. The other **hotels** – the *National* (2*A), *Karim* (2*A), *Essalam*, and *Turismo* – climb back behind the *place* along Avenues Hassan II and Abd el Krim, and the Rue de Rif. None are particularly noteworthy: the *Karim*, slightly pricier than most, is usually the last to fill up.

If none of these have rooms you're down to the two **campsites**, each of them positioned by a beach and reached along the main road (east) out of town. Nearest at 2km is the *Camping Plage el Jamil*, the best place around to swim but geared heavily towards caravans and outrageously expensive for tent-campers. The main and much more popular site is a little further down the road at the *Plage Cala Iris*; not, incidentally, a wise place to leave anything around. Swimming – and walking in the olive groved hills if you want change – is Al Hoceima's main attraction but if you wake early enough it is worth going down to the bay to watch the *lamparo* fishermen coming in; they work at night using acetylene lamps to attract and dazzle the fish. The town's other minor curiosity is the Spanish offshore islet of Peñon de Alhucemas, a perennial subject of dispute between Spanish and Moroccans since the C17.

As throughout the Rif **buses** leave early: to TAZA at 4am, to FES (via the Route de l'Unité), CHAOUEN and TETOUAN slightly later. If you're going to CHAOUEN try to take one of the private buses rather than the *CTM*, which stops at the turning 9km out of the village. If you need to get anywhere in a hurry there are plenty of *grands taxis*, negotiable even for Rabat and Casablanca. A small **ONMT** office, by the prominent Hotel Quemado, can give information and times.

NADOR

Entering or leaving Morocco at the Spanish enclave of MELILLA you will have to pass through **NADOR**. But beyond this it is hard to conjecture any reason for coming here. Landlocked by the shallow and useless inland sea of Mar Chica and rather rashly earmarked as a centre for economic development, it is characterised only by an annoying gritty wind floating down from the cement factory. A depressed as well as a depressing place, this was the site of the first and main troubles in the 1984 riots.

When the Spanish left in 1957, Nador was just an ordinary Riffian village, given work and some impetus by the port of Melilla. Its choice as a Moroccan provincial capital was probably unfortunate – there is little contact for the university students, while the iron foundry to fuel the Rif's mining industry has yet to materialise. Add to this the creation of a 45,000 population drawn from the mountain villages and you begin to see some of the problems.

The town is built on a drab and uniform grid, the **bus station** providing its main focal point. There are plenty of **hotels** close by if you need to stay: the better ones, past a string of real holes, about 100m down the Av. Ibn Tachfine. Moving off from the bus station in the opposite direction (towards the 'sea') you reach the main boulevard with its banks and post office. The best place to swim and make a quick exit is KARIET-ARKMANE, some 20km to the south: there's a campsite there, the *Karia Plage*, and a stretch of sandy coastline that extends to Algeria. If you have a car you can also get to the CAP DES TROIS FORCHES by leaving on the Melilla road; this has no campsite but Moroccan families descend with tents in the summer.

All **transport** leaves Nador from the bus station, including local buses and *grands taxis* to the MELILLA frontier. If you're going over the Rif to

FES, CHAOUEN or TETOUAN best break the journey in AL HOCEIMA (3½hrs): it is still 8hrs from there to Fes or Chaouen, even longer to Tetouan. Buses and *grands taxis* to OUJDA are fairly plentiful throughout the day; to get to SAIDIA you can connect at BERKANE.

MELILLA: A SPANISH POSSESSION

There ought to be an eccentric appeal to **MELILLA**, but even after Nador it's difficult to muster great enthusiasm. With Ceuta it is the last of Spain's Moroccan enclaves, a former penal colony which saw prosperous days under the Protectorate as a port for the Riffian mining industry. Since Independence – and its retention as 'sovereign Spanish territory' – Melilla's decline has been pretty wholesale. Resented by Morocco, whose claims are a fairly direct parallel to Spain's own on Gibraltar, it again survives today on little more than the army, the duty-free tourist trade, and of course what's left of the Spanish colonial instinct.

As at Ceuta, most of Melilla's streets still bear the names of Spanish generals who fought in the colonising campaign: and in good symbolic style they centre on the **Plaza de España**, above the port, and the **Avenida del Generalissimo Franco**, leading inland off it. This is the most animated part of town, though not noticeably so until the evening *paseo* when everyone promenades up and down or strolls about the neighbouring Hernandez Park. Many of the buildings around here were designed by a modernist contemporary of the Catalan architect Gaudi, Enrique Nieto, but their 1930s tile and stucco façades are often masked or swamped by the rows of duty-free shops. Unless you're after a digital radio it's none too dynamic a sight.

Probably more interesting – and certainly more picturesque – are the cramped white streets of the old town of **Medina Sidonia**, steeped above the port on a superb defensive promontory. At the beginning of the century this was all there was of Melilla: a self-contained little enclave, heavily walled and well able to resist the sporadic years of siege and attack. It was founded in 1497, a kind of epilogue to the expulsion of the Moors from Spain in the year that saw the fall of Granada. Blockaded throughout the reign of Moulay Ismail the Spanish came close to relinquishing ownership in the C18 and C19, and probably would eventually have done so had not colonial ambitions revived at the beginning of this century.

The walls of the old town suggest the Andalusian Medinas of Tetouan or Chaouen, though inside the design is much more formal, laid out along the lines of a Castilian fort after a major earthquake in the C16. Steps near the harbour lead you up to its main square, the **Plaza Maestranza** flanked by a tiny Gothic **chapel of Santiago** (St James 'the Moorslayer'), and beyond to an old barracks and armoury. If you follow the fortifications around you'll come to another small fort, now housing a somewhat miscellaneous **Museo Municipal** (open weekdays 9-1 & 3-6). Below this is the church of **La Concepçion**, crowded with Baroque decoration, including a revered statue of *Nuestra Señora de Victoria* (Our Lady of Victory), the city's patroness. None of this is especially striking – and there's nothing you can't afford to miss if you've just come over from Spain – but there is a certain curiosity in the **markets** up here. Although Melilla's population is almost 90% Spanish most are run by Moroccans – and in the Mantelat quarter across the moat by a small Indian community.

The border, boats and some practical details

It is difficult to imagine a slower and more unco-operative **border post** than Nador-Melilla. The Moroccans deeply resent the colony and its duty-free port, and they are more than happy to reflect this in the most annoying, time-wasting system it's possible to devise. If you're crossing on foot from Nador the bus takes you right to the frontier, but expect to hang about a good hour while your passport is collected, forgotten and eventually stamped; in a car things tend to work a little faster. Don't even consider going off to Melilla on a duty-free day trip from Nador: this the Moroccans like least of all. Crossing *into* Morocco at Melilla is usually more good humoured. Buses leave frequently for the border from the Plaza de España and you should be in Nador within an hour or so of setting out. If there's no bus on the Moroccan side of the frontier you can usually share a taxi at fairly nominal expense.

Ferries leave Melilla daily – *except Sundays* – for both Malaga (year round; 10hrs) and Almeria (summer only; 8hrs). The Almeria boat usually departs around 11.30am, the Malaga one at 8.30pm.

Except in preference to Nador there is no great reason to stay overnight in Melilla: **hotels** are quite expensive and beds often hard to find. Most of the cheaper possibilities are in streets leading off towards the far end of the Av. Gen. Franco: particularly c/General Pareja (3rd left) and its first intersection, c/Primo de Rivera. There are also a couple of **pensions** in the c/Ejercito Español (parallel with Gen. Franco, on the right-hand side) and another, the *Miramar*, right by the port. The **Oficina de Turismo**, second left past the bullring at the far side of Hernandez park, will sometimes give addresses of private rooms. There is no campsite.

BERKANE, THE ZEGZEL GORGE AND SAIDIA

The road between NADOR and OUJDA is fast, efficient and well served by both buses and *grands taxis*. It is not a tremendously interesting route but if you've time (or ideally a car) there's an attractive detour around BERKANE into **the Zegzel gorge**, a dark limestone fault in the Beni Snassen mountains – last outcrops of the Rif.

The Zegzel cuts down behind Berkane, a fertile shaft of mountain valleys which for centuries marked the limits of the Shereefian Empire. They are quite easily accessible today, though still forbiddingly steep: all traffic goes *down*, climbing up from the main road to TAFORALT and winding through from there to Berkane. If you've got transport this is the route to follow. If not, stay on the bus to BERKANE where you can get a place in a *grand taxi* to TAFORALT and there negotiate another place back, via the gorge road. Neither is an expensive operation, as they're locally used (and popular tourist) routes.

TAFORALT itself is a quiet and very clear mountain village, active (or as active as it ever gets) only for the Wednesday market. It does, though, have a fairly constant supply of taxis and you should be able to move on quite swiftly towards the Zegzel. Before settling a price get the driver to agree to stop off for a while at the **Grotte du Chameau** (15km), a cavern of really vast stalactites – one of them quite remarkably camel-like in shape. The gorge, or rather **gorges**, begin soon after, scrupulously terraced and cultivated with all kinds of citrus and fruit trees. As the road criss-crosses the riverbed they progressively narrow, drawing your eye to the cedars and dwarf-oaks at the summit, until you eventually emerge (28km from Taforalt) onto the plain of Berkane.

French-built and prosperous, **BERKANE** is a strategic little market town – right at the centre of an extensive region of orchards and vineyards. There is little to do except move on but this at least is a pretty painless operation. There are frequent buses and *grands taxis* both to OUJDA and to the small-scale Moroccan resort of **SAIDIA**, right on the Algerian border and a good choice to stopover a few days. A one-street sort of place, it rambles back from the sea in the shadow of an old and still-occupied C19 kasbah. The beach is immense and sandy, stretching downcoast towards the tiny Chafarinas islands, up across the Oued Kiss into Algeria. The Moroccans have a saying that at Saidia 'we swim together with Algerians', which isn't exactly true but not totally false either – there's a very similar resort over on the Algerian side. If you want to stay at Saidia in midsummer you'll probably end up camping; there are only three smallish **hotels** – *Al Kalaa* (2*A), *Hamour* (1*A) and *Select* (1*A) – and a number of terminally full family boarding houses. In classic local resort fashion Saidia has two **campsites**, one for families only (off the mainstreet), another (towards the kasbah) for single people: pick your category. Liveliest of the cafes are a group by the market, past the kasbah and looking across into Algeria.

There are regular buses and *grands taxis* between SAIDIA and OUJDA.

OUJDA AND THE ALGERIAN FRONTIER CROSSINGS

Most travellers arrive at **OUJDA** after a lengthy journey, which makes it all the more attractive. Open and easy-going, it has that rare quality in Moroccan cities of nobody making demands on your instinct for self-preservation.

As Morocco's most easterly town, Oujda became the capital of French 'Maroc Orient' and an important trading centre. This it remains, even if the 'Orient' tag shouldn't be taken too *un*literally; there's nothing more exotic here than the black market trade in Algerian currency and Melilla whisky. It is though a lively place – and prosperous too, strikingly so by Moroccan standards with a population of over a quarter of a million. Strategically positioned at the crossroads of eastern and southern routes, the town, like Taza, has always been vulnerable to invasion and it has frequently been the focus of territorial claims. The Algerian Ziyanids of Tlemcen occupied Oujda in the C13-14, and it was the first place to fall under French control when they moved into Morocco in 1907. In recent years its proximity to the Algerian border and distance from the government in Rabat has led to its being a minor centre of dissidence and unrest. This was particularly to the fore during the Algerian border war in the early 1960s and again, over the last couple of years, in a series of student strikes.

Oujda consists of the usual **Medina** and **Ville Nouvelle**, the latter highly linear in plan after starting out as a military camp.

The Medina, more or less walled, lies right at the centre of the town – the main square of the new town (**Place du 16 Août 1953**) at its north-west corner. Around the *place* you'll find all the main facilities, including the Post Office, banks, **CTM bus station**, and a tourist office which gives out free town plans. If you've arrived by **train** get there by walking straight out of the station along the prominent Boul. Zerktouni – turn left at its end onto the Blvd Mohammed V and you will emerge right on it. The **non-CTM Gare Routière** is also nearby: walk out onto the main road, Rue de Marrakesh, which follows the Medina walls to the square.

Most of the cheap **hotels** are along these two routes. *Hôtel Zegreg* (Rue de Marrakesh) is much the best of the bottom line; if you have a little more money try the *Royal* (2*A) on Blvd Zerktouni. For the really affluent, or those with dirhams to get rid of, the *Hôtel Terminus* (4*A by the railway station) is the traditional place to stay before going across the border. If you want to camp best go to one of the sites at SAIDIA.

The focus of evening activity – and best source of cheap eating holes – is around **Bab el Ouahab**, a prominent gate just below the *Gare Routière*, where you can get all kinds of grilled food. In latter days, more or less up until the French occupation, this was the gate where the heads of criminals were displayed. It is still a square where storytellers and musicians come to entertain, an increasing rarity in post-Independence Morocco.

The Medina itself is really more of a French reconstruction – revealingly obvious by the ease with which you can find your way about. Unusually it has retained much of the city's commercial functions and has an enjoyably active air. Entering from Bab el Ouahab you'll be struck by the amazing variety of food – and it's well worth a wander for that alone. If you want to add further direction head straight down the main street towards the **Place d' Attarine,** flanked by a *kissaria* and particularly grand *fondouk*. At the far end of the souks you come upon the **Souk el Ma,** the irrigation souk where the supply of water used to be regulated and sold by the hour. Following on from here you emerge back at the Place du 16 Août 1953

Sidi Yahia: an oasis Marabout

If you've got a couple of hours to fill and feel like avoiding the worst of the afternoon heat, **SIDI YAHIA** is a natural and rewarding option. Just 6km outside Oujda, it is an unexpected little oasis, immense palms and ancient baobab trees breaking the wide empty plain, clear springs and streams watering the grass and flowers.

This has been a holy place since pre-Islamic times, the main object of veneration being the tomb of **Sidi Yahia** – a shadowy marabout whom local tradition identifies with John the Baptist. Oujda's patron saint, he seems to have had a broad ecumenical appeal – Jews and even Christians paying pilgrimage to the tomb over the centuries. Nobody is quite sure where he is buried (several of the cafes stake an optimistic claim) but there is much reverence towards one of the great wells, said to be his water supply before the springs rose up after his death. On Fridays – and above all at the great *moussems* held here in August-September – this spot, together with almost every shrub and tree in the oasis, is festooned with little pieces of coloured cloth, a ritual as lavish and extraordinary as anything in the Mediterranean church. Scattered around the oasis are other lesser shrines – the tombs, *koubbas* and hermitages of numerous saints who followed Sidi Yahia to live within the grove. Among them is a former hermitage of **Sidi Bel Abbes,** one of the Seven Saints of Marrakesh, and here too is a sacred and haunted grotto, the **Ghar el Houriyat** or *Cave of the Houris* – the obliquely sensual hand-maidens of Paradise promised to good Muslims in the Koran.

Regular **buses** leave OUJDA for SIDI YAHIA from close by the Bab el Ouahab. Or if you've energy it is only a little over an hour's walk down a broad (signposted) avenue.

Crossing into Algeria

The state of Moroccan-Algerian relations, and that of their frontiers, changes so frequently that it is impossible to give any definitive instructions. At present, however, and for the forseeable future, the **Rabat-Algiers trains** (the *Trans-Maghreb Express*) do not go through the border.

Instead, the line terminates at OUJDA and re-starts inside Algeria at MAGHNIA. For the remaining 27km (15m in Morocco; 12km in Algeria) you're dependent on hitching, taxis or somewhat sporadic local buses. At times, too, there's an additional problem in that the Moroccans won't allow anyone to leave at Oujda except for car passengers: hitching can usually overcome this, though the most officious frontier guards demand that the date of entry to Morocco in your passport co-incides with that of the driver. If this happens to you there are two options: either hang about and try your luck with a new car and the next frontier shift, or give up, return to Oujda and take a bus down to the Figuig border where no such restrictions apply. You'll invariably find fellow-travellers in Oujda who will be able to give information on the current position, and the Tourist Office in the main *place* are usually well briefed and helpful.

If you decide to go through at OUJDA-MAGHNIA there are fairly regular buses from by the CTM office on Rue de Sidi Brahim. Better still, though, try and hitch a lift with other travellers – you can usually fix this up the night before by touting around the better hotels (the *Terminus, Al Massira* and *Oujda*) and it should take you through to TLEMCEN, the first Algerian town of any size and a place well worth stopping over.

Crossing over at FIGUIG (see p. 278) is by no means a bad option, though an unbelievably hot one in the midsummer months. Despite its uncertain appearance on some maps there's a fast new road down from Oujda – a 369km trek, but no more than seven hours by bus. Try and get the early morning departure (currently at 6am); there are two later on, but by noon things can be pretty stifling. All of these buses leave from the *Gare Routière* at the Place du Maroc.

Two final and important points. British citizens can enter Algeria on a routine passport stamp at the frontier, but Americans and Australians must have an **advance visa**. You can get one at any overseas consulate, at the UAE Embassy in Rabat (see p. 104), or – simplest and quickest – at the **Algerian Consulate** in Oujda (11 Boulevard de Taza). At the latter you will need four passport size photographs, 30dhs and the best part of a day. Once you have obtained this steer yourself to a bank and **change at least £130** into French *francs*. The Algerians demand that you change this amount into *dinars* at the frontier – a regulation they used to waive on production of a full and valid ISTC card (though at present this practice has been suspended). **NB** if you're intending to cross at FIGUIG that you'll need to change this money into *francs* beforehand – the bank there does not change travellers cheques, and the Algerian frontier banks (at either crossing) accept nothing other than crisp new French notes.

TRAVEL DETAILS

Trains
From Taza 4 trains daily to Oujda (3½hrs), and in the other direction to Fes (2hrs).
From Oujda 4 trains daily to Taza (3½hrs) and Fes (5½-6 hrs). Also a night train (mainly for freight) to Bouarfa (8hrs).

Buses
From Chaouen Ketama/Al Hoceima (2 daily; 5hrs/8hrs); El Jebha (2; 7hrs).
From Ketama Fes (2 daily; 3½hrs).
From Fes el Bali (village) Daily to Taounate and Aknoul.
From Taza Fes (3 daily; 2½hrs): Oujda (4; 4½hrs); Al Hoceima (2; 4½hrs); Nador (2; 5-5½hrs).
From Al Hoceima Nador (2 daily; 3½hrs); Fes (1; 11½hrs).
From Nador Berkane/Oujda (5 daily; 2hrs/3hrs); Melilla (local buses to the border).
From Berkane Oujda (6 daily; 1hr); Saidia (4; 1hr).

From Oujda Saidia (4 daily; 1hr20); Figuig (3; 7hrs).

Grands Taxis
From Taza Regularly to Fes (1½hrs) and Oujda (2½hrs). Occasionally to Al Hoceima.
From Al Hoceima Regularly to Nador (3hrs). Infrequently to Fes and Taza.
From Nador Regularly to Oujda (2½hrs) and Al Hoceima (3hrs).
From Oujda Regularly to Saidia (50mins) and Taza (2½hrs). Negotiable for the Algerian border.

Flights
From Oujda Casablanca (most days: *RAM* office at *Hôtel Oujda*).
From Melilla Malaga (2 daily; 25mins); Almeria (most days; ½hr).

Ferries
From Melilla daily except Sundays to Malaga (10hrs) and Almeria (11hrs).

Chapter three
RABAT, CASA AND AROUND

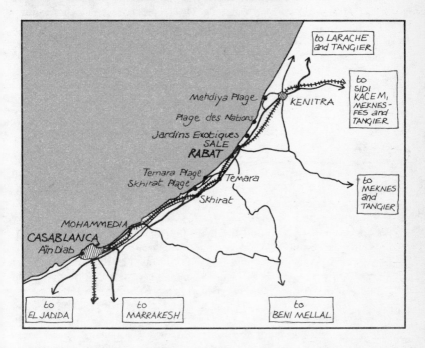

It gives a considerable sense of Rabat, Casablanca and this stretch of coast just to talk numbers. At the turn of the century, **Rabat**, the largest settlement, was a straggling port of 30,000 or so population; **Salé**, its twin-settlement, and **Casablanca** followed with another 20,000 each; the major towns of **Kenitra** and **Mohammedia** did not yet exist. Combined populations today run well above four million, with Casablanca and its suburbs alone accounting for a tenth of Moroccans and (excluding the country's mines) for some two-thirds of its industry. Inevitably, given this rapid and immense development, it is French and post-Colonial influences here which are dominant. You don't go to Casa – as it's known – expecting it to 'look Moroccan': it doesn't, it looks very much like Marseilles. And likewise in Rabat, which the French raised as a new capital to replace the old Imperial centres of Fes and Marrakesh, you emerge from the railway station to the cafes and broad avenues of a recognisably European city. This may not seem a very compelling option, yet if you want to get any real idea of what Morocco is about – and of how most Moroccans now actually live – these, at some stage, are both places to stop.

Casa is perhaps best visited after spending some time in the country, when you'll find its beach-clubs and bars a novelty, and appreciate both its differences and its fundamentally Moroccan character. Rabat, on the other hand, is one of the best points to make for as soon as you arrive in the country, well connected by train with Tangier (and on to Fes and Marrakesh) and an easy cultural shift in which to gain initial confidence. With the old port of Salé, facing Rabat across a river estuary, it has, too, some of Morocco's most interesting monuments – examples of both Almohad and Merenid architecture and good standards for any approach to the great Imperial Cities beyond.

RABAT

Capital of the nation since Independence – and of the Protectorate from 1912 to 1956 – RABAT is in many ways the city you'd expect: elegant in its spacious European grid, slightly self-conscious in its very civilised modern ways, and, as an administrative centre, a little dull. If you arrive during Ramadan you'll find the main boulevards an astonishing night-long, football-crowd-dense promenade; other times you'd be pushed to find a cafe open beyond ten at night. Rabat, as they tell you in Casa, is *provincial*.

None of this makes any difference to the city's very substantial historic and architectural interest, though it does leave you little choice but to act the tourist and go out to examine the sights: unlike Fes or Marrakesh there's no involved city-life to drift alongside. You can, however, get around the place quite happily without a guide, can talk with people who for the most part have no dependence on tourist money, and spend an easy few days around the monuments and on the excellent beaches a few kilometres to either side.

The monuments, more than those of any other town, punctuate the range of Moroccan history. The whole region, designated by the French *Maroc Utile*, has been occupied and cultivated since Paleolithic times, and it is probable that both Phoenicians and Carthaginians established trading posts on this site – naturally endowed with a low sheltered estuary. The original settlement, known as *Sala*, occupies the site of what is now Chellah. Here was created the southern-most Roman colony, lasting well beyond the break-up of the Empire in Africa and eventually forming the basis of an independent Berber state, which, by the C8, seems to have become of some local influence. Developing a code of government inspired by the Koran but adapted to Berber custom and needs, it represented a challenge to the Islamic orthodoxy of the Arab tribes of the interior. To stamp out the heresy a **ribat** – the fortified monastery from which the city takes name – was founded on the site of the present kasbah. The ribat's activities, a kind of Knights Templar-style persecution, led to Chellah's decline – a process hastened in the C11 by the founding of a new town, **Salé**, across the estuary.

With the arrival of the **Almohads** in the C12 the kasbah was rebuilt and a new city took form around it. The fort, renamed *Ribat el Fathi* (Stronghold of Victory), served as a gathering point for their Spanish campaigns, which by 1170 had brought virtually all of el-Andalus back to Muslim rule, and under the Caliph **Yacoub el Mansour** a new Imperial Capital was begun. The greatest of Almohad builders, el Mansour was responsible for the superb **Oudaia gate** of the kasbah, for the **Bab er Rouah** at the south-west edge of town, and for the **Hassan Mosque** – the largest ever undertaken in Morocco, its minaret, high above the river, still the city's great landmark. He erected, too, a vast enclave of walls over 5,000 metres in length – but neither his vision nor his success in the maintenance of a Spanish Empire were to be lasting. The Hassan Mosque was left unfinished, and only in the last sixty years has the city expanded to fill its dark circuit of pise walls.

Its significance dwarfed after Mansour's death by the Imperial Cities of Fes, Meknes and Marrakesh, Rabat fell into neglect. Sacked by the Portuguese, it was little more than a village when, as *New Salé*, it was resettled by C17 Andalusian refugees. In this revived form, however, it entered an extraordinary period of international piracy and local autonomy. Its Corsair fleets, '**the Sallee Rovers**', specialised in the plunder of merchant ships returning to Europe from West Africa and the Spanish Americas, but on occasion raided as far afield as Plymouth and the Irish coast – where they took captive whole village communities. Defoe's Robinson Crusoe began his captivity 'carry'd prisoner into Sallee, a Moorish port', and it is estimated that in a single decade (1620-30) over a thousand ships were seized. The Andalusians, owing no loyalty to the Moorish sultans and practically impregnable within their kasbah on a high rocky bluff above the river, established their own pirate state, the **Republic of the Bou Regreg**; they rebuilt the Medina below the kasbah in a style reminiscent of their homes in Spanish Badajoz, dealt in arms with the English and French, and even accepted European consuls. With the accession of Moulay Rashid, and of his successor Moulay Ismail, the town reverted to official government control, but the nature of its activity was little changed. As late as 1829 an Austrian ship is recorded as having been forced into the port and sacked.

Arriving, orientation and hotels
With its **Medina** and French-built **New Town** bounded by the river and

old Almohad wall, central Rabat never feels a big city. It's an easy place to find your way around, too, its points of interest all in walking distance. **Arriving by train** – much the simplest approach – you're at once in the heart of the New Town: the two main thoroughfares (**Avenue Mohammed V** and **Avenue Allal Ben Abdallah**) leading up from the station to the **Boulevard Hassan II** and (walled off beyond) the **Medina**. The main **bus terminal**, and the **grands taxis** for Casa, are now some way out of town – by the road junction for Casa and Beni Mellal; to get in to the centre you'll need to take a local bus (no. 30 and others stop along the Boulevard Hassan II) or a *petit taxi* (5dhs or so, usually metered, for up to three people).

Accommodation can be a slight problem in midsummer and especially July. Good rooms in cheap hotels tend to fill early in the day and by midafternoon many of the Medina places have inflated their prices almost as high as a 2* hotel in the New Town. If you're short on money you can do a lot worse than making straight for the *Youth Hostel* (34 Blvd Misr: one block above the Blvd Hassan II – see the map; YHA card obtainable on the spot). Otherwise, try the places listed – in roughly ascending price order – below. The best are keyed.

MEDINA
Hôtel France, Hôtel Algers, Hôtel du Marche. These three are all on the 2nd turning left off Rue Mohammed V – the continuation of Avenue Mohammed V; carry on around and there are several more. 'France' is easily the best.
Hôtel el Alam, Hôtel Marrakech, Hôtel Regina. One street beyond the previous group and off to the right, these are on Rue Gebbali. El Alam, outrageously decorated, is usually very cheap; Marrakech is good but overpriced.
Hôtel Darna (2*A), Blvd el Alou. Just inside the Bab el Alou at the far side of the Medina. Much the best in another small cluster of places.

NEW TOWN
Hôtel Majestic (1*A), 121 Blvd Hassan II. Probably the best cheap choice – when they have room.
Hôtel D'Orsay (1*A), 1 Av. Moulay Youssef. Behind the station; none too great.
Hôtel Central (1*A), 2 Rue el Basra. By the Balima Hotel.
Hôtel Splendid (2*B), *Hotel de la Paix* (2*A). Both on the Rue du 18 Juin/Rue Ghazza, near the top of Av. Mohammed V.
Hôtel Gauloise (2*B), 1 Zankat Hims. This and the two above are preferable among the eight 2* places around.
Hôtel Balima (3*B). Just back from the Av. Mohammed V this was

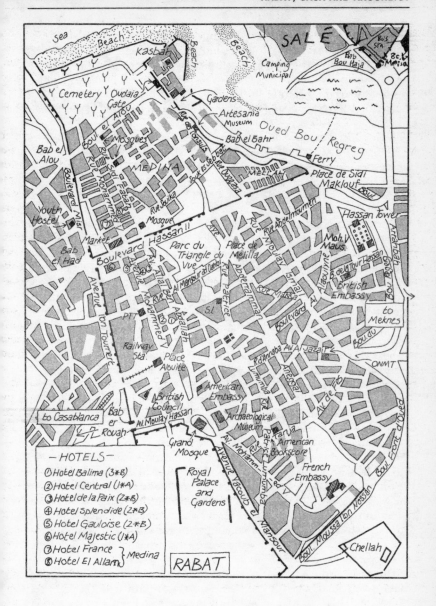

- HOTELS -
① Hotel Balima (3★B)
② Hotel Central (1★A)
③ Hotel de la Paix (2★B)
④ Hotel Splendide (2★B)
⑤ Hotel Gauloise (2★B)
⑥ Hotel Majestic (1★A)
⑦ Hotel France ⎱
⑧ Hotel El Allam ⎰ Medina

RABAT

Rabat's top hotel into the 1960s. Today it's faded and supplanted but still has a deco grandeur about it and absurdly cheap *suites*! Thami el Glaoui, Pasha of Marrakesh, stayed here when he came to ask pardon of Mohammed V in 1956, so too did just about everyone else doing business with the government. If you've the money follow them; or just hang out in the cafe – still the centre of life most evenings.

CAMPING

The *Camping Municipal*, stony and short of facilities, is across the river at Salé beach. Bus no.6 (and others) from the Blvd Hassan II will take you to the town gate – get off here and it's a 150m walk.

The Medina and Souks

Rabat's **MEDINA** – all that there was of the city until the French arrived in 1912 – is a compact quarter, wedged on two sides by the sea and river, on the others by Almohad and Andalusian walls. It is not among the country's most interesting – open and ordered in comparison to those of Fes or Marrakesh – but coming here from the adjacent avenues of the modern capital is always a surprise. In appearance it is still essentially the town created and settled in the C17 by Muslim refugees from Spanish Badajoz: and with these external features intact, its way of life seems at once traditional and un-Western.

That this is possible – here and throughout the old cities of Morocco – is largely due to **Marshal Lyautey**, the first and certainly the most sympathetic of France's Resident Generals. Colonising Algeria over the previous century, the French had destroyed most of the Arab towns, replacing their traditional structures (evolved through the needs of Islamic custom) with completely European plans. At Rabat Lyautey found this system already in operation, builders tearing out part of the Medina for the construction of a new town and of administrative quarters. Realising the aesthetic loss – and perhaps, too, the arrogance of 'Europeanising' – he ordered work to be stopped and the *Ville Nouvelle* to be built outside the walls. It was a precedent accepted throughout the French and Spanish zones of the colony: a policy which inevitably created 'native quarters', but one which also preserved continuity, maintained the nation's past, and, as Lyautey at least believed, showed the special relationship of the 'Protectorate'.

The basic gridlike regularity of the Medina, cut by a number of long main streets, makes this a good place to get to grips with the feel of a Moroccan town. In plan it is largely traditional, with a main market street (the **Rue Souika/Souk es Sebbat**) beside the Grand Mosque, and behind it a residential area scattered with smaller souks and 'parish' mosques. The buildings, characteristically Andalusian in the style of Tetouan or Chaouen, are part stone and part whitewash, with splashes of yellow and turqoise and great darkwood studded doors.

From the **Boulevard Hassan II** a series of streets give access to the Medina, all of them leading more or less directly through the quarter to emerge near the kasbah and the old hillside cemetery. The two on the left – **Rue Mohammed V** and **Rue Sidi Fatah** – are really continuations of the main *Ville Nouvelle* avenues; flanked by working-class cafe-restaurants and cell-like hotels, though, their character is immediately different. Entering here, past a modern food market and a handful of stalls for fruit, orange-juice and snacks, you can turn very shortly to the right to come out onto the cubicle shops of the **Rue Souika**. These, dominated by textiles and silverware along their first stretch, give way to a concentration of *babouche* and other shoe stalls as you approach the Grand Mosque. They are all fairly workaday shops, not for the most part geared to tourists, though generally quite affluent; the cheaper goods, and the *joutia*, or flea-market, are off towards the river around the old Jewish quarter of the Mellah. Along the way are few buildings of any particular note, most of the medieval city (which predated that of the Andalusians on this site) having been destroyed by Portuguese raids in the C16. The **Grand Mosque**, founded by the Merenids in the C14, is a partial exception but has been much rebuilt – its minaret, for example, having been completed only in 1939. Opposite, however, there is a small example of Merenid decoration in the stone façade of a public **fountain** – now forming the shopfront of an Arabic bookshop.

The most direct approach from Blvd Hassan II to the Grand Mosque is a broad tree-lined pedestrian way, about halfway along. Alternatively, continuing a couple of blocks (past the *Hôtel Rex*) you can go in by the Mellah, alongside Rue Ouqqasa. The poorest and most run-down area of the city, the **Mellah** no longer has a significant Jewish population, though some of its seventeen synagogues still survive in various forms; the only one active today is a modern building, a block away in the Ville Nouvelle. The quarter itself, where all of the city's Jews were once obliged to live, was created only in 1808; the Jews having previously owned several of the mansions along the Rue des Consuls, further on. With its meat and vegetable markets, it looks a particularly impenetrable area, but it is worth walking through towards the river. The **flea market** spreads out here along the streets below the Souk es Sebbat, down to the Bab el Bahr. There are clothes, pieces of machinery whose remaining parts can no longer exist, and (something you don't see too often) a number of sellers touting grand old 1950s and 1960s movie posters with titles like *Police Militaire* and *La Fille du Desert*.

Beyond the Mellah, **heading towards the kasbah,** you can walk out by the **Bab el Bahr** and follow an avenue near the riverside up to the Oudaia gate; to the left of this road is a small **artesania museum** (usually closed), to the right a rather dull *Centre Artesanal*. The **Rue des Consuls**, a block inland, is a more interesting approach; like the Mellah this too used to be a reserved quarter – the only street of the C19 city where European consulates were permitted. Many of the residency buildings survive, and there are too a few impressive old merchants' *fondouks*, in the alleys off to the left. The street, particularly at its top end, is today largely a centre for **rug and carpet shops** – most of them dependent entirely on the tourist trade but not without interest. Rabat carpets, woven with very bright dyes (which should, if vegetable-based, fade with time), are traditionally a cottage industry in the Medina, though they're now usually produced in factories, one of which you can take a quick look at on the kasbah's 'platform'. If you want some measure of quality for buying, you can see some classic examples in the kasbah museum (detailed below).

The Kasbah des Oudaias

Site of the original *Ribat* and citadel of the Almohad, Merenid and Andalusian towns, the **KASBAH DES OUDAIAS** is a striking and evocative place. Its principal gateway, the Bab el Kasbah (or *Oudaia Gate*), is the most beautiful surviving in the Moorish world; and within its walls are one of the country's best craft museums and a perfect Andalusian garden. Even if you've just a few hours between trains you should at least make it up here.

The **Oudaia Gate**, like all the great external monuments of Morocco, is of Almohad foundation. Built around 1195, concurrently with the Hassan Tower, it was inserted by Yacoub el Mansour within a line of walls already built by his grandfather Abd el Moumen. The walls in fact extended well to its west, cutting down to the sea at the edge of the Medina, and the gate cannot have been designed for any genuine defensive purpose – its function and importance purely ceremonial. It was to be a centre of the kasbah, its chambers acting as courthouse and staterooms, and everything of importance taking place within its immediate confines. The *Souk el Ghezel* – the main commercial centre of the medieval town with its wool and slave markets – was positioned just outside, whilst the original Sultanate palace stood immediately within.

The effect of the gate is startling. It doesn't impress so much by its size – which is not unusual for an Almohad structure – as by the visual strength and simplicity of its decoration. This is based on a typically Islamic rhythm, establishing a tension between the exuberant outward expansion of the arches and the heavy enclosing rectangle of the gate itself. Looking at the two for a few minutes you begin to sense a kind of optical illusion – the shapes appearing suspended by the great rush of movement from the centre of the arch. The basic feature is of course the arch, which here is actually a sequence of three, progressively more elaborate: first the basic horseshoe, then two 'filled' or decorated ones – the last with the distinctive Almohad *darj w ktarf* patterning. a cheek and shoulder design rather like a fleur de lis. At the top, framing the design, is a band of geometric ornamentation, cut off in what seems an arbitrary manner but which again creates the impression of movement and continuance outside the gate. The dominant motifs – scallop shell-looking palm fronds – are also characteristically Almohad, though without any symbolic importance; in fact there's very little that's symbolic in the European sense in any Islamic decoration, it's object being merely to distract the eye sufficiently to allow – hopefully religious – contemplation.

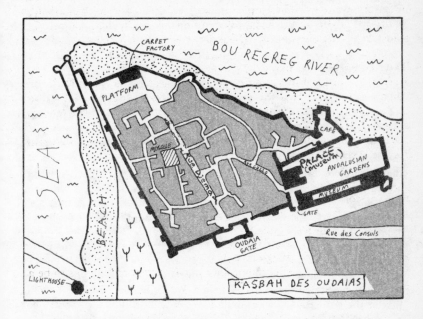

You can enter **THE KASBAH** proper through the Oudaia Gate (or, if it's closed, the small gateway on its right), or by a lower horseshoe gate at the base of the ceremonial stairway. This latter approach leads directly to the *Andalusian gardens* and *palace-museum*, but you can also reach these quite easily after a brief loop through the kasbah quarter. An airy, village-like part of the city, this is a pleasant place to wander – and not remotely dangerous or 'closed to visitors' as the hustlers around the gate try to suggest. Hardly more than 150 metres from one end to the other it's not somewhere you could really use a guide: but talk to the hustlers, be easy and explain you're only wandering down to 'le platforme'. Touting for business isn't too much fun, and tourist arrogance a just provocation.

Once inside the Oudaia gate it would actually be hard not to find the way down to the platform: there's just one main street, **Rue Djemaa**

(*Street of the Mosque*) and it runs straight down to a broad belvedere terrace commanding views across the river and sea. Along the way you pass by the minaret of the **Kasbah Mosque**, the city's oldest, founded in 1050, though much rebuilt in the C18 by an English renegade known as Ahmed el Inglizi – one of a number of European pirates who joined up with the Şallee rovers. El Inglizi was responsible, too, for several of the forts built below and around the **platform**, their gun positions echoed across the estuary by those of Salé. The Bou Regreg (literally 'Father of Reflection') is quite open at this point and would appear to have left the corsair fleets vulnerable, harboured a little downstream where the fishing boats today ferry people across to Salé beach. In fact, a long sandbank stretches submerged across the mouth of the estuary – a feature much exploited by the low-keeled pirate ships who would draw merchant ships into their pursuit to be stranded below the city's cannon. They are actions which you can still imagine, up here amid the low alleys and sea towers, though, as so often in Morocco, it is hard to come to terms with quite how recent is this past.

From the platform of the kasbah it is possible to climb down towards the **sea-beach**, crowded with locals throughout the summer – as too is that of Salé, across the water. Neither, however, are particularly inviting, and if you're more interested in swimming than in keeping mouth and ears above water you'll do a lot better at Bouknadel or Temara (see p. 108); these are also more relaxed – unlike Casa, the city beaches here are almost exclusively male.

Getting down to the *palace-museum* and *gardens* is fairly straightforward: from the main kasbah street just follow Rue Gazzo, which zigzags down towards them. Depending on which fork you take you'll either come out by the entrance to the Palace, or at the **Café Mauré** – at the side of the gardens. Oddly enough the cafe is not at all 'Moorish', but it's a wonderful place to retreat – high on a terrace above the river, with excellent mint tea, Turkish coffee and great trays of traditional pastries. It is used as much by Moroccans as tourists and ordinarily priced.

The Palace itself is C17, one of many built for the notorious Moulay Ismail (see p. 120), the first Sultan since Almohad times to force a unified control over the country. Ismail, whose base was at Meknes, gave Rabat – or *New Salé*, as it was then known – a relatively high priority. Having subdued the pirates' republic, he took over the kasbah as a garrison for the Oudaias – Saharan tribesmen who had accepted military service in return for tax exemption, and an important part of his mercenary army. This move was in part because they proved uncontrollable in Fes or Meknes but it also was an effective way of ensuring that the pirates using the port below kept up their tribute in a constant supply of slaves and booty.

Elegantly converted to a **Museum of Moroccan Arts** (open 8-12 & 4-

6; closed Tuesdays), the palace is an interesting building in its own right. Its design is classic: a series of reception rooms grouped around a central court, and giving access to the private quarters where you can take a look at the small *hammam* – a feature of all noble mansions. The displays within the main building include collections of Berber and Arab jewellery from most of the regions of Morocco, whilst the main reception hall has been furnished in the styles of C19 Rabat and Fes. All of this is well labelled and quite obvious, though there is a room just on your left as you're leaving which is often kept shut except by request: once the palace mosque, this has a very fine display of local carpets.

The collections – including groups of traditional costumes, which again reveal the startling closeness of a medieval past – are continued in a series of rooms along the side of the beautiful '**Andalusian garden**'. Occupying the old palace grounds, this was actually constructed by the French in the present century – its form, however, is entirely in the Spanish-Andalusian tradition with deep sunken beds of shrubs and flowering annuals. If you have come here from Granada it is illuminating to compare this (the authentic Moorish concept) with the neat box hedges with which the Alhambra has been restored. But such historical authenticity aside, this is a really delightful place, full of the scent of datura, bougainvillea and a multitude of herbs and flowers. It has a definite role, too, in modern Rabat as a meeting place for women, who gather here in dozens of small groups on a Friday or Sunday afternoon.

The Hassan Mosque and Tower

The most ambitious of all Almohad buildings, the **Hassan Mosque and Tower**, dominates almost every view of the capital – a majestic sight from the kasbah, from Salé, or glimpsed as you arrive across the river by train. If completed this would have been the second largest mosque in the Islamic world, outflanked only by that of Smarra in Iraq and even today its size seems a novelty.

Begun by Yacoub el Mansour in 1195 – contemporarily with the Koutoubia in Marrakesh and Giralda in Seville – the tower is one of the few Moroccan buildings which approach the European idea of monumentality. This is due in part to its site, on a level above the river and most of the city, but perhaps equally to its unfinished solidity. The other great Moroccan minarets, perfectly balanced by their platform decoration and lanterns, are left 'hanging' as if with no particular weight or height. The Hassan Tower, with no such movement, stands firmly rooted to the ground.

There is also the poignancy of its ruin. Designed by el Mansour as the centrepiece of the new capital, and as a celebration of his great victory over the Spanish kings at Alarcos, its construction seems to have been more or less abandoned at his death in 1199. The tower was probably left much as it appears today. The mosque, roofed in cedar, was actually used for some years, though its extent must always have seemed an elaborate folly. Morocco's most important mosque, the Kairaouine in Fes, is less than half this size but has long served a much greater population with adequate space for 20,000 worshippers. Bearing in mind that it is only men who gather for the weekly Friday prayer – when a town traditionally comes together in its Grand Mosque – Rabat would have needed a population of well over 100,000 to approach the Hassan's capacity. As it was, the city never really took off under the later Almohads and Merenids – and when Leo Africanus came here in 1600 he found no more than a hundred households, gathered for security within the kasbah.

The tower, or **minaret**, is unusually positioned at the centre rather than the northern corner of the rear of the mosque. Some 50m tall in its present state, it would probably have been around 80m if finished to normal proportions – a third again the height of the Koutoubia. Despite its apparent simplicity, it is perhaps the most complex of all Almohad structures. Each façade is different, with a distinct combination of patterning, yet the whole intricacy of blind arcades and interlacing curves is based on just two formal designs. On the south and west faces these are the *darj w ktarf* of the Oudaia gate; on north and east the *shabka* or 'net' motif, an extremely popular form adapted by the Almohads from the lobed arches of the Cordoba Grand Mosque and still in modern use. Although both are austere in comparison to some of the earlier exterior decoration of the Almoravides it is still hard to reconcile their exuberant and technically exacting display with the history and culture of a 'fanatical' puritan movement.

Facing the tower – in an assertion of Morocco's historical independence and continuity – are the **Mosque and Mausoleum of Mohammed V**, begun on the Sultan's death in 1961 and dedicated six years later. The *mosque*, spread between a pair of stark white pavilions, gives a somewhat foreshortened idea of how the whole site must once have appeared, roofed in its traditional green tiles. The *mausoleum*, designed for some reason by a Korean architect, was one of the great prestige projects of modern Morocco, but its brilliantly surfaced marbles and spiralling designs seem to pay homage to traditional Moroccan techniques while failing to capture their rhythms and unity. It is nevertheless an important shrine for Moroccans, and one which non-Muslims are permitted to visit. You file past the magnificently costumed Royal Guards to an interior balcony: the tomb is below, a series of old men squatting beside it to read perpetually from the Koran.

Around the New Town
French in construction, style and feel, the **NEW TOWN** provides the main focus of Rabat's life – above all in the cafes and promenade of the

broad, tree-lined Avenue Mohammed V. There's a certain grandeur in some of the old Mauresque public buildings here, raised with as much attention towards impressing as any earlier epoch, but it is the Almohad walls and gates, Chellah (see the following section) and the excellent archaeological museum which hold most interest.

More or less complete sections of **Almohad wall** run right the way down from the Kasbah to the Royal Palace and beyond, an extraordinary monument to Yacoub el Mansour's vision. Along its course four of the original **gates** survive. Three – the *Bab el Alou*, *Bab Zaer* and *Bab el Had* – are very modest. The **Bab er Rouah** ('gate of the Wind'), however, is on a totally different level, recalling and in many ways rivalling the Oudaia. Contained within a massive stone bastion, it again achieves the tension of movement (the sun-like arches contained within a square of koranic inscription) and a similar balance between simplicity and ornament. The east side, which you approach from outside the walls, is the main façade and must have been designed as a monumental approach to the city. It is perhaps slightly less imposing than the Oudaia gate, but the shallow cut floral relief between arch and square is reputed the finest anywhere in Morocco. Inside, you can appreciate its classic defensive structure – the three domed chambers aligned to force a sharp double turn on all who enter. Generally locked, they are used for occasional exhibitions.

From the Bab er Rouah it's about a 15-minutes walk down towards the last Almohad gate, the much restored **Bab Zaer**, and the entrance to the *Necropolis of Chellah*. On the way you pass a series of modern gates leading off to the vast enclosures of the **Royal Palace** – which is really more a suburb of palaces, built mainly in the C19 – and, off to the left (opposite the Hotel Chellah), the **Archaeological Museum**. The Museum (open daily except Tuesdays 8.30-12 & 2.30-6) is by far the most important in Morocco: small – surprisingly so in a country which saw substantial Phoenician and Carthaginian settlement and three centuries of Roman rule – but with one exceptionally beautiful collection. This is a series of *Roman bronzes* from the first and second centuries, found mainly at the provincial capital of Volubilis (see p. 130) but including a few from Chellah and the small coastal colonies of Banasa and Thamusidia. They are actually displayed in an annexe to the main part of the museum, and you may have to ask for it to be opened and lit. Highlights include superb figures of a guard dog and a rider, and two magnificent portrait heads, reputedly those of Cato the Younger (Caton d'Utique) and Juba II – the last significant ruler of the Romanised Berber kingdoms of Mauretania and Numidia before the assertion of direct imperial rule.

The Chellah Necropolis

The most beautiful of Moroccan ruins, **CHELLAH** is a startling sight as you emerge from the long avenues of the *Ville Nouvelle*. Walled and towered, it is a much larger enclosure than the maps suggest – and it seems for a moment as if you've come upon a second Medina. It is in fact a long unpeopled site – since 1154 when it was abandoned in favour of Salé across the Bou Regreg – but for almost a thousand years before, Chellah (or *Sala Colonia*) had been a thriving city and port, one of the last to sever links with the Roman Empire, and the first to proclaim Moulay Idriss, founder of Morocco's original Arab dynasty. An apocryphal local tradition maintains that the Prophet himself also prayed at a shrine here.

The site was already a royal burial ground under the Almohads, but most of what you see today, including the gates and enclosing wall, is the legacy of the Merenid Sultan **Abou el Hassan** (1331-51). The greatest of Merenid rulers, conquering and controlling the Maghreb as far east as Tunis, Abou el Hassan, 'the Black Sultan', was also their most prolific builder. In addition to Chellah he was responsible for important mosques at Fes and Tlemcen as well as the beautiful *medressas* at Salé and Meknes.

The **main gate** here is the most surprising of his monuments, its turreted bastions almost Gothic in appearance. The basis is still recognisably Almohad but each element has become inflated and the combination of simplicity with solidity has gone. In its original state, with bright coloured marble and tile decoration, the effect must have been incredibly gaudy – rather like the C19 palaces you see today in Fes and Marrakesh. An interesting technical innovation, however, are the stalactite (or 'honeycomb') corbels which make the transition from the bastions' half-octagonal towers to their square platforms; later to become a feature of Merenid building. The kufic inscription above the gate is from the Koran and begins with the invocation: 'I take refuge in Allah, against Satan, the stoned one . . .'.

There are usually a number of *guides* hanging around the gate, but once again they are not obligatory, nor is there any admission charge. Inside, things are clear enough. Off to your left, closed off in a state of long suspended excavation, are the main **Roman remains** – including the visible outlines of a forum, temple and artesans' quarter. The **Islamic ruins** are down to the right, within a second inner sanctuary approached along a broad path through half-wild gardens of banana, orange and ancient fig trees, sunflowers, dahlias and datura plants. Their most prominent and picturesque feature is a tall stone and tile minaret, a ludicrously oversized stork's nest invariably on its summit. Storks, along with swallows and crows, have a certain sanctity in Morocco, and their presence on minarets is a sign of good fortune.

The SANCTUARY itself looks a slightly confusing cluster of tombs and ruins but it is essentially just two buildings: the original **mosque** built on the site by the second Merenid sultan Abou Youssef (1258-86), and

a **zaouia**, or mosque-monastery, added along with the enclosure walls by
Abou el Hassan.

You enter directly into the *sahn*, or courtyard, of **Abou Youssef's
Mosque**, a small and presumably private structure built as a funerary
dedication. It is now very much in ruins, though you can make out the
colonnades of the inner prayer hall with its *mihrab* to indicate the direction of prayer. Off to the right is its minaret, now reduced to the level
of the mosque's roof. Behind, both within and outside the sanctuary
enclosure, are a series of scattered **royal tombs** – each aligned so that the
dead, dressed in white and lying on their right-hand sides, may face
Mecca to await the Call of Judgment. Abou Youssef's tomb has not been
identified, but you can find those of both **Abou el Hassan** and his wife
Shams ed Douna. Hassan's is contained within a kind of pavilion whose
external wall retains its decoration – the *darj w ktarf* motif set above
three small arches in a design very similar to that of the (unrelated)
Hassan tower. Shams ed Douna, 'Morning Sun', has only a tombstone –
a long pointed rectangle covered in a mass of verses from the Koran. A
convert from Christianity, Shams was the mother of Abou el Hassan's
rebel son Abou Inan, whose uprising led to the sultan's death as a fugitive
in the High Atlas during the winter of 1352.

The Zaouia is in a much better state of preservation: its structure, like

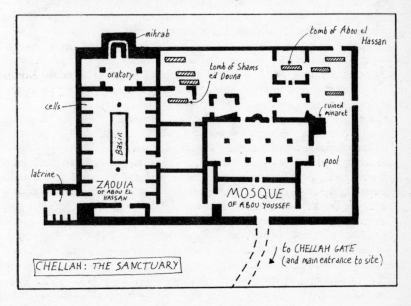

CHELLAH: THE SANCTUARY

Abou el Hassan's medressas, that of a long central court enclosed by cells, with a smaller oratory or prayer hall at the end. Each of these features are quite recognisable, along with those of the latrine, preceding the main court for worshippers' purification. There are fragments of zellij (mosaic tilework) on some of the colonnades and on the minaret, which again give an idea of its original brightness, and there are traces too of the *mihrab's* elaborate stucco decoration. Five-sided, the mihrab has a narrow passageway (now blocked with brambles) leading behind – built so that pilgrims might make their seven circuits around it. This was once believed to give the equivalent merit of the *hadj*, the trip to Mecca: a tradition, with that of Muhammad's visit, most likely invented and propagated by the zaouia's keepers to increase their revenue.

Off to the right and above the sanctuary enclosure are a group of **koubbas** – the domed tombs of local saints or marabouts – and beyond them a **spring-pool**, enclosed by low vaulted buildings. This is held sacred, along with the eels which lurk in its waters and women bring hard boiled eggs to invoke assistance in fertility and childbirth.

Practicalities

For a capital city, Rabat's potential for fun – and even for eating well – is none too impressive. As far as **restaurants** go you'll really do best heading for the ordinary workaday places on the edge of the MEDINA; these, at all events, are the cheapest – especially so at lunchtime when most offer very good value set meals. Among them, the *Restaurant-Café Jeunesse* is about the best (on the crossroads of Rue Mohammed V/Rue Souika, it's open for meals at lunchtime only) or, for only a few dirhams, you can pick up a range of snacks and juices just inside the Medina walls (by the *market* on our plan). Around the NEW TOWN most of the good cheaper places are around the railway station and Avenue Moulay Youssef (the diagonal street behind); *Le Clef*, just off the Avenue and slightly upmarket, is recommended. So too, in the 30-40dh range, are *Restaurant Saadi* (Av. Allal Ben Abdallah 87) and the *Balima restaurant* (on Mohammed V) – this last slightly pricey but with vast helpings and considerable style. Except during Ramadan all tend to stop serving around 9.30-10pm. Both avenues Mohammed V and Allal Ben Abdallah have some excellent **cafes**, though **bars** (outside of the main hotels) are few on the ground. Once again the *Hôtel Balima* is as good a place as any. When it's closed (usually at 10pm) about your only **late-night options** are the European style disco-bars around the Place de Melilla (right of the main park, below Blvd Hassan II).

Local bus services leave mainly from the Blvd Hassan II. Nos 1/2/4 run from here (via Allal Ben Abdallah) to the Bab Zaer, by Chellah; nos 6/12 cross the bridge to Salé; and no. 17 heads south to Temara Beach. For the **main bus terminal** (well outside the centre at Place Zerktouni on the road to Casa) take either bus 30 (which leaves near no. 6 on our plan) or a *petit taxi*. The **grands taxis** for Casa (which cost only a couple of dirhams more than the bus, and are considerably faster) also leave from the Place Zerktouni: just state your destination and you'll have to wait only a few minutes before there's a taxi full and ready to leave. Other *grands taxis* – to Tangier, Meknes, Fes and local destinations like Skhirat and Bouknadel – leave from the long anarchic rank on Blvd Hassan II.

AIRLINES *Royal Air Maroc* are just down from the Railway Station on Av. Mohammed V; *Air France* are at no. 281; *Iberia* at 104 (1st floor).

AIRPORT The local airport, for domestic flights, is just outside Salé. International flights go from the Mohammed V Airport, most of the way towards Casa; there's a very expensive airport bus from Av. Mohammed V (tickets from *RAM*) but with four or more people you'll save money and time by using a *grand taxi*.

ALPINE CLUB c/o *Librairie des Belles Images*, Av. Mohammed V.

AMERICAN EXPRESS have a bureau in the Rabat Hilton, miles out from the centre and a viciously expensive taxi-ride. Avoid having mail sent to them (see *Poste Restante* below).

BANKS Most are concentrated along Av. Allal Ben Abdallah; *Crédit du Maroc*, one of the most efficient, operate *Visa* transactions.

BEACHES Nearest are the Kasbah and Salé beaches, the latter best reached by boat ferry from down below the Mellah. For clearer waters head by bus to either the Plage des Nations or Temara, both detailed in the section following Salé (p. 108–109).

BOOKS The *American Bookstore* (Rue Tanja: see plan) have good selections of Penguin novels, etc., along with an enterprising shelf on Moroccan architecture, Islam and some of the Paul Bowles translations of Moroccan fiction. You can get the *Lamzoudi* Moroccan Arabic-French phrasebook – the only one of its kind (see p. 340) – from several of the bookshops along Av. Mohammed V.

CAR RENTAL *Leasing Cars*, usually the cheapest option, have an office in Casa (see p. 116) but not in Rabat. Here you're dependent on the usual standards: *Hertz* (467 Av. Mohammed V), *Europcar* (Hilton Hotel), *Avis* (7 Rue Abou Faris Al Mairini) and *Maroc/InerRent* (Hôtel Tour Hassan, Av. Annegai). *Tourist Cars* (c/o Hôtel Rex, 1 Rue de Nador) may be able to offer slightly better rates.

CAR REPAIRS Try *Concorde* (6 Av. Allal Ben Abdallah) or, particularly for Renaults, the garage at 14 Avenue Misr.

EMBASSIES & CONSULATES Britain (17 Blvd Tour Hassan; tel. 20-905); Ireland (representation c/o Britain); U.S. (2 Av. de Marrakesh – near the far end of Allal Ben Abdallah; tel. 62-265); Canada (13 Zankat

Joafar Essadik; tel. 71-375); **Australia** (representation c/o Canada);
Netherlands (40 Rue de Tunis; tel. 335-12); Sweden (159 Av. President
Kennedy; tel. 547-40). Most of these keep hours of around 8.30-11.30am,
Monday-Friday, though you can phone at any time in an emergency. The
Algerian Embassy at the time of writing remains suspended and for
Algerian visas you'll need to go to the United Arab Emirates *Special
Mission for Algerian Affairs* (8 Zankat Azrou; open 9.30-2.30). You'll
need four passport photographs and a good couple of days to hang
around. See Oujda (p. 85) for an alternative.

LIBRARIES   Both the *British Council* (6 Av. Moulay Youssef) and the
American Embassy (Annex on Av. Allal Ben Abdallah) have library rooms
where you can walk in and read newspapers and magazines. They can
also put you in touch with people if you want to take lessons in Moroccan
Arabic.

MAPS   Ordnance Survey type maps are erratically available from the
Institute Geographique National, 31 Av. Hassan I.

POLICE   Telephone 19; central office at Rue Soekarno, a couple of
blocks out from Av. Mohammed V.

POST OFFICE   The *PTT Centrale* – open 24hrs a day for phones – is
midway down Av. Mohammed V. The *poste restante* section is across
the road from the main building.

PUBLIC BATHS   Beside the Hôtel Rex, just off Blvd Hassan II.

TOURIST OFFICES   For larger scale, fold-out *map-pamphlets* of both
Rabat and Casa drop by either the ONMT office (22 Avenue Al Jazair)
or the *Syndicat d'Initiative* (Rue Patrice Lumumba). Both are marked on
our plan and are open Mon-Sat 8-12, the Syndicat on weekday afternoons
too.

Salé

Although it is now essentially a suburb of Rabat – just 2km by road
across the river – SALÉ was pre-eminent of the two right through the
Middle Ages, from the decline of the Almohads to the town's uneasy
alliance in the pirate Republic of Bou Regreg. Largely neglected since the
French creation of a capital in Rabat, it looks and feels today quite
distinct. The spread of a new town outside its walls has been restricted
to a small area around the bus station and the north gates, and the souks
and life within its medieval limits remain surprisingly traditional.

From Rabat you can cross the river by **boat** (see the plan on p. 91),
or take a **bus** (nos 6/12) from the Boulevard Hassan II. The boats charge
a dirham a person and drop you close to the Salé beach, a lively stretch,
though less enticing at close quarters; from here it's a steep walk up to
the **Bab Bou Haja**, one of the main town gates. Both buses drop you at
an open terminal just below the railway station and opposite another

major gate – the **Bab Fes**, which leads straight in towards the souks. There is a sketchy but functional **plan** of the town printed on the tourist board's standard 'Rabat-Salé' pamphlet.

Just down to your left, facing the ramparts from the bus station, is the high-curved arch of the **Bab Mrisa**, most interesting of the town's gates and a good point to start looking around. Its name – 'gate of the small harbour' – recalls the marine arsenal which used to be sited within the walls, and explains the gate's unusual height. A channel up here from the Bou Regreg, long silted, allowed medieval merchant ships to sail right into town. The device must have been a useful defence over the years of the Pirate Republic, though in fact Salé was much less of a corsair base than the Rabat kasbah and its trading traditions went back some centuries before the arrival of the Andalusians; in 1600 Leo Africanus reported the presence here of ships from Genoa, Flanders, Venice and England. The gate itself is a very early Merenid structure of the 1270s, its design and motifs (palmettes enclosed by floral decoration; bands of kufic inscription and *darj w ktarf*, etc.) still inherently Almohad in tone.

Through the gate you find yourself in a small square at the bottom of the old *Mellah* quarter. Turning to the left, and continuing close to the walls, you'll come out in about 350m at another gate, **Bab Bou Haja**, beside a strip of park. If you want to explore the souks – the route outlined below – take the road along the left-hand side of the park. If not, carry on just inside the walls to a long open area: as this starts to narrow into a lane (about 450m further on) cut in to your right into the town. This should bring you out more or less at the *Grand Mosque*, opposite which (see below) is the *Medressa of Abou el Hassan*.

The park-side street from Bab Bou Haja is known as **Rue Bab el Khabaz** ('street of the bakers gate'), a busy little lane which emerges right at the heart of the **souks** by a small *kissaria* – or covered market – given over mainly to textiles. Most of the alleys around are grouped about specific crafts, a particular speciality here being the pattern-weave mats produced for the sides and floors of Moroccan mosques. From the kissaria a kind of main road, the **Rue de la Grande Mosque**, leads uphill through the middle of town to the Grand Mosque. This is the simplest approach but you can take in more of the souks by following the **Rue Kechachin** – parallel but slightly above it (away from the river walls). Along Kechachin are, among other craftsmen, the carpenters and stone carvers. In **Rue Haddadin**, a fairly major intersection which leads off to its right up towards the Bab Sebta, you'll come upon gold and coppersmiths.

As far as buildings go, the **Grand Mosque** signals very much the most interesting part of town, its surrounding lanes fronting a concentration of aristocratic mansions and religious *zaouia* foundations. Almohad in origin, the mosque is one of the largest and earliest in Morocco: though what you can see as a non-Muslim – the gateway and minaret – are recent additions. You can, however, visit its **Medressa** (opposite the monumental stepped main entrance). Salé's main monument, this has recently been restored and there may well still be signs suggesting that it's closed: don't be put off, and if the gate's locked knock and ask the people around. Founded in 1341 by the sultan Abou el Hassan (see Chellah, p. 100), the building is more or less contemporary with the Bou Inania medressa in Meknes and Fes. Like them, it follows the basic Merenid plan of a central courtyard giving onto a prayer hall, with a series of cells for the students – for whom these 'university college halls' were endowed – around its upper storeys. If this is the first one you've seen it will come as a surprise after the sparse Almohad economy of the monuments in Rabat. The great Merenid medressas are all intensely decorated – in carved wood, stucco and zellij – and this is no exception. As you stand within the gate (itself highly elaborate with its stucco surround and painted carved portal) there is hardly an inch of space which doesn't draw the eye away into a web of intricacy. Even the pillars, here unusually rounded, are completely encased in zellij mosaic.

What is remarkable, though, despite a certain heaviness which the great Merenid medressas manage to avoid, is the way in which each aspect of the workmanship succeeds in forging a unity with the others – echoing and repeating the standard patterns in endless variations. The patterns, for the most part, derive from Almohad models, with their stylised geometric and floral motifs, but in the latter there is a much more natural- istic, less abstracted approach. There is also a new stress on calligraphy, with monumental inscriptions carved in great bands on the dark cedar- wood and incorporated within the stucco and zellij. Almost invariably these are in the elaborate cursive script and they are generally passages from the Koran. There are occasional poems, however, such as the beautiful foundation inscription, set in marble against a green background on the rear wall of the court, which begins:

Look at my admirable portal!
Rejoice in my chosen company,
In the remarkable style of my construction
And my marvellous interior!
The workers here have accomplished an artful
Creation with the beauty of youth . . . *

Only sporadically visited, you'll probably have the medressa to yourself save for the sparrows and the guardian – a quiet meditative place. Close to its entrance there is a stairway up to the old windowless cells of the students, and to the roof, where, looking out across the river to Rabat, you can really sense the enormity of the Hassan tower.

* Quoted in translation from a French book by Charles Terrasse in Richard B. Parker's *Islamic Monuments in Morocco* (see p. 327)

Out beyond the medressa, a street runs down the near side of the Grand Mosque to emerge amidst a vast and very ancient **cemetery** – at the far end of which you can see (though you should not approach) the white *koubba* and associated buildings of the **marabout of Sidi ben Achir**. Sometimes known as *at Tabir* 'the doctor', ben Achir was a C14 ascetic from Andalusia. His shrine, said to have the ability to attract shipwrecks and quieten storms – good pirate virtues – is also a reputed cure for blindness, paralysis and madness. Enclosed by C19 pilgrim lodgings, it still has its devotees and is the scene of a considerable annual *moussem*, or pilgrimage-festival.

The most important of Salé's moussems, however, is that of its patron saint, **Sidi Abdallah ben Hassoun**, whose *zaouia* stands just to the right of the road a few paces before you come out at the cemetery. The saint, who has a St Christopher-like role for Muslim travellers, lived at Salé during the C16, though the origins and significance of his moussem are unclear. Taking place each year on the eve of the Mouloud – the Prophet's birthday – it involves a spectacular procession through the streets of the town with local boatmen, dressed in corsair costume, carrying huge and elaborate wax lanterns mounted on great poles.

Since Salé is so close to Rabat, and has a bus and train station for most points to the north, there is little reason to stay. It is an interesting town to wander through for an afternoon, and you can eat at one of the many workers **cafes** along the Rue Kechachin, but, if anything, its streets empty even earlier than those of Rabat; as an alternative base it would be wilfully eccentric, though there is one small **café-hôtel** (the *Saadiens*, by the bus station) as well as the unalluring **camping municipal** by the beach.

NORTH OF RABAT: THE JARDINS EXOTIQUES, PLAGE DES NATIONS AND KENITRA

Respectively 12km and 18km from Rabat, the **Jardins Exotiques** and **Plage des Nations** provide the capital's most enjoyable excursion. The first, as its name suggests, is a French colonial creation of botanical extravagance; the second, an immense fine strand which, with Temara (see the next section), is the sophisticated local beach to hang out. Both can be reached by bus no. 28 from the *Salé terminal* (about every 20 mins). The bus stops and turns round a couple of kilometres before it reaches the turning to the *Plage* (which is where everyone will be going); for the *Jardins* you'll need to ask the driver to let you off – their entrance is just to the left of the road and there's a bus stop 20metres beyond it.

The **JARDINS**, laid out in what the French guides call 'une manière remarquable' by one M. François, have obviously seen better days – a fact which adds considerably to their charm. Full of precarious bamboo bridges and bizarre dot-directed routes, you wander through a sequence of brilliant regional creations. There is a Brazilian rain forest, dense with water and orchids, a formal Japanese garden, and then suddenly a great shaft of French Polynesia with rickety summerhouses set amid long pools, turtles paddling around you, palms all about and terrific flashes of bright red flowers. On a more local level there is also a superbly maintained Andalusian garden, but the appeal of this place has little really to do with Morocco. It is open daily from sunrise to sunset for a nominal (currently 5dh) admission fee.

There is a good modern road right down to the PLAGE DES NATIONS, but the no. 28 (which you can flag down outside the *Jardins*) stops some way before this turning – just after the village of BOUKNADEL, by a cafe in what seems to be the middle of nowhere. Everybody gets out here and takes the diagonal track off towards the sea and a cape: past a couple of farms, round a wood and then joining the tail end of the asphalt road down to the beach itself.

After this approach one's imagining a wild, Irish kind of beach with battered cliffs and a few picnic groups. **PLAGE DES NATIONS**, or SIDI BOUKNADEL as it's also known, is nothing of the kind. Flanked by the 5*A *Hôtel Firdaous*, a slick new complex with a freshwater pool (open to all for a small charge or, sometimes, a meal), it seems actually more Westernised than Rabat itself. Certainly, unlike the Kasbah or Salé beaches, it's a resort where young Rabat women feel able to come out for the day – outside the uncontested male domination of the city's beaches. And with everyone here to take a day's holiday, it's a very relaxed and friendly sort of place: the beach is excellent with big exciting rollers (said to be dangerous, but patrolled along a central strip) and there are a couple of reasonably-priced cafes.

If you're planning to go on north towards **KENITRA** you'll have to return to Salé or hitch, but the town is probably just as well bypassed. A major port established by the French, it is nowadays a considerable US and Moroccan military base – a drab-looking place with a rather self-conscious garrison prosperity (an unusual amount of bars, hotels, pizza joints and semi-discos). Not somewhere you'll want to get stuck for long: if you are, most of the cheaper **hotels** are along the main Av. Mohammed V from the bus station, or just off it (like the 2*B *Hôtel La Rotonde* at Av. Mohammed Diouri 60). **Mehdiya Plage**, Kenitra's local beach, is a dull greyish strip with a few beachside houses and summer crowds.

TOWARDS CASA: TEMARA, SKHIRAT AND MOHAMMEDIA

It's little over an hour by *grand taxi* from Rabat to Casa – an hour and a half if you go by train – and there's very little en route to delay your progress. The landscape, wooded in parts, is a low flat plain, punctuated only by the industrial port of Mohammedia and the turnings to a few local beach resorts. None of these are particularly memorable but they are each lively and popular escapes from the capital and being close remain so well into the evenings.

TEMARA PLAGE, 16km south-west of Rabat, is probably the best of the bunch – just 20 minutes by *grand taxi* (from the main rank on Blvd Hassan II) and flanked by a number of fairly late-night discos, a summer alternative to the lack of action in Rabat. Few people stay here overnight, though if you want to there should be no problem: there's a **campsite** and two **hotels**, the 3*A *La Felouque* and unclassified *Hôtel Casino*. Bus no. 17, incidentally, which leaves from Hassan II, goes only as far as the village (and old kasbah ruins) of TEMARA, a 4km walk from the beach. **ECH CHIANA**, another beach 9km further on, is in a smaller but similar vein; again with a luxury **hotel** (the 4*B *Kasbah Club*), cheap **auberge** (the *Gambusia*) and **campsite**. Beyond, there is a distinctly upmarket shift as you approach **SKHIRAT PLAGE** and its summer Royal Palace, site of the notorious coup attempt by senior Moroccan generals during the king's birthday celebrations in July 1971. Mounted with a force of Berber cadets, who took over the palace, imprisoned King Hassan and massacred a number of his guests, this came within hours of success – but was thwarted, ironically, by the accidental shooting of the cadets' leader, General Mohammed Medbuh. The palace today still forms the centre-piece of a rather exclusive resort. If you want to stop over and swim, there are two **hotels** – the 1*B *Auberge Potiniere* and 3*A *Amphitrite*. Easiest access is by train – from Rabat or Casa – to the town of SKHIRAT, only a couple of kilometres from the beach.

Lastly, before you move into the industrialised outskirts of Casablanca, there is **MOHAMMEDIA**: an industrial and commercial port now conclusively dominated by the refineries of its petro-chemical develop-ments. A town of some 70,000 population, it has also been a popular and somewhat elitist resort over the last few decades – a pleasure ground for Casa, with its excellent 5km beach, racecourse, 18-hole golfcourse, casino and yachting marina. The recent industrial growth has dampened enthusiasm, but only to an extent. There are a number of big luxury hotels along the beach, along with dozens of restaurants and discos. It isn't somewhere I'd personally choose to stay, though if you're curious there are cheaper **hotels** around the old C18 kasbah, close behind the **railway station**.

CASABLANCA (CASA, DAR EL BAIDA)

Neither in point of history nor situation, nor even for what it is in itself does Dar el Baida offer the slightest attraction. It has never been, and probably never will be, more than a provincial trading port.

Budgett Meakin: *The Land of the Moors* (1901)

Chief city of Morocco, and capital in all but administration, **CASA-BLANCA** (*Dar el Baida* in its literal Arabic form) is now the largest port of the Maghreb – busier even than Marseilles, the city upon which it was modelled by the French. Its development, from a town of 20,000 in 1906, has been astonishingly rapid, and quite ruthlessly deliberate. When the French landed their first forces here in 1907, and five years later established their protectorate, it was Fes which was Morocco's commercial centre, with Tangier its chief port. Had Tangier not been in international hands this would most likely have been perpetuated. Instead, the demands of an independent colonial administration forced the French to seek an entirely new base. Casa, at the heart of *Maroc Utile*, the country's most fertile zone and the centre of its mineral deposits, was a natural choice.

Superficially, Casa is much like any other large Western city – a familiarity which makes it quite easy to get an initial hang of, and a revelation as you begin to understand something of its life. It is a genuinely dynamic city, still growing at a rate of 50,000 a year, and coming here from the south, or even from Fes or Tangier, most of the preconceptions you've been travelling around with will be happily shattered. So, too will any illusions you might have about Casa's own movie mystique. Not a scene from any of the films which bear its name were shot here, there is no Rick's Bar (even as a tourist recreation), and sophisticated degeneracy is very thin on the ground.

Casa's Western image – its almost total absence of the veil and its smart beach clubs – shields, however, what is still substantially a 'first generation' city, and one which has an inevitable weight of problems. Alongside its wealth and a handful of showpiece developments – it has recently hosted the Mediterranean Games – it has had since its formation a reputation for extreme poverty, prostitution, *bidonville* shantytowns and social unrest. The 'bidonville problem' resulted partly from the sheer extent of the population increases (over 1million in the 1960s), partly because few of the earlier migrants intended to stay permanently – sending back most of their earnings to their families in the country. The pattern is now much more towards permanent settlement, and this, together with a strict control of migration and a limited number of self-help programmes, have eased and cleared many of the worst shanty areas. The problem of a concentrated urban poor, however, is more enduring and represents, as it did for the French, an intermittent threat to government stability. Casa, through the 1940s and 1950s, was the main centre of anti-French rioting, and it was the city's working class, too, which formed the base of Ben Barka's Socialist Party. There have been strikes here sporadically since Independence, and on several occasions, most violently in the 'food strikes' of 1982, they have precipitated rioting. Whether Casa's development can be sustained, and the lot of its new migrants improved, must decide much of Morocco's future.

Arriving and hotels

A large city by any standards, Casa can be a confusing place to arrive — particularly so if you're on one of the trains which stop at the main *Gare des Voyageurs* (2km out from the centre) rather than carrying on to the well-positioned *Gare du Port*. Once you're into the city, though, things are quite simple. There are two principal squares — the **Place Mohammed V** and **Place des Nations Unies** — and most of the places to stay, to eat and (in a rather limited way) to see are contained in and around the avenues to their sides. The **Old Medina**, *the* Casablanca until around 1907, remains largely within its walls behind the Place Mohammed V (which was formerly the site of its weekly souk). The **New Medina**, a slightly bizarre French creation, lies a couple of kilometres out to the south — easiest reached by following the Rue Hadj Amar Riffi. And beyond this it is only the the beach suburb of **Ain Diab**, west from the port, which you're likely to want to explore.

The *Casablanca tourist pamphlet* prints a fairly clear plan of the city, covering a much larger area than ours and detailing Ain Diab, the Gare des Voyageurs and the New Medina (labelled *Habbous*, its local name). You can pick this up in advance from any Moroccan tourist office, or here from the **ONMT** (Rue Omar Slaoui 55) or **Syndicat d'Initiative** (Boulevard Mohammed V 98), both marked on our plan.

Most of the **trains** from Marrakesh call at both stations, allowing you to stay on until the **Gare du Port** just 150m from Place Mohammed V. From Rabat (and Fes/Tangier), however, trains sometimes terminate at the **Gare des Voyageurs**, at the far end of Blvd Mohammed V. There's no bus into the centre from here and unless you move very sharply you'll wait hours for a *petit taxi*, so reckon on a 20min walk: Blvd Mohammed V runs straight ahead from the square in front of the station, curving slightly left as you come to the next main square (Place Albert 4er). **Bus stations** and **grand taxi ranks** are more central and straightforward. All the **CTM buses** come in at the *Gare Routière* on Rue Léon L'Africain (off Rue Colbert, centre right on our plan) and the **grands taxis** for Rabat usually stop just across the street behind. Non CTM buses use the **private lines** station down below the Place de la Victoire at the bottom of our plan.

HOTELS, unless there's a major event on in the city, are fairly easy to find. Many of the cheaper one and two-star places are also quite stylish in a faded deco sort of way, though don't expect too much choice if you're arriving late in the day. The cheapest place to stay – and quite a good option here – is the **Youth Hostel** at Place Admiral Philbert 6, just inside the Medina; from the Gare du Port or Place Mohammed V walk up to the corner of the walls and follow them down to the first entrance off the Boulevard – the hostel's on your right at the near side of the square. Among the cheaper hotels keyed on our plan the best value are usually the *Gallia* (19 Rue Ibn Batouta, off Av. Houman el Fetouaki), *Touring* (87 Rue Allal Ben Abdallah), *Lincoln* (1 Rue Ibn Batouta) and *Foucauld* (52 Rue de Foucauld). The *Excelsior*, on Place Mohammed V, is a little pricier (3*B) but recommended if you can afford it – another of those places which used to be *the* grand hotel until the big concrete Hiltons moved in.

Addresses of other cheap options, the first six keyed, include:
Hôtel du Perigord, 56 Rue de Foucauld (next to the *Foucauld*).
Hôtel Les Negotiants, Rue Allal Ben Abdallah (just up from the *Touring*), and in the same street the cheap if windowless *Kon Tiki*, at no.89, and *Bon Rêve*.
Hôtel Rialto (2*B) 9 Rue Claude. (Opposite is the *Hôtel de France* and a *hamman*.)
Hôtel du Louvre (2*B) 36 Rue Nationale.

As in Rabat the **Medina hotels** are comparatively expensive – most of them charging the equivalent of 1*A prices for fairly miserable rooms. The nearest **campsite**, if you're obsessively dedicated, is *Camping Oasis* on Avenue Mermoz, well out on the road to El Jadida; to get there by public transport take bus 31 from the *CTM* terminal.

Around the city

Unique among Moroccan cities, Casa lacks any kind of monument or 'sight' – not even a museum, though there is a sad-looking aquarium, flanked by penquin-less penguin pools, out on the way to Ain Diab. But it is an interesting enough city in its own right and with its obsessive beach life (detailed in the following section) you can spend a good few days without any tourist compulsion. After this, catching a train south to Marrakesh is all the more impressive.

Having said there are no monuments, the city in some ways feels full of them. The French city centre and its formal colonial buildings already seem to belong to a different and distant age. Grouped about the **Place des Nations Unies**, these have served as models for administrative architecture throughout Morocco, and to an extent still do; their style, heavily influenced by art deco, is known as *Mauresque* – a French idealisation and 'improvement' of Moorish design. The effect, orchestrated to a *son et lumière* fountain three nights a week, is actually most impressive, the

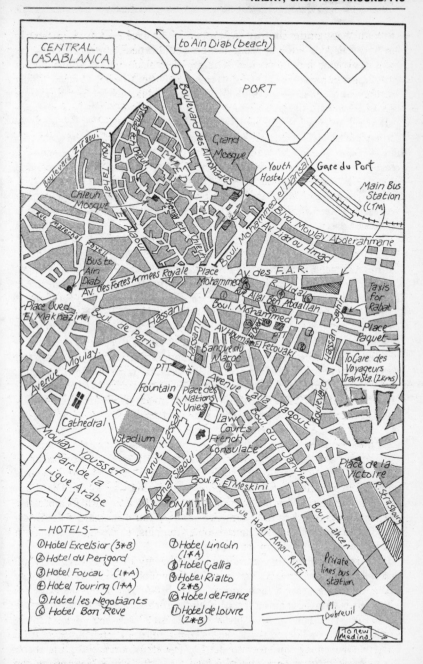

CENTRAL CASABLANCA

to Ain Diab (beach)

PORT

Boulevard des Almohades

Grand Mosque

Youth Hostel

Blvd. Mohammed el Hansali

Gare du Port

Main Bus Station (CTM)

Av Ziad ou Hmad

Blvd. Moulay Abderahmane

Chleuh Mosque

Boulevard Ziraoui

Boul Tahar El Alaoui

Rue Marechal Foch

Bus to Ain Diab

Av. des Fortes Armees Royale

Place Mohammed V

Av des F.A.R.

R. Vidal

Place Oued El Makhazine

Boul de Paris

Hassan I

Boul. Mohammed

Rue Allal Ben Abdallah

Taxis for Rabat

Place Paquet

Hassan Senir

Avenue Moulay

Av Houmam El Fetouaki

PTT

Banque du Maroc

To Gare des Voyageurs Train Sta. (2kms)

Avenue Hassan I

PTT

Fountain

Place des Nations Unies

Avenue Lalla

Boul du 11 Janvier

Cathedral

Stadium

Law Courts French Consulate

Place de la Victoire

Moulay Youssef

Parc de la Ligue Arabe

Avenue Hassan

Rue Omar Slaoui

Boul. R. El Meskini

Rue Hadj Amor Rifci

R. Strasbourg

Boul. Lahcen

Private lines bus station

Pl. Dubreuil

To new Medina

─ HOTELS ─
① Hotel Excelsior (3 ∗ B)
② Hotel du Perigord
③ Hotel Foucal (1 ∗ A)
④ Hotel Touring (1 ∗ A)
⑤ Hotel les Négotiants
⑥ Hotel Bon Reve
⑦ Hotel Lincoln (1 ∗ A)
⑧ Hotel Gallia
⑨ Hotel Rialto (2 ∗ B)
⑩ Hotel de France
⑪ Hotel de Louvre (2 ∗ B)

only intrusively French feature a clocktower in the *Prefecture*. More European in style, though again adopting traditional Moroccan forms, is the old **Cathedral of Sacre Coeur** at the far end of the **Parc de la Ligue Arabe**. Now used as a school, it is perhaps the one building in Casa worth seeing in itself – a wonderfully balanced and airy design quite out of character with the repressive colonialism of its age.

If you have time to fill, the **New Medina** (or *Quartier Habbous*) is a somewhat bizarre extension of this French-Mauresque interest. Built in the 1930s as a response to the first *bidonville* crisis, it is an extraordinary recreation of what the French felt domestic Moroccan architecture should be like. The streets, laid out in neat little rows, have today a rather folksy shopping centre feel about them – not at all Moroccan even with the years. Most unreal, however, is the quarter's mosque, flanked by a tidy stretch of green like any good French village church.

The **Old Medina**, lapsing into dilapidation above the port, is largely the product of the late C19 when Casa begun a modest growth as a commercial centre. Before that it was little more than a group of village huts, half-heartedly settled by local tribes after the site was abandoned by the Portuguese in 1755. *Casa Branca*, the city the Portuguese founded here in the C15, had been virtually levelled by the Great Earthquake of that year (which also destroyed Lisbon). Only its name – 'the White House', *Casablanca* in Spanish, *Dar el Baida* in Arabic – survives.

Now relatively underpopulated, the Medina has a slightly disreputable if also quite affluent air. It is said to be the place to go and look for any stolen goods you might want to buy back – a character well in keeping with many of the stalls. There's nothing sinister though, and it can be a good source for cheap snacks and general goods. A single main street, the Rue Djemaa ech Chleuh, edges its way right through the quarter, past most of the market stalls and the principal mosque from which it takes its name.

Ain Diab: the beach

You can get out to Ain Diab by bus (no.9 from the Boulevard de Paris: see our plan), by *petit taxi* (hang around Place Mohammed V) or by walking. The beach starts about 3km round from the port and Old Medina and stretches on for about the same distance.

A beach right within Casa may not sound exactly alluring, and it's certainly not the cleanest and clearest of the country's waters. But the big attraction of Ain Diab is not so much in the sea, in the shallows of which Moroccans gather in odd phalanx formations wary of the currents, as in the 'beach clubs' along the front. Each of these has one or more pools (usually of filtered seawater), a restaurant and a couple of snack-bars; in the more upmarket there'll also be additional sports facilities – tennis, volleyball, and maybe even a disco. On paper this must sound very ordinary and average, but its novelty in a Moroccan city is quite amazing. Country people and recent immigrants must reckon so, as well, and it's an odd sight to see women veiled from head to toe looking down on the cosmopolitan intensity below.

Prices and quality of the clubs vary enormously, and it's worth wandering around a while to check out what's on offer. Most locals have annual membership and for outsiders a day or weekend ticket can work out surprisingly expensive (£2-5). But there's quite often one place which has thrown its doors open for free in an attempt to boost its cafe business. *Piscine Eden Roc*, the first you come to from the port, is usually among the cheapest, though it's a little dull and away from the centre of things. If you're taking a *petit taxi* ask to be dropped off a kilometre or so beyond at one of the groups of clubs, around *Le Lido* or *Kon Tiki*.

Eating and nightlife

Casa has the reputation of being the best **place to eat** in Morocco – and if you can afford it this is certainly true. There are some excellent seafood restaurants along the corniche road at Ain Diab, and some very stylish old French colonial ones around the central boulevards.

Assuming you're not into blowing very large amounts of money, some of the best possibilities are in the smaller streets off Boulevard Mohammed V. Rue Mohammed el Quori, by the Cafe de France (no.9 on our plan), has a couple of cheap cafe-restaurants including *Brasserie el Sphinx* and, signposted off, *Restaurant Ouazarzate*. The area around the Syndicat, and especially Rue Colbert, is also good territory, and for rock-bottom Moroccan standbys there are the *Medina cafes* around the beginning of Rue Djemaa ech Chleuh and (further in) on Rue Centrale.

Slightly pricier, *Las Delicias* (168 Blvd Mohammed V) is a good Spanish place, with big salads and huge plates of fried fish. Or if you want a real chunk of Casablanca style, dressed up like a Parisian 1920s salon (which is really what it is), there's the *Petit Poucet* at 86 Blvd Mohammed V. The *Poucet*, one of those classic French restaurants of infinite portions and service, also has a (much cheaper) **snack-bar** next door: one of the best places around for straight drinking.

For less straight drinking you're likely to find Casa something of a disappointment. **Nightlife**, in the centre at least, is elusive, and beyond the Mohammed V bars is pretty much limited to a few seedy strip joints out towards the port. *La Fontaine*, on Blvd Mohammed el Hansali, is one of the more conspicuous if you're curious: belly dancing, live music and obligatory drinks for the barwomen. At **Ain Diab** there's usually more happening, though for the most part it's a question of Western-style discos, like *Le Balcon* or *Zoom Zoom*. If you want to stay out and eat at Ain Diab, incidentally, there are some good value places; the best, however, function more at lunchtime.

Casa also has a big reputation for its **icecream** and **patisseries**. For the former, two of the best places are *L'Igloo* and *Glacier Gloria* – each on Boulevard du 11 Janvier off below the Place des Nations Unies.

Listings

AIRLINES   *Royal Air Maroc*, 44 Av. des F.A.R.; *Air France*, 15 Av. des F.A.R.; *British Caledonian*, Hôtel Casablanca, Pl. Mohammed V.

AIRPORT   All international flights and most of the domestic leave from the *Aeroport Mohammed V*, some 30km south of Casa. There are fairly regular buses from the *CTM* terminal on Rue Léon l'Africain.

AMERICAN EXPRESS   *Voyages Schwarz*, 112 Av. Mouley Abdallah (743-33).

BANKS   *SGMB*, 84 Blvd Mohammed V; *Crédit du Maroc*, 48-58 Blvd Mohammed V; others along the same boulevard.

BOOKS & PAPERS   One of the best bookshops is on the corner of Rue de Foucauld, opposite the Air France building on Av. des F.A.R. British newspapers are available from the stands around Place Mohammed V.

CAR HIRE   Cheapest is *Leasing Cars*, 100 Blvd Zerktouni (tel. 265 331; and you'll need to go out by taxi). Others are concentrated along the Av. des F.A.R.

CAR REPAIRS   Garages inclue *Renault-Maroc* on the Place du Bandoeng (just off our plan below Place Paquet). For information and addresses contact the *Touring Club du Maroc* (3 Av. des F.A.R.) or *R.A.C. du Maroc* (3 Rue Lemercier).

CONSULATES   The British Consulate has been closed: you'll need to go to Rabat. US maintain their presence at 8 Blvd Moulay Youssef.

FOOTBALL   Casa's about the best place in Morocco to see some, at the Marcel Cedan stadium. Check local press.

GOING ON FROM CASA   CTM run **buses** to just about everywhere, including El Jadida, Agadir, Tiznit and various European destinations; tickets and times from the terminal on Rue Léon l'Africain (see plan). For Rabat you'll find **grands taxis** the most efficient service – they leave regularly from the block behind the CTM. For Tangier, Meknes, Fes or Marrakesh you'll probably want to go **by train**. Check times in advance at the *Gare du Port*, above Place Mohammed V, and try to find one that's leaving from this station rather than the *Voyageurs*. If you're going **to Marrakesh** this probably means the morning train, currently at 8.00. It's a fast journey across the plains, interesting in the gradual transition to the south but without anywhere to delay you en route. If you're driving or bussing it you might consider the coastal route via **El Jadida** and possibly Safi (see p. 245).

MEDICAL AID   Dial 15 for emergency services. Addresses of doctors from the larger hotels, or the *Croissant Rouge* (Cité Djemaa, 44 Av. E; 370 914). All night *pharmacie* in the Place des Nations Unies.

POLICE Phone 19. Main office is on Blvd Brahim Roudani.

POST OFFICE Central *PTT* (for phones/poste restante) is on the Place des Nations Unies.

TAXIS *Petits taxis* can be tricky to find: try the corner of Place Mohammed V/Av. des F.A.R. Very few are metred and you'll need to establish a price in advance for Ain Diab (15dhs) or the Gare des Voyageurs (10dhs).

TOURIST OFFICES *ONMT*, 55 Rue Omar Slaoui; *Syndicat d'Initiative*, 98 Blvd Mohammed V.

TRAVEL DETAILS

Trains

Rabat-Casablanca 8 trains daily in around 1½hr. Slightly under half run to the *Gare du Port*, the rest terminating at *Voyageurs*.

Casablanca-Tangier (via Rabat) 3 daily in around 7hrs (6hrs from Rabat), via Mohammedia, Salé, Kenitra and Asilah. The morning departure (currently 7.35 from Casa *Port*) is usually direct; on the other two (12.10 & 21.42) you generally have to change at Sidi Kacem.

Casablanca-Fes (via Rabat) 6 daily in around 6hrs (4½-5hrs from Rabat). All of these go via Salé, Kenitra and Meknes (3½-4hrs from Rabat). Occasionally there's a change at Sidi Kacem or Sidi Slimane.

Casablanca-Marrakesh 3 daily (currently 8.00, 17.10 & 1.00) in around 4hrs.

Buses

From Rabat: Tangier (2 daily; 5hrs); Larache (4; 3½hrs); Salé (frequently; 15mins); Casablanca (10; 1hr40); Meknes (3; 4hrs); Fes (6; 5½hrs).

From Casa: Dozens of destinations: including Tangier (2 daily; 6½hrs); Rabat (10; 1hr40); El Jadida (3; 2½hrs); Agadir (1; 10hrs); Marrakesh (3; 4hrs).

Grands Taxis

Rabat-Casablanca: Regular route, 1hr20.

Flights

Rabat/Casa Mohammed V Airport: International flights to London, Paris and most major destinations. Domestic flights to all Moroccan airports. Limited number of **domestic flights** from the local Casa and Salé airports.

Chapter four
FES, MEKNES AND THE MIDDLE ATLAS

Imperial Capital of the Merenids, Wattasids and Alouites, Fes has for ten centuries been at the heart of Moroccan history – and was for five of them one of the major intellectual and cultural centres of the West. It is today unique in the Arab world, preserving the appearance and much of the life of a medieval Islamic city. In terms of monuments, above all the university *medressas*, there is as much here as in the other capitals together; the souks, over a mile in extent, maintain the whole tradition of urban crafts; while you do not easily forget the sounds and smells. In all of this – and equally in the most mundane everyday aspects – there is enormous fascination and, for the outsider, a real feeling of privilege. But inevitably it is at a cost. Declared a historical monument by the French, and deprived of its political and cultural significance, Fes is beautiful but in drastic and evident decline; its university is now over-shadowed by Rabat, its commercial elite have left for Casa, and for survival the city is increasingly dependent on the tourists themselves.

Fes's claims are well known, and after Tangier it is by far the most touristed city of the north. **Meknes**, in contrast, sees comparatively few – despite being an easy and convenient stop en route by train from Tangier or Rabat, or by bus from Chaouen. The megalomaniac creation of Moulay Ismail, most tyrannical of all Moroccan sultans, it is again a city of lost ages – its abiding impression one of endless marches of wall. But Meknes is also a considerable market centre and its *souks*, if smaller and less secretive than those of Fes, are almost as varied and generally more authentic. There are, too, the local attractions of **Volubilis**, best preserved of the country's Roman sites, and the sacred hilltop town of **Moulay Idriss** forbidden to non-Muslims and unseen by Europeans, until 1916.

Beyond the two Imperial Cities stretch the cedar-covered slopes of the **Middle Atlas**, which in turn give way to the High Atlas and eventually the sub-Sahara. Across and around this region, often beautiful and for the most part remote, there are three main routes. The most popular, a day's journey by bus, skirts the range beyond Azrou to emerge via **Beni Mellal** at Marrakesh. A second climbs south-east from Azrou towards **Midelt**, an exceptional carpet centre, before passing through great gorges

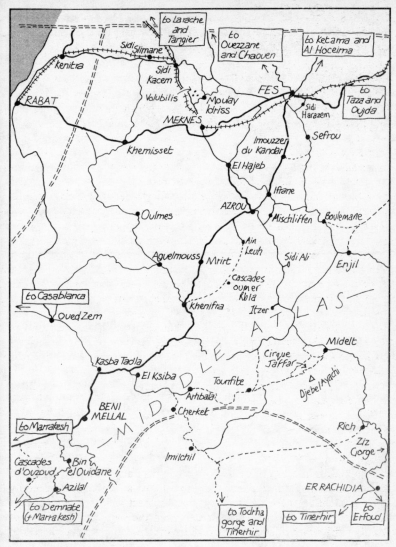

to Er Rachidia and the vast date-palm oasis of Tafilalt – the beginning of a tremendous southern circuit. The last, between these two, is much more adventurous and is detailed in reverse on p. 267; leaving the main Azrou-Marrakesh highway at **El Ksiba**, it follows a series of pistes, best negotiated by local Berber truck, which lead directly across the High Atlas to bring you out at Tinerhir.

If you're going for one or other of the main highways, and you've time, the Middle Atlas has attractions of its own. Close to Fes, **Immouzer** and **Ifrane** have each developed as summer resorts, their air and water a cool escape. Then there is the Berber market town of **Azrou**, and beyond, just off the Marrakesh road, the **Cascades d'Ouzoud** – waterfalls which crash down from the mountains even in midsummer, beside which you can swim, camp, hike and completely rest up.

MEKNES, VOLUBILIS AND MOULAY IDRISS

MEKNES

More than any other Moroccan town, **MEKNES** is associated with a single figure: that of the **Sultan Moulay Ismail**, in whose fifty-five year reign (1672-1727) the city was raised from a provincial centre to an immense and spectacular capital of 20 gates, over 50 palaces and some 25km of exterior wall. 'The Sultan', wrote his chronicler Ezziani, 'loved Mequinez, and he would have liked never to leave it.' But leave it he did, ceaselessly campaigning against the rebel Berber chiefs of the south until the entire country, for the first time in five centuries, lay completely under government control. On his return, with his Black Guard of negro troops gathered from across Morocco, the obsessive building programme would always be redoubled, the Sultan directing as architect and sometimes even working alongside the slaves and labourers.

A tyrant even by the standards of his day – and Europe was at this time actively burning, torturing and putting to the rack its enemies – Ismail was almost unbelievably violent and sadistic. His reign began with the display at Fes of 700 heads, most of them captured chiefs, and over the next three decades, outside of battles, it is estimated that he was responsible for over 30,000 killings. Many were quite arbitrary. Mounting a horse Ismail would generally slash the head off the eunuch who held his stirrup. Inspecting the work on his buildings he would carry a weighted lance, with which he would batter the skulls of men to encourage the others. 'My subjects are like rats in a basket,' he used to state, 'and if I do not keep shaking the basket they will gnaw their way through'.

The Imperial City
Time has not been easy on Moulay Ismail's constructions. Built mainly

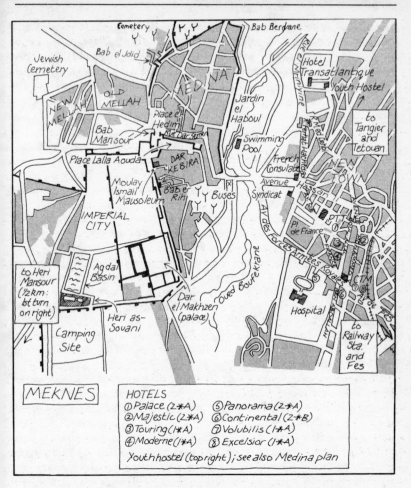

MEKNES

HOTELS
① Palace (2*A)   ⑤ Panorama (2*A)
② Majestic (2*A)   ⑥ Continental (2*B)
③ Touring (1*A)   ⑦ Volubilis (1*A)
④ Moderne (1*A)   ⑧ Excelsior (1*A)

Youth hostel (top right); see also Medina plan

of *tabia*, a mix of earth and lime, they were severely damaged by a hurricane within his lifetime, and since, with subsequent Alaouite sultans shifting their capitals back to Fes and Marrakesh, have been left to crumble and decay. Walter Harris, writing only 150 years after Ismail's death, found Meknes 'a city of the dead ... strewn with marble columns, and surrounded by great masses of ruin'. And even with its new town across the river, built as a military HQ by the French, there is still this feeling of emptiness.

The principal remains of Ismail's creation – the **Imperial City** of palaces and gardens, barracks, granaries and stables – sprawl below the Medina amid a confusingly manic array of walled enclosures. It's a long morning's walk if you intend to take everything in but a fairly straightforward one.

From the New Town (see p. 128 for this, hotels and general orientation) just make your way down to the main street at the edge of the Medina (**Rue Rouamazin/Rue Dar Semen**) and along to the **Place el Hedim** and its immense gateway of **Bab Mansour**. There are usually **guides** hanging around here if you want to use one: you don't need to but if you can find someone entertaining he'll probably flesh the walls out with superbly convoluted local legend.

The **Place el Hedim**, 'square of destruction', immediately recalls Moulay Ismail; originally it formed the western corner of the Medina, but the houses here were demolished to form a grand approach to the palace quarter, or *Dar Kebira*. The centrepiece of this ensemble of walls and gateways is the great **Bab Mansour**, startlingly rich in its ceremonial intent and almost perfectly preserved. Its name is that of the architect – one of a number of Christian renegades who converted to Islam and rose to high position at Ismail's court; there is a tale that when the Sultan inspected the gate he asked el Mansour whether he could do better, a classic Catch 22 whose response – yes – led to immediate and enraged execution. It is probably apocryphal, however, for the gate was actually completed under Ismail's son, the almost equally perverse Moulay Abdallah*. Whatever, the gate is the finest in Meknes and an interesting adaptation of the classic Almohad design – flanked by unusually inset and rather squat bastions, purely decorative with their marble columns brought here from Volubilis. The decorative patterns on both gate and bastions are basically elaborations of the *darj w ktarf* (see p. 00), the space between each motif filled out with a brilliant fricassée of zellij mosaic tiles. The darker, floral pattern between the arch and rectangle is created by a layer of cut-away black tiles, as is the ornamental inscription above which extols the triumph of Ismail and even more that of Abdallah, adding that there is no gate in Damascus or Alexandria which is its equal.

To the left of the Bab Mansour is a smaller gateway in the same style, the **Bab Jama en Nouar**. Through the Bab Mansour, and straight on through a **second gate**, you will find yourself in a large open square, on the right of which is a domed **koubba** – once a reception hall for ambassadors to the Imperial Court. Below it a stairway (small entrance fee to guide) descends to a vast series of subterranean vaults, known to popular tradition as the *prison of Christian slaves*. It was in fact probably a storehouse or granary, although there were certainly several thousand Christian captives at Ismail's court. Most were captured by the Sallee Rovers and brought here as slave labourers on the interminable construc-

---

*Moulay Abdallah was said to have 'a predilection for standing slaves in a row beside a wall he was about to demolish, and letting it fall about them'. He once had a European slave executed for refusing to serve as a footstool for him to fornicate with a mare.

tion programmes; reputedly any of them who died whilst at work were simply built into the walls which they were building.

Ahead of the *koubba*, set within the long wall at right angles to it (see MEDINA plan), are two quite modest **gates**. That on the right is generally closed and is at all times flanked by soldiers from the Royal Guard; within, landscaped across a lake and sunken garden of Ismail's last and finest palace, are the **Royal Golf Gardens** – private and *interdit*. The gate on the left opens onto an apparently endless corridor of walls and, a few metres down, the entrance to the **Mausoleum of Moulay Ismail**. With that of Mohammed V in Rabat, this is the only Moroccan shrine non-Muslims may visit. It is generally open from around 9-12 & 3-6 but even then admission is occasionally refused: women especially must dress with total modesty. That Ismail's mausoleum, completed within his lifetime, remained a shrine is itself perhaps puzzling. Yet, as Walter Harris wrote a century ago, this 'deceased Sultan who, having killed more men, Christians and Moors, than any of his predecessors, having wasted more money on impossible palaces and such-like than could ever be counted, and, when tiring of a wife, having her for amusement tortured and killed before his very eyes, is reverenced as one of the greatest saints of the Moorish religious calendar.' So it was, too, in Ismail's lifetime. His absolute tyranny of control, his success in driving out the Spanish from Larache and the British from Tangier, and his extreme observance of Islamic form and ritual all conferred a kind of magic.

Entering the mausoleum you are allowed to approach the sanctuary in which the Sultan is buried – though you cannot go beyond the annexe. Decorated in bright zellij and spiralling stuccowork, it is a fine if unspectacular series of courts and chambers. But what is most interesting, perhaps, is that the shrine was thoroughly renovated in the 1950s at the expense of Mohammed V, and that the sarcophagus is still the object of prayer. You will almost invariably see country people here, women particularly, seeking *baraka* and intercession.

Past the mausoleum, a gate to your left gives access to the ruinous quarter of the **Dar el Kebira**, Ismail's great palace complex. The Imperial structures, the legendary fifty palaces, can still be made out between and above the houses here – ogre-like creations whose scale is hard to believe. They were completed in 1677 and dedicated amid a tremendous celebration at midnight, the Sultan personally slaughtering a wolf so that its head might be displayed at the centre of the gateway. In the grandeur of the plan there is sometimes claimed a conscious echo of Versailles – its contemporary rival – though in fact it was another decade until the first reports of the French building reached the Imperial Court. When they did, Ismail was certainly interested, and in 1699 he even sent an embassy to Paris with the task of negotiating Louis XIV's daughter, Princess Conti, for his harem.

On the opposite side of the long-walled corridor, beyond the Royal Golf, sprawl more immense buildings – Ismail's last great palace, the **Dar el Makhzen**. Unlike the Kebira, which was broken up by Abdallah in 1733, this has remained in use as a minor royal residence. The most you can gain are a few brief glimpses over the heads of the bored guards posted by sporadic gates in the crumbling 20ft high wall. The corridor itself, which eventually turns a corner to bring you out by the *campsite* and *Heri as-Souani*, may perhaps be the 'strangee' which all the C18 travellers recorded. A mile-long terrace wall, shaded with vines, it was a favourite drive of the Emperor, taken, several sources relate, in a bizarre kind of chariot drawn by his women or eunuchs.

At its end, and the principal 'sight' of the Imperial City, is the **Heri as-Souani** – often introduced by local guides as Ismail's stables. These in fact are further afield (see below), and the startling series of high vaulted chambers here were again a series of storerooms and granaries, fulsome provision for siege or drought. 20mins walk from the Bab Mansour, they are certainly worth seeing, and give a powerful impression of the complexity of C17 Moroccan engineering. Ismail's palaces had underground plumbing (well in advance of Europe), and here you find a remarkable system with chain-bucket wells built between each of the storerooms. One on the left, near the back, has been restored: there are lights to switch on for a closer look. Equally worthwhile is the view from the roof of the as-Souani, approached by the second entrance, to the right. From the roof garden here, beautifully maintained with a good cafe, you can look out across much of the *Dar el Makhzen* and onto the wonderfully still Agdal Basin – built both as an irrigation reservoir and pleasure lake for boating parties. Behind you, in the distance, you can make out another C17 Royal Palace, the *Dar al-Baida* ('White House', now a military academy), and beyond it (to the right) the *Rouah*, or stables.

Known locally as the *Heri Mansour* ('Mansour's granary'), **the Rouah** are a further 20-30 mins walk. They are officially closed to visits, though if you hang around for a while you will probably find the local guide turns up to show you round. To get out here follow the road which runs diagonally behind the campsite and Heri as-Souani for about half a kilometre; when you reach a junction turn right and you should come out at the *Djemaa Rouah* (stable mosque), a large and heavily restored building preceded by a neat gravel courtyard. Walk round behind the mosque and you will see the stables off to your right – a massive complex perhaps twice as large as the as-Souani. In contemporary accounts it was often singled out as the greatest feature of all Ismail's building: some three miles in length, with a long canal running through, flooring built on vaults for grain, and space for over twelve thousand horses. Today, the province of a few scrambling goats, it's a more or less complete ruin – piles of rubble and zellij tiles lining the walls and high arched aisles of crumbling pise loping out in each direction. As such it perhaps recalls more than anything else in Meknes the scale and madness of Moulay Ismail's vision. From here, the Emperor once decreed, a wall should be built stretching right to Marrakesh – a convenient access for his carriage and a useful guide for the blind beggars to find their way.

Around the Medina

Meknes **MEDINA**, although taking much of its present form and extent under Moulay Ismail, bears less of his stamp. Its main sights are a Merenid medressa, the Boulnania, and a C19 palace-museum, the **Dar Jamai**. This latter stands directly on the Place el Hedim and is open daily from 9-12 & 4-7. Built by the same family of viziers as the Palais Jamai in Fes (see p. 161), it is in itself an interesting example of domestic architecture and craftsmanship – the best the late C19 could offer. The exhibits, some of which have been incorporated to recreate reception rooms of the period, are predominantly of the same age, though there are pieces of *Fes and Meknes pottery* which date back more or less to Ismail's reign. These ceramics, elaborate polychrome designs from Meknes, strong blue and white patterns from Fes, make interesting comparision, and the superiority of Fes's artesan tradition throughout the last two centuries is immediately apparent. The best display here, however, is of *Middle Atlas carpets*, particularly those of the Beni Mguild tribe. If at any time you're planning to buy a rug – and Meknes itself can be good – take a long and careful look at each of these: you won't find anything approaching their quality but you'll have a sound idea of what you're looking for.

To reach **the souks** from the Place el Hedim just follow the lane immediately behind Dar Jamai. You will come out in the middle of the Medina's major market street: to your right, leading to the Grand Mosque and medressa, is the *Souk es Sebbat* (b), to your left (a) the **Souk en Nejjarin**. Turning first to the left, you're in an area mainly of textile stalls, though they later give way to the carpenters' (*nejjarin*) workshops from which the souk takes its name. Shortly after you pass on your left a mosque, immediately beyond which is an entrance to a parallel arcade. The **carpet market**, or *Souk Joutiya as-Zerabi*, is just off here to the left. Quality can be very high (and prices too), though without the constant stream of tourists of Fes or Marrakesh dealers are much more willing to bargain. Don't be afraid to start too low.

Out at the end of Souk en Nejjarin you come out on a futher souk, the **Bezzarin**, which runs up at right angles to it, on either side of the city wall. This looks a rather shambling, run-down quarter but if you follow the outside of the wall you'll come upon an interesting variety of crafts, each grouped together in their trading guilds and often fronted by an old fondouk or warehouse. As you go on up there are *basket-makers*, *ironsmiths* and *saddlers*, whilst near the **Bab el Jdid**, at the top, you find *tent-makers* and a couple of *musical instrument* workshops.

Had you turned right beyond the Dar Jamai, onto the **Souk es Sebbat**, you would have been in a wealthier section of the market: starting off with the *babouches* sellers, moving into rather ritzier (and tourist-geared) goods around the medressa, and finally coming out into the covered **kissaria**, here much dominated by kaftans. The place to make for is inevitably the Bou Inania, whose imposing portal is quite easy to spot on the left-hand side of the street. If you want a break before this, there's a C19 **fondouk** a short way back which now doubles as a cafe and carpet/crafts emporium – look out for its open courtyard. Meknes mint, incidentally, is reputed the best in Morocco and exported all around the north for quality tea.

The **Bou Inania Medressa** was built around 1340-50, and is therefore more or less contemporary with the great medressas of Fes; it takes its name from the somewhat notorious Abou Inan (see p. 148) though was in fact founded by his predecessor, Abou el Hassan, the great Merenid builder of Chellah in Rabat. A modest and functional building, it follows the plan of Hassan's other principal works – the Chellah zaouia and Salé medressa – in a single *courtyard* giving onto a shallow *prayer hall;* these are enclosed on each storey by the *cells* for the students, with their beautifully worked cedarwood screens. It is all much lighter in feel than the medressa at Salé, and in the balance of wood, stucco and zellij achieves a remarkable combination of intricacy (no area is uncovered) and restraint. Architecturally, the most unusual feature is a ribbed dome over the *entrance hall*, an impressive piece of craftsmanship which extends right out into the souk. From *the roof*, to which there's generally access, you can look out and almost climb across to the tiled pyramids of the Grand Mosque. The souk is mainly obscured from view, but there is a good general sense of the town and the individual mosques of each quarter; inlaid with bands of green tiles, their minarets are distinctive of Meknes, those of Fes or Marrakesh tending to be more elaborate and multicoloured.

Beyond the Medressa and Grand Mosque, the Medina is for the most part residential, dotted with the occasional fruit and vegetable market, or, up past the mosque of Ben Khadra, a carpenters' souk for the supply of woods. If you carry on this way you'll eventually come out in a long open *place* which culminates in the monumental **Bab el Berdain**. The 'gate of the saddlers', this was another of Ismail's creations and echoes, in a much more rugged and genuinely defensive structure, the central section of the Bab Mansour. Outside, the city walls continue to march, up along the main road to Rabat and past (1500m out) the **Bab el Khemis** (or Bab Lakhmis) another very fine gate with a frieze of monumental inscription etched in black tiles on the brickwork. Between the two gates, within the wall to your left, you will catch occasional glimpses of an enormous **cemetery** – almost half the size of the Medina in its extent. Non-Muslims are not permitted to enter this enclosure, near the centre of which lies the shrine of one of the country's most famous and curious saints, **Sidi Ben Aissa**. Reputedly a contemporary of Moulay Ismail, Ben

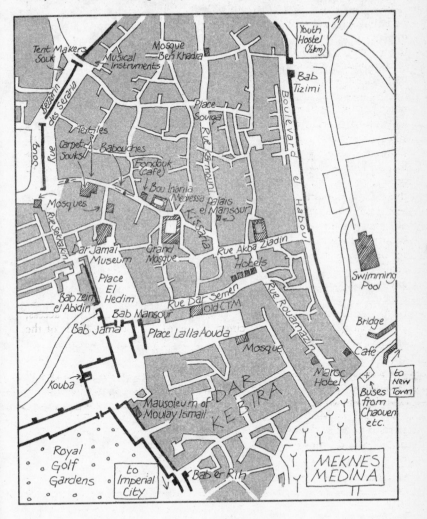

Aissa conferred on his followers the power to eat anything, even poison or broken glass, without ill effect. His cult, the *Aissaoua*, became one of the most important in Morocco – and certainly the most violent and fanatical. Until prohibited by the French, some fifty thousand devotees regularly attended the saint's annual moussem on the eve of Mouloud; attaining trance, they might pierce their tongues and cheeks with daggers, eat serpents and scorpions, and devour live sheep and goats. The only other confraternity to approach such frenzy were the *Hamacha* of Moulay Idriss, whose favoured rites used to include cutting their heads with hatchets and throwing up heavy stones or cannon-balls which they allowed to fall on their skulls. Both cults continue to hold moussems, though Moroccan governments have effectively outlawed their more extreme activities.

The New Town: orientation and details

Cut neatly in two by the wide river valley of the Oued Boufekrane, Meknes is simpler than it looks on the map. Its **New Town** stretches along a slope above the east bank of the river, the **Medina**, flanked by its former Mellahs. Focal point of the Medina is the **Place el Hedim**, and you'll do well to adopt this for all bearings: from here there are *petits taxis* and a regular shuttle of buses (nos 5/7/9) up towards the main New Town avenues.

Unless you arrive by **bus from Chaouen** (which will probably stop by the Medina side of the bridge) or by **grand taxi from Fes** (to the Place el Hedim), you should find yourself getting out at the New Town. The **CTM bus station**, marked on our general plan, is at the intersection of virtually all its main avenues; the **railway station** is a kilometre or so further out – along the Avenue de Gare which comes in to join with the Avenue de Fes/Avenue des Forces Armées Royales. Buses 5/7/9 all run to the Place el Hedim from close by the *CTM*.

Hotels, including a very reasonable youth hostel, are mainly in the New Town. But, comforts aside, this is a dull place to stay and if you're happy with a fairly basic room best make for the *Maroc Hôtel*, opposite the Apollo Cinema on Rue Rouamazin. Much the cleanest and quietest of the **Medina** places, and more often than not the cheapest, this is marked on our Medina plan – a short walk up from the bridge. The other Medina hotels, at the corner of Rue Rouamazin/Rue Dar Semen, are drab and airless.

In the **New Town** you'll find the *Youth Hostel* (Av. Okba Ibn Nafi) by following the signs to the luxury Hotel Transatlantique, a block further on. Other cheapish possibilities, all keyed on our general plan, are grouped in an area around the bus station and main avenues; best of the one star's is *Hôtel Moderne* (54 Blvd Allal Ben Abdallah), of the two's *Hôtel Panorama* (9 Av. des Forces Armées Royales). Other addresses are:

Hôtel Volubilis, Hôtel Excelsior, 45 & 57 Av. des Forces Armées Royales
Both 1*A.
Hôtel Continental (2*B), 92 Av. des Forces Armées Royales.
Hôtel Majestic (2*A), 19 Av. Mohammed V.
Hôtel Palace (2*A), 11 Rue du Ghana.
Alternatively there's an attractive if rather pricey and 'international' **campsite**, with a swimming pool which was due to open in 1986. It's well out from the centre of town (20mins walk from Place el Hedim, or an 8-10dh taxi ride) but imaginatively positioned (see general plan) opposite the Heri as-Souani. There are *chalet rooms* to let here, too, at around 2*B prices.

Eating in Meknes tends to be a functional affair: there's nothing very exciting, and, Ramadan aside, the town is pretty much closed by around ten at night. For straight Moroccan food pick from any of the grill-cafes along the Rue Dar Semen, towards the Place el Hedim, or try the slightly more expensive *Rotisserie Oumnia* behind the Maroc Hotel. In the New Town there are a handful of fair French-style restaurants on and around the Place de France. Rue du Ghana, which leads off from here past the PTT, has a couple of cheap places (*La Coupole*, towards the junction with Av. Hassan II is a good bet); so too does Av. Hassan II itself – the unnamed restaurant at no.12 in particular. **Bars** are few. You might try the *Roi de la Bière* near the beginning of Av. Mohammed V, but it's often closed in summer; otherwise there are the hotels *Rif* and *Nice* (both below the PTT on Rue d'Accra: the Rif has a nightly cabaret and disco) and the *Novelty bar-restaurant* at Rue de Marseilles 12.

Banks are concentrated on Av. Mohammed V (the *Crédit du Maroc* is at no. 33) and Av. des Forces Armées Royales; the **PTT**, just off the Place de France, is open Monday-Saturday 8am-2pm – its phone section until 9pm. There are two public **swimming pools** down by the river, reached along a lane from the Boulevard el Haboul or from the intersection of Av. Hassan II and Av. Moulay Ismail. The first you come to is very cheap; a little further on there's another – more elite, less crowded and three or four times the price. If you're staying in the Medina, the Maroc Hotel should be able to steer you towards a **hammam**; in the New Town you'll find a good one off Av. Hassan II at 4 Rue Patrice Lumumba, with separate sections for women and men (both 7am-9pm). Lastly, the **Syndicat** is just off to the left at the beginning of Avenue Hassan II (see the general plan).

Leaving Meknes for FES you've a choice of bus (8 *CTM* departures a day), train or quickest of all *grand taxi;* the latter depart more or less continuously from Place el Hedim and arrive in Fes el Jdid at the Place des Alaouites. *CTM* have at least daily departures, too, for AZROU, MIDELT, RABAT and MARRAKESH. Private line buses use a teminal just outside the Bab Zein el Abidin on Place el Hedim and another by the bridge below the Maroc Hotel. If you're making for CHAOUEN check out times with the *Syndicat* and try to buy a ticket in advance, preferably the night before.

VOLUBILIS AND MOULAY IDRISS

The classic excursion from Meknes, **Volubilis** and **Moulay Idriss** embody much of Morocco's early history: Volubilis as its provincial Roman capital, Moulay Idriss in the creation of the country's first Arab dynasty. They stand 4km apart, at either side of a deep and very fertile valley.

Unless you're driving – when you may want to go on to Fes or Ouezzane – Volubilis and Moulay Idriss are easiest visited by setting out from and returning to Meknes. You can take in both on a leisurely day's circuit, and at the **Bab Mansour** you've a choice of **grand taxi** (6dhs a *place* to Idriss: very frequent) or **private bus** (1dh less, but leaving only when full). Whichever way you go, ask to be dropped at the signposted turning to Volubilis, left of the road a couple of kilometres before you reach Moulay Idriss (or negotiate with the driver to drop you right at the ruins). 1½km from the main road turning you'll come to a fork signposted AIN EL JEMAA/COL DU ZEGOTTA: either road will bring you to the ruins in very similar distance by cutting (respectively) right/left about 2km on. From Volubilis you'll probably be able to get a lift into Moulay Idriss, where you can later pick up one of the taxis or buses back to Meknes. Moulay Idriss taxis do not as a rule run to Fes, unless you're willing to pay for a *course* (a white taxi).

Non-Muslims are still not permitted to stay overnight in Moulay Idriss but there is a good shaded **campsite** (with a bar and snacks) midway on the 'outer road' to Volubilis. Roads here are slightly confusing and you'd do well to ask directions: to *le refuge Zerhoun*.

Volubilis

A striking site, visible for some miles at turns in the approach, **VOLUBILIS** occupies the ledge of a long, high plateau. Below its walls, towards Moulay Idriss, stretches a rich river valley; beyond are the dark outlying spurs of the Zerhoun mountains. Except for a small trading post on the island off Essaouira, this was the Roman Empire's most remote and far-flung base. The roads stopped here, having reached across France and Spain and then down from Tangier, and despite successive emperors' dreams of 'penetrating the Atlas' the southern Berber tribes were never effectively subdued.

Direct Roman rule here in fact lasted little over two centuries – the garrison withdrawing early, in 285, to ease pressure elsewhere. But the town must have taken much of its present form well before the official annexation of North African *Mauretania* by the Emperor Claudius in AD45. Tablets found on the site, inscribed in Punic, show a significant Carthaginian trading presence in the C3BC, and prior to colonisation it was the western capital of a heavily Romanised but semi-autonomous Berber kingdom which reached into northern Algeria and Tunisia. After the Romans left, too, Volubilis saw very gradual change. Latin was still spoken in the C7 by its population of Berbers, Greeks, Syrians and Jews; Christian churches survived until the coming of Islam; and the city itself remained alive and active into the C18, when its marbles were carried away by slaves for the building of Moulay Ismail's Meknes.

What you see today, well excavated and maintained, are largely the ruins of C2-C3AD buildings – impressive and affluent creations from its period as a colonised provincial capital. The land hereabout is some of the most prosperous in North Africa, and the city exported wheat and olives in considerable bulk to Rome. So too, wild animals from the surrounding hills. Roman games, memorable in the sheer scale of their slaughter (9000 beasts were killed for the dedication of the Colosseum), could not have happened without the African provinces, and Volubilis was a chief source of their lions. Within just two hundred years, along with Barbary bears and elephants, they were virtually extinct.

You enter THE SITE through a minor gate in the city wall, built with a number of outer camps in AD168 after a prolonged series of Berber insurrections. Just inside are the *ticket office* (the ruins are open daily, sunrise-sunset), a shaded *cafe-bar*, and a small open-air **museum** of sculpture and other fragments. The best of the finds made here – which include a superb collection of bronzes – have all been taken to the Rabat museum. Volubilis, however, has retained in situ the great majority of its **mosaics**, some thirty or so in a good state of preservation. You leave with a real sense of Roman city life and its provincial prosperity, whilst in the layout of the site it is not hard to recognise the essentials of a medieval Arab town.

Following the path up from the museum and across a bridge over the Fertassa stream, you come out on a mixed area of housing and industry – each of its buildings with the clear remains of at least one **olive press**. Their extent and number, built into even the grandest mansions, reflect the olive's absolute importance to the city and indicate perhaps why it remained unchanged for so long after the Roman departure. A significant proportion of its 20,000 population must have been involved in some capacity in the oil's production and export.

Somewhat isolated in this suburban quarter is the **House of Orpheus**, an enormous complex of rooms which begin just beside the start of a paved way. Although substantially in ruins, this maintains a strong impression of luxury – a bourgeois mansion perhaps for one of the richer merchants. It divides into two main sections – public and private – each

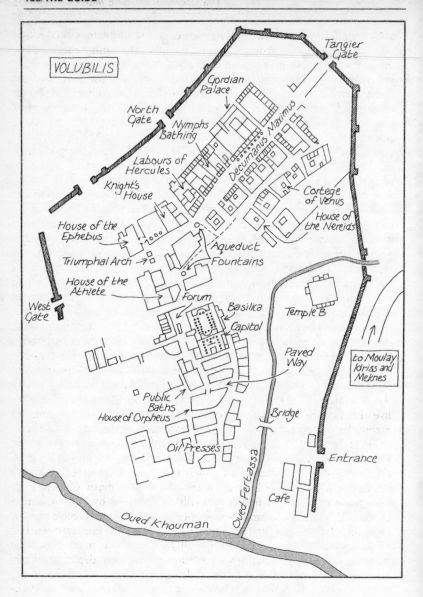

VOLUBILIS

Tangier Gate

Gordian Palace

North Gate

Nymphs Bathing

Decumanus Maximus

Labours of Hercules

Knight's House

Cortege of Venus

House of the Ephebus

House of the Nereids

Triumphal Arch

Aqueduct Fountains

House of the Athlete

Forum

Basilica

Capitol

West Gate

Temple B

Paved Way

to Moulay Idriss and Meknes

Public Baths

House of Orpheus

Bridge

Oil Presses

Entrance

Oued Fertassa

Cafe

Oued Khouman

with their separate entrance and interior court. The private rooms, which you come to first, are grouped around a small patio with a more or less intact *dolphin mosaic*. You can make out too the furnace and heating system (just by the entrance), the kitchen with its niche for the household gods, and the *baths* – a considerable system of hot, cold and steaming rooms. The public apartments, further round, are dominated by a great *atrium*, halfway a reception hall, halfway a central court, and again preserving a very fine mosaic (*the chariot of Amphitrite drawn by a seahorse*). The best example here, however, and the mosaic from which the house takes its name, is that of the *Orpheus myth*, off to the south in a room which was probably the *tablinium*, or archives.

Above the Orpheus house a broad paved street leads up towards the main group of public buildings – the *Capitol* and *Basilica* whose stork-topped, sand-coloured ruins dominate the site. Taking the approach to the left, though, you will pass first through remains of the city's principal **public baths**. Restored by the Emperor Gallienus in the C2, these are clearly monumental in their intent, though sadly the mosaics are only fragmentary. The arrangement of the **Forum** is typical of a major Roman town: built on the highest rise of the city and flanked by a triumphal arch, market, capitol and basilica. The **Capitol**, smaller and lower of the two main buildings, is dated from inscriptions to 217 – a time at which this whole public nucleus seems to have been rebuilt by the African-born Severian emperors. Adjoined by small *forum baths*, it is an essentially simple building, a porticoed court giving access to a small temple and altar. Its dedication – standard throughout the Roman world – was to the official state cult of Capitoline Jove, Juno and Minerva. The large five-aisled **Basilica** to its side served as a Hall of Justice, while immediately across the forum were the small court and stalls of the central **market**.

The **Triumphal Arch**, right in the midst of the town, held no particular purpose beyond creating a ceremonial function for the principal street, the Decumanus Maximus – on which side it is the more substantially ornamented. Erected in honour of the Severian Emperor Caracalla, its inscription records that it was orginally surmounted by a great bronze chariot. This and the nymphs which once shot water into its basins below are gone, though with its tall Corinthian columns (of imported marble) and unashamed pointlessness it is still an impressive monument. The medallions on either side, heavily eroded, presumably depict Caracalla and his mother Julia Donna, who is also named in the inscription.

The finest of Volubilis's mansions – and its mosaics – line the **Decumanus Maximus**, fronted in traditional Roman and Italian fashion by the tiny cubicles of shops. Before you reach this point, however, take a look at the remains of an **aquaduct** and **fountains** across from the triumphal arch: these once supplied yet another complex of public baths. Opposite are a small group of **houses**, predominantly ruined but retaining an impressive *mosaic of an athlete* or chariot-jumper; he is depicted receiving the winner's cup for a *desultor* race, a display of great skill involving leaping from and remounting a horse in full gallop.

First of the Decumanus Maximus mansions, the **House of the Ephebus** takes name from the bronze of a youth found in its ruins (and today displayed in Rabat). In general plan it is very similar to the House of Orpheus, once again housing an olive press in its rear section, though it is far grander – almost twice the size, with pictorial mosaics in most of its public rooms and an ornamental pool in its central court. Finest of the mosaics is a representation of *Bacchus being drawn in a chariot of panthers* – a suitable scene for the *cenacula* or banqueting hall in which it is placed. Separated from the Ephebus house by a narrow lane is a mosaic-less mansion, known after its façade as the **House of Columns**, and, adjoining this, the **Knight's House** with an incomplete mosaic of *Dionysos discovering Ariadne* asleep on the beach at Naxos; both houses are themselves largely ruined. More illuminating is the large mansion which begins the next block, similar again in its plan but featuring a very complete mosaic of the **Labours of Hercules**. Almost comic caricatures, these give a good idea of ordinary provincial Roman mosaics – immediate contrasts to the stylish Orpheus and Bacchus, and to the excellent **Nymphs Bathing** of the next but one house down.

Beyond, approaching the partially reconstructed *Tangier Gate*, is the **Palace of the Gordians**, former residence of the Procurators who administered the city and the province. Despite its size, however, with a huge *bath-house* and pooled courtyards, it is an unmemorable ruin. Stripped of most of its columns, and without mosaics, its grandeur and scale may have made all too obvious a target for Ismail's building mania. Indeed, how much of Volubilis remained standing before his reign is an open question; Walter Harris, writing at the turn of this century, found the road between here and Meknes littered with ancient marbles, left as they fell after the announcement of the Sultan's death.

Back on the Decumanus, cross to the other side of the road and walk down a block to a smaller lane below the street. Here, in the third house along, is the most exceptional ensemble of mosaics of the entire site – the **Cortege of Venus**. Zealously guarded by the custodians, not all of these are easily seen from the officially designated vantage points. But you can walk into the main section of the house, a central court preceded by a paved vestibule and giving way to another smaller patio, about which the main reception halls (and mosaics) are grouped. As you enter, the *baths* are off to your left, flanked by the private quarters, whilst immediately around the central court are a small group of mosaics, including a curious, very worn representation of a *chariot race* with birds in place of horses. But the outstanding examples are beyond, in the 'public' sections of the villa. To the left, in the corner, is a geometrical design with medallions of *Bacchus surrounded by the Four Seasons*; off to the right are *Diana bathing* (and surprised by the woodland god, Actaeon) and the *abduction of Hylas by nymphs*. Each of these scenes – the last two above all – are superbly handled in their stylised but very fluid animation. They date, like that of the **Nereids** (two houses along), from either the late C2 or early C3 and were obviously a very serious commission. It is not known for whom this house was built but its owner must have been among the city's most succesful patrons; here were found the bronze busts of Cato and Juba II which are now the centrepiece of Rabat's museum.

Leaving the site by a track below the forum you pass close by the ruins of a **Temple** on the opposite side of the stream. This was dedicated by the Romans to Saturn, but probably predated by worship of a Carthaginian god; in its excavation several hundred votive offerings were discovered.

Moulay Idriss

MOULAY IDRISS takes name from its founder, Morocco's most venerated saint and the creator of its first Arab dynasty. His tomb and zaouia lie right at the heart of the town, the reason for its sacred status and the object of constant pilgrimage and a great September *moussem*. Even today, open to non-Muslims for almost seventy years, it is a place which feels closed and introspective, continuing with some dignity the business of religion; for the infidel, barred from the shrines, there is little specific that can be seen, and nothing that may be visited. But coming here from Volubilis, the site alone is enough – a girdle of hills with no European building of any kind.

Moulay Idriss el Akhbar ('the elder') was a great-grandson of the Prophet Muhammad through the marriage of his daughter Fatima with his cousin and first follower Ali. Heir to the Caliphate at Damascus, he fled to Morocco around the year 787 after Ommayad victory in the great civil war which split the Muslim world into Shia and Sunni sects. At Volubilis, then still the main centre of the north, he seems to have been welcomed as an *Imam* – a spiritual and political leader – and within five years had succeeded in carving out a considerable kingdom. This town, easier defended than Volubilis, he created as a capital, and he also begun the building of Fes – continued and much extended by his son Idriss II, that city's patron saint. News of his growing power however filtered back to the East and in 792 the Ommayads had Idriss poisoned, doubtless assuming that his kingdom would likewise disappear. In this they were mistaken. Idriss had instilled with the faith of Islam the region's previously pagan – sometimes Christian or Jewish – Berber tribes and had been joined in this prototype Moroccan state by increasing numbers of Arab Shiites* loyal to the succession of his *Alid* line. After the assassin-ation, Rashid, the servant who had travelled with Idriss to Morocco, took over as regent, until in 807 Idriss II was old enough to assume the throne.

Arriving at Moulay Idriss you find yourself just below an elongated *place* near the base of the town: above, almost directly ahead, are the green-tiled pyramids of the shrine and zaouia, on either side of which rise the two conical quarters of *Khiber* and *Tasga*. The **souks**, such as they are, line the streets of the Khiber (the taller hill) above the zaouia but apart from the excellent local nougat, made and sold in great quanti-ties, they're not of great interest. The **shrine and zaouia**, rebuilt by Moulay Ismail, stands blocked from the street by a low wooden bar placed to keep out Christians and beasts of burden. To get any real idea of it you'll have to climb up towards one or other of the vantage points near the top of each quarter – ideally the *Terrasse Sidi Abdallah el Hajjam* right above the Khiber. It's not easy to find your way up through the streets, most end in abrupt blind alleys – and unless you're into the challenge of it all, you'll do well to enlist a young guide down in the *place*.

FES AND AROUND

FES

> *The history of Fes is composed of wars and murders, triumphs of arts and sciences, and a good deal of imagination.*
> – Walter Harris: *Land of an African Sultan*

The most ancient of the Imperial Capitals, and the most complete medi-eval city of the Arab world, **FES** is for the moment at least unique. It is a place of infinite senses – of haunting and beautiful sound, immense detail and uncovered smells – and it seems to exist in a time somewhere between the Middle Ages and the modern world. As ever there is a French-built New Town, but some 200,000 of the city's half-million or so inhabitants continue to live in an extraordinary Medina-city – *Fes el Bali* – which owes absolutely nothing to the West beyond its electricity and tourists.

---

*Although these are Shiite origins, the Moroccan tribes soon adopted the Sunni (or Malekite) system in line with the powerful Andalusian Caliphate of Cordoba. Present-day Morocco remains orthodox Sunni.

As a spectacle this is entirely satisfying, and it's difficult to imagine a city whose external forms (which are all that you can really hope to penetrate) could be so constant and enduring a source of interest. But stay in Fes a few days and it's equally hard to avoid the paradox of the place. Like much of 'traditional' Morocco, Fes was 'saved' and then re-created by the French – mostly under the auspices of General Lyautey, the Protectorate's first Resident-General. Lyautey took the philanthropic and startling move of declaring the city a historical monument: philan-thropic because he was certainly saving Fes el Bali from destruction (albeit from less benevolent Frenchmen), and startling because until then many Moroccans were under the impression that Fes was still a living city – the Imperial Capital of the Moroccan Empire rather than a preservable part of the nation's heritage. In fact this paternalistic protection conveniently helped to disguise the dismantlement of the old culture. By building a new European town nearby (the Ville Nouvelle) and then transferring Fes's economic and political functions to Rabat and the west coast, Lyautey successfully ensured the city's eclipse along with its preservation.

To appreciate the significance of this demise you have only to look at the Arab chronicles or old histories of Morocco, every one of which takes Fes as its central focus. The city had dominated Moroccan trade, culture and religious life – and usually its politics, too – since the end of the tenth century. It was closely and symbolically linked with the birth of an 'Arabic' Moroccan state through a mutual foundation by Moulay Idriss I, and was regarded, after Mecca and Medina, as one of the holiest cities of the Islamic world. Early European travellers wrote of it with a mixture of awe and respect – as a 'citadel of fanaticism' and yet the most advanced seat of learning in mathematics, philosophy and medicine.

At the death of Moulay Idriss I in 792, Fes seems to have been little more than a village on the east bank of the river. It was his son, **Idriss II**, who set the city's development underway at the beginning of the C9, making it his capital and allowing in refugees from Andalusian Cordoba and from Kairouan in Tunisia – at the time the two most important cities of Western Islam. The impact on Fes of these refugees was immediate and lasting: they established separate walled towns (still distinct quarters today) on either riverbank, and provided the superior craftsmanship and mercantile experience for Fes's industrial and commercial growth. It was at this time, too, that the city forged its intellectual reputation. The C10 Pope Silvester II studied here at the Kairouine University, and from this source he is said to have introduced Arabic mathematics to Europe.

The seat of government – and impetus of patronage – shifted south to Marrakesh under the Berber dynasties of the **Almoravides** (1068-1145) and **Almohads** (1145-1250). But with the conquest of Fes by the **Merenids** in 1248, and their subsequent consolidation of power across Morocco, the city regained its pre-eminence and moved into something of a 'golden age'. Alongside the old Medina the Merenids began the construction of a massive royal city – Fes el Jdid, literally 'Fes the New' – which reflected both the wealth and confidence of their rule. They enlarged and decorated the great Kairaouine Mosque, added a network of fondouks for the burgeoning commerical activity, and, above all, were responsible for the meteoric rise of the university – building the series of magnificent *medressas*, or colleges, to accommodate its students. Once again this was an expansion based upon an influx of refugees, this time from the Spanish reconquest of Andalusia, and it helped to establish the city's reputation as a haven of Islamic Moorish culture – 'the Baghdad of the West'.

It is essentially Merenid Fes which you witness today in the form of the city and in its monuments. From the fall of the dynasty in the mid C16 there was decline as both Fes, and Morocco itself, became isolated from the main currents of western culture. The new rulers – the **Saadians** – in any case preferred Marrakesh, and although Fes re-emerged as a capital again under the **Alaouites** it had lost its international stature. Moulay Ismail, whose hatred of the Fassis (the people of Fes) was legendary, almost managed to tax the city out of existence, and the principal building concerns of his successors were in restoring and enlarging the vast domains of the Royal Palace. Under French **colonial rule** there was preservation and relative prosperity in the Ville Nouvelle, but little progress: as a thoroughly conservative and bourgeois city, Fes became merely provincial. Since **Independence**, the city's position has been even less happy. The first Sultan, Mohammed V, retained the French capital of Rabat, and with it signalled the final removal of the Fassi political and financial elites. In 1956, too, the city lost most of its Jewish community to France and Israel. In their place the Medina population now has a predominance of first-generation rural migrants, poorly housed in mansions designed for single families but now occupied by four or five, and increasingly dependent on the craft and tourist trade. If UNESCO had not moved in over the last decades with their Cultural Heritage plan for the city's preservation, it seems likely that its physical collapse would have become endemic and much more obvious than it appears today.

Orientation

Even if you feel you're getting used to Moroccan cities, Fes is still bewildering. The basic lay-out is simple enough, with a Moroccan **Medina** and French-built **New Town**, but here the Medina is actually two physically separate cities – **Fes el Bali**, the oldest part in the main stretch of the Sebou valley, and **Fes el Jdid**, the 'new Fes' established on the lip of the valley in the C13. The latter, dominated by a vast enclosure of royal palaces and gardens, is quite easy to negotiate; Fes el Bali, however, where you'll want to spend most of your time, is an incredibly intricate net of lanes, blind alleys and souks, and it takes two or three days before you even start to feel confident in where you're going.

For this reason – and because there is such a concentration of interest – you may find it worthwhile to have a **guide** for your first encounter with Fes el Bali. A half-day tour from an *official guide* (who can identify himself with a round gold medallion) is probably the best option, and you'll be charged only 30dhs (50dhs for a full day) no matter how many people in your group. Official guides can be engaged at the *Syndicat d'Initiative* in the New Town, or outside the main hotels (such as the *Palais Jamai* or *Merenides* above the Medina). Anywhere else, guides who tout their services are likely to be *unofficial* and technically illegal.- This doesn't mean that they're any worse – and some who may genuinely be students (as they all claim to be) can be excellent. You'll need to pick carefully though, ideally by drinking a tea together before settling a rate (or even declaring real interest). And whether you get an official or unofficial guide it's essential to work out the main points you want to see in advance, making it absolutely clear that you're not interested in shopping – even 'just to look', this you can do quite happily, and much more effectively, on your own, later on.

The most straightforward way **to arrive** in Fes is by train. The **railway station** is in the New Town and only 10mins walk from the main concentration of cheap hotels around the Place Mohammed V. If you prefer to stay in the Boujeloud hotels (see the following section) walk down to the Avenue Hassan II where you can pick up the no.9 bus to the Dar Batha/Place de l'Istiqlal.

Coming in **by coach** can be more confusing as there are several different terminals. All of the *CTM buses* arrive at the main *CTM* Bus Station, again in the New Town, on Boulevard Mohammed V. Here too, you're right at the heart of the hotel region, or you can pick up the no.9 bus just a couple of blocks in at the Place Mohammed V. The *private bus lines*, however, might arrive at any one of three stations. If you're coming *from Taza or the East* it'll be the Bab Ftouh at the south-east corner of Fes el Bali (bottom right on our second map) – from here take bus no.18 for the Ville Nouvelle or a taxi to Boujeloud. *Buses and grands taxis from Meknes and Sefrou* stop at the Place des Alaouites on the edge of Fes el Jdid (bus no.3 for the New Town; no.1 for Boujeloud). All *the rest* operate through the Boujeloud/Place el Baghdadi terminal (bottom left-hand corner of our Fes el Bali plan), just around the corner from the Bab Boujeloud and its hotels – walk straight down the hill.

Hotels

Staying in Fes you've the usual choice between comfort (and water) out in the **New Town** or a number of much more basic places on the edge of the **Medina**. Neither option is perfect: the city can get very full in midsummer, the Medina places raise their prices to 2* rates while most of those in the New Town, stuck out on the plains, do little to cope with the heat. However, given these limitations, there's quite a range of rooms available.

BAB BOUJELOUD AND FES EL JDID
If you want to be at the heart of things – and to be able to walk out at night straight into the great main souk – the half-dozen hotels around **Bab Boujeloud** are the obvious choice. You're very well positioned here for exploring Fes el Bali, since the Bab (or gate) is the main approach in from Fes el Jdid and the Ville Nouvelle. In summer don't expect anyone to let you a 'single room', and at all times if you can possibly join up with two or three other people do so – you'll get a much better deal.

All six of the Boujeloud hotels are marked and keyed on our plan of Fes el Bali (see p. 146), and apart from the *Jardin Publique* – signposted down a short lane by the Boujeloud Mosque, friendly and noticeably cleaner – there's not a lot to choose between them. A second choice is probably the *Kaskades* with its flat roof-terrace, just on the right through the gate. The Bab Boujeloud itself, incidentally, is an easy and very obvious landmark – multicoloured on each of its sides with an elaborate bright blue and gold floral pattern.

As an alternative to the Boujeloud hotels – but remaining within easy walking distance of Fes el Bali – you might want to try the three small (and similarly basic) places in **Fes el Jdid**. Less well known, these are generally cheaper and even in mid-season you've a fair chance of an ordinarily priced single. Closest to Boujeloud is the *Hôtel du Parc*, way the most attractive (or at least the cleanest) and very good value. Keyed on our *Fes el Jdid/New Town* plan, you'll find it at the beginning of the Grand Rue des Merenides – Fes el Jdid's main street, about 10mins walk from the Bab Boujeloud. The other two, the hotels *du Croissant* and *Moulay al Chrif*, wouldn't win any health and safety awards but they've enough character to be more or less saved from squalor. They too are easily enough found, on either side of the Bab Semmarin at the far end of Grand Rue des Merenides.

The lack of effective showers in most of these Medina hotels isn't particularly a problem, for there's a fairly reasonable **hammam** (or Turkish bath) right opposite the Hotel L'Amrani, just inside Fes el Bali. The entrance, as often, is unmarked – a small wooden door in a whitewashed arch. Hours are 1pm-midnight for women, midnight-1pm for men; bring a towel and swimming trunks.

THE NEW TOWN (VILLE NOUVELLE)
The **New Town** has much the highest concentration of hotels and if you

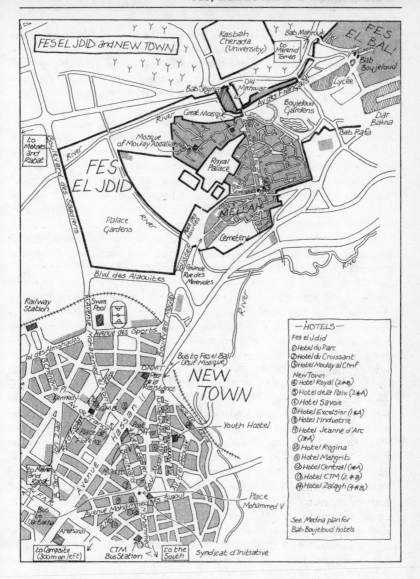

FES EL JDID and NEW TOWN

Kasbah Cherada (University)

to Merenid Tombs

Bab Mahrouk

FES EL BALI

Bab Boujeloud

Old Mechouar

Bab Segma

Av. des Français

Lycée

RIVER

Great Mosque

Boujeloud Gardens

Dar Batha

Mosque of Moulay Abdallah

Bab Rafa

to Meknes and Rabat

Boulevard des Saadiens

FES EL JDID

Royal Palace

RIVER

Bab Semmarin

MELLAH

Cemetery

Palace Gardens

RIVER

Blvd. des Alaouites

Grande Rue des Merenides

Railway Station

Swim Pool

Avenue des Sports

Bus to Fes el Bali (Rsif Mosque)

RIVER

NEW TOWN

Av. des Almohades

ONMT

Place de la Résistance

Youth Hostel

Pl. Kennedy

Place de Florence

Post Office

Market

to Meknes and Rabat

Avenue Hassan II

Place Mohammed V

Bus to Dar Batha

Avenue Mohammed V

Artesanal

to Campsite (300m on left)

CTM Bus Station

to the South

Syndicat d'Initiative

HOTELS

Fes el Jdid
1) Hotel du Parc
2) Hotel du Croissant
3) Hotel Moulay al Chrif

New Town
4) Hotel Royal (2*B)
5) Hotel de la Paix (2*A)
6) Hotel Savoie
7) Hotel Excelsior (1*A)
8) Hotel l'Industrie
9) Hotel Jeanne d'Arc (1*A)
10) Hotel Regina
11) Hotel Mahgrib
12) Hotel Central (1*A)
13) Hotel CTM (2*B)
14) Hotel Zalagh (4*B)

See Medina plan for
Bab Boujeloud hotels

arrive in the afternoon or evening you might as well settle for a room around here. Well apart from the life of the old city you will miss the real atmosphere of Fes – and the amazing sound of its dawn as the muezzins' calls are preceded by the chanting of other holy men, 'the companions of the sick'. But though you lose on style you will have the bars and restaurants – and a couple of swimming pools – close at hand. Below, in roughly ascending order of price are most of the options; through July or August don't expect too much choice.

Youth Hostel (Auberge de Jeunesse), 18 Blvd Mohammed el Hansali (see plan). New and friendly, they let out roofspace if the dormitories are full and travelling on your own you won't get a cheaper bed. Closes 10pm.

Hôtel Savoie, Just off Blvd Chefchaouni (keyed 6 on our plan). Tends to be the cheapest of the unclassifieds – if nothing else. Avoid like the plague, however, the *Volubilis* next door.

Hôtel Regina, Hôtel Maghreb, Av. Mohammed es Slaoui (keyed 10 & 11). Still unclassified but considerably better than the Savoie with cool, spacious rooms. Both up prices considerably in summer.

Hôtel Excelsior, Hôtel l'Industrie, Blvd Mohammed V (keyed 7 & 8). Standard 1*A type places, fairly clean and with functional showers.

Hôtel Jeanne d'Arc (1*A), 36 Av. Mohammed es Slaoui; *Hôtel Central* (1*A), Rue Nador, off Blvd Mohammed V. Keyed 9 & 12, these are the best one star places – though correspondingly popular and often full.

Hôtel Royal (2*B), 36 Rue d'Espagne (keyed 4). Usefully placed for the train station – just off the Av. de France – and tends to have space, perhaps due to its total lack of distinction.

Hôtel CTM (2*B), Av. Mohammed V (keyed 13); *Hôtel de la Paix* (2*A), 44 Av. Hassan II (keyed 5). Straight and very reasonable tourist hotels, considerably more comfortable than any of the above.

Hôtel Zalagh (4*B), Rue Mohammed Diouri (keyed 14). With fine views over Fes el Jdid and a swimming pool of its own, this is the place to make for if you've the money. It is also a favourite hang out for successful young Moroccans.

CAMPING

Camping Moulay Slimane, Rue Moulay Slimane. 10 minutes walk from the centre of the New Town, this isn't so far as it looks on the map. It's also cheap, reasonably secure (though don't camp around the perimeter), and has good facilities – cafe, bar, showers, occasionally filled swimming pool. To get there follow Av. Hassan II to the major intersection with Av. F.A.R.: turn left (onto Av. Youssef Ben Tachfine) and Rue Moulay Slimane is the first street off to your right. Even if you're not staying you might find it worthwhile wandering in to pick up information – and possibly a lift – as seemingly every campervan, landrover and Renault 4 travelling through Morocco puts in here.

TOTAL LUXURY/DIFFERENT WORLDS

Setting for Paul Bowles's brilliant novel *The Spider's House*, and one of the three most luxurious hotels in Morocco (the others are the *Mamounia* in Marrakesh and *Gazelle d'Or* in Taroudannt), the **Palais Jamai**. poised above Fes el Bali, is an experience in itself: 24hrs spent here – if you're loaded with money or feeling slightly crazy – leave you feeling like you've spent a week on a Presidential junket. On the other hand you do pay for this privilege, with the cheapest double rooms starting at some £40 a night, a rate you can bring down slightly with a group of three people. If you really have money, ask for a room in the old part of the hotel, originally a C19 Vizier's Palace and genuinely spectacular.

Fes el Bali

With its mosques, *medressas* and *fondouks*, and its mile-long network of souks, there are enough 'sights' in **FES EL BALI** to spend three or four days just searching them out. And some even then you'd be unlikely to stumble upon except by chance or the whim of a guide. In this – the apparently wilful secretiveness – is part of the fascination, and there is much to be said for Paul Bowles's rather lofty advice to 'lose oneself in the crowd . . . to be pulled along by it – not knowing where to and for how long . . . to see beauty where it is least likely to appear'. If you do so, be prepared to become quite lost: despite what the hustlers tell you, the Medina is not a dangerous place and you can always ask a boy to lead you out towards one of its landmarks – **Bab Boujeloud**, the **Talaa Kebira**, **Kairaouine mosque** or **Bab Ftouh**.

Making your own way in purposeful quest for the souks and monuments you should be able to find everything detailed in the following pages with a little patience and endurance. As a prelude it's not a bad idea to head up to the **Merenid tombs** on the rim of the valley, where you can get a spectacular overview of the city and try to fix its shape.

Down below, there are four principal entrances and exits – much the easiest at which to gather your bearings is the **Bab Boujeloud**. The others are an open square by the **Mosque er Rsif**, a few blocks below the Kairaouine mosque and connected by bus no.19 with the New Town; the **Bab Ftouh** at the bottom of the Andalous quarter (bus 18 from here goes to the Dar Batha, close by Boujeloud); and the **Bab Guissa**, an alternative approach to the Merenid tombs up at the top of the city by the Palais Jamai hotel.

The Merenid tombs and a view of Fes

A crumbling and rather obscure group of ruins, the **Merenid tombs** are not of great interest in themselves. Nobody knows any longer which of the dynasty's sultans had them erected and there is not a trace remaining of the 'beautiful white marbles' and 'vividly coloured epitaphs' which so struck Leo Africanus in his C16 description of Fes. Poised at the city's skyline, however, they are a picturesque focus and superb vantage point. All about you spread the Muslim cemeteries which ring the hills on each side of the city, while looking down you can delineate the more prominent among Fes's reputed 365 mosque minarets.

Getting up to the tombs is no problem. You can walk in about 20 minutes from Bab Boujeloud, or take a taxi (around 10dhs from the New Town). From the Boujeloud area leave by the **Bab el Mahrouk**, above the bus terminal, and once outside the walls turn immediately to the right. After a while you come to a sort of shanty-town area, above which (and accessible by a network of paths) is the stolid fortress of the **Borj Nord**. Despite its French garrison-like appearance this and its southern counterpart across the valley were actually built in the C17 by the Saadians; the dynasty's only endowment to the city, they were used to control the Fassis rather than to defend them. Carefully maintained, the Borj now houses the country's **arms museum** – an interminable display of row upon row of muskets, most of them confiscated from the Riffs in the 1958 rebellion.

Clambering across the hillside from the Borj Nord – or following the Route du Tour du Fes past the imposing and controversially sited *Hôtel des Merenides* – you soon emerge at **the tombs** and a hopeful cluster of guides. Wandering about here you are probably standing on the city's original foundations, before its rapid expansion under Moulay Idriss II. But it is the view across the deep bowl of a valley below which holds everyone's attention, Fes el Bali neatly wedged within, white and diamond-shaped, and buzzing with activity.

Immediately below is the *Adourat el-Kairaouine*, or **Kairaouine quarter**: the main stretch of the Medina where Idriss settled the first Tunisian refugees. At its heart, towards the river, stands the green-tiled courtyard of the **Kairaouine mosque**, the country's most important religious building, preceded and partially screened by its two minarets. The principal one of these is domed and whitewashed, an unusual (though characteristically Tunisian) design; the slightly lower one to its right (square with a narrower upper storey) is the *Borj en Naffara*, 'the trumpeter's tower', from which the beginning and end of Ramadan are proclaimed. Over to the right of this, and very easily made out, are the tall pyramid-roof and slender, decoratively faced minaret of the city's second great religious building, the **Zaouia of Moulay Idriss II**. The **Andalous quarter**, the other area settle by C9 refugees, lies some way over to the left of this trio of minarets – divided from the Kairaouine by the appropriately named **Bou Khareb**, the 'carrier of rubbish river', whose path is marked out by a series of minarets. The **Djemaa el-Andalous**, principal mosque of this quarter, is distinguished by a massive, tile-porched monumental gateway, behind which you can make out the roofs enclosing its great courtyard.

Orientation aside, though, there is a definite magic if you're up here in the early evening or best of all at dawn. The sounds of the city, the stillness and the contained disorder below: all seem to make manifest the mystical significance which Islam places on urban life as the most perfect expression of culture and society.

From the tombs you can enter Fes el Bali either through the Bab Guissa *(which brings you out at the Souk el Attarin, or by returning to the* Bab Boujeloud. *There is a* petit taxi *rank by the Bab Guissa.*

Bab Boujeloud and the Dar Batha

The area around the **Bab Boujeloud** is today the main entrance to Fes el Bali: a place where people come to talk and stare, and a great concentration of cafes, stalls and activity. Provincial buses leave through the day from a square (**Place Baghdadi**) just behind the gate, while in the early evening there are occasional entertainers and a vague flea market spreading out towards the **Bab el Mahrouk**.

This focus and importance is all comparatively recent, for only at the end of the last century were the walls joined up between Fes el Bali and Fes el Jdid and the area within developed. Nearly all the buildings here date from this period, including those of the elegant **Dar Batha** palace, designed for the reception of foreign embassies and now a very fine **museum of Moroccan art and crafts**. Open daily except Tuesdays from 9-11.30 & 3-6, this is well worth a visit and its gardens a useful respite from the general exhaustion of the Medina. Admission is free (though you'll tip at some stage) and the entrance is through a small door on its lower side, about 30metres along from the Place de l'Istiqlal. The displays here are probably the finest anywhere in Morocco, concentrating as they do on the local artesan traditions. There are stunning collections of *carved wood*, much of it rescued from the Misbahiya and other medressas; another magnificent room of *Middle Atlas carpets;* and excellent examples of *zellij-work, calligraphy* and *embroidery*. Above all, though, it is the *pottery* rooms which stand out – the pieces gathered from the C16 to the 1930s, showing the remarkable preservation of technique long after the end of any form of innovation. This in its own way is impressive and creates a kind of timeless quality which keeps being asserted as you wander about Fes. There is no concept of the 'antique': something is either new or it is old, and if the latter it may be anything from thirty years to three centuries.

Until you've got a cetain grasp of Fes el Bali you'll find it useful to stick with **Bab Boujeloud** as a **point of entry** and reference. Decorated with blue and gold tiles (green and gold on the inside face) it is a pretty unmistakeable landmark, and once inside things are initially straightfor-

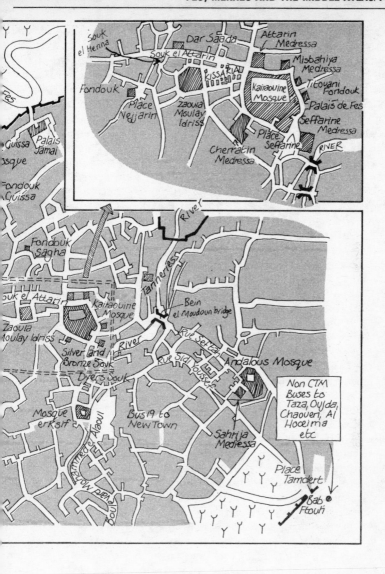

ward. You will find yourself in a small square, flanked by the *Hôtel Kaskades* (on your right) and with a couple of minarets almost directly ahead. Just beyond the Kaskades the square splits into two main lanes, cut by dozens of alleys but running in parallel for much of the Medina's length. The lower (right-hand) fork is the **Talaa Seghira**, or *Rue du Petit Talaa*, a street which begins with a handful of small foodstalls where you can buy chunks of pastilla – the great Fassi delicacy of pigeon-pie; beyond, it has little of specific interest until it rejoins the upper lane, the Talaa Kebira, just before the Place Nejjarin (see p. 153).

The **Talaa Kebira**, or *Rue du Grand Talaa*, is really the fork to take – bending round and off to the left of the two visible minarets. The major artery of the Medina, this, with its continuations, runs right through to the Kairaouine Mosque and for virtually the whole stretch it is lined with shops and stalls. About 100 metres down, too, it is host to the most brilliant of all the city's monuments – the **Medressa Bou Inania**. You will see the entrance to this, down a step on your right, just before you come to a white plastered bridge-arch over the road.

Bus no.18 *from the New Town will drop you more or less outside the* Dar Batha *in the Place de l'Istiqlal, two minutes walk below the Bab Boujeloud. Here and around the gate you'll be battered with offers of a guide. If you don't want one be firm but unagressive and explain you're only going down to the Bou Inania – which is probably your first move anyway. Most hustlers give up chasing your custom after about 50 metres or so. To pick up a* petit taxi *around Boujeloud walk up to the* Place Baghdad *by the Boujeloud bus terminal.*

The Bou Inania medressa and clock

If there is just one building you actively seek out in Fes – or even, not to put too fine a point on it, in Morocco – it should be this one. The most elaborate, extravagant and beautiful of all Merenid monuments, the **Bou Inania medressa** comes close to perfection in every aspect of its construction – its dark cedarwood is fabulously carved, the *zellij* tilework classic, and the stucco a revelation. In addition it is the city's only building in religious use which you are allowed to enter and so the nearest you will come to sharing a mosque with Moroccans. You cannot, of course, enter the prayer hall – which is divided from the main body of the medressa by a small canal – but you can sit in a corner of the marble courtyard and gaze across. The admission hours are daily from around 8am until 5pm, with the exception of Friday mornings (closed) and times of prayer (when you may be pushed out); as with all the medressas in Fes, you are expected to give a dirham each to the *guardien* as you leave.

The medressas – student colleges and halls of residence – were by no means unique to Fes and in fact originated in Khorassan in Iran, gradually spreading west through Baghdad and Cairo. They seem to have reached

Morocco under the Almohads, though the earliest surviving in Fes are C14 Merenid – possibly the last flowering of the system. The word *medressa* means 'place of study' and there may have been lectures delivered in some of the prayer-halls. In general, however, the medressas acted as little more than dormitories, providing a room and food to poor (male) students from the country and so allowing them to attend lessons at the mosques. In Fes, where students might attend the Kairaouine university for ten or more years, rooms were always in great demand and 'key money' often paid on their takeover. Although they had largely disappeared from the Islamic world by the late Middle Ages, most of these Fassi medressas remained in use right up to the 1950s and a few remain occupied today.

Set rather apart from the other medressas of Fes, the **Bou Inania** was the last and the grandest built by a Merenid sultan. It shares its name with the one in Meknes, which was completed (though not designed) by the same patron Sultan Abou Inan (1351-58), but it is infinitely more grand. Its cost alone was legendary, and Abou Inan is said to have thrown the accounts into the river upon its completion, claiming (not perhaps originally) that a thing of beauty is beyond reckoning. At first glance, Abou Inan doesn't seem the kind of sultan you would expect to have wanted a medressa – his mania for building aside, he was most noted for having 325 sons in ten years, for deposing his father and committing a number of unusually atrocious murders. The *Oulema*, the religious leaders of the Kairaouine mosque, certainly thought him an unlikely candidate and advised him to build his medressa on the city's rubbish dump – on the basis that piety and good works can cure anything. Whether it was this or merely the desire for a lasting monument which inspired him, he set up the medressa as a rival to the Kairaouine itself and for a while it became the most important religious building in the city. A long campaign to have the announcement of the time of prayer transferred here eventually failed in the face of the Kairaouine's powerful opposition; but the medressa was granted the status of a Grand Mosque – unique in Morocco – and retains the right to say the Friday *khotbeh* prayer.

The basic lay-out of the building is really quite simple with a single great courtyard flanked by two sizeable halls and giving onto an oratory – essentially the same design as the wealthier Fassi mansions. For its effect it relies on the mass of decoration and the light and space held within it. You enter the courtyard – the medressa's outstanding feature – through a stalactite-domed entrance chamber, a feature adapted by the Merenids from Andalusia. Off to each side here are stairs to the upper storey, lined with students' cells, and to the roof. Depending on how the restoration is going you may or may not be able to go up: if you can, press on to the roof for an excellent (and very useful) view across this part of the city. The cells, as is usual, are bare and monkish except for their windows and decorated ceilings.

In the court, the decoration covers every possible surface and is startlingly well preserved. Perhaps most striking in terms of craftsmanship is the wood carving and joinery; an almost unrivalled example of the Moorish art of *laceria*, 'the carpentry of knots'. For the rest, the elegant black kufic script that rings three sides of the courtyard and divides the zellij from the stucco is largely a list of the properties whose incomes were given as an endowment to the medressa, rather than the usual Koranic inscriptions. Abou Inan, too, is bountifully praised amid the inscriptions, and on the foundation stone he is credited with the title *caliph*, an emotive claim to leadership of the Islamic world followed by none of his successors.

More or less opposite the medressa, just across the Talaa Kebira, the Bou Inania's property continues with an extraordinary **water-clock** built above the stalls in the road. An enduring curiosity, this consists of a row of thirteen windows and platforms, seven of which retain their original brass bowls. Nobody has been able to discover exactly how it functioned, though a contemporary account details how at every hour one of its windows would open, dropping a weight down into the respective bowl. Clocks had great religious significance through the Middle Ages in establishing the time of prayer and it seems probable that this one was bought by Abou Inan as part of his campaign to assert the medressa's pre-eminence; there are accounts of similar constructions at Tlemcen, just across the border in Algeria. As to its destruction, there are classically involved Fassi conspiracy tales – most of which revolve around the miscarriage of a Jewess passing below at the time of its striking and a Jewish sorcerer casting the evil eye on the whole device. The building to which the clock is fixed, which was in fact once owned by a Rabbi, is popularly known as 'The house of the magician'. Completing the medressa complex and immediately adjacent to the clock, there are the original **public latrines** built for its Friday worshippers. These have recently been closed up, though it is possible that this will only be temporary. Pre-dating the West by some four centuries, the 'Turkish style' closets here are still quite functional, washed by vast quantities of running water. If they look open – and if you're male – take a look inside at the great central patio with its ablutions pool and unexpectedly rich stucco ceiling.

Further down the Talaa Kebira
Making your way down the **Talaa Kebira** – a street that is quite easy to follow – you will eventually emerge at the labyrinth of lanes around the Kairaouine mosque and Zaouia Moulay Idriss II. It's an interesting route, though less for any specific 'sights' than for the general accumulation of

senses. The diarist Anais Nin placed her reaction in terms of smells: ' . . . the smell of excrement, saffron, leather being cured, sandalwood, olive oil being fried, nut oil so strong at first that you cannot swallow'. To which might be added the sounds – the shouts of muleteers (*balak!* means 'look out!'), mantric cries from the beggars, the bells of water-sellers – and above all the people, seen in shafts of light filtered through the rushes which cover much of the Talaa's length.

Along the first (upward) stretch watch out for a very large **fondouk** – on your left, just after a row of blacksmith's shops, about 300m beyond the Bou Inania. This was originally a **Merenid prison**, fitted out with suitably solid colonnades and arches; today it's used as a kind of mule-park, for tethering animals while their owners go off and do business or visit the mosque. Before the advent of the French cafe at the beginning of this century, the fondouks (or *caravanserais* as they're called in the East) formed the heart of social life outside the home – providing rooms for traders and richer students and frequently becoming centres of vice, intrigue and entertainment. There were once some two hundred in Fes el Bali, but although many survive, often with beautiful C14-15 decoration, they tend now to serve as small factories or warehouses. Another **fondouk**, about 100m further on as you reach the crest of the Talaa hill, is today used for curing animal skins (and smells appalling).

Once over the top of the rise the street changes its name – to the **Rue ech Cherabliyyin** – and, passing the oldest **hammam** still in use in Fes, you find yourself in a district of leather stalls and shoe-makers. The Fassi *babouches*, thick leather slippers, are reputed the best in the country and here, unusually, you find rather sophisticated grey ones in addition to the classic yellow and white. If you want to buy a good pair you'll need to spend some while examining the different qualities: for the best, be prepared to bargain hard until you're down to around 80dhs. The **Cherabliyin** ('slipper makers') **mosque**, in the midst of the quarter, was endowed by the Merenid sultan Abou el Hassan, builder of Rabat's Chellah. It has been substantially restored, though the minaret, its decoration inspired by the Koutoubia in Marrakesh, is original. If you've gazed at Koutoubia, or the great Almohad monuments of Rabat, you'll recognise the familiar *darj w ktarf* motifs.

Onwards, the lane is flanked by a drab series of 'typical' craft shops before, at the bottom of the hill, reaching an arched gateway marked quite undramatically **Souk el Attarin**. The 'souk of the spice-sellers', this is the formal heart of the city, and its richest and most sophisticated shopping district. It is around the Grand Mosque of a city that the most expensive commodities are traditionally sold and kept, and approaching the Kairaouine, this pattern is more or less maintained. Spices themselves are still sold here, so too Egyptian and Japanese imports, while in the web of little squares off to the left you'll find all kinds of manufactured produce. There are a few small cafes amidst these, while back on the Attarin is the **Dar Saada,** a grand C19 mansion now housing an expensive carpet shop and restaurant – you can look in or drink tea with only moderate pressure. Just beyond, this time on the right of the street, is the **Kissaria,** or covered market, again dominated by textiles and modern goods; it had to be totally rebuilt after a fire in the 1950s and so lacks any particular character.

Reaching the end of the Souk el Attarin you come to a **crossroads of lanes** slightly askew from the direction of the street. On your right (and ahead of you) are the walls of the *Kairaouine mosque;* to your left, and entered a few yards up the lane, is the magnificent *Attarin medressa*: for both, see the next section. First, however, its seems logical to take a look at the area below the Souk el Attarin – dominated, as it has been for five centuries, by the *shrine and zaouia of Moulay Idriss II*, the city's patron saint.

Below the Souk el Attarin: the Zaouia of Moulay Idriss II, Place Nejjarin and Souk el Henna

Although enclosed by a highly confusing web of lanes, the **Zaouia Moulay Idriss II** is not itself difficult to find. Take the first lane to the right – the Rue Mjadliyin – as soon as you have passed through the arch into the Attarin and you will find yourself at a wooden bar which marks the beginning of its *Horm*, or sanctuary precinct. Until the French occupation of the city in 1911, this was as far as Christians or Jews, or mules, could penetrate, and beyond it any Muslim had the right to claim asylum from prosecution or arrest. These days non-Muslims are allowed to walk around the outside of the zaouia and, although you are not permitted to enter, it is possible to glimpse inside the shrine and even to see the saint's tomb. Passing to the right of the bar make your way around a narrow alleyway, emerging on the far side of the zaouia at the *women's entrance*. Looking in from the doorway you'll see the tomb over on the left, with a scene of intense and apparently high-baroque devotion all about. The women, who are Idriss's principal devotees, burn candles and incense here and then proceed around the corner of the precinct to touch, or make offering at, a round brass grille which opens directly onto the tomb. A curious feature, common to many zaouias but rarely within view, are the numerous European clocks – prestigious gifts, and very popular in the last century when many Fassi merchant families had them shipped over from Manchester (their main export base for the cotton trade).

There is no particular evidence that Moulay Idriss II was a very saintly marabout, but as the effective founder of Fes and the son of the founder of the Moroccan state he obviously has considerable *baraka*, the magical blessing which Moroccans invoke. Originally, it was in fact assumed that Idriss, like his father, had been buried near Volubilis but in 1308 an uncorrupt body was found on this spot and the cult launched. It was presumably an immediate success, for in addition to his role as the city's patron saint, Idriss has an impressive roster of supplicants. This is the place to visit for poor strangers who arrive in the city, for boys before their circumcision and for women to facilitate childbirth, while for some unexplained reason Idriss is also a national protector of sweetmeat-sellers. The shrine itself was rebuilt in the C18 by the sultan Moulay Ismail — his only act of pious endowment in this city.

Standing at the women's entrance to the zaouia you'll see a lane off to the left — the **Bab Moulay Ismail** — full of candle and nickleware stalls for devotional offerings. If you follow this to the wooden bar, go under it (turning to the right) and then keep to your left you should come out in the picturesque square of the **Place Nejjarin** ('Carpenters square'). There is a very imposing *fondouk* here, built in the early eighteenth century, and a beautiful canopied fountain which is probably its contemporary. The *fondouk*, crumbling about its court, is generally closed, though it was used until a few years ago as a hostel for Kairaouine students. In the alleys off this square you'll find the **Nejjarin souk**, the carpenters chiselling away at sweet-smelling thuya wood, and parallel to it a souk of **metal-workers**, hammering patterns into great iron tubs and implements. To return to the Souk el Attarin turn left at the point where you entered the square.

A similar arrangement of buildings characterises the **Souk el Henna**, a quiet tree-shaded square adjoining what was once the largest madhouse in the Merenid empire (and is now a modern storehouse). Not such an inappropriate setting this, as apart from the henna and the usual cosmetics (kohl, antimony, etc.) sold here, people still come to the souk's stalls to buy the more esoteric ingredients required for aphrodisiacs and other magical spells. Notice on one side of the square a huge pair of scales used for weighing the larger deliveries. On the others, *pottery stalls* are gradually encroaching on the traditional business. Cheap but often striking in design, the pieces here include Fassi pots (blue and white, or very simple black on earthenware) and others from Safi (heavy green glazed) and Salé (elaborate modern designs on a white glaze). To get down to the square, take the lane to the right immediately *before* the entrance-arch to the Souk el Attarin.

Around the Kairaouine: the Attarin and other medressas

The largest mosque in Morocco, and one of the oldest universities anywhere in the world, **el-Kairaouine** remains the fountainhead of the country's religious life. It was founded in 857 by a Tunisian woman, a wealthy refugee from the city of Kairouan. The present dimensions, with sixteen aisles and space for 20,000 worshippers, are essentially the product of C10 and C12 rebuildings: first by the great Caliph of Cordoba,

Abd er Rahman III, later under the Almoravids.

Even if all the roads in Fes el Bali do lead to the Kairaouine – an ancient claim which still has truth – the mosque remains a thoroughly elusive place to non-Muslims. The building is so enmeshed in the surrounding houses and shops that it is impossible to get any clear sense of its shape, and at most you can gain partial views from adjoining rooftops (best from the Attarin medressa) or through the four great entrances to its court. Surprisingly, for such an important religious building, nobody objects (publicly at least) to tourists craning around the gates to look inside; inevitably, however, the centrepieces that would order all the separate parts – the main aisle and mihrab – remain hidden from view.

The overall effect of this obscurity is compounded by the considerable amount of time you will spend, no doubt, lost around here – forever returning to familiar places you've been lost in before, in a kind of bewildered pilgrimage. The best **point of reference** around the Kairaouine – and the building most worth visiting in its own right – is the *Attarin medressa*, whose entrance (a bronze door) is just to the left at the end of the Souk el Attarin. From here you can make your way around the mosque to a succession of other medressas and *fondouks*, picking up glimpses of the Kairouine's interior as you go.

Open daily, except Friday mornings, from 9-12 & 2-6, the **Attarin medressa** is, after the Boulnania, the finest of the city's colleges. It has an incredible profusion and variety of patterning: equally startling in the zellij, wood and stucco yet handled with an apparent ease its proportions never under any threat of being overwhelmed. The building was completed in 1325 by the Merenid sultan Abou Said, and so is one of the earliest of Fes's medressas. Interestingly, its general lightness of feel is achieved by the relatively simple device of using pairs of symmetrical arches to join the pillars to a single weight-bearing lintel – a design repeated in the upper storeys and mirrored in the courtyard basin. The later Merenid design, as employed in the Bou Inania, was to have much heavier lintels (the timbers above the doors and windows) supported by shorter projecting beams; this produces a more solid, step-like effect, losing the Attarin's fluid movement.

The basic groundplan, however, is more or less standard: an entrance hall opening onto a long pooled court, off which to the left are the latrines, and directly ahead the prayer hall. On your way in, stop a while in the *entrance hall*, its zellij decoration perhaps the most complex in Fes. A circular pattern, based on an interlace of pentagons and five-pointed star, this perfectly demonstrates the intricate science – and the philosophy – employed by the craftsmen. As Titus Burckhardt explains (in his *Moorish Art in Spain*), this lies in direct opposition to the western arts of pictorial representation:

*with its rhytmic repetitions, [it] does not seek to capture the eye to
lead it into an imagined world, but, on the contrary, liberates it
from all the pre-occupations of the mind. It does not transmit specific
ideas, but a state of being, which is at once repose and inner rhythm.*

Burckhardt adds that the way the patterns radiate from a single point
serves as a pure simile for the belief in the oneness of God, manifest as
the centre of every form or being.

In the *courtyard* you'll notice change in the zellij base – to a combination of eight- and ten-pointed stars. This probably signifies the hand
of a different *maallem*, or master craftsman, for most had a single mathematical base which they worked with infinite variation on all
commissions. In comparison to these outer rooms, the actual *prayer hall*
is quite bare and meditative, focussing on its *mihrab* (or prayer niche)
flanked by marble pillars and lit by a series of small zellij-glass windows.

If you are allowed to go up the stairs in the entrance hall, do so.
Around the first floor there are *cells* for over sixty students, and these
operated as an annexe to the Kairaouine university until the 1950s.
Budgett Meakin (in 1899) estimated some 1500 students in the city's
various medressas – a figure which may have been overestimated since it
was based not on an actual count of the students but on the number of
loaves of bread prepared for them each day. Non-Muslims were not
allowed into the medressas until the French undertook their repair at the
beginning of the Protectorate, and were banned again (this time by the
colonial authorities) when the Kairaouine students became active in the
struggle for Independence.

Up on **the roof** of the medressa you can gain one of the most complete
views possible of the **Kairaouine mosque**. Looking out across the green
tiles of its roof there are three visible minarets. On the left, tall and
square, is that of the Moulay Idriss Zaouia, to its right, the Burj an-
Naffara (the Trumpeter's Tower) and finally the Kairaouine's original
minaret. Slightly thinner in its silhouette than is usual – most minarets
are built to an exact 5:1/width:height ratio – this is the oldest Islamic
monument in the city, built in 956. Below it, you can make out, too, a
considerable section of the central courtyard of the mosque – **the Sahn**.
For a closer glimpse at ground level the best vantage point is the Bab el
Wad gate: 20m down from the Attarin entrance (turn left as you step
out then immediately left again). At the end of the court a pair of
magnificent pavilions are visible – the last additions to the structure of
the mosque, added by the Saadians in the C16. They are modelled on
the Court of the Lions in Granada's Alhambra palace, and were perhaps
constructed by Spanish Muslim craftsmen.

There is another different angle onto the Sahn from a further gate, the
Bab Medressa, near the end of this first stretch of the mosque wall.

Opposite, as you'd expect, is another college – the semi-derelict (but occasionally open) **Misbahiya medressa**. If you can get in this has some fine details, though much of its wood carving is now displayed at the Dar Batha museum. The elegant central basin was brought over by the Saadians from Almeria in Spain; the marble floor in which it is set level, from Italy. Surprisingly large, with courts (and two latrines) at each corner, it was built a couple of years before the Bou Inania, again by the Merenid sultan Abou el Hassan.

Moving on round the corner of the Kairaouine, you pass the **Tetouani** (or *Istroihani*) **fondouk**, a well-preserved Merenid building where the traders from Tetouan – even then reputed for dishonesty – used to stay. Now partially occupied by a carpet-shop, you can look inside without pressure and will probably be shown the huge ancient doorlock which draws across its gateway. A few doors down, past another much smaller fondouk, is the so-called **Palais de Fes**, a grand C19 mansion now converted to an upmarket restaurant and rug shop. Again you can walk in, and if you ask you'll be allowed up to the roof for a different view of the Kairaouine and an interesting exercise in orientation across the immediate area.

There is another gate to the Kairaouine, essentially of Almoravid construction, right opposite the Palais de Fes; one of the ten which are opened only for the Friday prayers. Alongside, notice the cedarwood panelling, placed to guide the blind towards the mosque. If you follow this round, through a tight-wedged alley, you soon emerge into a very distinctive open square, metalworkers hammering away on each of its sides, surrounded by immense iron and copper cauldrons and pans for weddings and festivals. This is the **Place Seffarine**, – almost wilfully picturesque with its faience fountain and gnarled old fig trees. On the near side, a tall and quite simple entrance in the whitewashed walls leads into the **Kairaouine library**, one of the most frustrating buildings denied to non-Muslims. Established by the Kairouan refugees in the C9, and bolstered by virtually the entire contents of the medieval Cordoba library, this was once the greatest collection of Islamic, mathematical and scholarly books outside of Baghdad. Amazingly, and somewhat pointedly marking Fes's decline, much of the library was lost or dissipated in the C17, but, restored and in use, it remains one of the most important in the Arab world. The **university** here has had its function largely usurped by the modern departments established around Fes el Jdid and the Ville Nouvelle, though it was until recent decades the only form of Moroccan higher education. Entirely traditional in character, this comprised courses on Koranic law, astrology, mathematics, logic, rhetoric and poetry – very much as the medieval universities of Europe. Teaching was informal, with professors gathering a group of students around them in a corner of the mosque whilst they contrived to absorb and memorise the body of his knowledge. It was, of course, an entirely male preserve.

A major point to fix your bearings, the Place Seffarin gives way to various possible routes. You can continue around the mosque by taking the first lane to the right as you enter the square – *Sma't el Adoul*, 'the street of the notaries'. The notaries, professional scribes, are sadly out of business, but before looping back to reach the Attarin medressa you will catch a number of gates revealing the Kairaouine's rush-matted and round-arched interior. If you don't take this turning but instead pass straight on, you enter an area of souks specialising in *gold and silver jewellery* and secondhand metal goods – a magnificent range of *pewter teapots* among them. As this road begins to veer off left down the hill, a right turn will lead you up to the *Cherratin medressa* (and eventually to the Zaouia Moulay Idriss).

First though, right on the square, is the earliest of Fes's Merenid medressas – **the Seffarin**. Its entrance is quite inconspicuous, and you may need it pointed out: leaving the Seffarin square at the bottom left-hand corner you follow a short lane down to the left and then briefly to the right – the door (porched and studded) is on your left. Built around 1285 – twenty years before the Attarin, forty-two before the Bou Inania – the Seffarin is unlike all the other medressas in taking the exact form of a traditional Fassi house, with an arched balcony above its courtyard. It is heavily decayed, though still with suggestions of grandeur in the lofty prayer-hall. Elsewhere, the wandering vine and delicate ablutions pool give it a rather domestic air. If there is a student around – which is likely, as there are two newer medressas next door which house groups from the Lycée – ask him to unlock the door to the roof, an atmospheric place where you can look down on the Seffarin square and listen to the individual rhythms of the metalworkers. If you were to continue down the lane beyond the entrance to the medressa, swinging off down the hill to the right, you would reach the *Rue des Teinturiers* (the dyers' souk: see the following section) and a *bridge* over the Oued Fes, below which you can leave the Medina by the Place beside the *Mosque er Rsif*.

Very different from the Seffarin, and indeed all the previous medressas, **the Cherratin** (see directions above) dates from 1670 and the reign of Moulay er Rachid, founder of the Alaouite dynasty. The whole design represents a shift in scope and wealth – to an essentially functional style with student cells grouped around three corner courtyards and a latrine around the fourth. Comprising some 120 rooms (each with space for two students) it was in use until very recently and the cells are still partitioned and occasionally fitted up with electric light. The craftsmanship here represents a significant decline, though there is still impressive woodwork around the individual courts. It is interesting too in a general way as a rare surviving building from this period.

Below the Kairaouine: the dyers' souk and tanneries
If you're beginning to find the medieval prettiness of the central souks

and medressas slightly unreal then this region, just below the Kairaouine, should provide the antidote. For the dyers' and tanners' souks – basis of the city's trading wealth from the C10 to C19 – represent the nauseating underside of all you've seen before.

The **dyers' street** – *souk Sabbighin* – is directly below the Seffarine medressa. Continue down past the medressa to your left, and then turn right immediately before the bridge ahead. Short and very weird, the souk is draped with fantastically coloured yarn and cloth drying in the heat. Below, workers in grey chimney-sweep clothes toil over ancient cauldrons of multicoloured dyes. The atmosphere is thick and mysterious, and not a little disconcerting so close to one of the city's main entrances.

At the end of the souk Sabbighin you come to a second bridge – the hog-backed **Qantrat Sidi el Aouad** – almost disguised by the shops built upon and about it. Walking across, you'll find yourself in the *Andalous quarter* (see below) and if you follow the main lane up to the left, Rue Sidi Youssef, you'll come out at the Andalous mosque. Staying on the Kairaouine side of the river and taking the lane down to your right at the end of the souk, you should emerge at the open *square by the Rsif Mosque;* from here if you want to return to the New Town you can get a no.19 bus, or a *petit taxi.*

For the **tanneries quarter** – the *Dabbaghin* – return to the Place Seffarine and take the right-hand lane at the top of the square (the second lane on your left if you're coming from the Palais de Fes). This street is known as the *Darb Mechattine,* 'comb makers road' and it runs more or less parallel to the river for 150m or so, eventually reaching a fork. The right-hand branch of this goes down to the river and the *Bein el Moudoun bridge* – another fairly direct approach to the Andalous mosque. The left winds up amid a maze of C18 streets for another 150–200m until you see the tanneries off to your left; it sounds a hideously convoluted route but in fact is a well trodden one – the most physically striking sight in Fes, the tanneries are constantly being visited by groups of tourists, whom you can tag on to for a while if you get lost. Otherwise, follow your nose or accept a guide up from the Seffarine. Once outside the quarter, there are always small boys about who will show you round for a couple of dirhams.

Within, there is a compulsive fascination about everything. Great streams of water pour through holes that were once the windows of houses; hundreds of skins lie spread out to dry on the rooftops; whilst amid the vats of dye and cows urine (to treat the leather) an unbelievably Gothic fantasy is enacted. The rotation of colours in the great honey-combed vats still follows the traditional sequence – yellow (saffron), red (poppy), blue (indigo), green (mint) and black (antimony) – though most of the vegetable dyes have now been replaced by chemicals. This innovation and the odd rinsing machine aside, there can have been little change since the sixteenth century when Fes took over from Spanish Cordoba as the pre-eminent city of leather-production. As befits such an ancient system, the ownership here is also quite feudal: the foremen running a hereditary co-operative and the workers passing down their specific jobs from generation to generation.

All of this can best be seen from one of the surrounding terrace rooftops, where you'll be directed along with the other tourists. There is, oddly enough, a kind of sensuous beauty about it – for all the stench and for all the voyeurism involved – though sniffing at the mint you are given as you go in, and looking across to see others doing the same, there can be few more pointed exercises in the nature of comparative wealth. Like it or not, this is tourism at its most extreme.

The Andalous quarter

Coming across the **Bou Khareb** (or Oued Fes) from the Kairaouine to the **Andalous bank** is not quite the adventure it once was. For the first three centuries of their existence the two quarters were entirely separate walled cities and the intense rivalry between them often resulted in factional strife. The rivalry still lingers enough to give each a distinct identity, though since the C13 this has been a somewhat one-sided affair: as the Fassi ordering of events goes, the Andalusians are reputed for the beauty of their women and the bravery of their soldiers while the Kairaouinis have always had the money. Whatever the reasons, the most famous Andalusian scholars and craftsmen have nearly all lived and worked on the other side of the river and as a result the atmosphere here has a rather provincial character. Monuments are few and comparatively modest, and the streets quieter and predominantly residential.

Each of the **approaches** detailed above is quite straightforward and gives more or less direct access to the area around the Andalous mosque. Across the **El Aouad bridge** take the Rue Sidi Youssef, up the hill to the right, and keep going straight to the top when you come into line with the minaret of the Andalous mosque: at this point veer left and you will see (on your right) the elaborate facade of the *Sahrija medressa*. Across the **Bein el Moudoun** ('the bridge between the cities'), follow the main street, the *Rue Seftah*, all the way up the hill as it winds round to the Andalous mosque. In addition, there are two other main entrance-routes. From the square by the **Mosque er Rsif** you can get onto the *Rue Sidi Youssef* by going in at the gate opposite the mosque entrance, then taking a first left by the first mosque you come to (the *Sidi Lemlili*), followed by a right turn up the hill. Or you can go in at the bottom of the quarter by the **Bab Ftouh** (connected by bus no.18 with Dar Batha).

The **Sahrija** (or *es-Sihrij*) **medressa** is by far the quarter's most interesting monument and is generally rated third in the city after the Attarin and Bou Inania. Anywhere else but Fes it would be a really major sight, though here, perhaps because of its state of dilapidation, it fails to stand out as much as it should. Still, it is currently undergoing restoration, and there's a considerable range and variety of original decoration. The zellij is among the oldest in the country, whilst the wood-carving harks back to Almohad and Almoravid motifs with its palmettes and pine cones. Built around 1321 by the sultan Abou el Hassan, it is very slightly earlier than the Attarin and a more or less exact contemporary of the medressa in Meknes – which in many ways it resembles.

Once again it is worth going up to the roof of the medressa for the view across the city, though there's frustratingly little to be seen of the **Andalous mosque**. Down below, however, you see almost nothing of the building other than its monumental entrance gates, for it's built right at the highest point of the valley. Like the Kairaouine, it was founded in the late C9 and saw considerable enlargement under the Almoravids and Merenids. The Sahrija and the adjoining *Sebbayin medressa* (which is currently in use for Lycée students) both served as dormitory-annexes for those studying at its library and under its individual professors.

Out behind the mosque – and towards the **Bab Ftouh** – you enter a strange no-man's land of **cemeteries** and run-down houses. Once a leper colony, this is traditionally a quarter of necromancers, thieves, madmen and saints. At its heart, close by the Bab Ftouh, is the whitewashed **koubba of Sidi Harazem**, a C12 mystic who has been adopted as the patron saint of students and the mentally ill. The saint's *moussem*, held in the spring, is one of the city's most colourful and was in the past a frequent spark for rioting.

About 1500m out beyond the Bab Ftouh, and easily distinguished by the smoke from its kilns, is the **Potters' quarter** (*quartier de potiers*). If you're interested in the techniques – the moulding, drying and decoration of the pots and tiles – follow the road and wander up to some of the workshops. The quarter itself is actually quite new, the potters having been moved out from an enclosure by the Bab Ftouh only a few years back, though the designs and workmanship remain traditional.

At Bab Ftouh *you can pick up a* petit taxi *to any part of town (the route up to the Merenid tombs is good for its views), or you can catch* bus no.18 *back to the Ville Nouvelle.*

Up from the Kairaouine

This region – up towards the *Bab Guissa* and the *Palais Jamai* hotel – is something of a tailpiece to Fes el Bali. It is not a route which many tourists take, scattered as it is with curiosities rather than monuments, but in this alone there's an obvious interest. Additionally, leaving the city at the Bab Guissa you can walk out and round to the *Merenid tombs*.

From the **Souk el Attarin** there are dozens of lanes leading up in the general direction of Bab Guissa – a good many of them blind alleys which send you scuttling back to retrace your steps. For one of the more interesting and unproblematic approaches, take the first lane to your left just inside the entrance arch to the Souk (i.e. about 15m before you come to the *Dar Saada* palace-restaurant). Following this as directly as seems possible you will soon emerge at the **Joutia**, the ancient fish and salt market. Spreading out above here is the **Sagha** – the *jewellers' quarter* – which bends around to the right into a small square flanked by an C18 fondouk and fountain. The fondouk is now used as a wool storehouse, though you can wander in to take a look at the elegant cedar-work and (heavily restored) stucco.

Back at the main lane – the *place* and *fondouk* Sagha are about 20m off to its right – you pass a series of small cafe-restaurants and a cinema, close by which is the **Place Achabin**, 'the herbalists square', where remedies and charms are still sold. The cafe-restaurants are among the best value in Fes el Bali, serving good solid meals, many double up as *patisseries*, good for a tea or fresh orange juice in the course of rambling around the Attarin/Kairaouine area. The official name of this lane, in which most are sited, is Rue Hormis. Beyond, the road continues uphill through an area of carpenters' workshops towards the Bab Guissa. On your way, look out for the *Fondouk Guissa* – or **Fondouk el Ihoud**, 'the Jews fondouk', on the left-hand side of the road. This dates back to the C13 and was at the centre of the city's Jewish community until their removal to the Mellah in Fes el Jdid. It is used today for sorting and storing skins brought up from the tanneries.

The **Bab and Mosque Guissa**, at the top of the hill, are of little interest – rebuilt in the C19 to replace a string of predecessors which have occupied this site for 800 years. A quick right just before the gate, however, takes you up to the **Palais Jamai Hotel** – one of the most glamorous in Morocco and originally a Vizier's palace. It was built towards the end of the last century by the Jamai brothers, viziers to the Sultan Moulay Hassan and in effect the most powerful men in the country. Fabulously rapacious, even by the standards of their age, the brothers eventually fell from power amid spectacular intriguing at the accession of Abdul Aziz in 1894. Walter Harris records the full story in *Morocco that Was*, dwelling in great detail on the brothers' ignominious fate – 'perhaps the blackest page of Moulay Abdul Aziz's reign'.

They were sent in fetters to Tetouan, and confined, chained and fettered, in a dungeon. In the course of time – and how long those ten years must have been – Hadj Amaati [the elder] died. The governor of Tetouan was afraid to bury the body, lest he should be accused of having allowed his prisoner to escape. He wrote to the court for instructions. It was summer, and even the dungeon was hot. The answer did not come for eleven days, and all that time Si

Mohammed remained chained to his brother's corpse! The brother survived. In 1908 he was released after fourteen years of incarceration, a hopeless, broken, ruined man. Everything he had possessed had been confiscated, his wives and children had died; the result of want and persecution. He emerged from his dark dungeon nearly blind, and lame from the cruel fetters he had worn. In his days of power he had been cruel, it is said – but what a price he paid!

In overt and dramatic contrast to this tale, you can, with a little confidence and a fistful of dirhams to spare, wander in to the Jamai hotel to take tea. Ask to do so on the terrace beside the old palace, now dwarfed by a huge modern extension. The palace quarters are still used as special suites, but if they're unoccupied the waiters may be willing to show you around one or two.

From the Bab Guissa *you can take a short cut across through the hill cemetery to the Merenid tombs, or you can follow the road up and round. At the* Bab Ferdaous, *just outside the Palais Jamai, there's a* petit taxi rank, *and from here* bus no.10 *runs to the Place des Alaouites in Fes el Jdid.*

Fes el Jdid

Unlike Fes el Bali, whose development and growth seem almost organic, FES EL JDID, 'Fes the New', was an entirely planned city – built by the Merenids at the beginning of their rule as both a practical and symbolic seat of government. It was begun around 1273 by the dynasty's second ruling sultan, Abou Youssef, and in a manic feat of building was completed within three years. The capital for much of its construction came from the Meknes oil presses; the Jews were taxed to build a new Great Mosque; and the labour, at least in part, was supplied by Spanish Christian captives.

The site which the Merenids chose for el Jdid lies some distance apart from Fes el Bali. In the chronicles this is presented as a strategic move for the defence of the city, though it is hard to escape the conclusion that its main function was a defence of the new dynasty against the Fassis themselves. It was not an extension for the people in any real sense, being occupied largely by the *Dar el Makhzen*, a vast royal palace, and by a series of army garrisons. With the addition of the Mellah – the Jewish ghetto – at the beginning of the C14, this process was continued. Moved out from Fes el Bali following one of the periodic pogroms, the Jews could provide an extra barrier (and scapegoat) between the Sultan and his Muslim faithful, as well as a useful source of income close to hand.

Over the centuries, Fes el Jdid's fortunes have generally followed those of the city as a whole. It was extremely prosperous under the Merenids and Wattasids, fell into decline under the Saadians, lapsed into virtual ruin during Moulay Ismail's long reign at Meknes, but revived with the commercial expansion of the C19 (at which point the walls between the old and new cities were finally joined). Events this century, largely generated by the French Protectorate, have left Fes el Jdid greatly changed and somewhat moribund. As a 'government city', it had no obvious role after the transfer of power to Rabat – a vacuum which the French filled by establishing a huge *quartier reservé* (red light district) in the area around the Great Mosque. This can have done little for the city's identity, but it was not so radical or disastrous as the immediate aftermath of Independence in 1956. Concerned about their future status, and with their position made untenable by the Arab-Israeli war, virtually all of the Mellah's 17,000 Jews left for Israel, Paris or Casablanca; today only a small community remains in the Ville Nouvelle.

You can reach Fes el Jdid in 10mins walk from the Bab Boujeloud (*the route outlined below*), *or from the* New Town *by walking up or taking a bus (no.3 from Pl. de Resistance) to the* Place des Alaouites *beside the* Mellah.

Down from Boujeloud
Walking down to Fes el Jdid from the **Bab Boujeloud** involves a shift in scale. Gone are the labyrinthine alleyways and souks of the Medina, to be replaced by a massive expanse of walls. Within them, to your left, are a series of gardens: the private **Jardins Beida**, behind the Lycée, and then the **Jardins de Boujeloud** with their pools diverted from the Oued Fes. These latter have an entrance towards the end of the long Av. des Français, and they are sometimes open to the public.

Moving on, you pass through twin arches to reach a kind of square, the **Petit Mechouar**, which was once the focus of the city's life and still sees the occasional juggler or storyteller during Ramadan evenings. To its left, entered through another double-arch, begins the main street of Fes el Jdid proper – the *Grande Rue*. Up to the right is the monumental **Bab Dekakine** ('gate of the benches'), a tremendous Merenid structure which served until the last decade* as the main approach to the royal palace and to Fes itself. It was on this gate that the Infante Ferdinand of Portugal was hung, upside down, for four days in 1437; he had been captured in an unsuccessful raid on Tangier and his country had failed to raise the ransom required – as a further, salutary warning, when his corpse was taken down from the Bab it was stuffed and displayed for the next 29 years. Through the three great arches you will find yourself in another, much larger **Mechouar**, laid out in the C18 and flanked along the whole of one side by an old arms factory – the Italian-built *Makina*

*In 1967-71 Hassan II re-orientated the royal palace and the city, developing the *Place des Alaouites* (which faces the Ville Nouvelle) as the principal approach.

– which is today partially occupied by a rug factory and various local clubs. A smaller gate, the C19 **Bab as Smen**, stands at the far end of the court, forcing an immediate turn as you leave the city through the Merenid outer-gateway of the **Bab Segma** (whose twin octagonal towers slightly resemble the contemporary Chellah in Rabat). If you are making your way up to the *Merenid tombs* from here, turn sharp right. Directly ahead, and closed to the public, is the huge **Kasbah Cherrada**, a fort built by the Sultan Moulay Rashid in 1670 to house – and keep at distance – the Berber tribes of his garrison. It is now the site of a hospital, school and annexe to the Kairaouine university.

Back at the Petit Mechouar – and before turning through the double arch onto the Grande Rue – a smaller gateway leads off to the right at the bottom of the square. This is the entrance to the old *quartier reservé* of **Moulay Abdallah**, where the French built cafes, dance-halls and brothels; the prostitutes themselves were mostly young Berber girls, drawn by a rare chance of quick money and usually returning to their villages when they had earned enough to marry or keep their families. The quarter today has a slightly solemn feel about it, the main street twisting down to Fes el Jdid's **Great Mosque**.

Within the main gateway, the **Grand Rue** zigzags slightly before leading straight down to the Mellah. There are **souks**, mainly for textiles, fruits and vegetables, along the way but nothing very much to delay you. Just by the entrance though, immediately to the left after you go through the arch, a narrow **lane** curves off into an attractive little area on the periphery of the Boujeloud gardens. There's an old waterwheel here which used to supply the gardens, and a small cafe nearby. On the way down you pass a handful of stalls, among them, traditionally, the *kif* and *sebsi* (kif pipe) sellers.

The Mellah

With under a dozen Jewish families remaining, **the Mellah** is a rather melancholic place. It has been resettled by Muslim emigrants from the countryside, though as with all of these old Jewish quarters you sense a slightly squatting (and stigmatised) air. The name *mellah* – 'salt' in Arabic – came to be used of Jewish ghettoes throughout Morocco, though it was originally applied only to this one at Fes; in derivation it seems to be a reference to the job given to the Fassi Jews of salting the heads of criminals before they were hung on the gates.

The enclosed and partly protected position of the Mellah fairly accurately represents the Moroccan Jews' historically ambivalent position. Arriving, for the most part, with compatriot Muslim refugees from Spain and Portugal, they were never fully accepted into the nation's life. Nor, though, were they quite the rejected people of other Arab countries. Within the Mellah they were under the direct protection of the Sultan (or the local Caid) and maintained their own law and governors. Whether the creation of a ghetto ensured the need for one is of course debatable. Certainly it was greatly to the benefit of the reigning Sultan, who could both depend on Jewish loyalties and manipulate the international trade and finance which came increasingly to be dominated by them in the C19. For all this importance to the Sultan, however, even the rich Jews had to lead incredibly circumscribed lives. In Fes before the French Protectorate no Jew was allowed to ride or even to wear shoes outside the Mellah, and they were severely restricted in their travel elsewhere.

Since the end of the Protectorate, when many of the poorer Jews here left to take up an equally ambivalent place at the bottom of Israeli society (though this time above the Arabs), memories of their presence have faded rapidly. What does remain are their C18 and C19 **houses** – immediately and conspicuously un-Arabic, with their tiny windows and elaborate ironwork. Cramped even closer together than in Fel el Bali, they are interestingly designed if you are offered a look inside. At some point too, it is worth weaving your way down towards the **Hebrew cemetery**, its neat white rounded gravestones restored to pristine condition as part of the UNESCO plan. There are two surviving **synagogues:** the *Fassiyin* (which is now a carpet workshop) and the *Serfati*, slightly grander but currently occupied by a Muslim family. If you take up a guide, offer a few dirhams and you may be able to see them both.

At the far end of the Mellah's main street – the **Grand Rue des Merenides** (or Grand Rue de Mellah) – you come into the **Place des Alaouites**, fronted by the new ceremonial gateway to the **Royal Palace**. In the 1970s it was sometimes possible to gain a permit to visit part of the palace grounds – described in Christopher Kininmonth's guide as 'the finest single sight Morocco has to offer . . . many acres in size and of a beauty to take the breath away'. This practice, however, seems unlikely to be restored under the present king, Hassan II, who divides most of his time between his palaces here and at nearby Ifrane.

The New Town and some practical details

By day at least, there's absolutely nothing to hold you in the **VILLE NOUVELLE**, the new town established by Lyautey at the beginning of the Protectorate. Unlike Casa or Rabat, where the French adapted Moroccan forms to create their own showplaces, this is a straightforward and rather dull European grid. It is, however, home to most faculties of the city's university, and is very much the business and commercial centre. If you want to talk with Fassis on a basis other than that of guide and tourist you'll stand most chance in the cafes here. It's more likely, too, that the *students* you meet are exactly that – rather than the 'friends' who want to walk with you, fare-meters rolling, in the Medina.

Cafes are plentiful throughout the Ville Nouvelle, with some of the most popular around the Place Mohammed V and in particular along the Av. Mohammed es Slaoui and Blvd Mohammed V (both of which run between the Place and the main Av. Hassan II). For **bars** – which are totally absent from Fes el Bali and Jdid – you have to look a little harder. There are a couple along the Av. Slaoui (the *Es Saada* here is usually lively); a rather pricier outdoor one at the *Hôtel Zalagh* swimming pool; and the somewhat seedy, but cheap *Dalilla* at 17 Blvd Mohammed V, its upstairs bar a place for serious Moroccan drinking.

Eating, too, is generally best in the New Town, though there are few restaurants which go any way towards justifying the city's reputation as the home of the country's most exotic cooking. Most places here serve fairly standard French-Moroccan food and you have to pay pretty heavily (see below) if you want the works. For a cheap, solid option try one of the handful of cafe-restaurants round by the municipal market – on the left-hand side of Blvd Mohammed V as you walk down from the Post Office. The Rue Kaid Ahmed, here, has two of the best: *Restaurant Chamonix* (at no.5) and *Casse-Croute Balkhaiat* (at 41). Moving a little upmarket there are two good restaurants on the Blvd Mohammed V itself, each with 'Moroccan salon' type decor and vaguely enterprising food: the *Voyageurs* (at 49) and *Roi de la Bière* (59). Along the Av. Slaoui there is another concentration – best of which is the once-famous (but now unlicensed) *Tour d'Argent* (no.40), where you still get considerable style and massive portions of food.

If you're **eating in Fes el Bali** there are two main areas: around Boujeloud, and along the Rue Hormis (which runs up from the Souk el Attarin towards the Bab Guissa: see p. 161). The places around Boujeloud have seen too many tourists to remain particularly good or cheap, though there is always plenty going on. *Restaurant Bouayad*, next to the Hotel Kaskades, is about the best there, with a good standby tajine; it's also open pretty much through the night. If your money doesn't run to a full meal you can get a range of snacks around Boujeloud, including chunks of *pastilla* from the stalls near the beginning of the Talaa Seghira: ask prices before you're served, they fluctuate considerably. In **Fes el Jdid** there are fewer – but much less touristy – places, most of them concentrated around the Bab Semmarine. The unnamed restaurant opposite the Hotel Moulay al Chrif is basic but quite wholesome.

For a real **Fassi banquet,** in an appropriate palace setting, you'll need to reckon on upwards of 60dhs a head. If you're interested try the *Dar Saada* (21 Souk el Attarin: see the Fes el Bali plan), where you can get a wonderful *pastilla* or (ordered in advance) *mechoui;* all their portions are vast and two people can do well by ordering one main dish and a plate of vegetables. The *Hôtel Palais Jamai* (up by the Bab Guissa) also has a distinguished restaurant, and with its terrace outside above the Medina there are few more stylish ways to spend an evening. Count on at least 80dhs each, though; and considerably more if you go the full course. Less ethereal, but with music and belly dancing, is the nearby *Restaurant Firadaous* (just below the gate); 45dhs buys admission and a drink here, 90dhs a full meal.

Listings

ARTISANIA Fes has a rightful reputation as the centre of Moroccan traditional crafts – but if you're buying rather than looking bear in mind that it also sees more tourists than any of its rivals. Rugs and carpets, however much you bargain, will probably come cheaper in Meknes, Midelt or Azrou; and although the brass, leather and cloth here is the best you'll find, you will need energy, humour and a lot of patience to stake a reasonable price. Fassi dealers are experts in intimidation techniques – making you feel an idiot for suggesting so low a price, jumping up and pushing you out of a shop, lulling you with mint tea and displays. All of this can be fun but you do need to develop a certain confidence and to have some idea of what you're buying and how much you should be paying. As a preliminary check on quality (which may put you off buying anything new at all) take a look round the *Dar Batha* museum; as a check on official prices (which are themselves on the high side) visit the state-run *Centre Artisenal* in the new town (on Blvd Allal Ben Abdallah: bottom left-hand corner of our plan).

BANKS Most are grouped along Blvd Mohammed V – including *Crédit du Maroc* (for VISA/Change). *SGMB* are at the junction of the Av. de France and Rue d'Espagne. Crédit du Maroc also have a branch in Fes el Bali, in the street above the Cherratin medressa.

BOOKS The *Librairie de l'Oasis* (68 Av. Hassan II; by the Pl. de Resistance) has a tremendous selection of English novels stocked for the Fes students, and a fair number of Islamic/African writers. *Librairie du Centre* (60 Blvd Mohammed V; near the Post Office) and the *Hôtel de Fes* (Av. des F.A.R.) can also be worth trying.

BUS STATIONS *CTM* operate services to Meknes, Casa, Rabat, Tangier, Chaouen, Ouezzane, Oujda and Marrakesh. Their main terminal is at the lower end of Blvd Mohammed V (see our plan), though some of the buses also call in at the Place Baghdadi near Boujeoud: check, and preferably buy tickets, in advance. *Buses for Azrou and Sefrou* leave from a small terminal known as 'Laghzani' near the CTM. *Private Buses* for Taza, Oujda, Al Hoceima, Ketama and Chaouen leave from a terminal at the *Bab Ftouh* (south-east corner of Fes el Bali); other private ones including those for Marrakesh, Midelt, Azrou and most of the CTM destinations, leave from the *Place Baghdadi* terminal, just above Boujeloud. For times and clarification call in at either of the tourist offices (see below).

CAR HIRE Fes has quite a number of hire companies, though none as cheap as the best deals in Casa. Phone round the following, all of whom allow return delivery to a different centre: *Zeit* (35 Av. Slaoui; tel. 236-81/255-10); *Transcar* (21 Rue Edouard Escalier; 217-76); *Avis* (23 Rue de la Liberté; 227-90); *Tourist Cars* (Grand Hôtel, Blvd Mohammed V; 229-58); *Hertz* (Hotel de Fes, Av. des F.A.R.; 228-12); or *Caravan Maroc* (21 Rue de la Liberté).

CAR REPAIRS Most of the garages are close to the centre of town, a few blocks out from the Place Mohammed V (whose auto-parts shops will point you to the right specialist for any given make). If you have problems, or want advice, contact either the *R.A.C. du Maroc* (Av. Hassan II) or the *Touring Club* (Rue de Beyreuth).

CITY BUSES Useful routes are detailed in the text but as a general guide these are the ones you're most likely to want to use:

no.1: Place des Alaouites – Dar Batha (by Bab Boujeloud).

no.2: Rue Escalier (below the Post Office) – Dar Batha.

no.3: Place des Alaouites – Place de la Résistance (Ville Nouvelle).

no.9: Place de la Résistance – Dar Batha.

no.10: Bab Guissa – Place des Alaouites.

no.18: Place de la Résistance – Bab Ftouh (via Rsif Mosque square).

no.19: Train station – Place des Alaouites.

Note that these numbers are marked on the side of the buses, not on the back.

CULTURAL EVENTS are relatively frequent, both Moroccan and French sponsored. Call in and ask for details at one of the tourist offices.

FESTIVALS The city's two big events are the *students moussem of Sidi Harazem* (Spring) and the *Moulay Idriss II moussem* (September). There are others locally if you can persuade the tourist office to look out their lists, make a couple of phonecalls and explain . . .

GUIDES See the comments on p. 140, and if you take an unofficial guide be wary. A favourite trick, here and elsewhere, is to take tourists deep into the Medina and, towards evening, disorientate them. You're guided out, of course, but possibly after agreeing on a more than generous payment for the privilege.

GRANDS TAXIS For *Sefrou* from the Place de l'Atlas (a block below the CTM station in the Ville Nouvelle); for *Meknes* from the Place des Alaouites (Fes el Jdid); for *Taza* from the Bab Ftouh.

MAPS You should find the plans that we've printed as functional as any that you can buy. The free *ONMT map* (on the back of their Fes pamphlet) is a useful complement, folding out to show how each of the three cities (*el Bali, Jdid* and *Ville Nouvelle*) relate.

MEDRESSAS are open daily, though not necessarily everyday and all day – depending on their *gardiens*. Most stay closed on Friday mornings. Standard – and compulsory – tip is 1dh each.

NEWSPAPERS British ones are sold at the *Hôtel de Fes bookshop* and at some of the stalls around Boulevard Mohammed V.

PETIT TAXIS on the whole use their meters, so they're very good value. Useful *ranks* include Place Mohammed V and the Post Office (in the Ville Nouvelle), Place des Alouites (Fes el Jdid); Place Baghdadi (by Boujeloud), Dar Batha, Bab Guissa, Mosque er Rsif square, and Bab Ftouh (all in Fes el Bali). After 9.30pm there's a 50% surcharge on top of the price registered on the meter.

PHARMACY Among numerous ones dotted about the Ville Nouvelle, there's an all-night *Pharmacie du Municipalite* just up from the Place de la Résistance on Blvd Moulay Youssef.

POLICE *Commissarat Central* is on Av. Mohammed V. Tel. 19.

POST OFFICE The main *PTT* is on the corner of Blvd Mohammed V/Av. Hassan II in the Ville Nouvelle (open summer 8-2; winter 8.30-12.00 & 2.30-6). *Poste restante* is next door to the main building; the *phones section* (open until 9pm) has a separate side entrance when the rest is closed.

SWIMMING POOLS Cheapest is the *Municipal Pool* (on the Av. des Sports, just west of the railway station; open mid-June until mid-September). For more space you can pay more to use the pool at the *Hôtel Zalagh* (close by the Youth Hostel), and if they're filled, the pools at the *Campsite*.

TOURIST OFFICES Most central is the *ONMT* on the Place de la Résistance; The *Syndicat d'Initiative* (where you can arrange an official guide) is halfway down towards the CTM on the Place Mohammed V. The ONMT is open Mon-Sat 8-12 & (not Sat.) 2-6; the Syndicat Mon-Sat 8-7pm.

TRAINS You'll find the railway station marked on our plan – 5mins walk from the centre of the Ville Nouvelle. Trains from Fes are useful for Tangier, Taza/Oujda, Meknes, Rabat, Casablanca and Marrakesh (for which you'll need to change at Casa). Try to avoid the *night train* to Marrakesh, which has gained a reputation for tourists having their baggage ripped off.

AROUND FES: SIDI HARAZEM AND SEFROU

It needs a definite sense of purpose to break out from the all-enveloping atmosphere of Fes's Medina. The countryside around – the foothills of the Middle Atlas – is pleasant but is easiest explored by car; local bus services can be laborious and daytrips something of an effort.

If you just want a quick escape from the city, the easiest option is to head off to the eucalyptus-covered oasis of **SIDI HARAZEM** – a shrine first made famous by the Sultan Moulay er-Rachid in the C17 and more recently as the home of Morocco's best selling mineral water. 15km from

Fes, it is served by frequent **buses** from the CTM station in the Ville Nouvelle and by private ones (and *grands taxis*) from the Bab Ftouh. Unfortunately, though, the oasis and its old thermal baths have been all but overwhelmed by the bottling factory and modern hotels which support the village's health industry, and it's crowded out right through the summer.

SEFROU, 28km (and an hour by bus) to the south, is an altogether more interesting proposition. A very ancient, walled town, this was the first stop on the caravan routes from Fes to the Tafilalt, and, up until the Protectorate, marked the mountain limits of the *Bled el Makhzen* – the governed lands. Into the 1950s it was also a predominantly Jewish town: there was an indigenous Jewish-Berber population here long before the coming of Islam and although subsequently converted a large number of Jews from the south again settled in the town under the Merenids. All of this made Sefrou a classic case study for post-war French anthropologists – who found a convenient contrast 8km to the north in BHALIL, a small village which has claims to pre-Islamic Christian origins and, more visibly, a number of troglodyte (cave) dwellings. If you're mobile it's worth a brief detour on your way from Fes: the village is signposted to the right 5km before Sefrou, the cave-houses are in the backlands behind, reached by a dirt track.

Although Sefrou itself is not a large place (pop. 40,000), its general layout is confusing. If you are coming in by bus the first stop is usually the **Place Moulay Hassan** – the main entrance to the Medina, whose walls (and two gates) you see below. Beyond, the road and most of the buses continue around a loop above the town and valley, crossing the river and straightening out onto the **Blvd Mohammed V**. This, as you'd expect, is the principal street of the New Town and contains all the usual facilities. On the right, about 300m along, is the **Post Office**, next door to which is the *Hôtel des Cerises*, the only cheap and central **place to stay** (though see below). Ask to be dropped here if possible – it'll save the kilometre's walk from the *place*. If you can afford it, there's an alternative choice (with a pool) halfway between the two: the 3* *Hôtel Sidi Lahcen Lyoussi*. Back by the bridge, as well, you'll find a sporadically open **Syndicat d'Initiative** in the isolated white building.

In many ways it's a pity that Sefrou's MEDINA is so close to Fes el Bali – in comparison with which it inevitably suffers. It is, though, on its own modest scale, equally well preserved, and the relaxed, untouristed atmosphere makes it a much more believable place to be in. The **Thurdsay souk**, for instance, remains very much a local affair, drawing Berbers from the neighbouring villages to sell their garden produce and buy up basic goods. The one time the town draws crowds is for the annual **Fête des Cerises** – the cherry festival, usually held in June and accompanied by various music and folklore events.

Enclosed by its C19 ramparts and split in two by the river, the **Medina** isn't difficult to find your way about. Coming from the post office/Blvd Mohammed V you can take a short cut down to the right of the road before you reach the bridge: the gate here, the **Bab Der Omar**, leads straight into the Mellah (or if you turn up to the left will bring you out eventually to the Place Moulay Hassan). The most straightforward approach, though, is through the **Bab M'Kam** in Place Moulay Hassan – on your left as you face the walls. Entering here you are on the main street of the old Arab town, which winds down to the river, passing through a region of **souks**, to emerge at the **Grand Mosque**. The souks include some impressive ironwork stalls and, reflecting the traditional Jewish heritage, a number of silversmiths.

The Mellah, a dark and cramped conglomeration of tall, heavily shuttered houses and tunnel-like streets, lies across the river from the Grand Mosque. It is today largely occupied by Muslims, though many of Sefrou's Jews only left for Israel after the June 1967 'Six-day war' and the quarter still seems very distinct. Over the years of the French Protectorate the Jews had become quite well off, owning good agricultural land around. But when most of the houses were built, in the mid C19, their condition must have been fairly miserable. Edith Wharton, visiting in 1917, found 'ragged figures . . . in black gabardines and skull-caps' living a family to a room in most of the mansions, and the alleys lit even at midday by oil lamps. 'No wonder', she concluded, '[that] the babies of the Moroccan ghettoes are nursed on date-brandy, and their elders doze away to death under its consoling spell.'

High enough into the Middle Atlas to avoid the dry summer heat of Fes, Sefrou's a place where you might actually want to walk. There are dozens of springs in the hills above the town and for at least part of the year there are active cascades. For a relatively easy target, take the road up behind the Post Office – which forks in two after about a kilometre. The right branch goes up to a semi-maintained **campsite** (signposted); the right to a small French-built fort (known as *Prioux*) and the **Koubba of Sidi Boualserghin**. At the *koubba* a strange annual *moussem* takes place involving the ritual sacrifice of a black hen and a white cock. Close by, with a cool and tremendous view over the valley, is the *Hôtel-Café Boualserghin* – a cheap, attractive but somewhat remote option. Another possible walk is up in the hills above the river, a path followed by the **Rue de la Kelaa** (just before the bridge, coming from the Post Office). There are gorges, caves and waterfalls in this direction (for which the Syndicat may be able to give more detailed directions or suggest a guide).

Moving on **south from Sefrou** can be a frustrating business. There is no bus direct to AZROU or MIDELT and the *grands taxis* travel only the routes to Fes and the military garrison town of BOULEMANE. The simplest solution is probably to backtrack to Fes, or to come out here for the day: though if you can muster a group of people you might be able to persuade a taxi driver to take you over to IMMOUZER DU KANDAR (see below), over the mountainous **Massif du Kandar** (piste 4620; 34km). This, if you've a car, is definitely a tempting option, though check out the state of the road with the Syndicat before setting out – in winter it can be impassable. The P4620 turns off from the Midelt road 12km after Sefrou, climbing up into the hills around the Djebel Abad (1768m) before descending to Immouzer. If you reckon your car can make it – or you feel like walking – there's a rough track almost to the summit of the mountain (4km each way), to the right of the road 10km down the P4620.

THE MIDDLE ATLAS

Heading south from Fes most people take a bus straight to **Marrakesh** or to **Er Rachidia**, beginning of the great desert and *ksour* routes. Both, however, involve some 10-12hrs continous travel, which in summer at least is reason enough to break the journey. The additional lure, if you've time (or ideally a car), is getting off the main routes and up into the mountains. Covered in forests of oak, cork and giant cedars, the **Middle Atlas** is a surprising part of the country which few tourists get to explore. The brown-black tents of nomadic Berber encampments immediately establish a shift from the European north, the plateaus are pock-marked by dark volcanic lakes, and at **Ouzoud** and **Oum er Rbia** there are spectacular waterfalls.

You will probably hear that it's difficult to stop en route to Marrakesh, many of the **buses** arriving and leaving full. But though this is true to an extent, taking the occasional *grand taxi* or stopping over a night to catch a dawn bus you shouldn't find yourself stuck for long. Along the Fes-Azrou-Midelt-Er Rachidia route, buses are no problem.

IMMOUZER DU KANDAR, IFRANE AND THE MISCHLIFFEN

The first hills of the Middle Atlas, rising from the plains about Fes, seem perversely un-Moroccan: at Ifrane the king has a summer palace, at Mischliffen there's a ski-centre, and the road up to both of them is almost ceremonial.

Just under an hour by bus from Fes, **IMMOUZER DU KANDAR** is slightly more mundane – a one-road, one-square kind of place where the

Fassis come up to swim and picnic, and spend a few days. There are a handful of cheap **hotels** if you feel like doing the same: the 1*A *Hôtel des Truites*, near the beginning of town, is probably the best, with a bar and restaurant; slightly cheaper is the *Hôtel du Centre* right beside the bus stop. The municipal **swimming pool**, too, is near the centre – open from mid-June to mid-September and filled, like everything here, with a natural spa-water. There's a famous **restaurant**, the *Auberge de Chambotte;* a small Monday **souk**; and a July **festival**, the *Fête de Pommes*, which takes in a number of music and dance events. Otherwise, the main thing to do is to get a lift (or the Ifrane bus) up to the **Dayet Aouwa** – a beautiful freshwater lake just to the left of the Ifrane road, 9km to the south. You can camp around the lakeside here, and float about in pedal-boats run by the 2*A *Chalet du Lac* – the one source of rooms, meals and drink.

With a car it's possible to reach Ifrane by following the track (4628) up behind the Dayet Aouwa, looping round to the right past another lake (Dayet Ifrah) before joining the last section of the road in from Boulemane. By bus the approach is simpler, the main road climbing through more and more dense shafts of forest before emerging in a bizarre clearing of pseudo-Alpine chalets and broad suburban streets. This – created in 1929 – is **IFRANE**, a deliberate 'poche de France' whose affluent villas have now been taken over by the Moroccan government ministries and the wealthier bourgeoisie. For the average traveller there's not a lot going here beside a certain ironic insight and a glimpse of the Royal Hunting Lodge across the valley. If you're into **ski-ing**, though, and here between January and March, this is the main base for the slopes of the Mischliffen: there are taxis up to the *refuge/club* (food, drink, no accommodation) and *ski-lifts*, and you can hire equipment in town from the *Café-Restaurant Chamonix*. The rest of the year, Ifrane's cool air and excellent **swimming pool** are the main attractions. If you find yourself stranded here – which, with four buses daily to Azrou and Fes, is unlikely – finding a **room** can be a problem. Besides the *youth hostel* (which may or may not be open: ask at the Syndicat in the centre of town), the only cheap place is the 1*A *Hôtel Tilleuls*, which in midsummer (and in the ski season) is frequently full. A summer alternative, though again somewhat upmarket, is the **Camping**, signposted just off the principal street through the town. There is nowhere to stay, or to eat, in the 'Medina quarter' of Ifrane, a drab modern estate built at some distance from the villas to house the resort's domestic servants and workers.

Ski-ing aside, **MISCHLIFFEN** has nothing to draw you – it is merely a low bowl in the mountains, enclosed all about by more cedar forests. There's no village and few buildings, though there is said to be a brothel. French *Michelin* readers rather manically charge up here as an excursion: if one offers you a lift, try to dissuade them.

AZROU

AZROU, the first real town of the Middle Atlas, stands at a major junction of routes – north to Meknes and Fes, south to Khenifra and Midelt. As you might expect, it's an important market centre (the main souk is held on Tuesday) and it has long held a strategic role in the control of the mountain Berbers. Moulay Ismail built a kasbah here, remains of which survive, while more recently the French established a prestigious high school – the *College Berbère* – as part of their attempt to split the country's Berbers from the urban Arabs. The college, still a dominant building in the town, provided many of the Protectorate's interpreters, local administrators and military officers, but in spite of its ban on Arabic and any manifestation of Islam the policy proved a failure. Azrou graduates played a significant role in the Nationalist Movement – and were uniquely placed to do so, as a new French-created elite. Since Independence, however, their influence has been slight outside of the army; many of the Berber student activists followed Mehdi Ben Barka's ill-fated socialist UNFP party (see p. 315).

Arriving at the town the most immediate feature is a massive outcrop of rock – the *Azrou* from which it takes name. By bus you are dropped just in front of this at the end of the main square, **Place Mohammed V**. The best of the cheap **hotels**, the 1*A *Hôtel des Cèdres* is here; or you can walk round the corner into a smaller adjacent square where you'll find the more basic *Hôtel Ziz* and *Hôtel Beausejour*. There are cheap **foodstalls** around the bus station, an erratic **restaurant** in the *Cèdres* and a bar/restaurant right next door – *Le Relais Forestier* (whose meals can be pricey). An alternative place to stay, quiet but slightly out of town, is the *Auberge de Jeunesse:* to get there walk back out towards the crossroads to Fes and Midelt, it's about 1km uphill on the left.

If you can manage to do so, much the best time to be in Azrou is for the **Tuesday market**, which draws in Berbers from all the surrounding mountain villages. It's held a little above the main part of town – just follow the crowds up to a separate quarter across the valley. The fruit and vegetable stalls spread over the principal area and at first seem to be all that there is: look up, though, and you'll see a stretch of wasteland (usually manned by musicians or storytellers), beyond which is a smaller section for carpets, textiles and general goods. The carpet stalls, not particularly geared towards tourists, can turn up some beautiful items, reasonably (if not exactly bargain) priced. For a modern selection – including high quality heavy wool rugs – take a look, too, at the **Cooperative artisanale** (open daily 8.30-12.00 & 2.30-6.00), back at the Place Mohammed V, to the left of the rock. This is one of the best craft cooperatives in the country, and a considerable contrast to the usual tourist-shop tat. In addition to the rugs, bright geometric designs based on the traditional patterns of the Beni M'Guild tribe, there is impressive cedarwood and stone carving.

There is little else to do in the town, though you can spend a good day clambering about the hills (which again have seasonal springs) or wandering down to the river, reputedly well stocked with trout. Local guides tout the cedar forest and above all a very ancient tree known as the **Cèdre Gouraud**: if this appeals, it's a 14km hike or taxi-ride – 8km up the Midelt road and then down a signposted track to the left. Stopping off for a respite from the Fes-Marrakesh/Midelt journey, you may find the **swimming pool** (behind the rock and main square) equally tempting.

Azrou has two **bus stations**, both of them in the Place Mohammed V. Between them, there are some five runs a day to Midelt, Er Rachidia and Rissani, and it's not usually a problem to get a bus to Fes (or, less frequently, to Meknes). For Marrakesh you should ask around and try to buy tickets the night before you want to leave: several of the buses tend to arrive full, though there is one (currently leaving at 4am, arriving Marrakesh 10.30-11am) which starts at Azrou. Around the other side of the rock there is a **grand taxi** rank, with routine departures for Ifrane and Fes, sporadic (but possible) ones for Khenifra.

Ain Leuh and the Cascades of Oum er Rbia

Directly south of Azrou lies some of the most remote and beautiful country of the Middle Atlas – at its heart the magnificent cascades of Oum er Rbia, source of Morocco's greatest river. There's a daily bus from Azrou to Ain Leuh, 30km along this route, but beyond this (over the most interesting section) you're down to *pistes*, feasible only with a car. Even then it's an adventurous run, boggy and impassable in the winter months.

AIN LEUH (17km down the main Khenifra road; then left for 13km on the paved S303) is a large Berber village, typical of the Middle Atlas with its flat-roofed houses tiered above a valley. As at Azrou there are ruins of a kasbah built by Moulay Ismail, and there are springs (with a more or less year-round cascade/fountain) up in the hill behind. Market day here is basically Wednesday, though it can spread out a day in either direction as the weekly gathering point of the Beni M'Guild tribe – still semi-nomadic in this region, camping out beside their flocks in heavy, dark tents. As a colonial *zone d'insécurité*, this part of the Atlas was relatively undisturbed by French settlers and the traditional balance between pasture and forest has largely remained.

The track towards the Oum er Rbia, partially surfaced along its initial stretch, begins just before you reach Ain Leuh and should be signposted 'AGUELMANE AZIGZA/KHENIFRA'. It runs for the most part through mountain forest, where you sometimes see groups of monkeys – indigenous to the Middle Atlas and ancestors of the famous apes of

Gibraltar. There is a small lake, **Lac Ouiouane**, to the left of the road about 20km out of Ain Leuh, whilst at the 33km mark you reach a sizeable **bridge** above the **Oum er Rbia river**. The traditional barrier between north and south, this eventually reaches the sea at Azzemour, near El Jadida. Its source is just a 15min walk down the footpath to your left: a fabulous spray of over forty **cascades**, shooting out from an enormous limestone cliff. The basin below, sculpted by the rapids, looks enticing – though be warned that the currents here are extremely strong.

On past the bridge a number of tracks lead off to either side of the main piste. Keep straight (which initially means left) and you should in about 18km reach a turning left to the previously signposted **Aguelmane Azigza** – a dark, very deep and extremely poisonous lake 2km from the road. Pressing on (ignoring the turning) there is a larger junction of pistes about 3km beyond. Off to the left a very rough track climbs up into the heart of the mountains, emerging eventually on the road to Midelt. Unless you're into landrover exploration, however, keep to the right-hand track, which reaches KHENIFRA in a further 24km. If it doesn't – and you feel you've gone wrong somewhere – you want to head west, the general direction of sunset if the day's fading about you.

MIDELT AND THE ROUTE TO ER RACHIDIA

If you're travelling the southern circuits of the *ksour* and kasbahs of the sub-Sahara, you're almost certain to cover this route in one or other direction. It's 125km from Azrou to Midelt and a further 154km on to Er Rachidia: quite possible distances for a single bus journey or a day's driving, but much more satisfying taken in a couple of stages. You cross passes over both the Middle and High Atlas ranges, catch a first glimpse of the south's extraordinary *pisé* architecture and end up in the desert.

Climbing out of AZROU, the road follows a magnificent stretch of the **Middle Atlas**, winding through the pine and cedar forests around the town to emerge at the river valley of the *Oued Gigou*, the view ahead taking in some of the range's highest peaks. By bus you've little alternative but to head straight to Midelt, which you reach in around 2hrs. With a car, though, there are two very brief and worthwhile detours. 52km from Azrou, as the road levels out onto a strange volcanic plateau littered with dark pumice rocks, there's a turning to the left marked '**Aguelmane Sidi Ali**'. This is a mountain lake, the largest of many formed in the extinct craters of this region. It's only a kilometre from the road – long, still and eerily beautiful. Beyond a marabout's tomb on the far shore (from which the lake takes its name) and perhaps a shepherd's tent and flock, there is unlikely to be anything or anyone in sight; if you can improvise a fishing rod, there are reputed to be shoals of trout, pike and perch. The other point you may want to leave the road is 24km further on, just before the junction with the old road (and caravan route) from Sefrou and Boulemane. 6km off to the right here is the small village of **ITZER**, whose **market** remains one of the most important in the region. Held on Mondays and Thursdays, it can (like Midelt) be a good source of local Berber rugs and carpets.

At **MIDELT**, approached through a bleak plain of scrub and desert, you have left the Middle Atlas behind. Suddenly, though, through the haze, appear the much greater peaks of the High Atlas – rising sheer behind the town to a massive range, the *Djebel Ayachi*, at over 3,700m. The drama of this site, tremendous in the clear, cool evenings, is probably the most compelling reason to stop over: for the town itself initially looks rather drab, a one-street affair with a couple of cafes and hotels and a small souk. In fact it's a very pleasant place to stay – partly because so few people do, partly as the first place you become aware of the much more relaxed southern atmosphere. There are foodstalls and a cheap unnamed **hotel** by the bus station (midway through the town); another, the *Hôtel Excelsior* (with a rather stylish *brasserie/bar*), back about 50m on the Azrou road; and a third (the *Roi de la Bière*) near the **campsite** a kilometre or so out in the other direction towards Er Rachidia. The most interesting section of town, however, and well worth at least a stop between buses, is the old souk – the **Souk Jdid** – off behind the stalls opposite the bus station. This is exclusively a **carpet market**, the wares slung out in rotation in the sunlight (for natural bleaching) and piled up in bewildering layers of pattern and colour in the various shops behind. It's a laid-back sort of place, startlingly so after Fes, and one of the best places to buy rugs or carpets anywhere in the country. Most of those here are local – bright, closely woven geometric designs from tribes of both the Middle and High Atlas. Ask to see the 'antique' ones – few are more than ten or twenty years old but they are usually the most idiosyncratic and inventive.

More carpets – and traditionally styled blankets and textiles – can be seen or bought at the **Atelier de tissage** run by a group of French Franciscan nuns in a convent just off to the left of the road to **Tattiouine** (signposted *Cirque Jaffar*, first right after the bus station). If you follow this road a while further – two or three kilometres is enough – you find yourself in a countryside quite different to that around Midelt, with eagles wheeling above the hills and mule tracks leading down to valleys and an occasional kasbah. There are more ambitious walks up into the Djebel Ayachi, if you get a taxi to take you up to the village of Tattiouine.

The most adventurous possibility at Midelt, however, is the **Cirque Jaffar** road – a very poor piste, practicable only in dry weather, which leaves the Tattiouine road to edge its way through a kind of hollow in the foothills of the Ayachi. If you're mobile there's a classic route around the Cirque, which loops back to the Midelt-Azrou road after 34km (turn right, onto the 3426, near the *maison forestière de Mitkane*); this is only 79km all in all back to Midelt, though it'll take you a good half day to get round. Alternatively – and highly recommended by a couple of hikers I met – you can continue along the *Cirque* track right **over the backbone of the Atlas**, eventually reaching ARHBALA and EL KSIBA (see p. 267) or IMILCHIL (see p. 269). Along this route you don't necessarily need a car, for as long as you have the time it's possible to get Berber trucks (for which you pay as if they're buses) over the various stages. Bear in mind, though, that you'll be largely dependent on the patterns of local markets and reckon on three, perhaps four days up to Imilchil, and a similar number from there down to the fabulous TODRHA GORGE and TINERHIR (see p. 265). It will help, too, if you decide that for at least part of the way you're going to walk. If, incidentally, you set out to walk the whole way you might want to acquire one of the two French *CAF hiking guides* which detail the whole zone between Midelt and the Toukbal massif, and will certainly want some of the *Carte de Maroc* national grid sheets.

There's less adventure in continuing the journey **south from Midelt to Er Rachidia** though it is still a memorable route, marking as it does the transition to the south and the sub-Sahara. You cross one of the lower passes of the High Atlas, the **Tizi n'Talrhmeht** (*Pass of the She-camel*) some 30km beyond Midelt, descending to what is essentially a desert plain. At AIT MESSAOUD, just beyond the pass, there's an old, thoroughly Beau Geste-like military fort, and a few kilometres further on you come upon the first southern *ksar*, AIT KHERROU, a river oasis at the entrance to a small gorge. After this the *ksour* – plural form for these high-walled fortified villages – begin to dot the landscape as the road follows the path of the great Ziz river. En route there is a possible, if distinctly Quixotic, prospect for a stopover at **RICH**: a small, inappropriately named market town which is approached from the main road by a vast and bizarre red-washed esplanade. Utterly desolate, with mountains stretching off into the distance, this seems a perfect stage for some fatalistic gesture. Staying here would probably be enough. On a more prosaic level, the *piste* behind the town (trailing the last section of the Ziz) offers an alternative approach to IMILCHIL – less dramatic than that from Midelt but said to be passable for most of the year.

One last highlight. 25km on from the Rich turning, and 54km before Er Rachidia, begins the **Ziz gorge** – a tremendous, Gothic piece of erosion that cuts its way through a final stretch of the Atlas. Impressive at any time of day, it's unbelievably majestic in the late afternoon with great blocks of light shining through the valleys. ER RACHIDIA (see p. 271) sprawls out ahead as you emerge, past a huge dammed reservoir. Unless you arrive late in the day you'll probably want to press straight on from here to MESKI (p. 272) or ERFOUD (p. 273).

TOWARDS MARRAKESH: THE ROUTES FROM AZROU AND THE CASCADES D'OUZOUD

The main route from Azrou to Marrakesh, the P24, is an unusually dull one. It skirts well clear of the mountains, while the towns along the way – hot, dusty, functional market centres – are unlikely to tempt you to linger. Once again, for any contact with the Middle Atlas you're going to have to leave the road and take to the pistes. A great network of them spread out behind the small town of EL KSIBA, itself 8km off the P24 but easily hitched from the turning or reached by bus from KASBA TADLA.

It is unlikely that you'll be stranded in **KHENIFRA** and difficult to think of any other reason to stay. A small town, for all its prominence on the maps, it springs into occasional life with the weekly souks (Wednesdays and Sundays); otherwise there's not much going. If you're following this chapter in reverse (from Marrakesh) note that you can approach the Cascades of Oum er Rbia (see p. 176) from here. If you've just done this, or plan to do so, there's a particularly gloomy hotel by the CTM station at the end of the town, or a couple of rather more enticing ones (each with restaurants) down by the river – the *Voyageurs* and *France*.

EL KSIBA, a sizeable and busy Berber village, is again no great target in itself – though the approach up here, hemmed in by thick woods, is a promise of the countryside beyond. There's quite an attractive small hotel, the 2*B *Hostelerie Henri IV*, on a kind of ring road which bypasses the main part of the village. But if you arrive here in the morning you should be able to get a bus straight on to **ARHBALA** (it leaves currently at 9.30am and 1.30pm), another important market village, at the beginning of the piste to MIDELT. If you are heading for IMILCHIL and the PLATEAU DES LACS (see p. 267) you can either try and get a lorry here (most likely on a Wednesday when Arhbala has its souk, or Saturday for Imilchil's) or chance your luck by getting dropped at the Imilchil turning – 50km from El Ksiba and 13km before Arhbala. The usual route from the turning to Imilchil – see the map on p. 266 – goes via the villages of CHERKET and TASSENT; there's a Berber truck-bus along each stage at least every other day.

Created by Moulay Ismail, and taking name from a fortress which he built here, **KASBA TADLA** is much the most interesting town on the direct route to Marrakesh. It is not perhaps worth a special detour: however, if you're mobile or between buses, take time and look around. The kasbah is only a few blocks from the bus station – a massive, crumbling quarter whose palace and even mosque have lapsed into dereliction, their shells squatted by small farmholdings and cottages. It owed its original importance – as did Khenifra – to the site beside the Oum er

Rbia river. Ismail, the first Sultan since the Almoravids to impose order on the whole country, billeted here a considerable garrison of Sudanese troops.

There are two cheap **hotels** right by the bus station in Kasba Tadla, and another, the spacious and friendly *Hôtel des Alliés*, just around the corner. And given the choice, this is really a more pleasant place to stop a night than the larger, modern town of **BENI MELLAL**, market town for the broad, prosperous flatlands to its south. Beni Mellal, though, is the base for setting out to the Cascades d'Ouzoud, and it does have a very considerable **Friday market** (good for blankets, sold here with unusual designs). If you're staying, there are a couple of cheapish **hotels** just up the road from the bus station in the 'New Medina': the unclassified *Hôtel Afrique* and (with a lively and rather seedy bar) the 1*A *Hôtel de Paris*. The town's kasbah, again built by Moulay Ismail, is much restored and of no great interest. If you want to fill out an evening though – and evenings here do need filling out – you can walk up to the smaller, ruined **Kasbah de Ras el Ain**, set above the gardens, and the spring of **Ain Asserdoun**, to the south of the town.

The **CASCADES D'OUZOUD** are a long and rather tricky detour from the Beni Mellal-Marrakesh road – a good half-day's journey if you're going by local bus and taxi. But there are few places in Morocco so enjoyable and easy-going, and in midsummer it's incredible to come upon the cool here, the springs crashing down amid a great drop of dark red rocks and thickets of lush-green trees and vegetation, flocks of birds wheeling above. There is a small **hotel-cafe**, just beside the road as you arrive, but much more attractive are two makeshift **campsites** (open March-September) on trellis-covered terraces poised right above the springs. There's not much commercialisation beyond this, though both campsites sell drinks and cook meals and there are a series of posted trails down to the valley and to the great basins below the cascades. You can swim in one of these – a tremendous natural pool, and if you don't mind the occasional monkey (still quite a common sight in this stretch of hills) could pitch a tent under the oaks and pomegranates alongside.

Getting to Ouzoud (which, beside the spring, consists only of a few houses) involves taking a bus or *grand taxi* from Beni Mellal to AFOURER, at the beginning of the secondary route to Marrakesh. Here, you can take a *grand taxi* (or very long bus ride) to the roadside village of AZILAL (63km) and bargain for another to Ouzoud itself. When you come to leave, you will probably be able to fix a lift (with other tourists) back to Beni Mellal/Azilal or even on to Demnate or Marrakesh. There is also a very poor piste which goes beyond Ouzoud to rejoin the main Marrakesh road at El Khemis des Oulad Ayad: you might be able to hitch this way but there are no regular buses.

On the way from Beni Mellal to Azilal the road climbs almost sheer from the plain, zigzagging through the hills and crossing an immense dammed lake at **BIN EL OUIDANE** (where there's a small 1*A **hotel**, the *Auberge du Lac*, with a bar, restaurant and river fishing/swimming, and a **campsite**. One of the earliest (1948-55) and most ambitious of the country's irrigation schemes, the barrage has changed much of the land around Beni Mellal – formerly as dry and barren as the phosphate plains to its west – and provides much of central Morocco's electricity.

If you've read Ernst Gellner's *Saints of the Atlas* (see p. 327), you might be tempted by one of the pistes up towards the village of **ZAOUIA AHANESAL** – centre of a still remote region, populated in part by transhumant shepherds who bring their flocks up here in summer from the oases beyond the mountains. There are two possible approaches. At the Bin el Ouidane a small road turns off to OUAOUIZARNT, crosses to the south of the lake and then gives out into an extremely rough track, practicable only by jeep or truck: this winds through the mountains for some 70km before reaching Ahanesal, passing (after 40km) the ZAOUIA TEMGA, above which are strange rock formations shaped like a Gothic cathedral (and known as such – *la cathédrale des rochers*). Alternatively – and rather easier – there's a track south-east of AZILAL to the village of AIT MEHAMMED and on to TAMDA, which joins the piste running south from Ahanesal. Continuing straight across the Atlas from Ait Mehammed, a difficult *piste* leads to the Bou Goumez valley – a possible walking/climbing base for the 4000m peaks of the **Irhil M'Goun**, the highest in Morocco outside the Toubkal massif. Some details of this, and of rock-climbing around the Zaouia Ahanesal, are given in Robin Collomb's very helpful *Atlas Mountains* guide.

Having come as far as Azilal and the Cascades, it is easier to carry on along this secondary road to Marrakesh – in any case the more interesting – rather than to try and cut back onto the main route from Beni Mellal. You will probably have to change buses along the way at **DEMNATE**, a walled market town whose **Sunday souk** is by far the largest in the region and an interesting, unaffected event with which to coincide. It is held just outside the ramparts, the stalls sprawling up into the townstreets with their secondhand goods and clothes and great piles of fresh vegetables and fruit. There is a small **hotel** here, close by the bus station, and if you've time or transport a track above the town climbs up in 6½km to a curious-looking natural bridge – the **Imi n'Ifri**. Close beside a series of springs, which account for the Demnate valley's prosperous and intense cultivation, this is the site of a large *moussem* held two weeks after the Aid el Kebir.

The land between Demnate and Marrakesh is generally poor and stony, distinguished only by a sporadic outcrop of farmsteads or shepherd huts. If you take the bus it may follow either of the routes to Marrakesh – via Tamelelt (where you rejoin the P24) or, a perfectly well-surfaced road, via Tazzerte and Sidi Rahhal. Given the choice, go for the latter. An old Glaoui village, **TAZZERTE** is fronted by four crumbling kasbahs from which the clan (see p. 234 for their history) used to control the region and the caravan routes to the north. There is a small Monday market held here, and a larger one on Fridays at **SIDI RAHHAL**, 7km on. Sidi Rahhal, named after its marabout, is also a point of considerable local pilgrimage and host to an important week-long *moussem* (flexible summertime date). The saint in whose honour the festivities take place has an unusual Judaeo-Muslim tradition. He seems to have lived in the C15 but the stories told about him are all timeless in their evocations of magic and legend. The most popular record his power to conduct himself and other creatures through the air – a gift which led to a minor incident with the Koutoubia minaret in Marrakesh, whose upper storey one of his followers is supposed to have knocked off with his knee.

Coming into Marrakesh from either Demnate or Beni Mellal you skirt round part of the huge **palmery** which encloses the northern walls of the city. Arriving by bus you will almost certainly find yourself at the main **bus station** by the Bab Doukkala – 10mins walk from the centre of the Gueliz (or New Town), 20mins (or an 8-10dh taxi ride) from the Place Djemaa el Fna and the Medina.

TRAVEL DETAILS

Trains
Fes-Meknes 7 daily in each direction (around 45mins).
Fes-Rabat/Casablanca 6 daily in around 4½-5hrs/6hrs; all via Meknes, Sidi Kacem (2¼hrs), Kenitra (3½hrs) and Salé (4hrs).
Fes-Taza/Oujda 4 daily 2-2¼hrs/5¾-6hrs.
Fes-Tangier 3 daily in around 6hrs; all via Meknes, Sidi Kacem (3½hrs), and Asilah (5hrs).
Fes/Meknes-Marrakesh 3 daily via Marrakesh in around 11½hrs/10¾hrs.

Buses
From Meknes Fes (hourly; 50mins); Larache/Tangier (2 daily; 5½hrs/7hrs); Rabat (3; 4hrs); Ouezzane (2; 4hrs); Chaouen (1; 5½hrs); Azrou (4; 3½hrs); Midelt (1; 5½hrs); Beni Mellal/ Marrakesh (1; 6hrs/9hrs).
From Fes Chaouen (2; 7hrs); Larache/Tangier (2; 6½hrs/8hrs); Rabat (6; 5½hrs); Casa (8; 7hrs); Taza (3; 2½hrs); Al Hoceima (1; 11½hrs); Sefrou (3; 1½hrs); Immouzer/Ifrane (5; 1hr/ 1½hrs); Azrou (5; 3½hrs): Midelt/Er Rachidia (3; 5½hrs/8½hrs); Beni Mellal/Marrakesh (3; 8½hrs/11hrs).
From Azrou Ifrane/Immouzer (4 daily; 1hr/1½hrs); Midelt/Er Rachidia (5; 2hrs/5hrs); Khenifra/Kasba Tadla/Beni Mellal/Marrakesh (3; 3hrs/4hrs/ 4½hrs/7hrs).
From Kasba Tadla El Ksiba (3 daily; 20mins); Beni Mellal (4; 1hr).
From Beni Mellal Demnate (4 daily; 3hrs); Marrakesh (6; 6hrs).

Grands Taxis
From Meknes Regularly to Fes (40mins) and Volubilis/Moulay Idriss (35mins).
From Fes Regularly to Meknes, Sefrou (1hr), Immouzer/Ifrane (1hr20/1hr40) and Taza (1hr40).
Other **local and Middle Atlas** routes specified in the text.

Flights
From Fes Daily to Casablanca (and thence to Marrakesh etc).

Chapter five
MARRAKESH, THE HIGH ATLAS AND THE WEST COAST

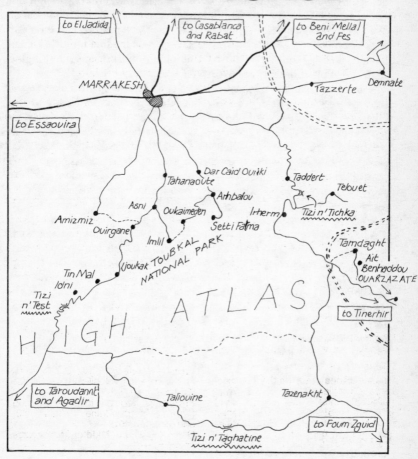

to El Jadida

to Casablanca and Rabat

to Beni Mellal and Fes

MARRAKESH

Tazzerte

Demnate

to Essaouira

Dar Caid Ouriki

Taddert

Telouet

Tahanaoute

Asni

Oukaimeden

Arhbalou

Irherm

Tizi n'Tichka

Amizmiz

Ouirgane

Setti Fatma

Imlil

Tamdaght

Ujoukak TOUBKAL NATIONAL PARK

Ait Benhaddou

OUARZAZATE

Tin Mal

Idni

Tizi n'Test

H I G H   A T L A S

to Tinerhir

to Taroudannt and Agadir

Taliouine

Tazenakht

to Foum Zguid

Tizi n'Taghatine

Marrakesh – Morocco City as the early travellers called it – has always been something of a pleasure city, a marketplace where the southern tribesmen and Berber villagers bring in their goods, spend their money and find entertainment. For tourists it's an enduring fantasy – a city of immense beauty, low, pink and tentlike before a great shaft of mountains, and immediately exciting. At the heart of it all is a square, the **Djemaa el Fna,** really no more than an open space in the centre of the city, but a long established ritual where shifting circles of onlookers gather about groups of acrobats, drummers and pipe musicians, dancers, story-tellers and comedians. However many times you come it remains compelling – as too do the city's architectural attractions: the immense, still basins of the **Agdal** and **Menara** parks, the delicate Granadine carving of the **Saadian tombs,** and above all the **Koutoubia minaret,** for me the most perfect Islamic monument in North Africa.

Some 40km south of Marrakesh rise the **High Atlas,** the highest and the most rewarding Moroccan range. You can reach its foothills and lush **Ourika valley** in just an hour's ride by bus or *grand taxi*, or inside a morning can leave the city and get up to the village and hiking centre of **Imlil** where trails begin for **Djebel Toubkal** – at 4165m the tallest Atlas peak and one of the loftiest in Africa. To explore the massif you don't have to be a serious climber; there are well-established walking trails to *refuge* huts. It is too a surprisingly populated region: the slopes drop away to valleys and streams, small Berber villages (where you can usually stay) terraced at their sides.

The remoteness of these mountain villages – easily maintained despite the growing popularity of trekking – is reflected also in the two High Atlas passes, the *tizis* n'Test and n'Tichka. **Tizi n'Test,** the pass beyond Toubkal over to Taroudannt, is the steepest: a crazy, adrenalin-plugged switchback of almost continuous hairpin bends. If you drive this road be aware of what's in store – it's pretty alarming even by bus. On the way, however, are definite attractions. You can stop over in **Idni,** virtually at the summit, and backtrack to the dramatic valley and C12 mosque ruins of **Tin Mal,** the base from which the Almohads swept down to take Marrakesh and ultimately to reconquer Spain. The **Tizi n'Tichka,** which today takes most of the traffic, has a more recent but equally evocative history. The old caravan route to Tafilalt, it was controlled over the last century and for much of the present by the legendary Glaoui family, 'the Lords of the Atlas'. Their kasbah, a bizzare cluster of crumbling towers and kitsch 1930s reception halls, is still to be seen at **Telouet,** just an hour from the main road.

From Marrakesh you are also within a couple of hour's bus ride of **the coast.** This for most travellers means **Essaouira,** an extremely laid-back resort popularised in the 1960s by, among others, Jimi Hendrix and Cat Stevens, and a target for all the *Marrakesh Express* hippies. Nearly twenty years on, it's not far different – enjoyable, slightly ramshackle and with a tremendous sweep of beach. The one disadvantage, here more than usual on the Atlantic coast, is the wind, which for much of the year is remorseless. At **Oualidia** and **El Jadida** it's less of a problem, and these have become quite sophisticated resorts – the favoured choice of *Marrakchis* and popular too with people from Casablanca. Even at Jadida, however, it's all pretty low key, and there's still only one high rise hotel at the edge of town.

MARRAKESH AND AROUND

MARRAKESH (MARRAKECH, MARRAKCH)

Unlike Fes – so long its rival as the nation's capital – **MARRAKESH** exists very much in the present. Its population is rising (and stands today at perhaps half a million), it has a thriving industrial quarter and remains the most important market and administrative centre of southern Morocco. None of this is to suggest a bland prosperity – there is heavy unemployment here, as throughout the country, and intense poverty – but travelling through you leave with a predominant impression of life and activity. And for once this doesn't apply exclusively to the new town, *Gueliz;* the *Medina,* part-ruin at the beginning of this century, was renewed and expanded over the years of French rule and retains no less significant a role in the modern city.

Indeed the Koutoubia excepted, it is not a place of great monuments, gaining its beauty and pull in the whole atmosphere and situation – the latter really spectacular with the tallest, sheerest peaks of the Atlas stacked hard behind the town and towering through the haze. The feel, as much as anything, is a product of this. Marrakesh is a Berber rather than an Arab city: the traditional metropolis of Atlas tribes, Mahgrebis from the plains, Saharan nomads, and of former slaves from Africa beyond the desert – from the Sudan, Senegal and the ancient kingdom of Timbuctou. All of these strands have shaped the souks and the way of life, and in the crowds and performers of the Djemaa el Fna they can still occasionally seem distinct.

The original **foundation** of the city is disputed, though it was certainly close to the onset of **Almoravid** rule – around 1062-70 – and must have taken the initial form of a camp and market, a *ksour* or fortified town gradually developing roundabout. Its founder (as that of the Almoravid

dynasty) was **Youssef bin Tachfine,** a restless military leader who conquered northern Morocco within two years and then turned his attention
towards Spain, defeating the Christian kings to bring Andalusia under
Moroccan rule. Tachfine maintained as bases for the empire both Fes
and Marrakesh but under his son, the pious **Ali Ben Youssef,** Marrakesh
became very much the dominant centre. Craftsmen and architects from
Cordoba worked on the new city: palaces, baths and mosques were built,
a subterranean system of channels constructed to provide water for the
growing palmery, and in 1126-7 the first 7km *circuit of walls* were raised,
replacing an earlier stockade of thorn bushes. These, many times rebuilt,
are essentially the city's present walls, raised from *tabia* – the red mud
of the plains, mixed and strengthened with the addition of lime.

Of the rest of the Almoravid building there is scarcely a trace. The
new dynasty who replaced them – the orthodox and reforming **Almohads**
– sacked the city for three days after taking possession of it in 1147.
Once again, though, Marrakesh was adopted as the Empire's pre-eminent
capital – its domain this time stretching as far as Tripolitania (modern
Libya) in the wake of phenomenal early conquests, and with the accession
in 1184 of **Yacoub el Mansour,** the third Almohad sultan, entering its
greatest period. Under this massively prolific builder, *Kissarias* were
constructed for the sale and storage of Italian and Oriental cloths, a new
kasbah quarter was begun housing twelve separate palaces, mosques and
gardens, and a succession of scholars and poets arrived at the court –
among them Averroes, the most distinguished Arabic medieval philosopher. Mansour's reign too, saw the construction of the *Koutoubia
mosque* and minaret.

It is astonishing though to reflect that this whole period of Almoravid
and Almohad rule – so crucial to the city and the nation's rise – lasted
barely two centuries. By the 1220s the empire was fragmenting amid a
series of factional civil wars, and Marrakesh fell into the familiar pattern
of pillage, ruination and rebuilding. It revived for a time to form the
basis of an independent **Merenid** kingdom (1374-86) but overall lost way
to Fes until the emergence of the **Saadians** in the early C16. Taking
Marrakesh, then devastated by famine, in 1521, and Fes in 1546, they
provided a last burst of Imperial splendour. Their first sultans regained
the Atlantic coast, which had been extensively colonised by Portuguese;
Ahmed el Mansour, the great figure of their dynasty, led a conquest of
Timbuctou, seizing control of the most lucrative caravan routes in Africa.
The *El Badi palace* – the city's largest and greatest – was constructed on
the proceeds of this new wealth, though again it was a victim of dynastic
rivalry and, its mausoleum (the *Saadian tombs*) apart, reduced to a ruin
by Moulay Ismail.

Subsequent history under the **Alaouites** – the dynasty perpetuated today
by King Hassan – is for the most part less distinguished. Marrakesh

remained an Imperial Capital, and the need to maintain a southern base against the tribes ensured the regular, alternating residence of its sultans. But through the C17 to the C19 it shrunk back from the medieval walls and lost much of its old trade. A British traveller's description of the city at the turn of this century – 'a squalid, straggling mazy kind of open cesspool about the size of Paris' – is probably not inaccurate, though for the last decades before the Protectorate it enjoyed a return to favour with the Shereefian court; **Moulay Hassan** (1873-1894) and **Moulay Abder Aziz** (1894-1908) both exercised government from here in a bizarre closing epoch of the old ways which was accompanied by a final bout of *palace building*.

On the arrival of **the French**, Marrakesh gave rise to a short-lived Pretender, the religious leader El Hiba. For the remainder of the Colonial period it was a virtual fief of its Pasha, **T'hami el Glaoui** – the most powerful, autocratic and extraordinary character of his age (see p. 234). Then, and since **Independence**, it has undergone considerable change: rural emigration from the Atlas and sub-Sahara, new methods of cultivation in the plains and the development of a sizeable tourist industry combining to make it today the largest modern trading centre outside Casablanca.

Orientation and hotels

Despite its size – and the tortuous maze of its souks – Marrakesh is not too difficult to find your way around. The broad, open space of the **Djemaa el Fna** (or 'big square' as the guides call it) lies right at the heart of the Medina and almost everything of interest is concentrated in the net of alleys above and below it – the two areas detailed on our individual plans. Just to the west of the Djemaa, and an unmistakeable landmark, is the minaret of the **Koutoubia** – in the shadow of which begins the **Avenue Mohammed V**, leading out of the Medina and up the length of the new town, **Gueliz**. Going from the Djemaa to the Gueliz is a fair walk, but there are plenty of *petits taxis* (from the Post Office in Gueliz, and from the Djemaa) and a regular *bus* (no. 1: between the Koutbouia/Sq. de Foucauld and the main squares in Gueliz along Av. Mohammed V).

Points of arrival are straightforward. There is now a single **bus terminal** (both for *CTM* and private lines), positioned just outside the walls of the Medina by the Bab Doukkala. You can walk into the centre of Gueliz from here in about 10mins by following the Av. des Nations Unies; to the Djemaa it's a 20-25min haul, easiest accomplished by walking down beside the Medina walls to the Place de la Liberté and then following the Av. Mohammed V towards the Koutoubia. Alternatively catch *bus no. 3 or 8* which run in one direction to the Koutoubia, in the other to the

to Meknes and Fes

Souk el Khemis

Bab el Khemis

> Bab Taghzout →

Zaouia of Sidi Bel Abbes

SEE PLAN OF SOUKS

Mosque and Medressa Ben Youssef

Dar el Glaoui

Bab Debbagh (Tanneries)

Bab Aylen

MEDINA

Souks

Place Djemaa El Fna

...toubia

CHEAP HOTELS

Dar Si Said

SEE PLAN OF MEDINA

Bab Aghmat

Palais de la Bahia

Bab er Robb

Saadian Tombs

Badi Palace

MELLAH

Royal Palace

Agdal Gardens

Bab Ahmar

to Ourika

MARRAKESH

— HOTELS —
1. Oasis (1*A)
2. Renaissance (3*B)
3. Koutoubia (2*A)
4. Marrakesh (4*A)
5. Foucauld (2*A)
6. Tazi (2*A)
7. Es Saadi (5*)

Youth hostel – 3 blocks below train station. For cheap hotels see plan of Lower Medina.

centre of Gueliz and the train station; or save a lot of sweat by taking a *petit taxi* (about 10dhs to the Djemaa, for up to three people). Getting into the Djemaa from the **railway station** you'll certainly want transport (bus no. 3 or 8; or 10-12dhs for a *petit taxi*), though you are here within easy reach of the campsite and youth hostel, and only 10mins walk from the middle of Gueliz.

From the city's **airport**, 5km out to the south-west, bus no. 11 is supposed to run every half-hour to the Djemaa. In reality you may decide to go for a *petit taxi*, in which case you're basically at the mercy of the day's going rate: anything above 30dhs is beginning to get unreasonable but, whatever you do, establish a price before you start.

One form of transport unique to Marrakesh are the **calèches**, horsecabs which assemble beside the Koutoubia, the Badi palace and some of the smarter hotels. These can take up to five people and are often no more expensive than *petits taxis*, though again fix and haggle charges in advance.

See the *souks* section for advice on **guides**: you won't really need them anywhere else.

Hotels
ON AND AROUND THE DJEMAA EL FNA
Virtually all the **cheap hotels** in Marrakesh are grouped in a triangular grid of streets below the Djemaa el Fna: the area (see our plan on p.206) bounded by Rue de Bab Agnaou, Rue Zitoun el Qedim and Av. El Mouahidina. A few of them are miserable, overpriced flea-pits but most are really quite nice – small, family-run places with eight or ten rooms gathered around a cooling central courtyard. The big advantage, however, is their position: staying out at the youth hostel or campsite, or around Gueliz, you spend half your time and a lot of energy getting in to the Djemaa and the souks. Here you're right in the midst of it all.

Hôtel CTM (1*A), *Hôtel du Café de France, Hôtel Oukaimeden.* These three are actually on the Djemaa el Fna and all have some rooms which overlook the square. The CTM, above the old bus station, is perhaps the best – and like the Café de France easily found. Oukaimeden is over on the far side of the square, beside the huge, strictly guarded Club Med.

Hôtel Chellah Facing the CTM Hotel turn down the arched lane to its left, the Rue Zitoun el Kedim, near the beginning of which you pass a different Hôtel de France and the Hôtel des Amis, neither much recommended; Chellah is signposted down an alleyway to the right about 50m down – one of the best cheap options around, and clean, safe and surprisingly cool. A couple of doors down from the Hôtel de France, and useful compensation for the sporadic showers in many of these hotels, are public *hammams* for both women and men.

Hôtel Central, Hôtel Afrique, Hôtel Eddakla. Best in a zigzagging lane of small, cheap hotels whose entrance (coming from the Djemaa) is the first alley on the left of the Rue Bab Agnaou. Rue Bab Agnaou doesn't have a very prominent streetsign but it's on our map of the Lower Medina – near its beginning is an easily spotted branch of the Crédit du Maroc bank.

Hôtel Souria, Hôtel Hillal, Hôtel El Farah, Hôtel El Al-lal, Hôtel Gallia (2*B). These are all scattered along the next lane down off Rue Bab Agnaou – reached through a smaller, arched entrance opposite the Hôtel du Tourisme (and just before you come to the Banque Populaire). Of the cheap places, Souria is far and away the best – better perhaps than Chellah, though often full. The Gallia, to the left at the end of the lane, is quite pleasant and if you get one of its better rooms might be worth the extra money.

Grand Hôtel Tazi (2*A), Rue Bab Agnaou/angle of Av. Hoummam el Ftouaki. If you can afford it, this is an excellent and superior option – very well run, with hot showers in every room, a garage behind and a rooftop bar. Tel. 221-52/53.

Hôtel de Foucauld (2*A), Rue El Mouahidine. Same prices and management as the Tazi though smaller rooms, no bar and frequent problems with the water supply. Still a good bet, though. Tel. 254-99.

GUELIZ (THE NEW TOWN)

There are two reasons why you might want to stay in Gueliz: **arriving late** at night, or feeling an overriding urge to have a **swimming pool** close at hand. Given regular summer temperatures of 100°F – and not uncommon midday bursts of 120-130°F – the latter can be a powerful impulse. Apart from the **Youth Hostel** and **Campsite**, however, there's nothing particularly cheap: all hotels in Gueliz are officially graded and there are only seven in the 1*/2* categories, all of which are listed below.

Auberge de Jeunesse (Youth Hostel), Rue el Jahid. Quiet, clean and a useful first-night standby if you arrive late by train – it's 5mins walk (and three blocks) below the railway station: take any of the roads opposite down to Rue Ibn el Qadi and follow this along, turning left a block before you reach the park behind the campsite. Closes 10pm in winter, around midnight in summer. To get to the Djemaa from here take bus 3/8 from up by the station.

Camping Municipal, Av. de France. Nothing special, though useful for the same reasons above – and for meeting people for information and possible lifts. There's a cafe-restaurant and small pool (with admission charge). Again, bus 3/8 to the Djemaa.

Hôtel Franco-Belge (1*A), *Hôtel des Voyageurs*, 62 & 40 Boul. M. Zerktouni. Unexciting but cheap, on a main traffic thoroughfare.

Hôtel Oasis (1*A), 50 Av. Mohammed V (keyed 1). Ditto.

Hôtel du Haouz (1*A), 66 Av. Hassan II. (Near the railway station).

Hôtel la Palmeraie (1*A), 8 Rue Souraya. (Parallel, 2 blocks below, Boul. Zerktouni).

Hôtel Excelsior (2*A), Tarik Ibn Zaid/Ibn Aicha. Popular French-run place with Moorish kitsch decor. (Parallel, a block above, with Avenue Mohammed V: and a block above Boul. Zerktouni).

Hôtel Koutoubia (2*A), 51 Av. El Mansur Eddahbi (keyed 3). Distinctly stylish with a bar and gardens, this is also the cheapest hotel with its own swimming pool. Recommended and near the railway station. Tel. 309-21

UPMARKET (AND WAY UPMARKET)
The interesting thing about upmarket Moroccan hotels – 4*A places with palm-shaded swimming pools – is that they tend to cost rather less than your average London B&B, so a double room for a night or two's total respite is, well, possible. Way upmarket hotels (5* luxury class) are a different proposition, but since Marrakesh has two of the best in the country, and you might always stumble on a 500dh note, they're here recorded.

Hôtel le Marrakech (4*A), Place de la Liberté (keyed 4). Very much the best among its class – and some can be surprisingly tacky – this is a good, modern hotel with a decent-sized pool, individual *hammam* and a useful position just outside the Medina. Tel. 333-51.

Hotel Es Saadi (5*), Av. Qadissia, Hivernage (keyed 7). Hivernage is a whole garden suburb of luxury villas and hotels: the Es Saadi is the most elegant among them. Tel. 720 42.

Hotel Mamounia (5*), Av. Bab Jdid. Something of a legend, set within its own palace grounds, this is the most beautiful and also the most expensive hotel in Morocco. Room prices drop slightly out of season (which means the summer months, people *winter* in Marrakesh) but if you're curious, tea in the gardens comes a lot cheaper. If you're serious about staying you might consider a double room between three people, but to keep all this in proportion it's worth noting that a *taxi ride* to the Mamounia (from anywhere in Marrakesh) is well above the cost of a room in any of the unclassified hotels around the Djemaa.

Djemaa el Fna and the Koutoubia

There's nowhere in North Africa like the **Djemaa el Fna** – nowhere which so effortlessly involves you, blows aside travel cynicism and keeps you returning for as long as you stay. By day it's basically a market, with a few snake charmers and an occasional troup of acrobats. In the evening (and during Ramadan, through the night) it becomes a whole carnival of musicians, clowns and street entertainers. When you arrive in Marrakesh, and when you've found a room, come out here and you're straight into the ritual: wandering about, squatting amid the circles of watchers, giving a dirham as your due. If you get tired, or the patterns slow, you shift to the terrace of the *Café de France* to look out across it all and to the frame of the Koutoubia minaret.

What you are part of is a strange process. Tourism is probably now vital to the Djemaa's survival, yet apart from the snake charmers and watersellers (who live by posing for photos) and the hustlers (who have more subtle ways) there's little that has compromised itself for the West. In many ways it actually seems the opposite. Most of the people gathered into circles around the performers are Moroccans – Berbers from the villages and kids – and you often feel an intruder. There is no way that any tourist is going to have a tooth pulled by one of the dentists here, for all the neat piles of molars displayed on their square of carpet. Nor are you likely to use the scribes or street barbers, or understand the convoluted tales* of the story-tellers, around whom are perhaps the most animated crowds in the square.

Nothing of this, though, matters greatly. There is a fascination in the story-tellers beyond the concealment of language, just as in the spells and remedies of the herbalists, their bizarre concoctions spread out before them. There are, too, **performers** whose appeal is universal. The acrobats, itinerants from the Tazeroualt, have for years supplied European circuses – though they are probably never so spectacular as here, thrust forward into multiple somersaults and contortions in the late afternoon heat. There are child boxers and rather sad trained monkeys, clowns and Chleuh boy dancers – their routines, to the climactic jarring of cymbals, totally sexual (and a traditional invitation to clients). And last, the Djemaa's enduring sound, there are the dozens of **musicians**. Late into the night, when only a few people are left in the cafe stalls at the centre of the square, you come upon individual players, hammering away on their *ginbris* – the skin covered, two- or three-string guitars. Earlier, there are full groups: the *Aissaoua*, blowing oboe-like *ghaitahs* beside the snake charmers, the Andalusian influenced groups with their *aouds* and crude violins, and the predominantly black *Gnaoua*, trance-healers who beat out hour-long shafts of rhythm with hard iron clashers and tall drums hit with long curved sticks.

If you become interested in the music there's a small section in the Djemaa, close by the entrance to the souks, where stalls sell recorded **tapes**. Most of these are actually Egyptian, the pop music which dominates Moroccan radio, but if you ask they'll play you Berber music from the Atlas, classic Fassi pieces and even Gnaoua – which sounds even

---

*According to the novelist/translator Paul Bowles these repertoires tend to be 'rather grandiose stories about the Sultan and his daughter and the rich Jew who tries to get her . . . very full of plot . . . with lots of magic and transportation'.

stranger on tape, cut off only by the end of the reel and starting off almost identical on the other side. These stalls apart, and those of the nut-roasters whose massive braziers line the immediate entrance to the potters souk, the **market** activities of the Djemaa are mostly quite mundane. Not to be missed, however, even if you have no stomach to eat at them, are the avenue of makeshift **restaurants** which come into their own towards early evening. Lit by great lanterns and their tables piled high with massive bowls of cooked food, each calls out extolling their range or specialities. You can eat, sitting at benches along their sides, for next to nothing, though even sticking to vegetables you probably won't escape the effects. If you're wary, head for the orange and lime juice sellers opposite the Café de France, or go for a handful of cactus fruit, peeled in a couple of seconds from the stalls nearby. For details on more substantial eating in the Djemaa and elsewhere see p. 214.

Nobody is entirely sure when or how the Djemaa el Fna came into being – nor even what its name means. The usual translation is *assembly of the dead*, a suitably epic title which seems to refer to the public display here of the heads of rebels and criminals. This is certainly possible, for the Djemaa was a place of execution well into the last century, though the phrase may just mean 'the mosque of nothing' (*Djemaa* means both mosque and assembly: interchangeable terms in Islamic society), a recollection of an abandoned Saadian plan to build a new Grand Mosque on this site. Whichever, as an open area between the original kasbah and souk's, the *place* probably played very much its present role from the earliest days of the city. It has often been the flashpoint for rioting – even within the last decade – and every few years there are plans to close it down and to move its activities outside the city walls. This in fact happened after Independence in 1956, when the new 'modernist' government built a corn market (which remains) over part of the square and tried to turn the rest into a carpark. The plan, however, lasted only for a year. Tourism was falling off and it was clearly an unpopular move – taking from the people a very basic psychological need, and perhaps too a necessary expression of the past.

The Koutoubia
The absence of any architectural feature to the Djemaa – which even today seems a random clearing – serves to emphasise the drama of the **Koutoubia minaret**, focus of every approach to the city. Nearly seventy metres in height and visible for miles on a clear morning, this is the oldest of the three great Almohad towers (the others are in Rabat and Sevilla) and the most complete. Its proportions – a 1:5 ratio of width:height – established the classic Moroccan design. Its scale, rising from the low city buildings and the plains to the north, is extraordinary – and the more so the longer you stay and the more familiar its sight becomes.

Completed by the sultan Yacoub el Mansour (1184-99), work on the minaret probably begun shortly after the Almohad conquest of the city, around 1150. It displays many of the features which were to become widespread in Moroccan architecture – the wide band of ceramic inlay near the top, the pyramid-shaped castellation of *merlons* above, the use of *darj w ktarf* (fleur de lis) and other motifs – and it established, too, the alternation of patterning on different faces. Here, the top storey is similar on each of the sides but the lower two are almost eccentric in their variety; the most interesting is perhaps the middle niche on the south-east face, a semi-circle of small lobed arches which was to become the dominant decorative feature of Almohad gates. If you look hard, you will notice that at around this point the stones of the main body of the tower become slightly smaller. This seems odd today but originally the whole minaret would have been faced with plaster and its tiers of decoration painted. To see just how much this can change the entire effect – and, to most tastes, lose much of the beauty – take a look at the Kasbah mosque (by the Saadian tombs, p. 207) which has been carefully but completely restored in this manner; there have been plans over the years to do the same with the Koutoubia, though for the present they have been indefinitely shelved. The only part of the structure which has really been renovated are the three copper gilt balls at the summit. The subject of numerous legends – mostly of supernatural interventions to defy thieves – these are thought originally to have been of gold, the gift of the wife of Yacoub el Mansour and presented as a penance for breaking three hours of the Ramadan fast.

The souks and northern medina

It is spicy in the souks, and cool and colourful. The smell, always pleasant, changes gradually with the nature of the merchandise. There are no names or signs; there is no glass . . . You find everything – but you always find it many times over.
                                    – Elias Canetti: *The Voices of Marrakesh.*

The SOUKS of Marrakesh sprawl immediately above the Djemaa el Fna. They seem vast the first time you venture in, and almost impossible to navigate, though in fact the area which they cover is quite compact. A long, covered street, the **Rue Souk Smarine**, runs for half of their length and then splits in two – becoming the **Souk el Attarin** and **Souk el Kebir**. Off these are virtually all the individual souks: alleys and small squares devoted to specific crafts, where you can often watch part of the production process. At the top of the main area of souks, too, you can visit the Saadian **Ben Youssef Medressa** – the most important monument in this northern half of the Medina and arguably the finest building in the city after the Koutoubia minaret.

If you are staying for some days, you'll probably return often to the souks – and this is a good way of taking them in, singling out a couple of specific crafts or products to see rather than being swamped by the whole. To get to grips with the general layout, though, you may find it useful to walk round the whole area once with a **guide**. Despite the pressure of offers in the Djemaa don't feel this is essential, but until the hustlers begin to recognise you (and that you've been in the souks before) you will probably be followed in; if and when this happens try to be easy and polite and confident – qualities which force most hustlers to look elsewhere. The liveliest **times** to visit are in the very early morning (between 5-8am if you can make it) and in the late afternoon, at around 4-5pm, when some of the souks auction off goods to local traders.

Towards Ben Youssef: the main souks

On the corner of the Djemaa el Fna itself there is a small potters' souk, but the main body of the markets begins a little way beyond this. Its **entrance**, usually lined with hustlers, is initially confusing. Standing at the *Café de France* (and facing the mosque opposite) look across and you'll see the *Café el Fath* and, beside it, a building with the sign 'Tailleur de la Place': the lane between them will bring you out at the beginning of Rue Souk Smarine.

Busy and crowded, **Souk Smarine** is an important thoroughfare, traditionally dominated by the sale of textiles. Today upmarket tourist 'bazaars' are moving in, American Express cards displayed in their windows for the guided hordes, but there are still dozens of shops in the arcades selling and tailoring shirts and kaftans. Along its whole course the street is covered by a broad iron trellis which restricts the sun to strats of light; it replaces the old rush (*smar*) roofing which with many of the souks' more beautiful features was destroyed in a fire in the 1960s.

Just before the fork at its end, the Souk Smarine narrows and there is a glimpse through the passageways to its right of the **Rahba Kedima**, a small and rather ramshackle square with a few vegetable stalls set up in its midst. Immediately on the right, as you go in, is the **Souk Larzal**, a wool market feverishly active in the dawn hours but pretty much closed for the rest of the day. Alongside, easily distinguished by smell alone, is the **Souk Btana** which deals with whole sheepskins – their pelts laid out to dry and for display on the roof. You can walk up here and take a look at the methods, though the most interesting aspect of the Rahba Kedima are the **apothecary stalls** around the near corner of the square. These sell all the standard traditional cosmetics – earthenware saucers of cochineal (*kashiniah*) or rouge, powdered *kohl* or antimony for darkening the edges of the eyes, *henna* (the only cosmetic unmarried women are supposed to use), and the sticks of *suak* (walnut root or bark) with which you see Moroccans cleaning their teeth. But in addition to such essentials the stalls sell the herbal and animal ingredients which are still in widespread use for manipulation, or spell-binding. There are roots and tablets used as aphrodisiacs, and there are stranger and more specialised goods – dried pieces of lizard and stork, fragments of beaks, talons and gazelle horns. Magic, white and black, has always been very much a part of Moroccan life, and there are dozens of stories relating to its effect, nearly always carried out by a wife upon her husband.

At the end of the Rahba-Kedima there is a corridor to the left which gives access to another, smaller square – a bustling, carpet-draped area known as **la Criée Berbère**. It was here that the old *slave auctions* were held, just before sunset every Wednesday, Thursday and Friday, until the French occupation of the city in 1912. They were conducted, according to Budgett Meakin's account of 1900, 'precisely as those of cows and mules, often on the same spot by the same men ... with the human chattels being personally examined in the most disgusting manner, and paraded in lots by the auctioneers, who shout their attractions and the bids'. Most had been kidnapped and brought in by the caravans from Guinea and Sudan; Meakin saw two small boys sold for £5 apiece, a girl of eight for £3.10s and a 'stalwart negro' for £14, though a beauty, he was told, might exceptionally fetch £130-150.

These days **rugs and carpets** are the almost exclusive business of the square and if you've the time and willpower you could spend the best part of a day here while endless (and often identical) stacks are unfolded and displayed before you. Some of the most interesting are the Berber rugs from the High Atlas – bright, geometric designs which look quite different after they have been laid out on the roof and bleached by the sun. The dark, often black backgrounds usually signify rugs from the Glaoua country – up towards Telouet; reddish-backed carpets from Chichaoua, a small village on the way to Essaouira, are also quite common. There is usually a small **auction** in the criée at around 4pm, an interesting sight with the auctioneers wandering about the square shouting out the latest bids but not very promising for rug-buying – it's devoted mainly to heavy brown-wool djellabas.

Cutting back to the **Souk el Kebir**, which by now has taken over from the Smarine, you emerge at the **Kissarias**, the covered markets at the heart of the souks. The goods here, apart from the numerous and sometimes imaginative *couvertures* (blankets), aren't especially interesting: the kissarias traditionally hold the more expensive products, which today means a sad predominance of Western designs and imports. Off to the right, near the beginning, is the **Souk des Bijoutiers**, a modest jewellers' lane which is rather less varied than that established in the Mellah (see p.209) by the old Jewish artisans. At the top end of the kissarias is a convoluted net of alleys which comprise the **Souk Cherratin**, essentially a leather-workers' souk (with dozens of purse-makers and sandal cobblers) though interspersed by smaller alleys and souks of carpenters, sieve-makers and even a few tourist shops. If you bear left through this area and turn out towards your right you should arrive at the open space in front of the Mosque Ben Youssef; the medressa (see the section below) is off to its right-hand side.

Had you earlier taken the left fork along **Souk el Attarin** – the spice and perfume souk – you would have hit the other side of the **kissarias** and the long lane of the **Souk des Babouches** (slipper-makers). The main attraction in this area, and infinitely the most colourful sight in the city, is the souk of the dyers, or **Teinturiers**. To reach it, turn to your left just a couple of paces before you come to the Souk des Babouches; Working your way down this lane (which comes out in a square by the Mouassin mosque) look out to your left and you'll see the entrance to the souk about halfway down – its lanes rhythmically flashed with bright skeins of wool, hung from above. If you have trouble in finding it just follow on the first tour you see, or ask one of the kids to lead you. There is a reasonably straightforward alternative route back to the Djemaa el Fna from here, following the main street down to the **Mouassin mosque** (which is almost entirely concealed from public view, built at an angle to the square beside it) and then turning left onto the Rue Mouassin. As you approach the mosque, the street widens very slightly opposite an elaborate, triple-bayed **fountain**. Built in the mid C16 by the prolific Saadian builder Abdallah el-Ghalib, this is one of many such fountains in Marrakesh with a basin for humans set beside two larger troughs for animals; to install it was a pious act, directly sanctioned by the Koran in its charitable provision of water for men and beasts.

Below the Mouassin mosque is an area of coppersmiths, the **Souk des Forgerons**. Above it sprawls the main section of **carpenters'** workshops – beautiful in their draughts of cedarwood smells – and beyond them a small souk for oils (*Souk des huivres*) and the **Souk Haddadine**, ironsmiths and metalworkers whose industry you hear long before arriving.

The Ben Youssef medressa and Almoravid koubba

One of the largest buildings in the Medina, and preceded by a rare open space, the **Ben Youssef mosque** is quite easy to locate. Its **medressa** – the old college-annexe for students taking courses in the mosque – stands off a sidestreet just to its east, distinguishable by a series of small, grilled and rather dilapidated windows. Over the last year or so it has been closed intermittently for restoration but it is well worth coming up to see if anyone will let you in. The entrance porch is a short way down the side street, covering the whole lane at this point: hammer on the doors, wait around and look generous. If normal hours have been resumed they

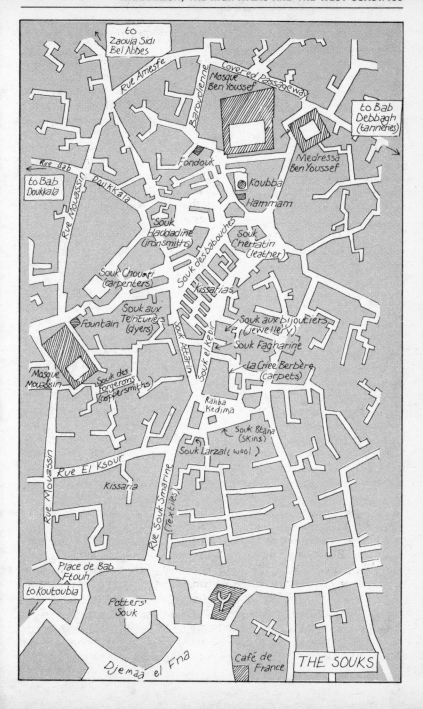

to Zaouia Sidi Bel Abbes

Rue Amesfe

Baroudienne

Covered Passageway

Mosque Ben Youssef

to Bab Debbagh (tanneries)

Rue Bab Doukkala

Fondouk

Medressa Ben Youssef

to Bab Doukkala

Rue Mouassin

Koubba

Hammam

Souk Haddadine (ironsmiths)

Souk Cherratin (leather)

Souk Chouari (carpenters)

Souk des babouches

Kissarias

Souk aux Teinturiers (dyers)

Fountain

Souk aux bijoutiers (Jewellery)

Souk Fagharine

Souk Attarin

Souk el kebir

La Criee Berbère (carpets)

Mosque Mouassin

Souk des Forgerons (coppersmiths)

Rahba Kedima

Souk Btana (Skins)

Rue El Ksour

Souk Larzal (wool)

Rue Mouassin

Kissaria

Rue Souk Smarine (Textiles)

Place de Bab Ftouh

to Koutoubia

Potters' Souk

Café de France

Djemaa el Fna

THE SOUKS

should be from around 8-12 & 2.30-6 daily, except for Mondays and Friday mornings (closed).

Like most of the Fes medressas (see p. 148 for a description of their development and function), the Ben Youssef was a Merenid foundation, established by the sultan Abou el Hassan in the C14. It was, however, almost completely rebuilt under the Saadians, and it is this dynasty's intricate, Andalusian-influenced art which has left its stamp. As with the slightly later Saadian tombs, no surface of the architecture is left undecorated, and the overall quality of its craftsmanship, whether in wood-carving, stucco work or zellij, is startlingly rich. That this was possible in C16 Marrakesh, after a period in which the city was reduced to near ruin and the country to tribal anarchy, is remarkable. Revealingly, parts of it have exact parallels in the Alhambra palace in Granada, it seems likely that Muslim Spanish architects were here directly employed.

Once admitted to the medressa, you reach the main court by means of a long outer *corridor* (an unusual feature in a college, though quite common in palace architecture) and a small entry *vestibule*. To the side of this are stairs to the *student cells*, arranged around smaller internal courtyards on the upper storeys, an *ablutions hall* and *latrine*. At the corner of the vestibule is a very rare and most un-Islamic marble *basin*, rectangular in shape and decorated along one side with what seem to be heraldic eagles and griffins; an inscription amidst the floral decoration records its origin in C10 Cordoba, then the centre of the Western Muslim world. The Ommayad caliphs, for whom it was constructed, had few reservations about representational art. What is surprising is that it was brought over to Morocco by the Almoravid sultan Ali Ben Youssef and, placed in his mosque, was left untouched by the Almohads before finally being moved to the medressa in the Saadian rebuilding.

The *central courtyard*, weathered almost flat on its more exposed side, is much larger than usual. Along two sides run wide, sturdy-columned arcades which were probably used to supplement the space for teaching in the neighbouring mosque; above are some of the windows of the student quarters, an interesting perspective if you are allowed up – and an enigmatic exercise in fathoming how over eight hundred students were once housed in the building. At its far end the court gives onto a *prayer hall*, where the decoration, mellowed outside with the city's familiar pink tone, is at its best preserved and most elaborate. You notice here, as on the court's cedar-wood carving, a predominance of pine cone and palmette motifs, and around the *mihrab* (the horseshoe-arched prayer niche) they've been applied so as to give the frieze a highly three-dimensional appearance. This is unusual in Moorish stucco-work, though the inscriptions themselves, picked out in the curling vegetative Arabesques, are familiar Koranic texts. The most common, here and throughout Moroccan stucco and zellij decoration, is the ceremonial *bismillah* invocation: 'In the name of Allah, the Tender-hearted, the Merciful . . .'.

After the medressa or the souks, the **Almoravid koubba** doesn't look much – a small, two-storey kiosk which at first sight seems little more than a grey dome and a handful of variously shaped doors and windows. Look closer, though, and you begin to understand its significance and even fascination. For this, the only intact Almoravid building, is right at the root of all Moroccan architecture. The motifs you've just seen in the medressa – the fircones, palmettes and acanthus leaves – are all carved here for the first time. The windows on each of the different faces became the classic shapes of Almohad and Merenid design. So too the *merlons*, the Christmas-tree-like battlements; the complex 'ribs' on the outside of the dome; and the dome's interior support, a sophisticated device of a square and star-shaped octagon which is itself repeated at each of its corners. Once you see all this, you're only a step away from the eulogies of Islamic art historians, who sense in this building, which was probably a small ablutions annexe to the original Ben Youssef mosque, a powerful and novel expression of form.

Excavated only in 1952 – having been covered over amid the many rebuildings of the Ben Youssef – the koubba lies just to the south of the present (mainly C19) mosque. It lies mostly below today's ground level, though standing with your back to the mosque you can make out the top of its dome (quite probably scaffolded) behind the long, low brick wall. There is an entrance-gate, down a few steps, where a *guardien* will emerge to escort you around what little there is to be seen; if this is closed you can get almost as good a view from the roof of a very ancient (but still active) *hammam* down to the right. Either way you'll be expected to tip.

Beyond Ben Youssef: the tanneries and northern gates

The main souks – and the tourist route – stop abruptly at the Ben Youssef medressa. Above, in any direction, you'll find yourself in the ordinary **residential quarters** of the Medina. There are few particular 'sights' here, but if you've time there's an interest of its own in following the crowds, and a relief in moving away from the blocks of Marrakesh where you are (quite legitimately) expected to come in, *look* and buy.

Probably the most interesting targets are the **Bab Debbagh**, or tanners' gate and the **Souk el Khemis**, the 'Thursday market'. From Ben Youssef you can reach these quite easily: it's about 15 mins walk to the first, another 15-20 mins on round the ramparts to the second. As you pass the entrance porch to the medressa you'll quickly reach a fork in the sidestreet. To the left a covered passageway leads round behind the mosque to join the Rue Amesfah (see below). Head instead to your right and then keep as straight as possible until you emerge at the ramparts by the Bab Debbagh; on the way you'll cross a small square and road junction, the Place el Moukef, where a busy and sizeable lane goes off to the left – a more direct approach to (and alternative route back from) the Bab el Khemis.

Bab Debbagh is supposed to be Almoravid in design, though over the years it must have been almost totally rebuilt. Going through, you become aware of its very real defensive purpose: three internal rooms placed so as to force several turns on anyone attempting to storm it. To the left of the first chamber there's a stairway which (for a small fee) you can use to climb up onto the roof. Looking down there's an excellent view over the tanneries, built out here at the edge of the city for the access to water (the summer-dry Oued Issil runs just outside the walls) and for the obvious reason of smell. If you want to take a closer look at the processes come in the morning when the co-operatives are at work. Any of the kids around will take you in. Following the road from here outside the ramparts is the simplest approach to the Bab el Khemis, ('gate of the Thursday market') another reconstructed Almoravid gate, built at an angle in the walls. The Thursday market now seems to take place more or less daily, about 400m to the north, above a cemetery and marabout's tomb. It is really a local provisions market, though odd items of craft interest occasionally surface.

The area immediately north of the Ben Youssef mosque is cut by two main streets: the Rue Assouel (which leads up to Bab el Khemis) and the Rue Bab Taghzout, which runs up to the gate of the same name and to the Zaouia of Sidi Bel Abbes. These were, with the Bab Doukkala, the principal approaches to the city until the present century and along them you find many of the old fondouks used as storage and lodgings by merchants visiting the souks. There is one just below the mosque and a whole series along the Rue Amesfah – the continuation of Baroudienne – above and to the left. Most are still used in some commercial capacity, as workshops or warehouses, and the doors to their courtyards often stand open. Some date from Saadian times and there are often fine details of wood carving or stuccowork. If you are interested nobody seems to mind if you wander in.

The Rue Amesfah runs for about 150m above the intersection with Baroudienne before reaching the Y- junction of Rue Assouel (right) and Rue Bab Taghzout (left). Following the latter you will pass another *fondouk*, opposite a small recessed fountain known as *Chrob ou Chouf* ('drink and admire'), and, around ½km further on, the old city gate of Bab Taghzout. This was the original extent of the Almoravid Medina, and remained such into the C18 when the sultan Mohammed Abdallah extended the walls to enclose the quarter and Zaouia of Sidi Bel Abbes. Sidi Bel Abbes, a C12 marabout and a prolific performer of miracles, is the most important of the city's Seven Saints, and his zaouia, a kind of monastic cult-centre, has traditionally wielded very great influence and power, often at odds with that of the Sultan, and a traditional refuge for political dissidents. The present buildings, which are strictly forbidden to non-Muslims, date largely from a rebuilding by Moulay Ismail – an act which was probably inspired more by political manipulation than piety. You can see something of the complex and its activities from outside the official precinct: do not, however, try to pass through the long central corridor. The zaouia still owns much of the quarter to its north and continues its educational and charitable work, distributing food each evening to the blind. There is a smaller, though still significant, Zaouia dedicated to **Sidi Slimane**, a Saadian marabout, a couple of blocks to the south-west.

A third alternative from the Ben Youssef is to strike west, off **towards the Bab Doukkala**. This route, once you have found your way down through the Souk Haddadine to the **Rue Bab Doukkala**, is quite a sizeable thoroughfare and very straightforward to follow. Midway, you pass the **Dar el Glaoui**, the old palace of the Pasha of Marrakesh and a source of legendary exoticism throughout the first half of this century. The Glaoui, cruel and magnificent in equal measure, was the last of the great southern tribal leaders; an active and shrewd supporter of French rule, and a personal friend of Winston Churchill. He was also one of the most spectacular party-givers around – in an age where rivals were not sparse. At the extraordinary *difas* held at the Dar el Glaoui 'nothing', as Gavin Maxwell wrote, 'was impossible': hashish and opium were available for experiment for the Europeans and Americans, and 'to his guests T'hami gave, literally, whatever they wanted, whether it might be a diamond ring, a present of money in gold, or a Berber girl or boy from the High Atlas'. Not surprisingly, there has been little enthusiasm for showing off the palace since El Glaoui's death in 1956, but there are said to be plans to open it as a museum of some sort. You might ask at the tourist office in Gueliz, for by all accounts the combination here of traditional Moroccan architecture and 1920s chic is unique and rather wonderful.

The lower medina: the Palaces, Saadian tombs and Mellah

Staying in Marrakesh even for a few days you begin to sense the different appearance and life of its various Medina quarters: and nowhere more so than in the shift from north to south, from the area above the Djemaa el Fna to the area below. At the base here – a kind of stem to the mushroom shape of the city walls – is the **Dar el Makhzen**, the Royal Palace. To its west stretches the old inner citadel of the **Kasbah**; to the east, the **Mellah**, once the largest Jewish ghetto in Morocco; whilst rambling above are a series of mansions and palaces built for the C19 elite. It's an interesting area to wander, particularly the Mellah, though you will probably do time trying to figure out the sudden and apparently arbitrary ramparts and enclosures. If you want direction there are two obvious highlights: the **Saadian tombs**, preserved in the shadow of the Kasbah mosque, and the ruined palace of Ahmed el Mansour – **El Badi**, 'the Incomparable'.

The Saadian tombs and El Badi

Sealed in by Moulay Ismail after he had destroyed the adjoining Badi palace, the **Saadian tombs** lay half-ruined and half-forgotten at the beginning of this century. In 1917, however, they were rediscovered on a French aerial map and a passageway constructed to give access at the side of the Kasbah mosque. Restored, they are today the city's main 'sight' – over-lavish, maybe, in their exhaustive decoration, but dazzling nonetheless. Friday mornings excepted, they are open daily from around 8am-7pm; go either early or late, if possible. On arrival you are given a quick tour: names are named, pavilions pointed out and a tip dutifully earned. You are then left to look about on your own, or even just to sit and gaze. A quiet, high-walled enclosure, shaded with shrubs and palms, and dotted with bright zellij-covered tombs, it seems as much pleasure garden as cemetery.

Some form of burial ground behind the royal palace probably predated the Saadian period though the earliest of the tombs here is dated 1557 and all the principal structures were built by the sultan Ahmed el Mansour. This makes them virtual contemporaries of the Ben Youssef medressa – with which there are obvious parallels – and allows a revealing insight into just how rich and extravagant the El Badi must once have been. Their escape from Moulay Ismail's systematic plundering was probably due to superstition – Ismail having to content himself with blocking all but an obscure entrance from the Kasbah mosque. Despite this, a few prominent Marrakshis continued to be buried amid the mausoleums; the last, in 1792, was the 'mad Sultan' Moulay Yazid, whose brief 22-month reign was probably the most violent, vicious and sadistic in the nation's history.

There are two main **mausoleums** in the enclosure. The finest is on the left as you come in – a beautiful group of three rooms, built to house el Mansour's own tomb and completed within his lifetime. Moving round from the courtyard entrance, the first hall is a *prayer-oratory*, a room probably not intended for burial though now almost littered with the thin marble stones of Saadian princes. It is here that Moulay Yazid was laid out, perhaps in purposeful obscurity, certainly in ironic contrast to the cursive inscription around the band of black and white zellij: 'and the works of peace they have accomplished', it reads amid the interlocking circles, 'will make them enter the holy gardens'. Architecturally the most important feature is the *mihrab*, its pointed horseshoe arch supported by an incredibly delicate arrangement of columns. Opposite this face is another elaborate arch, through to the domed *central chamber* and el Mansour's own tomb which you can glimpse from the next door in the court. The tomb, slightly larger than those around, lies right in the middle, flanked on either side by the sultan's sons and successors. The room itself is spectacular: half-light filtering onto the tombs from an interior lantern in a tremendous vaulted roof, the zellij full of colour and motion, and, beyond, the undefined richness of a third chamber almost hidden from view. Throughout there are echoes of the Alhambra in Granada, from which its style is clearly derived; oddly, though, it was completed nearly two centuries later and except in detail and exuberance seems hardly to show any development.

The *other mausoleum*, older and less impressive, was raised by Ahmed in place of an existing pavilion above the tombs of his mother, Lalla Messaouda, and of Mohammed esh Sheikh, the founder of the Saadian dynasty. It is again a series of three rooms, though two are hardly more than loggias. Lalla's tomb is the niche below the dome in the outer chamber. Mohammed is buried in the inner – or at least his body is, for he was murdered in the Atlas by Turkish mercenaries, who salted his head and took it back for public display on the walls at Istanbul.

Outside, around the garden and courtyard, are the tombs of over a hundred more Saadian princes and members of the royal household. Like the privileged sixty-six accorded space within the mausoleums, their gravestones are brilliantly tiled and often elaborately inscribed. The most usual inscription reads quite simply:

> *There is no God but God. Mohammed is God's envoy.*
> *Praise to God.*
> *The occupant of this tomb died on. . . .*

But there are others, epitaphs and extracts from the Koran, that seem to express more the turbulence of the age – which with Ahmed's death in 1603 was to disintegrate into nearly seventy years of constant civil war. 'Every soul shall know death', reads one tombstone; 'Death will find you wherever you are, even in fortified towers', another. And, carved in gypsum on the walls, there is a poem:

> *O mausoleum, built out of mercy, thou whose*
> *walls are the shadow of heaven.*
> *The breath of asceticism is wafted from thy tombs*
> *like a fragrance.*
> *Through thy death*
> *the light of faith has been dimmed,*
> *the seven spheres are fraught with darkness*
> *and the columns of glory*
> *broken with pain.*

Getting to the Saadian tombs, the simplest route from the Djemaa el Fna is to follow **Rue Bab Agnaou** outside the ramparts. At its end you come to a small square flanked by two gates. Directly ahead is the **Bab er Robb** – behind which the *grands taxis* and private line buses leave for Ourika and other local destinations. To the left, somewhat battered and eroded, is the city's only surviving Almohad gateway, **Bab Agnaou** (*gate of the Gnaoua*: the blacks). This is an impressive structure, smaller than

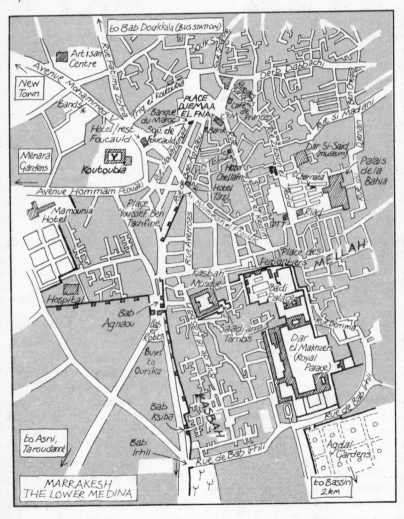

MARRAKESH
THE LOWER MEDINA

the monumental gates of Rabat but sharing much of their force and apparent simplicity: notice how the semi-circular frieze above its arch creates a strong three-dimensional effect without any actual depth of carving. On construction it was the only stone building in Marrakesh apart from the Koutoubia minaret. Passing through, the **Kasbah mosque***
is in front of you; the narrow *passageway to the Saadian tombs*, insignificant and not really signposted, at its near right-hand corner.

To reach the ruins of the **El Badi** palace – which seems originally to have sprawled across the whole area east of the Kasbah mosque – you have to backtrack slightly. At the Bab Agnaou follow the ramparts up again, this time taking the road just inside them, until you come to a reasonably sizeable street on your right (just before the walls temporarily give out). Turn into this, keeping more or less straight, and in about 550m you emerge at the Place des Ferblantiers – a major intersection of roads. On the south side of the *place* is a gate known as the Bab Berrima which opens onto a long rectangular enclosure, flanked on either side by walls: go through and to your left and you'll come to the Badi's entrance. Hours are generally 9-12 & 2.30-5.30; again a guided tour is pushed, though far from essential.

Though substantially ruined, and reduced throughout to its red *pisé* walls, enough remains of **El Badi** to suggest that its name – the Incomparable – was not immodest. It took Moulay Ismail over ten years of systematic work to strip the palace of everything moveable or of value and even so there's a lingering sense of luxury and grandeur. The scale, with its sunken gardens and vast 90m pool, is certainly unrivalled, and the odd traces of zellij and plaster evoke a decor that was probably as brilliant as the Saadian tombs.

Begun shortly after Ahmed el Mansour's accession, the palace's initial finance came from the enormous ransom paid out by the Portuguese after the 'Battle of the Three Kings' at Ksar el Kebir. Fought in the summer of 1578, this was one of the most disastrous battles in Christian medieval history: ostensibly in support of a rival Saadian claimant but to all intents a Portuguese crusade, led by the king, Sebastiáo, and supported by almost the entire nobility. Few escaped death or Moorish capture. Sebastiáo himself was killed, so too were both the Saadian claimant and the ruling Sultan. As a result Ahmed – dubbed *el Mansour*, 'the Victorious' – came to the throne, undisputed and commanding immediate wealth. He reigned for twenty-five years, trading in sugar and slaves with Britain, Spain and Italy, seizing the gold route across the Sahara with the capture of Timbuctou (which earned him the additional epithet *El-Dhahabi*, 'the golden'), and maintaining peace in Morocco through a loose confeder-

*The mosque's minaret looks gaudy and modern but is in fact contemporary with both the Koutoubia and Hassan towers. It was restored, exactly to its original state, in the 1960s.

ation of tribes. It was the most prosperous era in the country's history since Almohad times – a cultural and political renaissance reflected in the coining of a new title, the Shereefian Empire, which was to remain the country's official name until Independence in 1956.

What you see today is essentially the ceremonial part of the Badi, planned on a grand scale for the reception of embassies, though not for everyday living. It seems likely that El Mansour and the multiple members of his court each had private palaces – smaller, though built to a similar groundplan – to the west and south, covering much of the area today occupied by the Dar el Makhzen. The *entrance* in current use was probably not the main approach. Going through, you find yourself at the side of a *mosque*, like everything else within this complex of an enormous height. Beyond extends the great *central court*, over 130m long, almost as wide, and entirely constructed on a substructure of vaults to allow the circulation of water through the pools and gardens. When they are full – as for the June folklore festival (see p. 215) – the pools are an incredibly majestic sight: the main one above all with its island, originally surmounted by an elaborate double-fountain. At each side there were once summer pavilions, traces of which survive; the most prominent is at the far end, a monumental hall which was used by the sultan on occasions of state and known as the *Koubba el Hamsiniya* ('the fifty pavilion') for the number of its columns. Strangely enough, the size and splendour of these is documented by a quite separate source to the Arab chroniclers who extolled their beauty: the French philosopher Montaigne, travelling in Italy, saw craftsmen preparing them, 'each of an extreme height . . . for the king of Fes and Barbary'.

North of the courtyard are ruins of the *stables*, and beyond them, leading towards the intriguing walls of the present royal palace, a series of *dungeons*, used until quite recent years as a state prison. You can explore part of these, and might easily spend an afternoon wandering about the various inner courts above with their fragments of marble and zellij and their water-conduits for the fountains and *hammams*. Like the Saadian tombs, the Badi-inspired contemporary poets, and there is an account, too, by the chronicler El-Ifrani, of its construction:

> El Mansour made workmen come from all the different countries . . .
> He paid for the marble sent from Italy in sugar, pound for pound
> . . . awarded his workers very generously . . . and paid attention even
> to the entertainment of their children, so that the artisans might devote
> themselves entirely to their work without being distracted by any
> other preoccupation.

If this is half true there can have been few greater contrasts to the next great Moroccan builder, and the dismantler of the palace, Moulay Ismail, whose workmen, beaten about, starved and abused, were buried in the walls where they fell. But C16 crèches aside, the most enduring account of the palace concerns its state opening, a fabulous occasion attended by ambassadors from several European powers and by all the sheiks and caids of the kingdom. Surveying the effect, Ahmed turned to his court fool for an opinion on the new palace. 'Sidi', the man replied, 'this will make a magnificent ruin.'

The Mellah, Bahia and Dar Si Said

It was in 1558 – five years before Ahmed's accession – that the city's **Mellah**, the separate Jewish quarter, was created. There is no exact record of why this was done at this particular time. Possibly it was the result of a pogrom, the Sultan moving the Jews to the protection of his Kasbah – and they in turn forming a useful buffer-zone (and scapegoat) between palace and populace at times of social unease. But as likely as not it was simply determined for ease of taxation. The Jews of Marrakesh were an important financial resource: they controlled most of the Saadian sugar trade, and comprised practically all of the city's bankers, metalworkers, jewellers and tailors. In the C16, at least, their quarter was almost a town in itself, supervised by rabbis, and with its own souks, gardens, fountains and synagogues.

The present Mellah, much smaller in extent, is almost entirely Muslim – the Marrakchi Jews having left for Casablanca (where some 6,000 or so still live), or emigrated to France or Israel. The few who remain, outwardly distinguishable only by the men's small black skullcaps, are mostly poor or old, or both. Their quarter, however, is immediately distinct: its houses taller than elsewhere, the streets more enclosed, even the shop-cubicles smaller. Until the Protectorate, Jews were not permitted to own land or property – nor even to ride, or to walk except barefoot – outside the Mellah; a situation greatly exploited by their own landlords who resisted all attempts to expand its walls. Today's air of neglect and poverty – this not being an elevated quarter in which to settle – is probably less than at any time during the past three centuries.

The main entrance, in what is still a largely walled district, is at the **Place des Ferblantiers**. This square, formerly the Place du Mellah, was itself part of the old Jewish souk and an arch (to your right if you stand at Bab Berrima) leads into its midst. Near the top end is a jewellers' souk, one of the traditional Jewish trades though now more or less taken over by Muslim artisans; further on are good spice and textile souks. Right at the centre – and positioned very much as the goal of a maze – is a small square with a fountain in the middle, the Place Souweka. You will almost certainly find yourself here if you wander about for a short while and manage to avoid the blind alleys. To your east, 200m or so away, is the old Jewish **cemetery**, the *Mihaara*. Closer at hand, though you'll need to enlist a guide to find them, are a number of **synagogues** (*s'noga*).

Even when in active use many were as much private houses as temples – 'serving also as places in which to eat, sleep and to kill chickens', according to Budgett Meakin – and they are today generally lived in. One of the larger ones, attached to a kind of hostel financed by American Jews, can usually be visited, and, depending on who your guide knows, a couple of others.

Heading north from the Mellah – back towards the Djemaa el Fna – there are three direct and quite simple routes. To the left of the Place des Ferblantiers the **Avenue Hoummam el Ftouaki** will bring you out by the Koutoubia. Above the *place*, two parallel streets, the *rues* **Zitoun el Kedim** and **Zitoun el Jdid** lead up to the Djemma itself. El Kedim is basically a shopping street, lined with general goods stores, barber shops and at its top end a couple of *hammams* (open all day: one each for women and men). El Jdid is more residential, and it is here that you find the major concentration of **palaces and mansions** built in those strange, closing decades of the last century, and the first few years of this, when the sultans Moulay Hassan and Moulay Abd el Aziz held court in the city.

By far the most ambitious and costly of these was **El Bahia**, residence of the Grand Vizier Si Ahmed Ben Moussa. Shrewd, wilful and cruel in the tradition of his age, Bou Ahmed (as he was better known) was a negro slave who rose to hold massive power in the Shereefian kingdom and for the last six years of his life exercised virtually autocratic control.

He was first Chamberlain to Moulay Hassan, whose death whilst returning from a *harka* he managed to conceal until the proclamation of Abd el Aziz at Rabat (see p. 332 for the dramatic account). Under Abd el Aziz just twelve years old at his accession, Bou Ahmed usurped the position of vizier from the ill-fated Jamai brothers (see p. 161) and then proceeded to rule. The Bahia he began in 1894, enlarging it, as land and property around was acquired, until his death in 1900. Its name means 'the Effulgence', or Brilliance, which after a **guided tour** around various sections of the rambling palace courts and apartments seems a near-total misnomer. There is reasonable craftsmanship in the main *reception halls*, and a pleasant arrangement of rooms in the *harem quarter*, but for the most part it is all fabulously vulgar and hasn't aged too well. Perhaps this is the main reason for a visit: for you come away realising just how much mastery and sophistication went into the Saadian medressa and tombs, and how corrupt and dull their traditions became. But there is also a certain pathos to the empty, echoing chambers – and the inevitable passing of Bou Ahmed's influence and glory. Walter Harris, who knew the Vizier, described his demise and the clearance of his palace in *Morocco that Was*, published just twenty years later, but by which time his name was already 'only a memory of the past':

*For several days as the Vizier lay expiring, guards were stationed
outside his palace waiting in silence for the end. And then one
morning the wail of the women within the house told that death had
come. Every gateway of the great building was seized, and no one
was allowed to enter or come out, while within there was
pandemonium. His slaves pillaged wherever they could lay their
hands. His women fought and stole to get possession of the jewels.
Safes were broken open, documents and title-deeds were extracted,
precious stones were torn from their settings the more easily to be
concealed, and even murder took place. . . . A few days later nothing
remained but the great building – all the rest had disappeared into
space. His family were driven out to starvation and ruin, and his
vast properties passed into the possession of the State. It was the
custom of the country.*

For some years of the Protectorate the palace was in fact used again as
a house for the Resident-General. Today it would probably be best
adapted as a hotel, for the tours only bother to take you around a third
or so of the rooms. To find it is quite straightforward: from the Rue
Zitoun follow the signs to the *Palais Gharnata*, keeping straight when
they suddenly direct you to the right under an arch. The **Gharnata**, and
nearby **Riad**, are among a number of mansions in this part of the city
which have been converted into 'Tourist-Spectacle' restaurants; they're
all expensive – and the shows hideously unauthentic – though interesting
for a quick look at the buildings themselves.

Worth some time, too, on this route, is the **Dar Si-Said**, a smaller
version of the Bahia which was built by a brother of Bou Ahmed. The
brother, something of a simpleton, nonetheless gained the post of royal
chamberlain. The palace is today a **museum of Moroccan arts**, particularly strong on its collections of southern *Berber jewellery and weapons*
– large, boldly designed objects of real beauty. There are also excellent
displays of C18 and C19 *wood-carving* from the Glaoui Kasbahs, *modern
Berber rugs*, and a curious group of traditional *wedding-chairs* – once
widely used for carrying the bride, veiled and hidden, to her new home
– and *fairground swings*, used at Moussems until the 1940s. The Dar Si
Said is just a block to the west of the Rue Zitoun el Jdid (turn right
opposite a mosque, getting on for half-way down); like the Bahia its
normal *opening hours* are from 9.30-12 & 2.30-5.30, closed Tuesdays.

The gardens

With summer temperatures of 90-100'F – and peaks well above that –
it seems best to devote at least the middle of a Marrakesh day to total
inactivity: and if you want to do this in style, it means finding your way
to a garden. There are two – the Agdal and Menara – which are designed

for this exact purpose. Each begins near the edge of the Medina, rambles through acres of orchard and olive groves, and comes, near its centre, to an immense, lake-sized pool of water. This is all – they are not flower gardens – but, cool and completely still, they seem both satisfying and luxurious, and in perfect contrast to the close city streets.

The **Agdal**, considerably the larger, is the best: some 3km in extent and with half a dozen smaller irrigation pools in addition to its *grand bassin*. Beginning just south of the Mellah and Royal Palace, it is watered by an incredible system of wells and underground channels which reach to the base of the Atlas in the Ourika valley and which date, in part, from the earliest foundation of the city. Over the centuries these have often fallen into disrepair and the gardens been abandoned, but the present (C19) layout probably differs little from any of its predecessors. It is walled about, with gates at each of the near corners whilst, inside, the orchard of oranges, figs, lemons, apricots and pomegranates are divided into square irrigated plots by an endless series of raised walkways and great avenues of olive trees. If you come out here by yourself the simplicity of all this can be confusing – and it's over 2km before you reach the main series of pools at its heart. The big one to ask for is the *Sahraj el Hana* ('tank of health'), which was probably dug by the Almohads and is flanked by a ramshackle old *menzeh*, or summer pavilion, where the last few pre-Colonial sultans held picnics and boating parties. You can climb up to its roof for a fabulous view over the park and across to the Koutoubia and Atlas, and if the caretaker's around you'll be shown the steam-launch in which, in 1873, the Sultan Sidi Mohammed capsized – or, as his epitaph put it, 'departed this life, in a water tank, in the hope of something better to come'. These days probably the most dangerous thing you could do here would be to swim, though the kids do and it looks unbelievably tempting. Better to pick up some food, maybe a bottle of wine from the Gueliz, and spread yourself out in good local tradition on the paved, shaded pathway around its edge.

The **Menara** is in a similar vein – though it has a single tank, is closer to the city and much more visited. If you just want a glimpse of one of these still sheets of water come out here, it's a lot easier to get to than the Agdal (and a cheaper ride). Like the Agdal, the Menara was restored and its pavilions rebuilt by the Sultan Abd er Rahman (1822-59). By tradition the famous poolside *menzeh* is supposed to have replaced an original Saadian structure.

To get to the Menara and particularly the Agdal would be a pretty enthusiastic walk – from the Djemaa el Fna, respectively 3½km and nearly 6km. You might therefore take at least this opportunity of hiring a **calèche**, which in summer can come surprisingly cheap and is far from exclusively tourist transport. Alternatively, for the chance to take in both gardens and tour round the ramparts and palmery you could rent a **bike** for the day: there are several places along the Av. Mohammed V (try

Peugeot at no. 225) and it'll set you back less than the cost of a return to the Agdal by *petit taxi*. The Menara couldn't be simpler to find: just follow the Av. de la Menara from the Bab Jdid (see the plan on p. 206). For the Agdal, take the road outside the ramparts below the Bab Agnaou/Bab er Robb and then turn left as you are about to leave the city at the Bab Irhli: this route will take you through a *mechouar* (parade ground) by the Royal Palace and to the corner gate of the garden, once inside keep going and ask directions. The best section of the **palmery** is signposted ('Route de Palmerie'), about 2km out on the Avenue el Jadida after its intersection with Av. Yacoub el Mansour; it is impressive, though not for very long if you are planning to head south. On the way, however, you could stop and take a look at the subtropical **Jardin Majorelle**, or *Bou Saf Saf* as it's now officially known, a small botanical garden created in the 1920s by the minor French painter, Louis Majorelle. A sobering afterthought, as you pass **Bab Doukkala**, is the shanty-town just outside the walls above the bus station – a quarter with its own industry, scrap and general goods souks, which is the direct descendent of the city's old leper colony. Even in the early years of the Protectorate lepers from here used to beg at the gates of the Medina, from which they were forbidden entrance.

Lastly – and much closer to hand – are the spectacularly elite gardens of the **Mamounia hotel**. Walled from the outside world, yet only five minutes walk from the Djemaa, these were once royal grounds, laid out by the Saadians with a succession of pavilions and follies. They are today slightly Europeanised in style, but have retained the traditional elements of shrubs and walkways. For the cost of a drink or tea on the terrace – neither exactly cheap options – you can walk in. Be prepared to resist the swimming pool, which is strictly reserved for residents, but if the waiters aren't too busy you can ask to be ushered up to the *Winston Churchill suite* – preserved complete with his books, Sultanic bed and photos of him painting in the gardens. Churchill was a frequent visitor to Marrakesh through the 1930s-1950s, and the Mamounia, so it is said, was his favourite hotel in the world. Though it's been rebuilt and enlarged since his day, it's not hard to understand the appeal.

Practicalities

Other than picking up mail at the main post office, or arranging car hire, there's no particular reason to hang around the French-built new town, **Gueliz** – you can cash money, eat well and even drink in the **Medina**. Listings that follow are largely geared to this.

Eating, drinking and nightlife
You may decide against eating at them – as even the hustlers caution – but at some stage wander down the makeshift lane of **eating stalls** near

the top of the Djemaa el Fna. These tend to specialise in a few main dishes (though they often have a larger range on display) and it's worth watching the crowds for a while to check out what is best eaten where. If you go for it, take a seat on one of the benches, ask the price of a plate of food, and order all you fancy; if you want to wash it down with a coke or mineral water, the owners will send a boy off to fetch one for you.

No more expensive and a lot healthier are some of the **cafes** on the side of the Djemaa. The best of these is an *unnamed café-restaurant* with a small terrace beside the Café Montreal (about 10m past the Café de France in the direction of the souks); this serves excellent kefta and brochettes, harira, salad and fresh yoghourt, all very cheaply. Somewhat pricier, though a good variation, are the rooftop-restaurants of the *Café el Fath* – directly opposite at the entrance to the souks – with a good line in tajines, and the *L'Etoile de Marrakech*, just off the square in Rue Bab Agnaou. The *Café de France* itself is really a place to drink tea or soft drinks on the terrace; the meals it serves, both here and in a cushioned salon downstairs, are dull and overpriced.

Well **upmarket** from all of these – but serving some of the best food you'll find in the country – is the *Hôtel-Restaurant Foucauld* (on the Square de Foucauld: see the plan on p. 206). This is a French-Moroccan restaurant in the old tradition, with a palace-type salon (but no kitsch entertainment) and massive portions of all that they serve. Pastilla (pigeon/chicken/vegetable pie) here is exceptional, so too the soups, pâté and vast pots of vegetables. The Foucauld's sister-hotel, the *Grand Tazi*, has a similar restaurant on its roof – just down the road at the corner of Rue Bab Agnaou/Av. Hoummam el Ftouaki. Though its food isn't usually quite so good, this is a pleasant place and worth visiting as a **bar** – the only one in the Medina apart from the Mamounia hotel.

Among the **Gueliz bars**, the *Renaissance* (by the hotel of the same name – see our key – on Av. Mohammed V) and *Petit Poucet* (56 Av. Mohammed V) are probably the liveliest: none, however, keep especially late hours. The *Poucet*, if you can afford it, also has an excellent French **restaurant**; or, if you're desperate for a change from French/Moroccan food, there's a Chinese (*Restaurante Chinois*, 134 Av. Mohammed V) and a couple of Italian places (*La Trattoria*, Rue Mohammed Beqal; and *La Pizza*, 63 Av. Mohammed V). Cheaper Gueliz options include the *Café Chaabia* (Blvd Moulay Rachid: a good choice if you're staying at the Campsite or Youth Hostel) and *Café de l'Union* (Rue Ibn Aicha: the road which cuts across from the end of the Av. Yacoub el Mansour/beginning of Blvd Zerktouni to the Charia Mohammed Abd el Krim – above no. 1 on our main plan).

Entertainment and **nightlife** in Marrakesh revolve around the Djemaa el Fna and its cafes. Sometimes, though, there might be a Berber **rock**

band playing in an enclosure behind the Koutoubia on Av. Mohammed V (see the plan on p. 206), and in Gueliz there are half a dozen or so **discos**. These include the *Pub Laurent* on Rue Ibn Aicha (see above for instructions) and *L'Atlas* and *Le Flash* on Av. Mohammed V.

Finally, if you can possibly coincide, there's an annual **Folklore Festival** held in the Badi palace. Despite its tourist-sham name, this can be tremendous, with groups of musicians and dancers brought in from all over the country and performances spanning the whole range of Moroccan music – from the Gnaoua drummers and the Pan pipers of Jajouka, across Berber *ahouaches* from the Atlas and southern oases, to classic Andalusian music from Fes. The shows are held each evening; before they start, towards sunset, there is also a **fantasia** at the Bab el Jdid – a spectacle by any standards with dozens of Berber horsemen firing their guns in the air at full gallop. The festival usually takes place for a fortnight, around the end of May/beginning of June.

Transport

TRAINS are the quickest and most comfortable way of getting to Casa and Rabat. If you're heading back to Tangier it's possible to do the journey in one haul, but you'll be travelling for most of the day. If you're confident – and look after your bags – you *could* do this journey by night.

BUSES to all except local destinations leave from the main terminal at the Bab Doukkala. Buy tickets in advance for the more popular destinations such as Fes, Essaouira and El Jadida or you could find yourself waiting for the second or third bus that's leaving, and turn up early if you're making for Idni or Taroudannt over the Tizi n'Test route – the *SATAS* bus currently leaves at 5am. Bear in mind, too, that *CTM* and all the private lines have their own individual windows – choices can be more extensive than at first appears. The local exceptions are buses to Ourika and to Asni (for Toubkal): these *all* leave from down by the Bab er Robb.

GRANDS TAXIS can also be useful for getting to Ourika or to Asni – negotiate for these by the Bab er Robb. Other destinations are less frequent but you can try asking some of the drivers at the ranks in the Djemaa el Fna and by the Bab er Raha (between the Av. Mohammed V and Bab Doukkala).

FLIGHTS *Royal Air Maroc* (197 Av. Mohammed V) operate internal flights to Casa, with onward connections to Tangier and Fes. There is supposed to be a student discount but to obtain it you must buy tickets in advance at the Mohammed V office – rather than at the airport, as is sometimes advised. The **airport** is 5km out, off the Av. de Menara: bargain hard with the *petit taxi* drivers but don't expect 'normal' rates.

Listings

AMERICAN EXPRESS c/o *Voyages Schwarz*, Rue Mauritania (off Av Mohammed V: 2nd left after the Place de la Liberté as you're coming from the Medina). Business hours Mon-Fri 9-12.30 & 3-4.30 but stays open until 7pm for mail.

BANKS *Crédit du Maroc, Banque Populaire* and the *SGMB* all have branches on Rue Bab Agnaou – just off the Djemaa el Fna. In the new town try the main stretch of Av. Mohammed V. For currency exchange there is a desk at the Bab Doukkala bus station.

BERBER MARKET A favourite tout of the Djemaa and souk hustlers: 'the Berber market – only today', they tell you, and off you go. In fact all the main souks are open every day, though they're quiet on Friday mornings. Even the big Souk el Khemis ('the Thursday market', see p. 202) now operates most days of the week.

CAR HIRE Marrakesh is the city where you're most likely to want to hire a car – and its rates are generally the most competitive after Casablanca. One of the cheapest is usually *Leasing Cars* (59 Blvd Mansour el Eddahbi: parallel with Blvd Mohammed V; Tel. 331-84) but you'd do well to ring round half a dozen. Companies include: *LVS*, 41, Rue Yougouslavie (Tel. 332-14); *Budget Cars*, 213, Blvd Mohammed V (Tel. 334-24); *Europ-Car*, 189 Blvd Mohammed V (Tel. 303-68); *Sud Cars*, 213, Av. Mohammed V (Tel. 309-97); *Transcar*, 10 Blvd Zerktouni (Tel. 316-47); *Tourist Cars*, 64, Blvd Zerktouni (Tel. 315-30) and *Hertz*, 154 Blvd Mohammed V (Tel. 346-80).

CAR REPAIRS The garage beside the Tazi hotel in Rue Bab Agnaou fix Renaults – and should be able to point you elsewhere for other makes which they don't have parts for.

CRAFTS Like Fes, Marrakesh can be an expensive place to buy – though if you've goods to bargain (design T-shirts, training-shoes, trousers . . .) you'll find people eager enough to arrange an exchange. Before setting out in search of rugs and blankets or whatever, check out the classic designs in the Dar Si Said museum and take a look at the (higher than you should pay) prices in the official state-run *Artisanal centre* – just inside the ramparts beside the Av. Mohammed V.

FESTIVALS Ramadan sees the Djemaa at its liveliest and most enjoyable: a great time to be in the city. Otherwise, the big tourist event is the Folklore Festival (see p. 215) held in late May/early June. Local *moussems* include Setti Fatma (Ourika; August), Sidi Bouatmane (Amizmiz; September) and Moulay Brahim (Asni; over the Mouloud).

GUIDES Official guides can be arranged at the ONMT or S.I. tourist offices (see below), unofficial ones in the Djemaa el Fna and almost anywhere you're seen looking unpurposeful.

HITCHING As ever, the campsite can be a good place to arrange lifts, or find people to share car hire or petrol costs. There are always people setting out for Ouarzazate and the southern kasbah/oasis routes.

MAPS In addition to those we've printed, and for an overview of the town and Medina, you might find the free ONMT leaflet-plan helpful. Maps of Toubkal can be bought up in Imlil (see p. 224).

MARKETS Local markets around Marrakesh include Amizmiz (Thursday; see below), Dar Caid Ouriki (Monday; see p. 218), Ait Ourir (on the road to Ouazarzate; Monday) and Tamasloht (on the road to Amizmiz; Tuesday). There is said to be a camel market every Tuesday, 4km out on the road to Essaouira: I've never made this, though it's probably a small one and for selling camels for slaughter/camel meat.

NEWSPAPERS Occasional British ones, plus *Time, Newsweek*, etc., from the stalls along Av. Mohammed V in Gueliz, and from the smart hotels.

PHARMACY There are several along the Av. Mohammed V, including a good one just off the Place de la Liberté who often have a doctor on call. Most Gueliz pharmacies will in fact be able to give you the name of an English-speaking doctor.

POST OFFICE The main PTT is on the Place 16 Novembre, midway down Av. Mohammed V: service hours are Mon-Sat 8am-2pm. The telephones section, with a separate entrance, stays open 24hrs a day.

SWIMMING POOLS There's a large, very popular municipal pool on the Rue Abou el Abbes Sebti – the first main road to the left off Av. Mohammed V as you walk past the Koutoubia towards Gueliz. In low season you might try asking one of the 4* hotels if they'll let you in for a fee.

TOURIST OFFICES Both the *ONMT* and *Syndicat d'Initiative* are on Av. Mohammed V – the first at the Place Abd El Moumen Benali, the second a little way up towards the Medina at no.170. Open daily 8.30-12 & 3-6 (S.I. closed Sat afternoons and Sundays).

OUT OF MARRAKESH: OURIKA, OUKAIMEDEN AND AMIZMIZ

Staying a few days in Marrakesh you're bound to hear about Ourika – a long and beautiful valley where the young breeze out on their mopeds to escape the city heat and lie about beside the streams and waterfalls. It is not a particularly dramatic 'sight', nor much touted by any of the tour guides, but for a day or two's break it's pretty much ideal. Access is simple. Taxis, buses and a fast transit-van leave the Bab er Robb fairly regularly from around 6am-midday and return in the late afternoon/early evening. The place to make for is SETTI FATMA, right at the end of the road and some 67km from Marrakesh: the journey takes a little under two hours (more by bus) and taxi fares start about 12-14dhs one way. Keep in mind that some of the Ourika taxis only run as far as DAR CAID OURIKI (33km) or ARHBALOU (50km), and unless it's market day (Monday – when lifts are easy) hold out for one going the whole way or to ASGAOUR (63km), the last village before Setti Fatma. Returning to Marrakesh you may have to walk up to Asgaour to pick up the bus.

The valley actually begins at **DAR CAID OURIKI,** a small roadside village with a mosque and zaouia clumped into the rocks to the left of the road. Beyond, scattered at intervals over the next 40km, are a series of very small hamlets, a few summer homes and cafe-restaurants and one sizeable settlement – **ARHBALOU,** where most of your fellow passengers will get off. There are some good walks around here and the possibility of serious hiking into the Djebel Yagour (see below), but it is at **SETTI FATMA** that things get really tempting. Here, a little over a kilometre before you arrive, the road and taxis give out and you climb down into a shallow stream of clear, icy water, flowing across the track even in the middle of August. On the far side is a cafe – the village focus – and below it an incredible flank of grassy terrace. People camp here for weeks on end through the summer – a real oasis as you arrive from the dry plains around Marrakesh – and in the rocky foothills behind there is a series of six, sometimes seven, **waterfalls,** the walk everyone suggests and points you towards. The first few falls are an easy 20 minute scramble over the rocks, the three highest slightly more tricky; walking up this way you can loop back to Setti Fatma's twin hamlet of Zaouia Mohammed, a few hundred metres further down the valley. If you want to stay there are three options besides the makeshift campsite; the *cafe* rents a few simple rooms and arranges others in village houses for longer periods, there's a small inn, the *Hôtel Atlas,* just at the edge of the village where the road gives out; and lastly, a couple of kilometres further back, a positively luxurious and fabulously sited 2* hotel, *La Chaumière.* The main **market** in the valley is on Mondays at NIRKE OURIKA, 10 km back towards ARHBALOU: a good day to come out. Even better, if you can establish the date at the ONMT in Marrakesh, is Setti Fatma's annual **moussem.** This takes place for four days round about the middle of August – as much a fair and market as religious festival, it brings in villagers from the isolated hamlets dotted all over the mountains and valleys of this region.

Ourika in fact cuts right into the High Atlas, whose peaks begin to dominate the land almost as soon as you draw clear of Marrakesh. At Setti Fatma they rise on three sides to 12,000ft: a startling backdrop which, to the south-west, takes in the main **hiking/climbing zone** of Morocco, the *Toubkal National Park.* The usual approach to this is from Asni and Imlil (detailed with the main walks in the following section) but it is possible to set off from here to reach either Tachedirt (a 2-day hike via the little-used refuge at Timichi) or the mountain lake of Ifni. If you are interested – and these are much harder, longer hikes than those from the west side – ask at the cafe in Setti Fatma for Bouifraden Mohammed Bella. Mohammed lives in the village (his father runs the transit-van taxi) and will guide you over any number of hikes in the region – from an easy day's excursion to a 10-12 day expedition to Ouazarzate; Possibilities between the two include striking up into the Djebel Yagour with its mass of prehistoric rock-carvings, or cutting through the Zat valley to emerge just below Taddert (see p. 236) on the n'Tichka pass.

An alternative and rather easier base from which to set out towards Toubkal is the village and ski-centre of **OUKAIMEDEN**, reached via a good modern road which veers off from Ourika just before Arhbalou. The village is a motley grouping of hotels, chalets and a few seasonal facilities (post office, ski hire, food-shops, restaurants), but the route up, carved from the mountainside, is spectacular and in midsummer, when Marrakesh can be up in the 120°sF, here it's a cool 60-70°F. The obvious place to stay the night is the large *CAF (Club Alpin) hut*, an extremely well-equipped building with a bar, kitchens (bring food if you don't want to pay inflated prices) and an informative resident warden who will give you advice and directions for the 3½-4hr trail to Tachedirt. Filling in time – or as an end in itself – the one interesting feature of Oukaimeden itself is the various clusters of prehistoric rock-drawings scattered around the sides of the plateau and mountain. There is a diagram, showing where to find these, displayed in the CAF hut: some, depicting animals, weapons and geometric designs, are to be seen only 20mins walk away.

The **trail to Tachedirt** is generally reckoned clear and easy-going. It begins a little way beyond the *teleski* (chairlift) carpark, veering off to the right of the dirt road that continues for a while past this point. The col, or pass, is reached in about 2hrs: on the descent the trail divides in two, either of which will lead you down to Tachedirt (for details on which see p.227).

As a ski-resort and hiking-centre Oukaimeden is a distinctly **seasonal** place. There are buses up from Marrakesh in winter, a less regular service in the summer and a completely dead season from mid-March until the beginning of July. At these times you'll have to hitch or take a taxi up from Arhbalou. The CAF hut is open all year round. Oukaimeden's **skiing** is reputed the best in Morocco (one major slope, three dormitory slopes: all served by chairlifts), though the fall of snow can be enormously erratic and the surfaces often very icy.

Another easy daytrip from Marrakesh is to the small town of **AMIZMIZ**, over to the west of the Tiz n'Test and the site of an important and long-established Tuesday market. This, one of the largest Berber souks of the Atlas, attracts only a few sporadic tourists though it is quite well served by bus. The town itself is interesting in a modest way: a cluster of distinct quarters – including a Mellah, zaouia and kasbah – separated by a small ravine.

THE HIGH ATLAS

The High Atlas, the greatest mountain range of north Africa, is perhaps the most beautiful and intriguing part of Morocco. An historical (and physical) barrier between the northern plains and the pre-Sahara, it has maintained a remoteness which until recent decades was virtually complete. When the French began their 'pacification' in the 1920s the Atlas way of life was essentially feudal, based upon the control of the three main passes (the Tishka, n'Test and Imi n'Tanaout) by three 'clan' families, 'the Lords of the Atlas', and even with the co-operation of these warrior-chiefs it was not until 1933 (21 years after the establishment of the Protectorate) that they were able to subdue and conquer the tribal lands. Today the region is under official government control through a system of local caids but in many villages the role of the state is still largely irrelevant – the Atlas Berbers are not generally taxed nor do they have any national benefits or services.

If you go walking into the Toubkal region – or even just stop for a day or two in one of the Tizi n'Test or Tishka villages – you soon become aware of this, and of the quite distinct culture and traditions of the mountains. The oldest-established inhabitants of Morocco, the Berbers here never adopted a totally orthodox version of Islam (see p. 322) and the Arabic language made virtually no impression on their indigenous Tachelhait dialects. Their music and the *ahouache* dances (in which women and men join together in broad circles) are unique; so too the village architecture, with its stone or clay houses tiered on the rocky slopes and craggy, fortified *agadirs* (collective granaries) and *kasbahs*, which continued to serve as kind of feudal castles for the community's defence right into the present century. Berber women in the Atlas are unveiled and have a much higher profile than their rural counterparts in the plains and the north. They perform virtually all the heavy labour – working in the fields, herding and grazing the cattle and goats, and carrying about vast loads of brushwood and provisions. Whether they have any greater status or power within the family and village, however, is questionable. The men, who often seem totally inactive by day, retain the 'important' tasks of buying and selling goods and the evening/night-time irrigation of the crops.

As an outsider in the mountains, one is constantly surprised by the friendliness and openness of the Berbers, and by their amazing capacity for languages – there's scarcely a village where you won't find someone who speaks French or English or both. In the areas where tourism has become a strong presence, particularly around Toubkal, there's exploitation too (initial prices can be unbelievable) but given the struggle of life up here this is hardly surprising.

HIKING IN THE ATLAS: TOUBKAL NATIONAL PARK

Hiking in the Atlas is one of the best possible experiences of Morocco, and in summer at least it's completely accessible for anyone reasonably fit. The mule trails around the mountain valleys are well-contoured and kept in excellent condition, the main ridges of the range are usually quite broad and there's a surprising density of villages and refuge huts. Unless you're undertaking a particularly long or ambitious hike you don't need any special equipment (beyond what's detailed below), nor will you need to do any actual climbing. The only physical problems are the high altitudes (from 10-12,000 ft throughout the Toubkal region), the midday heat and the tiring progress of walking over long sections of loose 'scree' – the mass of small volcanic chippings and stones which cover much of the mountains' surface.

The **Toubkal National Park,** a more or less roadless area enclosing the Atlas's tallest peaks, is the goal of 95% of people who hike in Morocco. It's easy to get to from Marrakesh (Asni, the 'first base', is just 2hrs by bus) and is reasonably well charted. It has not, however, been turned into an African version of the Alps: walking even quite short distances you get the sense of excitement and remoteness – and you feel very much the visitor in a rigidly individual world. Mount Toubkal itself, the highest peak in North Africa, is walkable right up to its summit and requires only two or three days all in from Marrakesh. Further afield and much less often visited is the high plateau-lake of Ifni, or much closer – a feasible daytrip from Asni – you can explore the beautiful valley between Imlil and Aremd. The villages too look amazing, their houses stacked one above another in apparently organic growth from the rocks, and, corny though it may sound until you arrive, absolutely nothing rivals the costume of the Berber women, which seem routinely to be composed of ten or twenty different and brilliant-coloured strips of material.

SOME DETAILS

Getting to Asni The most frequent buses from Marrakesh (about every 2hrs) leave from the Bab er Robb, *not* from the main Bab Doukkala station; the journey takes around 1½hrs.

Seasons Toubkal is usually under snow from November until mid-June, a good time to hike but only if you're seriously prepared (with full alpine clothes, tent, iceaxe, etc.). For ordinary, non-expedition walking only the four summer months (July-October) are really practicable. At all times of year Toubkal's weather can change very abruptly – with occasional snow-showers, mist, rain and intense night cold even in midsummer. Fortunately these shifts are usually very short-lived, generally for a few hours at most and rarely for more than a day. There are a few strategically sited refuges run by the French *CAF* Alpine Club.

Altitude Toubkal is 4,167m (13,750ft) above sea level and much of the surrounding region above 3,000m so it's possible you may get altitude sickness and/or headaches. Aspirins can help but just sucking sweets or swallowing is as good as anything. If you experience more than slight breathlessness and really feel like vomiting, go down straight away.

Clothes Even in the summer months you'll need a warm jersey or jacket and preferably a kagoul but tents at this time aren't necessary if you have a good sleepingbag and bivibag/groundsheet. Hiking boots are ideal – you can get by with a pair of trainers, though not sandals or gym shoes. Some kind of hat is essential and sunglasses helpful.

Other things worth bringing You can buy food at Asni, Imlil and some

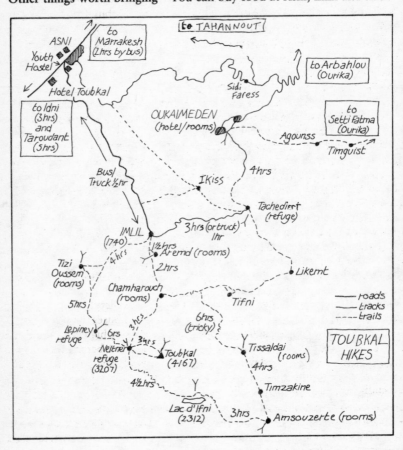

of the other villages – though it gets increasingly expensive the higher and the more remote you are so you may want to bring a few tins (sardines, tea, etc.) from Marrakesh. A 2-pint water bottle is enough since you can refill it fairly regularly; water purification tablets are probably worthwhile on longer trips, stomach pills, too, and insect repellent. You are constantly asked for cigarettes, *bon-bons* and cadeaux – and it's good if you can oblige: very basic medicines are always appreciated while, if you plan to hike for some time, local guides are always in great need of decent equipment.

Maps A 1:50,000 survey map of the Toubkal-region is sold at Imlil, and is certainly useful for anything more than the straightforward Imlil-Neltner-Toubkal hike. Also available there is Robin Collomb's very thorough and detailed *Atlas Mountains Guide*, the only book of its kind in English and invaluable if you really get interested in the walking/climbing possibilities.

The bases: Asni, Imlil and Aremd

The bus terminus for Toubkal, **ASNI** is really little more than a roadside village and marketplace – and a place many hikers pass straight through to get up into the mountains proper. If you're in a hurry this is good reasoning, though it's no disaster if you have to stay overnight: there's a very pleasant, shaded *Auberge de Jeunesse* (open all year: slightly higher charges for non IYHF members) near the far end of the village and, just beyond it, the amazingly luxurious 3*A *Grand Hôtel du Toubkal*, complete with bar, swimming-pool and reputedly excellent French cooking. Staying in the hostel you can cook for yourself (there are half a dozen food and provisions shops in the village) or try to persuade one of the cafe-stalls to rustle up a vegetable tajine or harira. The offers of 'couscous meals' – with which you'll be flooded here and also in Aremd – are another option, though bargaining down a price to anything half-way reasonable can be a tedious business.

The initial persistence of Asni's meal (and jewellery) touts is a little offputting, but it's all very shortlived and between buses the village drifts back into a smallholding/farming existence. The one big event – and the most interesting and convenient time to be around before making for Toubkal – is the **Saturday market** when the whole enclosure behind the row of shop-cubicles is crowded out with fruit, vegetable and livestock stalls, an occasional storyteller and a rather bizarre assembly of Berber barbers. The advantage of arriving on a Saturday morning (or Friday night) is that you can stock up with good cheap supplies and catch the bus – which runs throughout the morning – on to Imlil. Other days of the week getting to Imlil means waiting for the blue *camion*, which leaves whenever twenty or so passengers are assembled, or finding some fellow travellers to share the village's one taxi – a pricier approach, even after haggling, but probably your only choice if you want to move on in the late afternoon.

Whichever way you travel, the 17km of road and track to Imlil is a beautiful journey and a startling transition. Almost as soon as it leaves Asni the road begins to climb, while below opens up the brilliant and fertile valley of the Oued Rhirhaia, villages and hamlets crowded into the rocky slopes above its course. At **IMLIL** the air feels quite different – silent and rarefied at some 1740km – and trails and streams head off in all directions. The village itself is a small cluster of houses, along with three or four provisions shops, a prominent CAF hut and a **cafe terrace**, beside which a sign above a tiny stall announces 'welcome to the Shopping Centre'. This, whatever you're planning to do, should be your first stop. You can buy almost anything here, from left-behind bits of camping gear to the Toubkal survey maps and, more importantly, can talk over any doubts or queries you might have with the cafe-shopkeeper, Lahcen Easqarray. Lahcen has worked as a guide throughout the Toubkal area, speaks good English, and is an extremely trustworthy source of knowledge about any possible route you might be thinking of trying, or on virtually any other matter: if you want to make a camping base at Aremd, for instance, he should be able to recommend someone to act as a 'guardien' for your tent and equipment. The other source of information in Imlil, apart from the steady flow of hikers passing through, is the **CAF hut**, its noticeboard and book, and its wardens. Open all year and providing bunkbeds and foam mattresses (no blankets), kitchen and washing facilities, the hut is really a more useful place to spend the night than the Asni youth hostel if you want to make an early start for the Neltner hut and the ascent of Toubkal. You can leave your main pack/baggage at the hut (as too at Asni) or, if you're planning to set up a base for a number of expeditions, you can hire a mule and porter to transport it along with a supply of food and provisions. Rates for **porters/mules** are displayed on the outside of the hut, along with those for the official CAF approved guides. One mule can usually be shared among several people – and if you're setting out for Lac d'Ifni, Lepiney or Neltner can be a rewarding investment; there are two extras on the price – a fee to the supervisor in Imlil and a tip to the porter at the end. **Guides** aren't necessary for the trek up Toubkal (which is a fairly clear and very well-trodden trail) but can be invaluable for a group trying some of the more ambitious routes. The 'chief guide' in Imlil, who by general consent is the best for any serious expedition, has adopted the name Tensing.

AREMD (or AROUND as it's sometimes spelt) is 1-1½hr walk from Imlil – the first stage on the trail to Neltner and Toubkal and the largest village of the Mizane valley. It is an easy hike and if you arrive mid-afternoon at Imlil makes a good initial target. There are quite a number of **rooms** let out in the village houses and it's possible to **camp** slightly upstream. For camping you should ask permission and, as is usual, pay a small fee; the payment is really a compensation for non-production of crops since all possible land in this valley is cultivated. There is only one shop in Aremd – despite a population of some 500 – so if you lack the energy to negotiate a meal it's best to bring food from Asni or Imlil.

To get to Aremd from Imlil you basically follow the course of the Mizane river. On the west side (i.e. the right bank, coming from Imlil) there's a well-defined mule-track which switchbacks above the river for about 2km before dropping to the floor of the valley just before a crossing point to Imlil; over on the east bank (the Imlil side of the river) is a much rougher footpath – about the same distance but slightly harder to follow.

Even if you haven't time – or energy – for the hike up to Toubkal it can still be worth coming out for a day or so to Aremd. There are some fabulous trails down the path of the river valley and beside some of its seasonal streams, and the village itself, though increasingly geared towards tourism (one British holiday company maintains a base here), is an interesting community and an important agricultural centre for the region. It is built on a spur of loose rock above the valley, a site that resembles nothing so much as a landslide but which commands one of the most fertile stretches of the Atlas – terraced fields of maize, potatoes, onions, barley and various fruits. There is grazing about here too, and the village streets are often blocked by goats or cattle – and permanently coated in animal excrement and flies. Village life in the mountains is a lot poorer and less picturesque than it appears.

Imlil/Aremd to the Neltner refuge – and the ascent of Toubkal
One of the most surprising aspects of the hike to Neltner and Toubkal is just how straightforward it is: there's no climbing involved anywhere along the line, though some of the stonier stretches are a pretty energetic scramble. From Imlil the refuge at Neltner is about 12km (7 miles), a walk that should take you about 5½hrs if you set out early enough to benefit from the morning cool and shade. Once at Neltner most people stay the night, setting out at first light for Toubkal to get the clearest possible panorama from its heights. And since this *is* the tallest peak in Northern Africa it seems a shame to rush it any more than this.

From Aremd (see above) the Neltner trail follows the east (i.e. the Aremd) side of the Mizane river valley, climbing and zigzagging around the hard grey rocks. At intervals some of the larger rocks have been marked with red dots to reassure you that you're on the right track. If you have been following the main mule track on the west side of the valley from Imlil to Aremd you can join the trail without going into Aremd: it crosses over and merges with the section from Aremd a short distance after you pass the village to your left. The river is crossed once more 1½-2hrs further on, just before you arrive at the hamlet of **SIDI CHAMHAROUCH:** a cluster of houses, all built into one another, whose seasonal population of ten or twelve people run soft-drinks/basic-provisions shops for the tourist hikers and for the Moroccan pilgrims who come to visit the hamlet's marabout shrine. This lies just across the gorge from the hamlet, reached by a modern concrete bridge, which non-Muslims are strictly forbidden to cross. It is probably a survival of a very ancient nature-cult – which in these parts are often thinly veiled in the trappings of Islam. On the approach to the hamlet you may have noticed a tree, sacred to local tradition, where the Berbers hang strips of cloth and make piles of stones.

Beyond Sidi Chamharouch the Neltner trail continues along (and above) the course of **the Mizane** – drinkable now, unlike the earlier section of the valley. The track is pretty clear the whole way to the **NELTNER REFUGE,** which at 3,207m marks the spring snowline. Even in mid-August it gets pretty cold up here after the sun has disappeared behind the ridge and you'll probably want to take advantage of its shelter (open all year: about 20dhs to non-Alpine club members). It is quite possible, however, to camp on the grassy ridge below the hut or, if you're really committed, further up towards the summit. The first site is none too enticing – and there's no real vegetation above – but the night skies can be tremendous.

At Neltner you're almost bound to meet people who have just come down from **TOUBKAL** – the best source of description on the routes and on the state of the vaguely defined south corrie trail to the summit. The **south corrie** is the most popular and straightforward ascent and, depending on your fitness, should take between 2½-3½hrs (2-2½hrs coming down). With reasonable instructions and directions from the Neltner wardens or from fellow hikers it's easy enough to follow without hiring a guide, though there are confusing paths going off all over the place and you need to be careful finding the right track down. The trail actually begins just below the Neltner hut, dropping down to cross the stream and then climbing over a short stretch of grass and rock to reach the first of Toubkal's innumerable fields of boulders and scree. These – often needing three steps to gain one – are the most tiring (and memorable) feature of the hike up. The summit, a triangular plateau of stones marked by a tripod, is reached after much zigzagging through a gap in the ridge.

Robin Collomb, in his *Atlas Mountains* guide, recommends the **north corrie** as an alternative – though longer (4½hrs) and more ambitious – ascent. It's a bad way down, however, virtually guaranteeing periods of sliding and scraping down the scree. The **west-south-west corrie,** a third possible approach, is only for serious rock-climbers.

Lac d'Ifni: the route from Neltner

One of the largest mountain lakes in the Atlas – and the only one of any size in the Toubkal region – **LAC D'IFNI** is an impressive and satisfying target. From Neltner it's a 4-4½hr hike, an easy enough walking route though again involving long, tedious hauls over loose rock and scree. Coming back this is even more pronounced, and unless you're a very keen rock-scrambler you'll want to take enough food for a couple of day's camping to make the trip worthwhile.

The **Ifni trail** begins immediately behind the Neltner hut, climbing a rough stony slope and then winding up the head of the Mizane valley towards the imposing col (or pass) of **Tizi n'Ouanoumss.** The col is reached in about an hour and the track reasonably easy to follow: there is just one vague division, a little before the col ascent, where a path veers off right along the final stretch of the Mizane. The trail up the col itself is a good gravelly path, zigzagging continually until you reach the summit (3,664m), a narrow platform between two shafts of rock. The views from here are superb, taking in the whole route that you've covered and, in the distance to the south, the hazy green outline of the lake. At this point it looks as if you've completed the hard work – a totally false impression! The path down the valley to Ifni is slow, steep progress, the scree slopes apparently endless, and the lake often completely out of sight. It is in fact virtually enclosed by the mountains around and by what seem to be demolished hills – great heaps of rubble and boulders.

There is no village at **Lac d'Ifni,** just a few shepherds' huts and the sound of the water idly lapping at the shore. You can camp on vague scrubby terraces, somewhat fly-ridden by day, or up at the huts. If you've tackle (and, officially, permit) you can also fish: there are apparently plentiful trout. Be warned, however, that the lake is exceptionally deep – 50m over much of its area – and some of the sides drop sheer.

Most people return to Neltner by the route they came but it's said to be feasible to loop back via AMSOUZERTE (3hrs: food/sleep at Omar's house) and TISSALDAI (a further 4hrs: sleep/eat at Dilh Ahmed's) to SIDI CHAMHAROUCH (6hrs quite difficult hiking over the Tizi n'Tagharat). If you plan to do this route without a guide, talk to Lahcen or one of the wardens in Imlil before setting out: and please send us details – we'd like to include it in our next edition.

Tachedirt and beyond

TACHEDIRT, to the east of Imlil, is another village with a *CAF* refuge and a good range of local hikes and onward routes. But despite its now easy access – a piste has recently been blasted from Imlil and is covered by a daily Berber **truck** – only a handful of the tourists who charge up to Toubkal bother to head this way. If you're interested, the truck leaves Imlil each morning around 10am (a bumpy hour's ride), or you can walk the route, over the **Tizi n'Tamatert**, in 3hrs. There are no shops as yet in the village (though cokes are sold) so bring in your own food. The **CAF hut** is just above the track on the left hand side as you enter the village: it's kept locked but the warden should soon appear.

The two most rewarding hikes from Tachedirt are to **Oukaimeden** and along the **ridge of Anngour**. The first is relatively straightforward – a 3-4hrs walk over a reasonable mule track by way of the 2,960m Tizi n'Ou Addi; for details of Oukaimeden itself see p. 219. The Anngour hike is more demanding, taking a full day and (if the weather turns on you) demanding a night's bivouac. From the village the track zigzags up the left-hand side of the Imenane valley up towards the Tachedirt col (which is visible the whole way). At the col (3½hrs steep walk, taking you up to 3,616m) a path climbs due north, up a rough grass slope, to a ridge plateau giving access to the summit. The ridge – which is cut by a deep plateau – can be walked, allowing you to loop back to Tachedirt via the Tizi n'Ou Addi. Once again, detailed instructions should be sought before setting out. The description here is essentially to give an idea of the possibilities.

Less ambitious, but still demanding a lot of care on the loose, steep scree paths is an alternative route back from **Tachedirt to Imlil** by way of the **TIZI N'AGUENSIOUAL**. This takes you first by a tricky-surfaced path to the hamlets of TINERHOURHINE (1hr) and IKKISS (15mins on: cokes/rooms). From Ikkiss a good track (ask to be pointed) leads up to the Aguensioual pass; over the other side it's another stony scramble down to the village of AGUENSIOUAL, from where you can follow the road from Asni back up to Imlil.

A note on the Lepiney hut

Some 6½-7½hrs from Imlil, the **LEPINEY HUT** is essentially a rock-climbing base, above all for the barren cliffs of Djebel Tazarhart with its year-round snow. Details of a number of climbs are in the Collomb guide.

The village of **TIZI OUSSEM** (4hrs from Imlil) stands midway along this route if you're interested in trying an extended loop towards (or back from) Neltner. Rooms can be rented in the village from Omar Abdallah, who is also the guardian of the Neltner hut. The track up to Tizi Oussem and on to Neltner is quite reasonable: the difficult section is from Lepiney to Neltner, a very slow-going 5-6hr scramble over the rocks.

THE TIZI N'TEST: IDNI AND TIN MAL

The Tizi n'Test: the road that extends beyond Asni to TAROUDANNT and TALIOUINE – is unbelievably impressive. Cutting right through the heart of the Atlas, it was blasted out from the mountains by the French in the first years of their 'pacification' – the first modern route to link

Marrakesh with the Souss plain and the desert and an extraordinary feat of pioneer-spirit engineering. Until then it had been considered impracticable without local protection and knowledge: an important pass for trade and for the control and subjugation of the south, but one that few sultans were able to make their own. Through much of the last century – and the first years of this – it was the personal fief of the Goundafi family, whose huge kasbahs still dominate many of the crags and strategic turns along the way. Much further into the past it had served as the refuge and power-base of the Almohads, and it was from the holy city of Tin Mal, up towards the col that they launched their attack on the Almoravid dynasty.

Tin Mal, as remote and evocative a mountain stronghold as could be imagined, is the main 'sight' of this route: an excursion well worth making in its own right for the chance to see the ruined C12 mosque, a building close in spirit to the Koutoubia and for once accessible to non-Muslims. The real drama though, is in **the road** itself – perhaps most spectacular when approached from the Taroudannt direction, but a startling, dizzying ride, however, whichever way you take it. Not least, too, there is the powerful attraction of the **Hôtel Alpina** at **Idni**: a wondrous place to stop over a night or six, and of which more below. First, **some practicalities**. If you are setting out by **bus from Marrakesh** you should have four choices, leaving at either 5am, 6am, 2pm or 6pm. The 5/6am buses are the only ones direct to Taroudannt (7½hrs) but they all go as far as Idni (4hrs): the 2pm bus stops there, the 6pm goes on to Taliouine (arriving, after a scary night descent, at around 1-2am). If you're coming from Asni you can pick up any of these buses a little over an hour after they leave Marrakesh. For anyone **driving**, some experience of mountain roads is essential. The route is well contoured and, despite an unsurfaced passage between Ijoukak and the col, is in good condition, but between the col (the summit of the pass) and the intersection with the P32 Taliouine-Taroudannt road it is extremely narrow (1½car's width) with almost continuous hairpin bends and blind corners. Since you can actually see for some distance ahead this isn't as dangerous as it sounds – but you still need a lot of confidence and have to watch out for suicidal local drivers burning down on you without any intention of stopping or slowing. Bus and lorry drivers are fortunately more considerate.

The road to Idni and beyond

Heading out on the dawn bus from Marrakesh (which sometimes leaves at 5am, sometimes at 6am, and sometimes both: check and buy tickets a day early) you have the least interesting part of the Taroudannt journey to catch up on lost sleep. The landscape over the first couple of hours – before you come to the village of OUIRGANE and the beginning of the **Oued Nfis** gorges – is fairly monotonous. OUIRGANE itself is a tiny place but long-touted by the French guidebooks as a beautiful valley and 'étape gastronomique'. In the early hours of an Atlas morning this may not exercise great pull, but if you've a little money to blow after hiking around Toubkal you could do a lot worse than come up here to lie about and recover. There are two hotels, both with reputedly excellent restaurants and bars, and both with swimming pools. The big one, *Residence la Roseraie*, is an extremely grand 4*A place, complete with sauna and tennis courts, but the other, the curiously named *Au Sanglier qui Fume* ('the boar that smokes') is old-style French auberge and only 2*A.

Neither, however, are a patch on the *Alpina*. And unless you're into a surge of luxury, or serious hiking (in which case IJOUKAK'S CAF *hut* and access to the Toubkal massif via the Agoundis valley and Zaout pass may be of interest: see the *Guide Collomb*), you'll want to stay on the bus at least until Tin Mal or Idni. TIN MAL lies just to the right of the road 8km south of Ijoukak and is detailed (with the nearby Goundafi kasbahs) in the section below. To visit it you have two basic choices: either you can get off the bus at the village and then later hitch/walk/wait for another bus on, or you can wait until Idni and backtrack from there. There's no particular problem – except the midday heat – either way.

If it seems that IDNI and the Hôtel Alpina are beginning to dominate this account, this is no more than their due. The last hamlet and the last bus stop before the summit of the pass – the *Col du Tizi n'Test* at 2,100m – Idni was once a major staging-post for travellers crossing the Atlas* and it is still the place where the bus drivers choose to break their journey, juddering to a halt beside the ramshackle and wonderfully stylish *Alpina*. The bus drivers know this by the name of its *patronne* – Madame Gipolou – and indeed it is this long-established Frenchwoman who seems to be the guiding spirit of the whole neighbourhood. The hotel, she manages in totally idiosyncratic style. There is no running water or electricity – despite the lamps and bidets in each room – but you are given vast quantities of candles, huge dinners fresh from the cottage farm below, and limitless quantities of good dark Moroccan wine. There are no set charges and you pay, quite simply, what Madame considers you can afford.

With just four other houses and a Berber cafe, Idni is in some ways an odd place to stay. But there is no sense of being stranded. Above the hamlet there are dozens of trails – to the source of a river and to villages trapped within the mountains – and, in addition to visiting Tin Mal, you can take one of the buses up in the other direction to check out the views from the col. Going by bus – it's 18km beyond Idni – you can get dropped off (and picked up) at a *Café Restaurant* just over the pass. Walk back

---

*Most people travelling between Marrakesh and Taroudannt (or Agadir) now use the modern and much more mundane S511 road over the Imi n'Tanoute pass to INEZGANE.

a kilometre and you'll find a track leading straight up from the col – which is itself dark and restricted – towards a platform mounted by a TV relay station. From here, 20 mins walk, the views over the Souss plain and back towards Toubkal can be stunning.

Over the col, the **descent towards Taroudannt/Taliouine** is hideously dramatic: a drop of some 1,600m in little over 30km. Throughout, there are stark, fabulous vistas of the peaks, and occasionally, hundreds of feet below, a mountain valley and cluster of villages. TAROUDANNT is reached in around 2½-3hrs on the descent, TALIOUINE in a little more; coming up, needless to say, it all takes a good deal longer. For details on Taroudannt and Taliouine see pp. 288/290.

Tin Mal and the Goundafi kasbahs

The **TIN MAL MOSQUE**, quite apart from its historic and architectural importance, is an extraordinarily beautiful ruin – isolated above a sudden flash of river-valley, with stack upon stack of pink Atlas peaks towering beyond its roofless arches. If you feel like an easy day trip from Idni it is perfect: leaving on one of the mid-morning buses you can get dropped below the modern village of TIN MAL (or IFOURIREN), later walking on to the old Goundafi kasbah at TALAAT N'YACOUB (5km beyond Tin Mal) and catching a bus or hitching back from IJOUKAK (a further 3km: 26km in all from Idni). To reach the Tin Mal mosque from the road you cross a stream and walk up the valley to the village: the mosque, a massive, square kasbah-like building, is kept locked, but the *guardien* will soon arrive to take you up and let you look around at leisure.

The site seems now so remote and the land hereabout so unpromising that it is difficult to imagine a town ever existing in this valley. In some form, however, it did. For it was here that Ibn Toumert and his lieutenant Abd el Moumen preached to the Berber tribes and welded them into the Almohad (or 'unitarian') movement; here that they set out on the campaigns which culminated in the conquest of all Morocco and of southern Spain, and here, too, a century and a half later, that they made their last stand against the incoming Merenid dynasty.

This **history** – so decisive in the development of the medieval Shereefian Empire – is outlined in the general account on pp. 308-9. More particular to Tin Mal are the circumstances of Ibn Toumert's arrival and the appeal of his puritan, reforming teaching to the local tribes. Known to his followers as the *Mahdi* – the 'sinless one' whose coming is prophesied in the Koran – Toumert was himself born in the High Atlas, a member of the Berber-speaking Masmouda tribe (who held the desert-born Almoravids, the ruling dynasty, in traditional contempt). He was an accomplished theologian and studied throughout the centres of eastern Islam – a period in which he formulated the strict Almohad doctrines, based on the assertion of the Unity of God and on a verse of the Koran in which Muhammad set out the role of religious reform, 'to reprove what is disapproved and enjoy what is good'. For Toumert, Almoravid Morocco contained much to disapprove and, returning from the East with a small group of disciples, he began to preach against all manifestations of luxury (above all the use of wine and performance of music) and, inevitably, against women mixing to any degree in male society. In 1121 he and his group arrived at Marrakesh, the Almoravid capital, where they immediately began to provoke the Sultan. Ironically, this was not an easy task: Ali Ben Youssef, one of the most pious rulers of Moroccan history, accepted many of Toumert's charges and forgave his insults. It was only in 1124, when the reformer struck Ali's sister from her horse for riding (as was desert tradition) unveiled, that the Almohads were finally banished from the city and took refuge in the mountain fastness of Tin Mal.

Here, from the beginning, Ibn Toumert and Abd el Moumen set out to mould the Atlas Berbers into a religious and military force. They taught prayers in Arabic by giving each follower as his name a word from the Koran and then lining them up to recite, and they stressed the significance of the 'second coming' and Toumert's role as *Mahdi*. But more significant, perhaps, was the savage military emphasis of the new order. Hesitant tribes were branded 'hypocrites' and were massacred – most notoriously in a Forty Day Purge of the mountains – and within eight years none remained outside Almohad control. In the 1130s, Ibn Toumert himself having died, Abd el Moumen began to attack and 'convert' the plains. In 1145 he was able to take Fes and in 1149, just twenty-five years after the march of exile, his armies entered and sacked Marrakesh.

The mosque was built by Abd el Moumen around 1153-4: partly as a memorial and cult centre for Ibn Toumert, and partly as his own family mausoleum. Obviously fortified, it probably served also as a section of the town's defences, for in the first years of Almohad rule Tin Mal was entrusted with the state treasury. Today it is the only part of the fortifications – indeed of the entire Almohad town – that you can make out with any clarity. The rest was sacked and largely destroyed in the Merenid conquest of 1276: a curiously late event, since all of the main Moroccan cities had been in the new dynasty's hands for some thirty years. That Tin Mal remained for this long, and that its mosque was maintained, says much of the power Toumert's teaching must have continued to exercise over the local Berbers. Even two centuries later the historian Ibn Khaldun found Koranic readers employed at the tombs, and when the French began the work of restoration in the 1930s they found the site littered with the shrines of marabouts.

Architecturally, Tin Mal presents a unique opportunity for non-

Muslims to take a look at the interior of a traditional Almohad mosque. It is roofless, for the most part, and two of the corner pavilion-towers have disappeared, but the *mihrab* (or prayer niche) and the complex pattern of internal arches are substantially intact. The arrangement is a classic Almohad design– the T-shaped plan with a central aisle leading towards the mihrab – and is virtually identical to that of the Koutoubia, more or less its contemporary. The one element of eccentricity is in the placing of the *minaret* (which you can ascend for a view of the general lay-out) over the mihrab: a weakness of design which meant it could never have been much taller than it is today. In terms of decoration, the most striking feature is the variety and intricacy of the *arches* – above all those leading in to the mihrab, which have been sculpted with a stalactite-vaulting. In the *corner domes* and the *mihrab-vault* this technique is extended, with impressive effect despite their crumbling state. Elsewhere, and on the face of the mihrab, it is the slightly austere geometric patterns and familiar motifs (the palmette, rosette, etc.), of Almohad decorative gates which are predominant.

The **GOUNDAFI KASBAHS** don't really compare with Tin Mal – nor with the Glaoui kasbah at Telouet detailed in the following (Tizi n'Tishka) section. As so often in Morocco, though, they provide an extraordinary assertion of just how recent is the country's feudal past. The first you see, a massive fortress that straddles a spur to the right of the road 3km on towards Ijoukak, dates only from 1907, and others along the valleys of this pass were built only a decade or two earlier. The most important – and the only one which really repays a visit is the former Goundafa stronghold and headquarters at the village of **TALAAT N'YACOUB**. Half an hour's walk beyond Tin Mal, this is easily enough reached: down a short, tree-lined (and very French-looking) lane left of the main road 6km towards (and 3km before) IJOUKAK. **The kasbah**, decaying, partially ruined and probably quite unsafe, lies at the far end of the village. Nobody seems to mind if you take a look inside, though you need to avoid the dogs near its entrance. The inner part of the palace-fortress, though blackened from a fire, is reasonably complete and retains traces of its decoration. It is difficult to establish exact facts with these old tribal kasbahs but it seems that this one was constructed in the late C19 for the last-but-one Goundafi chieftain – a feudal warrior in the old tradition who was constantly at war with the Sultan through the 1860s and 1870s and a bitter rival of the neighbouring Glaoua clan. His son, Tayeb el Goundafi, also spent most of his life in tribal warfare – though he threw in his lot with the Sultan Moulay Hassan and later with the French. At the turn of the century he could still raise some five thousand armed Goundafa tribesmen within a day or two's notice but his power and fief eventually collapsed in 1924 – the result of El Glaoui's manoeuvrings – and he died three years later. The kasbah here at Talaat must have been already in decay; today it seems no more linked with the village than any medieval castle in Europe.

TELOUET AND THE TIZI N'TISHKA

Tizi n'Tishka – the direct route from MARRAKESH to OUAZARZATE – is less remote and less spectacular than the Test pass. It is an important military approach to the south (and to the war with Polisario) so the roads are modern, well-constructed and comparatively fast. Only a short way off the modern highway, however, this current role is underpinned by an earlier political history, scarcely three decades old and unimaginably bizarre. For this pass and the mountains to its east were the stamping ground of the extraordinary Glaoui brothers, the greatest and the most ambitious of all the Berber tribal leaders. Their kasbah-headquarters, a vast complex of buildings abandoned only in 1956, lies at TELOUET, now a 44km detour from the main road, and fast crumbling into the dark red earth, but visitable still and a peculiar glimpse of the style and melodrama of recent Moroccan government and power.

The extent and speed of **Madani** (1866-1918) and **T'Hami** (1879-1956) **el Glaoui's rise to power** is remarkable enough. In the mid C19 their family were simply local clan leaders, controlling an important Atlas pass – a long-established trade route from Marrakesh to the valleys of the Dra and Dades – but with little influence outside. Their entrance into national politics began, dramatically, in 1893. In the terrible winter of that year the Sultan Moulay Hassan, returning from a disastrous *harka* (subjugation/burning raid) of the Tafilalt region, found himself thrown on the mercy of the brothers for food, shelter and safe passage. With shrewd political judgment they rode out to meet the Sultan, fêting him with every detail of protocol and, miraculously, producing food enough to banquet the entire 3,000 strong force for the duration of their halt. The extravagance was well rewarded. When Moulay Hassan returned to Marrakesh he had given caid-ship of all the lands between the High Atlas and the Sahara to the Glaoui, and most important of all, had seen fit to abandon vast amounts of the royal armoury (including the first cannon to be seen in the Atlas) at Telouet. By 1901 they had dispensed with all opposition in the region, and when in 1912 the French arrived in Morocco, they were able to dictate the government of virtually all the South, putting down the attempted nationalist rebellion of El Hiba, pledging loyalty throughout the First World War, and having themselves appointed pashas of Marrakesh and their family caids of the main Atlas and desert towns. The French were happy enough to concur, arming them, as Gavin Maxwell wrote, 'to rule as despots, (and) perpetuating the corruption and oppression that the Europeans had nominally come to purge'.

The strange events of this age – and the legendary personal style of T'Hami El Glaoui – are brilliantly evoked in Gavin Maxwell's *Lords of the Atlas* (Century reprint; 1983), the brooding romanticism of which almost compels a visit to Telouet:

> *At an altitude of more than 8,000ft in the High Atlas, (the castle) and its scattered predecessors occupy the corner of a desert plateau, circled by the giant peaks of the Central Massif. . . . When in the spring the snows begin to thaw and the river below the castle, the Oued Mellah, becomes a torrent of ice-grey and white, the mountains reveal their fantastic colours, each distinct and contrasting with its neighbour. The hues are for the most part the range of colours to be found upon fan shells – reds, vivid pinks, violets, yellows, but among these are peaks of cold mineral green or of dull blue. Nearer at hand, where the Oued Mellah turns to flow through the valley of salt, a cluster of ghostly spires, hundreds of feet high and needle-pointed at their summits, cluster below the face of a precipice; vultures wheel and turn upon the air currents between them . . .*
>
> *Even in this setting the castle does not seem insignificant. It is neither beautiful nor gracious, but its sheer size, as if in competition with the scale of the mountains, compels attention as much as the fact that its pretension somehow falls short of the ridiculous. The castle, or kasbah, of Telouet is a tower of tragedy that leaves no room for laughter.*

And that's about how it is. If you've read the book, or if you've just picked up on the fascination, it's certainly a journey worth making: though it has to be said that there's little of aesthetic interest, that many of the rooms have fallen into complete ruin, and that without a car it can be a tricky and time-consuming trip. Nevertheless, even after thirty years of decay, there's still vast drama in this weird and remote eyrie, and in the painted salon walls, often roofless and open to the wind.

Once there, make your way to the second **kasbah** on the hillside – beyond a desolate and total ruin which is all that remains of the original castle built by Madani and his father in the mid C19. The castle-palace above is almost entirely T'Hami's creation and it is here that the road stops, before massive double doors and a rubble-strewn courtyard. Wait a while and you'll be joined by a *caretaker-guide*, necessary in this case since the building is an unbelievable labyrinth of locked doors and connecting passages, which, so it is said, no single person ever completely knew their way around. Sadly, these days, you're shown only the main halls and reception rooms. You can ask to see more – the harem, the kitchens – but the usual reply is *dangereux*, and so most likely it is: if you climb up to the roof (this is generally allowed) you can look down upon some of the courts and chambers, the bright zellij and stucco enclosing great gaping holes in the stone and plaster. The reception rooms – 'the outward and visible signs of ultimate physical ambition' – at least give a sense of the quantity and the style of the decoration, still in progress when the Glaoui died and the old regime came to a sudden halt. There are delicate iron window-grilles and fine wood-carved ceilings, though the overall result is once again the late C19/early C20 combination of sensitive classical imitation (the Saadian tombs, etc.) and out and out vulgarity. There is a tremendous scale of affectation, too, perfectly demonstrated by the use of green Salé tiles for the roof – usually reserved for mosques and royal palaces. The really enduring impression, though, is the wonder of how and why it ever came to be built at all, for, as Gavin Maxwell wrote:

> It was not a medieval survival, as are the few European castles still occupied by the descendants of feudal barons, but a deliberate re-creation of the Middle Ages, with all their blatant extremes of beauty and ugliness, good and evil, elegance and violence, power and fear – by those who had full access to the inventions of contemporary science. No part of the kasbah is more than a hundred years old; no part of its ruined predecessors gorlgoes back further than another fifty. Part of the castle is built of stone, distinguishing it sharply from the other kasbahs that are made of pise, or sun-dried mud, for no matter to what heights of beauty or fantasy these may aspire they are all, in the final analysis, soluble in water.

If you decide **to get to Telouet** there are several options open. At Marrakesh you'll need to take the OUAZARZATE bus as far as either IRHERM or TADDERT. At **IRHERM**, 10km beyond the Tishka col, there are shared *grands taxis* out to Telouet, and a small, basic hotel and bar if you need to stay the night. **TADDERT**, on the Marrakesh side of the pass, is in fact a more interesting place to stay: a terraced roadside hamlet with beautiful walks around (to the hamlet of TAMGUEMEMT, for example, ½hr away above a mountain stream) and a good cheap *auberge*. The problem here, though, is that you'll need to hitch on to Telouet: there's no bus or taxi and many of the buses on towards the pass and turning are often full. *Getting back* from Telouet should be less of a problem. There is usually some traffic – and a handful of tourists – and most people find it hard to turn down a lift. **By car** you can quite easily set out from Marrakesh in the morning, take in Telouet and perhaps also the kasbahs of AIT BENNHADOU (towards Ouazarzate, see p. 255). and reach OUAZARZATE in the early evening.

One last possibility, at least for committed walkers, is to continue **beyond Telouet**. Before the construction of the Tishka road the main pass here over the Atlas actually went through the village and extended towards Ouazarzate by way of AIT BENHADDOU. It was only the presence at the Telouet kasbah of T'Hami's xenophobic and intransigent cousin Hammou ('the Vulture') that caused the French to construct a road along the more difficult route to the west. Today there is a piste beyond Telouet as far as the hamlet of ANEMITER. Here the trails and tracks take over. It is said to be a 2-3day walk over to Ait Benhaddou, or, more ambitiously, you could even set out across the backbone of the High Atlas — a route I've heard taken as far as MIDELT.

THE OTHER ATLAS PASSES: MARRAKESH TO AGADIR, AND THE EASTERN PISTES

The direct route from MARRAKESH to AGADIR -- the **Imi n'Tanoute**, or *Tizi Maachou*, pass – is the least interesting of the Atlas roads. It is a reasonably fast (5hrs) journey if you're pushed for time, and a pretty enough route, but you'll be missing out on all the drama of the Test or Tishka — something that can't be recommended.

Leaving Marrakesh, the Agadir buses normally follow the Essaouira road as far as **CHICHAOUA**, a small roadside village and administrative centre famed in a small way for its locally produced carpets. These – brightly coloured and often using stylised animal forms – are sold at the *Centre Co-Operative* and also at the *Sunday market*. Beyond Chichaoua the road to Essaouira continues efficiently across the drab Chiadma plains. For Agadir you begin a slow climb towards IMI N'TANOUTE, another administrative centre (Monday market), and then cut through the last, outlying peaks of the High Atlas. The pass, *Tizi Maachou*, is at 1,700m (5,500ft); beyond there are occasional gorges and a handful of difficult tracks up into the mountains. The buses usually take a break at one of the hamlets on the way but there's nowhere very compelling or interesting to stop.

Quite different are the 'passes' to the **east of the Tizi n'Tishka**: remote and adventurous *pistes* which climb up above KASBA TADLA and BENI MELLAL to the high plateaus around IMILCHIL and eventually emerge in the fabulous gorges of the Dra and Todra. These are really exciting – well off the standard circuits of the country and taken for the most part by organised landrover expeditions. But despite this, they are actually quite feasible for independent travel, and with the patience to fit in with local market patterns you can go all the way across by Berber trucks and transit lorries. Details of some of these routes, and an account of what it's like to try them, can be found in the next chapter pp. 267-9).

THE WEST COAST RESORTS

One obvious solution to the heat and intensity of Marrakesh – or to the rather spartan isolation of the Atlas – is to make straight for the coast. **El Jadida**, **Safi** and **Essaouira** each have excellent beaches, good fast bus connections, and surprisingly individual characters. Essaouira, the closest to Marrakesh, is the best known to travellers and probably the most

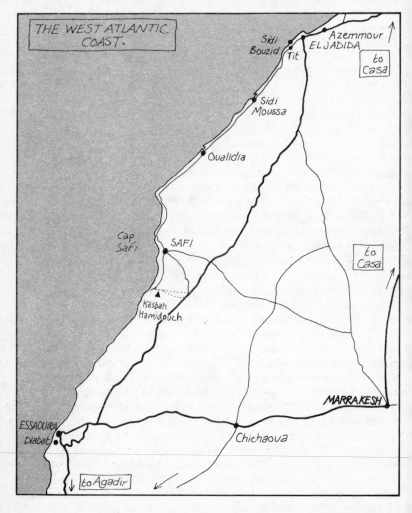

THE WEST ATLANTIC COAST.

attractive: a remarkable mix of traditional, provincial town and young, western resort. El Jadida, in contrast, was a beach-resort established by the French which is now immensely popular with Moroccans; while Safi, between the two, is solidly industrial, an interesting but rather depressing base unless you have your own transport.

Buses to all three towns leave through the day from Marrakesh's main Bab Doukkala station. For the early morning ones, in summer at least, it's worth buying tickets a day in advance. **Oualidia**, a smaller resort in the El Jadida mould, is easiest reached by bus from Safi.

ESSAOUIRA (MOGADOR)

Apart from the immediate impact of the sea air and the friendly animation of the town, the predominant images of **ESSAOUIRA** are of the Atlantic – of the rugged coast and offshore islands, the vast expanse of empty sands trailing back along the promontory to the south, and the almost Gothic scenery of the C18 fortifications. It is a powerful place, windblown and distinctly melancholic out of season but, with its whitewashed and blue-shuttered houses and lines of arcaded shops, thoroughly likable. For once, too, there's something of an atmosphere of openness and tolerance. The mixture of Berber villagers, sardine fishermen and Marrakchi and European tourists seems easy and uncomplicated, and even the handful of local hustlers half apologetic.

Getting around the town couldn't be easier. Nearly all the **buses** arrive at the **Bab Doukkala**, at the northern edge of the ramparts, and once inside the gates you come upon the two main streets, the **Rue Mohammed Zerktouni** and the **Av. Mohammed Ben Abdallah** – parallel with each other and running all the way down to the **harbour** and CTM terminal. At the far end, flanking the CTM and the small town **tourist office**, is a long, open square, the **Place Moulay el Hassan**, off and about which are most of the cafes, restaurants and hotels. Walk down here when you arrive and you'll get a pretty good sense of the layout.

Accommodation is not generally a problem, even in July-August, though as elsewhere it's better to arrive early in the day. Best by far, if you don't mind a little sea-dampness, is the *Hôtel des Remparts* (1*B) which, as the name suggests, is built right into the walls overlooking the sea. This used once to be quite grand but has since marvellously decayed: the style remains, however, along with two additional bonuses – a bar where most of the local drinking goes on and a roof-terrace to sunbathe out of the wind. To reach the hotel leave the Place Moulay Hassan along the road opposite of the Grand Mosque; at its end turn right and then immediately left onto the Rue Ibn Rochd – the hotel is on the left at its far end. Other reasonable options include the *Hôtel Atlantique* (signposted – down a blind alley – just around the corner from the Remparts), the *Beau Rivage* (on Pl. Moulay Hassan) and the *Hôtel du Tourisme* (at the corner of the ramparts right of the Place). These are all cheap and quite clean. Slightly more upmarket – and a little tacky – are the *Mechouar* (1*A) and *Sahara* (2*A), more or less next door to each other on the Rue Zerktouni/Av. de l'Istiqlal, or there's the *Hôtel Tafraout* (1*A; just off Ben Abdallah), again nothing much in itself but with a *hammam* right next door. If all of these are full – which is unlikely – there are half a dozen other basic hotels in the alleys between the two main streets, and, 600m along the seafront, a cheap, reasonably protected *Camping Municipal*.

Around the town

With its dramatic sea-bastions and fortifications, Essaouira seems a lot older than it is. For although there were a series of forts here from the C15 on, it was only in the 1760s that the town was established and the

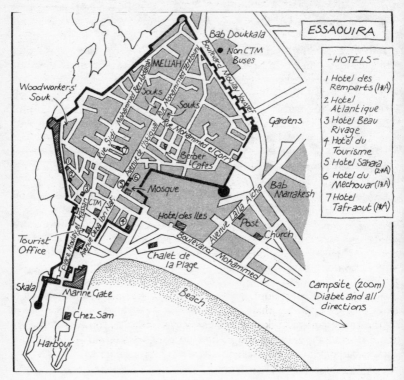

present circuit of walls raised around it. Its original function was military – Agadir was in revolt at the time and Sultan Mohammed Ben Abdallah needed a base – but this was soon pre-empted by commercial concerns. Through the C19, then known as *Mogador*, it was the only southern port open to European trade: its harbour was free from customs duties, British merchants lived in the town, and a large Jewish community was settled. With the French Protectorate, and the emergence of Casablanca, came decline, and with its end, and the exodus of the Jews, still more. Today, a fishing port and market town, it has lapsed into a rather genteel obscurity, boosted a little by its growing popularity as a resort.

There are few formal 'sights' around the town: it's more of a place just to be, looking about the souks and ramparts or wandering along the immense strand of beach. At some point, though make your way down to the **harbour** where fresh sardines are cooked on the quayside, and climb up to the **Skala**, the great sea bastion which runs back from it along the western cliffs. Orson Welles filmed much of his *Othello* here, staging a bizarre (but very Moroccan) 'punishment' of Iago, suspended above the sea and rocks in a cramped metal cage. Along the top are a collection of European cannon, most of them presented to the Sultan by ambitious C19 merchants, while out across the bay is the equally theatrical backdrop of the **Isles Purpuraires** – two rocky islets, the larger dominated by a fortress-like building which saw intermittent use as a state prison and a quarantine station for pilgrims returning from Mecca. These days the islands are 'interdit', though it's difficult to work out exactly why. The tourist office say they are used by the military, others that they're an officially designated bird sanctuary. Take your pick.

Underneath the Skala, towards the 'angle' of the ramparts, are a group of cedar and thuya **wood craftsmen**, long-established artesans in Essaouira, who produce some amazingly painstaking and beautiful marquetry work. Quite justifiably, they claim this is the best in the country – and if you see good examples elsewhere they've probably come from here. If you're thinking of buying – boxes and chess sets are made, as well as the traditional furniture – this is the best place to do it. Perhaps because they are craftsmen and not shopkeepers, however, bargaining is low-key: don't expect to pay a lot less than they ask.

The town's **other souks** spread around two arcades, on either side of the Rue Mohammed Zerktouni, and up towards the old Mellah – an interesting area and a good place to start thinking about food. Off to the right (if you're walking up from the harbour) are a series of '**Berber Cafes**', a unique Essaouiran institution amounting to little more than a street of tiny rooms covered with matting and serving soup and a variety of tajines. In a way it's a bit of a tourist trap, and travellers here have been badly ripped off (and not just for tajines), but on the other hand local fishermen and workers also eat here and it is by far the liveliest place around. Among the various mainstream tourist **restaurants**, about the best value is the *Café-Restaurant Essalam* in the Place Moulay Hassan. If you fancy a blow-out, however, there is also *Chez Sam* down at the end of the harbour: a terrific seafood restaurant and bar, serving huge portions of fish, proverbial wisdom, and (at a price) lobster. Beyond *Sam's* and the bar at the *Remparts*, other places to drink are limited. There is a restaurant-bar, the *Chalet de la Plage*, just back from the beach opposite the imposing *Hôtel des Iles*, and there's another attached to the *Iles* itself, where Moroccans gather to drink beer and play chess and draughts. Neither are too hot.

The beach – and Diabat
The beach at Essaouira extends quite literally for miles south of the town, culminating, about 10km downcoast, in the dramatic sand dunes of **Cap Sim**. As has been said before, the wind here can be annoyingly relentless – above all in early summer – but it does keep temperatures cool (70°F – 21°C – is about average) and it's a complaint you could level in some degree at anywhere along the Atlantic coast. Certainly here there are compensations, for only the hundred metres or so beside the town ever gets remotely crowded. The rest, beyond the sand-sunk remains of an old fort and royal summer pavilion, is yours for the walking.

In the direction of Cap Sim, an hour's walk along the beach and then up a kilometre-long track through thorny scrub, is the village of **DIABAT**, an old and legendary hippy-hangout where Jimi Hendrix rolled up some eighteen or so years ago. These days it's reverted to a straight Berber farming hamlet, a ragged sort of place nursing bad memories. In the mid 1970s a handful of hippies were killed here by (reputedly) local junkies and the police closed down all its rooms. There is still a **campsite** but this is another 3km past the village (follow the only track, parallel to the sea) and a half-hour trek from the sea. It is, however, a beautiful position, amazingly isolated and peaceful, and an attractive option of you've got your own transport. Still more so is the French-owned and distinctly chic **Auberge Tangaro**, next door: a small and rather wonderful place, little used except at weekends when groups of French and German windsurfers come down from Casablanca and Marrakesh. If you're interested in staying, you'll need to bring food – they don't usually cook during the week. To get there by car take the Agadir road for about 6km out of Essaouira and then turn off to the right; the 'direct' approach from Essaouira is no longer possible after the collapse of a bridge just below Diabat.

NORTH TO EL JADIDA: SAFI AND OUALIDIA

For one reason or another, few tourists take the road between ESSA-OUIRA and EL JADIDA. For while Jadida itself is an attractive, lively resort, you probably wouldn't want to spend time both here and Essa-ouira – and, with this in mind, there are more direct and more interesting routes between Marrakesh and the north.

What you'll be missing is, for the most part, a rather barren coastal plain – the periphery of the phosphate mining country, whose industry (despite a recent slump in the commodities market) has transformed the old Portuguese town of Safi into a major industrial port. The road there from Essaouira runs inland – the coast is inaccessible cliff – though beyond, and particularly around Oualidia, the landscape softens and you drop down to the sea and long, flat sweeps of sand. If you've a car, there is one possible excursion en route to Safi: to the **Kasbah Hamidouch**, a large and isolated fortress raised as ever by Moulay Ismail. It is positioned near the fishing hamlet of DAR CAID HADJI, 22km from the main road and signposted to the left as you pass DAR TAHAR BEN ABBOU. You can continue on from Dar Caid Hadji to Safi along the coast road by taking the dirt track to SOUIRA KEDIMA (7km: then 20km tarmac to Safi).

Approached from the south by a long trawl of sulphurous chimneys and vast sardine-canning factories, **SAFI** is not the prettiest of Moroccan towns. It does, however, provide a glimpse of an active, modern and working community – albeit a predominantly poor one – and, on a tourist level, the old Medina at its heart, walled and turreted by the Portuguese, has a certain interest. Here too there is an industrial tradition, with a whole quarter above the walls still devoted to the town's potteries – the workshops which have a virtual monopoly in the green, heavily-glazed rooftiles used on palaces and mosques.

Arriving by bus, you'll find yourself at one of the terminals in the Place Ibnou Sina, a busy traffic square 300m or so outside **the Medina:** to get there, and to find a room, follow any of the streets leading down towards the sea and bear to the right. You'll soon come to the old port, with its waterfront **Dar el Bahar** fortress, the main remnant of the town's brief Portuguese occupation (1508-41) and still in good repair after long use as a fortress and prison. It's open sporadically. Back from here, the old walls climb up, enclosing the Medina, to another, larger fortress known as **Kechla** – again Portuguese in origin but this time housing the town's modern prison. The **quartier des potiers** sprawls above it to the left, impossible to miss with its dozens of whitewashed kilns and chimneys. The processes here, certainly for the tile-production, remain traditional and are worth at least the time it takes to wander up. The colour-dyes, however, and the actual pottery designs are mostly pretty drab – hardly recognisable from the beautiful old pieces you see around the country's artesan museums.

The potteries apart, there's little particular to say about Safi's Medina – or about the long suburbs of the new town. The **souks**, workaday food and domestic goods markets, are grouped around the Medina's one main street – the **Rue du Socco**, which runs up from a small square by the Dar el Bahar to the old town gate of Bab Chaaba and the potteries. Most of the cheap **hotels** are around this street, too or on the street to its right (almost directly opposite the Bahar). All are fairly basic, though the *Hôtel de Paris* and *Hôtel Majestic* (both unclassified) are clean enough. If you want to **camp**, there's an all-year site near the beach of Sidi Bouzid, 3km to the north of the town.

Polluted and industrialised though it is to the south, the coast immediately north of Safi is a quite different proposition. I wouldn't personally recommend swimming as close to the town as **SIDI BOUZID** (4km: the most popular local beach) but once you've rounded Cap Safi things improve fast. 15km from Safi is a superb, cliff-sheltered beach known as **LALLA FATMA** – totally undeveloped, with nothing more than a koubba (and a few Moroccan campers) in sight. If you try it, you'll need to take food and drink; ideally you'd have transport, too, though it would be possible to get by through hitching and using the Safi-Oualidia bus. 12kms kilometres on, just before the next cape (Beddouza), there's another camping possibility by the hamlet of **SIDI BOUCHTA**. There's a roadside auberge here, though the beach itself is much more exposed – the cliffs by now giving way to long stretches of weed-strewn sands, flanked by burnt Irish-looking moor.

OUALIDIA, 66km from Safi, signals a change of scenery (salt-marshes and intense greenhouse cultivation) and also the first real resort since Essaouira. It's a picturesque little resort – a small fishing port and bay, flanked by an old kasbah and recent royal villa – and, in its own way, enjoyable. Most of the people who come here are Moroccan families and they settle into fairly permanent summer colonies in the two sizeable **campsites** – a standard *Camping Municipal* and, fancier and nearer the beach, the *International Camping Tourist Centre*. The latter, with bungalows, rooms and a restaurant, is a bit like Torbay – and Oualidia does have a rather staid middle-of-the-road feel about it. However, the beach is a good one and it's all pretty relaxed. If you want a room, there are two **hotels**, both of which have enticing (though expensive) seafood restaurants: cheapest is the *Auberge de la Lagune* (2*A; Tel. 105), right by the roadside.

From Oualidia it's 76km further to El Jadida, a swift, flat road broken by occasional new developments of holiday bungalows. If you are driving, you might want to take in the Almohad ruins of **Tit**, close by the fishing village of **MOULAY ABDALLAH** – 13km before Jadida on the smaller coastal-loop road. This is described in the El Jadida section: from which, without a car, it is easiest reached.

EL JADIDA AND AZZEMOUR

Far the most popular of these 'central Moroccan' resorts, **EL JADIDA** is also a stylish and rather beautiful town. Like Safi, it retains the lanes and ramparts of an old Portuguese medina, but here the beach, rather than any port or industry, is the focal point. Moroccans from Casablanca and from Marrakesh, even from Tangier or Fes, come in force, and there's an almost unique sense of licence. The bars are crowded (an unusual enough feature in itself): women, heavily veiled in Essaouira, are for once visible and active; and the summer evenings see an amazing and frenetic promenade. 'We are very European here', one of the Marrakchis told

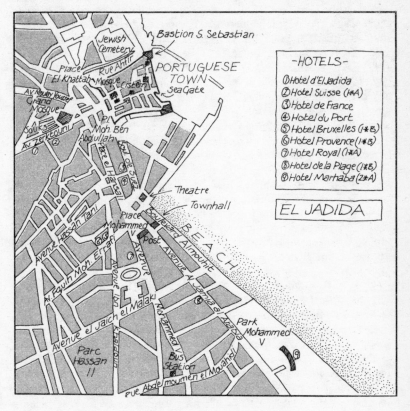

-HOTELS-

① Hotel d'El Jadida
② Hotel Suisse (H*A)
③ Hotel de France
④ Hotel du Port
⑤ Hotel Bruxelles (1*B)
⑥ Hotel Provence (1*B)
⑦ Hotel Royal (1*A)
⑧ Hotel de la Plage (1*B)
⑨ Hotel Marhaba (2*A)

EL JADIDA

me. They're not – it's a very Moroccan scene for all the casting off of traditions – but it is a young, very open and can be quite a fun place. The only problem – and a real difficulty in July or August – is finding a room: hotels, in all categories, can be packed to the gills.

Some details: arriving and hotels

El Jadida extends for some distance along the seafront and you might find it easier to make some phonecalls before setting out to get yourself a room. Numbers anyway are listed below. You will almost certainly be arriving at the main **bus station** – at the southern end of the town (bottom centre on our plan). From here it's a 10-15min walk to most of the central possibilities, or, 5mins in the other direction, to the well-equipped but somewhat pricey *Camping International* (Av. des Nations Unies, Tel. 25-47).

Best of the **cheap hotels**, if they've space, is the British-run, 1*B *Hôtel Provence* (42 Av. Fquih Mohammed Errafi, Tel. 23-47). Others are fairly standard: there are two 1*A's – *Hôtel Royal* (108 Av. Mohammed V, Tel. 28-39) and *Hôtel Suisse* (145 Blvd Zerktouni, Tel. 28-16); two 1*B's – *Hôtel Bruxelles* (40 Rue Ibn Khaldoun, Tel. 20-72) and *Hôtel de la Plage* (Av. Al Jamia al Arabia, Tel. 26-48); and, usually the last to fill, three unclassified in the ONMT lists – *Hôtel d'el Jadida* (Av. Zerktouni), *Hôtel de France* (Blvd de Suez) and *Hôtel du Port* (also Blvd de Suez but pretty seedy). Jadida has only two other hotels at present: the 2* A *Hôtel Mahraba* and 4*B *Hôtel Doukkala;* Mahraba, unusually elegant (French deco), with a bar and pool, could be good if you've the money.

A few other details. The **PTT** is on Place Mohammed V. **Bus tickets** for Casa or Marrakesh are best bought in advance (from the main station). There's a **Wednesday souk**, held out by the lighthouse s.w. of the town. And there's no tourist office. For a largish resort, it's surprisingly hard to find anywhere good **to eat:** try around the Place el Hansali (the real centre of town) or by the fairly mundane town souks, just off Av. Zerktouni. **Bars** are mainly in hotels – liveliest at the *de la Plage* and *Mahraba.*

The town, the beaches and Tit

El Jadida's Medina is the most European-looking in Morocco; a quiet, walled and bastioned sea-village, with a handful of churches scattered about its lanes. It was founded by the Portuguese in 1513 – and retained by them until 1769 – and it is still propularly known as the Cité **Portugaise,** The Moors who settled here after the Portuguese withdrawal tended to live outside the walls. Budgett Meakin, writing in the 1890s, found an 'extensive native settlement of bee-hive huts, or *nouallahs*' spreading back from the harbour, whilst European merchants had re-established themselves in the 'clean, prosperous and well-lighted streets' of the

Medina. As with all the 'open ports' of this coast there was also an important Jewish community, handling the trade with Marrakesh and the interior, and here, for once, they were reasonably treated. Almost uniquely, Jadida (or Mazagan, as it was known until Independence) had no separate Jewish quarter, or Mellah.

The cité today – decaying and insignificant – is not of enormous interest, though it does have one distinct and very beautiful sight. This is the **Portuguese cistern**, a dramatic subterranean vault which mirrors its roof and pillars in a shallow film of water covering the floor – a startling effect which, again, Orson Welles used in his *Othello*, staging a riot and filming from above. These days you'll see it on virtually all the town's postcards. It is normally open weekdays from around 9.30am until 6.30 or 7pm: the entrance is midway down the main street, on the left opposite a small souvenir shop. Walk further up this street and you'll come to the old **Porte de la Mer**, a sea-gate giving onto the port. The churches and chapels, long converted to secular use, are generally closed; the **grand mosque** here was once a lighthouse – and looks it.

El Jadida's **beach** spreads north from the cité and port, well beyond the length of the town. It's a popular strip, though from time to time polluted by the ships in port. If it doesn't look too good, or you feel like a change, take a *petit taxi* 3km south along the coastroad to PLAGE SIDI OUAFI, a broader strip of sand where dozens of Moroccan families set up tents for the summer. There is good swimming here, and cheap temporary food stalls, or, if you want to press on further, you can usually find *grands taxis* leaving for SIDI BOUZID and MOULAY ABDALLAH (5km and 11km respectively from El Jadida). Sidi Bouzid is another beach, but much more developed than Sidi Ouafi with smart villa-bunga-lows and a flashy bar-restaurant. Moulay Abdallah, in contrast, is hardly more than a fishing hamlet – dominated, to its left, by a large zaouia complex and partially enclosed by ruined circuit of walls. These span the site of a C12 ribat, or fortified monastery, known as **Tit** ('eyes', or 'spring', in the local Berber dialect) and built, so it is thought, in prep-aration for a Norman invasion: a real threat at the time – the Normans having launched attacks on Tunisia – but one that was never to materi-alise. Today there is little enough to see, though the minaret of the modern zaouia (prominent and whitewashed) is Almohad in origin, and behind it, up through the graveyard, you can walk to a second isolated minaret which may be still earlier. If it is, then it is perhaps the only one surviving from the Almoravid era – a claim considerably more impressive than its simple, blocklike appearance might suggest. At the zaouia an important *moussem* is held towards the end of August.

Azzemour

16km to the north of El Jadida, **AZZEMOUR** has an altogether different feel and appearance – oddly remote, considering its strategic site on the great Oum er Rbia river, and thoroughly Moroccan. It was occupied for under three decades by the Portuguese, remained closed to C19 European trade, and today sees possibly fewer tourists than any other Moroccan coastal town.

There is no very obvious attraction here – no particular reason to stay – but Azzemour is one of the more striking towns of the region. The Portuguese stayed long enough to build its walls, stacked directly over the banks of the river, and these are dramatically extended by the white, cubic line of the **Medina**. The best view of all this – and it is impressive – is from across the river, on the way out of town towards Casablanca. To look around, however, make your way down the bus station to the main (landward) side of the ramparts. At the far corner are the former **kasbah** and **Mellah** quarters, now largely in ruins but quite safe to visit. If you wait around, the local *guardien/syndicat-manager* will probably arrive, open things up and take you around; if nothing happens he can be found by asking up at the 'Tourist Office' at 141 Av. Mohammed V. Once inside you can follow the parapet walk around the ramparts, with its views of the river and the gardens (including henna orchards) along its edge, and you'll be shown the **Dar el Baroud** (the 'House of the Powder') with its ruined Gothic window, and the old town **synagogue**. It may not sound a great deal, and you'll need to bargain the final tip, but it's an interesting, enjoyable break from El Jadida, and easily combined with a swim. The river is notoriously dangerous, but there's a fabulous stretch of **beach** half an hour's walk through the eucalyptus trees above the town. If you go by road, this is signposted 'Balneaire du Haouzia', a small complex of cafes and bungalows that occupies part of the sands. If you want to stay in Azzemour you're probably best off camping: there's only one small, basic **hotel** – close by the bus station on Av. Mohammed V.

TRAVEL DETAILS

Trains
Marrakesh-Casablanca (3 daily; currently at 1.20, 6.50 & 17.27; 4hrs).
Marrakesh-Fes/Meknes (via Casablanca) (3 daily; 10¾/11½hrs).
Marrakesh-Tangier (2 daily; currently 1.20 & 17.25; 15½hrs).
Marrakesh-Safi (1 daily; 3hrs 40, but this is essentially a phosphate/goods train).

Buses
From Marrakesh Asni (8 daily; 1/1/2hrs); Taroudannt (2 at dawn; 8½hrs); Taliouine (1; 7-8hrs); Ouazarzate (4; 6hrs); Agadir (10; 3½hrs); Essaouira (6; 3hrs); Safi (4; 3½hrs); El Jadida (9; 3½hrs); Casablanca (Hourly; 4hrs); Rabat (8 daily; 5½hrs); Meknes (1; 9hrs); Fes (3; 11hrs); Beni Mellal (9; 3hrs); Azrou (4; 5½hrs); Demnate (4; 3hrs).
From Essaouira Agadir (6 daily; 3½hrs); Safi (2; 6hrs); El Jadida (2; 8hrs); Casablanca (4; 11hrs); Tiznit (1; 7hrs). Nb. Most of the Essaouira-Marrakesh services (6 daily; 3hrs) are non-*CTM* buses.
From Safi Oualidia/El Jadida (3 daily; 1¼/2½hrs).
From El Jadida Casablanca (3 daily; 2½hrs); Rabat (2; 4hrs).

Grands Taxis
From Marrakesh Frequent and useful services to the Ourika valley; negotiable elsewhere, though no particular standard runs.
From El Jadida Negotiable to Casablanca.

Flights
From Marrakesh Daily (except Tuesdays) to Casablanca with a connection on to Tangier. International flights via Tangier or Casablanca.

Chapter six
THE GREAT SOUTHERN ROUTES

Immediately when you arrive in the Sahara, for the first or the tenth time, you notice the stillness. An incredible, absolute silence prevails outside the towns; and within, even in busy places like the markets, there is a hushed quality in the air, as if the quiet were a constant force which, resenting the intrusion of sound, minimizes and disperses it straightaway. Then there is the sky, compared to which all other skies seem faint-hearted efforts. Solid and luminous, it is always the focal point of the landscape. At sunset, the precise, curved shadow of the earth rises into it swiftly from the horizon, cutting it into light section and dark section. When all daylight has gone, and the space is thick with stars, it is still of an intense and burning blue, darkest directly overhead and paling toward the earth, so that the night never really grows dark.

Paul Bowles: *The Baptism of Solitude*

The **Moroccan Sahara** begins as soon as you cross the Atlas to the south. It is not for the most part sand – more a wasteland of stone and scrub – but it is powerfully impressive. The quote from Paul Bowles may sound like romantic exaggeration, quasi-mysticism, but then staying at Figuig or Rissani, or just stopping in the desert between towns somehow has this effect. There is, too, an irresistible sense of wonder as you catch a first glimpse of the great river valleys – the **Drâa, Dades, Todrha** or **Tafilalt**. Long belts of date-palm oases, scattered with the fabulous mud-architecture of kasbahs and fortified *ksour* villages, these are the old caravan paths which reached back to Marrakesh and Fes and out across the Sahara to Timbuctou, Niger and the Sudan. They are beautiful routes – even today, tamed by modern roads and with the oases in obvious decline – and if you're travelling in Morocco for any length of time this is the part to make for. The simplest circuit (**Marrakesh-Zagora-Marrakesh**, or **Marrakesh-Tinerhir-Midelt**) takes a minimum of five days; to do them any degree of justice, or merely to see the highlights, a lot longer.

Although the old trading routes are now redundant, and the date production not what it was, the southern valleys were long a mainstay of the pre-colonial economy. Their wealth, and the arrival of tribes from the desert, allowed three of the royal dynasties to rise to power – including, in the C17, the present ruling family of the Alaouites. By the C19, however, the advance of the Sahara and the uncertain upkeep of

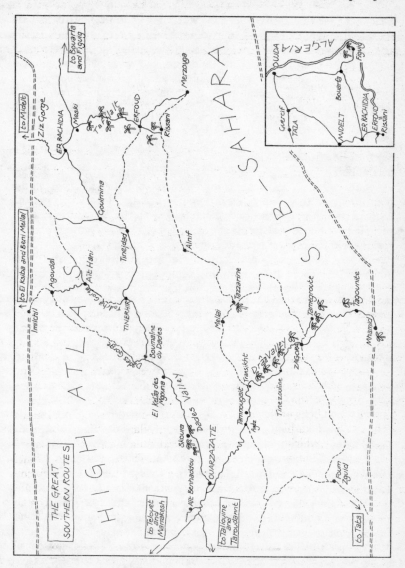

the water channels had led to a bare subsistence even in the most fertile strips. Under the French, with the creation of modern industry in the north and the new exploitation of phosphates and minerals, they became less and less significant, and subject to massive emigration to the cities. Today there are a few urban centres in the south – **Erfoud, Ouazarzate** and **Er Rachidia** are the largest – but these seem only to point the end of an age. For though the date harvests in late October can still employ the *ksour* communities, and tourism itself brings in a little money, the rest of the year sees only modest production of a handful of crops – henna, some grain cereals, citrus fruits and roses (a French introduction for the *attar*, or rosewater, produced in the spring). To make the position still more critical, in recent years the seasonal rains have failed, and perhaps as much as half the male population of the *ksour* now seek work in the north for at least part of the year.

Saharan practicalities

The popular image of the Sahara as a difficult land to travel, with long expedition style routes, doesn't on the whole apply to Morocco. All the main routes in this chapter are covered by ordinary **local buses** and on most of the others there are regular **Berber trucks** or **landrover taxis** (detailed in the text). There are, however, a few really adventurous *pistes* – such as the direct route from Zagora to Rissani, or up into the Atlas beyond the Dades or Todhra gorges – and if you plan to drive these you'll need to be decently equipped and able to look after your car.

Travelling by bus the only real disadvantage is the sheer physical exhaustion involved: most journeys tend to begin at dawn to avoid the worst of the heat, and for the rest of the day it can be difficult to summon up the energy to do anything. If you **hire a car** you'll lose out in cutting yourself off from the country and people, but you will get the chance to take in a lot more, with a lot less frustration, in a reasonably short space of time. Nearest agencies are in Marrakesh and Agadir: most allow you to complete a circuit and return a car to Casablanca or Fes.

A FEW OTHER POINTS

Temperatures can climb well above 120°F (50°C) in midsummer and you'll find the middle of the day best spent totally inactive. If you've any option, spring is way the most enjoyable time to travel – particularly if you're heading for Zagora (reckoned the hottest town in the country), Rissani-Merzouga or Figuig. Autumn – with the date harvests – is also good. In winter the days remain hot, though it can get quite cool at night and further south into the desert can actually freeze. Some kind of hat or cap, and sunglasses, are pretty much essential.

Rivers in the south are reputed to contain bilharzia, a parasite that can enter your system through the soles of your feet. Even walking by streams in the oases take care to avoid contact.

Petrol/car repairs Garages are regularly spaced along all the main routes, but they're not exactly plentiful. Fill up with petrol whenever and wherever you have the opportunity; carry water in case of overheating; and above all be sure you've got a good spare tyre – punctures tend to be frequent on all southern roads. As throughout the country, mechanics are excellent (particularly at Er Rachidia: see p. 272) and most minor problems can be quickly patched up.

OUAZARZATE AND THE DRÂA

Ouazarzate, easily reached from Marrakesh (6hrs by bus) or Taroudannt (6½hrs – via Taliouine, see p. 290), is the standard jumping-off point for the south. East from here stretches the river Dades, the 'valley of the kasbahs' as the ONMT promotes it. South, over a tremendous ridge of the Anti Atlas, begins the Drâa – 125km of date-palm oases, which eventually give out to the Sahara near the village of M'hamid.

Although it is possible to make a circuit on towards Rissani, for most people (and anyone relying on buses alone) the Drâa means going down to Zagora and then returning to Ouazarzate by the same route. If you're pushed for time this might sound a little gratuitous, but it is a route that really shouldn't be missed, taking you well south of anywhere in the Tafilalt and flanked by an amazing series of turreted and cream-pink coloured ksour. These – **ksour** is the plural, **ksar** singular – are found throughout the southern valleys, and to an extent in the Atlas. They are essentially fortified, tribal villages: massive but temporary structures built, in the absence of other available materials, from the mud-clay pisé of the riverbanks and lasting only as long as the seasonal rains allow. A unique and probably indigenous development of the Berber populations, they are often monumental in design and fabulously decorated, with bold, geometric patterns incised or painted on the exterior walls and slanted towers. The **kasbah**, in its southern form, is similar to the ksar, though instead of sheltering a mixed village community they are traditionally the domain of a single family and their dependents. **Agadirs** and **tighremts**, also variants on the ksar structure, used to serve villages as a combination of tribal fortress and communal granary or storage-house.

OUAZARZATE AND AIT BENHADDOU

At some stage, you're almost bound to spend a night at **OUAZARZATE** and it can be a useful base to visit the ksour and kasbahs of Ait Benhaddou or Skoura. It is not exactly compelling in itself, however. Like most of the new Saharan towns, it was created as a garrison and administrative centre by the French and remains pretty much the same today: a deliberate line of functional buildings, set along the main highway and lent an odd sort of permanence by the use of concrete in place of the mud-pisé of the ksour. Before the French arrived there was only the riverbed – now channelled into a large, shallow lake beyond the town – and, guarding the route, the inevitable Glaoui kasbah, fast eroding but the one local 'sight'.

The **bus station**, a block back from the highway/main street, more or less marks the centre of town. Most of the **cheap hotels** and rather sparse roster of cafe-restaurants are grouped round about. The one exception is 2*B *Hôtel Gazelle*, 1500m or so out, on the road to Agadir – a small, comfortable place with overpriced meals but the undeniable attraction of its own swimming pool. A little further out, this time in the other direction, the *Camping Municipal* also has a pool – though it's not always full; to reach it walk past the 'triumphal arch' across the road leading to Tinerhir, it's on the left and has self-contained facilities including a reasonable restaurant. The other places in the centre, apart from a Club Med and a couple of luxury 4*As, are all unclassified, though not a great deal cheaper than the Gazelle. Pick from the *Es Salam* and *Royal*, facing each other on the main highway, Mohammed V; the *Atlas* on parallel Rue du Marche; or the *Es Saada*, left out of the bus station and next door to the town cinema. **Eating**, the cheapest cafes are along Rue du Marché, which, as its name suggests, culminates (or rather leads off) a small *souk* for fruit and other food. Much better, though slightly pricey, is *Chez Dimitri*, in the centre on Mohammed V – the one place with any character and a survival from the days when this was a French Foreign Legion post. Even if you don't eat a meal at Dimitri's you'll probably want to take advantage of its breakfasts (good coffee) and its unusually cheap *Flag Specials*. If you want to stock up for the dry road ahead, there's also a grocers (right opposite Dimitris) which sells, along with various provisions, discreet newspaper-wrapped bottles of wine.

Taourirt, the old Glaoui kasbah, looms to the right of the highway near the Tinerhir end of town: a dusty, 20 minute walk from the bus station. It was never a residence of the Glaoui chiefs – as Telouet or Marrakesh – but, positioned at this strategic junction of the southern trading routes, was always controlled by a close relative. In the 1930s, when the Glaoui were the undisputed masters of the south, it was perhaps the largest of all Moroccan kasbahs – an enormous family domain housing numerous sons and cousins of the dynasty, along with several hundred of their servants and labourers, builders and craftsmen, even semi-itinerant Jewish tailors and moneylenders. Since, and with its take-over by the government at Independence, it has fallen into drastic decline. Parts of the structure have simply disappeared, washed away by heavy rains; others are completely unsafe; and it is only a small section of the original, a kind of village within the kasbah, that remains occupied today. That part is towards the rear of the rambling complex of rooms, courtyards and alleyways. What you are shown, if you visit, is just the main reception courtyard and a handful of principal rooms, quite lavishly decorated but not especially significant or representative of the old order of things. With an eye to tourist demands, and fantasy, they have become known as the harem. Opening hours are daily (except Sundays) 9-12 & 3-6.

There is little else in – or to – Ouazarzate, and really the most interesting option is to get out for the day: either to Ait Benhaddou (which is detailed below) or a little along the Dades to Skoura (see p. 000). The kasbah at Tifoultoutte, which the tourist office may recommend, is nicely sited but unless you've a car and a strange sense of humour is hardly worth the time. 9km outside Ouazarzate, on the P31 road which bypasses the town en route for Zagora, it was again a former Glaoui kasbah, though a much smaller one than Taorirt, built (or at least re-built) only this century. In the 1960s it was converted to a hotel, and it was used – claim of all claims in this region – by the cast of *Lawrence of Arabia*. Today, with various luxury hotels (and a huge Club Med) in Ouazarzate itself, it has been reduced to the role of 'traditional entertainments annexe' to the various hotel tour groups. It is all fabulously inauthentic – mock banquets and German bellydancing – and just a little gross.

On a slightly more genuine note, Ouazarzate also has a **crafts co-op** (*Coopérative des Tisseuses*) – on the crossroads leading out of town to Zagora. There is no really local craft tradition, but stone-carving, pottery and the geometrically-patterned, silky wool carpets of the region's Ouzguita Berbers are all displayed and sold here. Hours are Mon-Fri 8.30-12 & 1-6, Sats 8.30-12. A new co-operative is under construction opposite the Taorirt kasbah.

Ait Benhaddou

The first thing you hear about AIT BENHADDOU – at least the first thing you hear when you've finally arrived at the village – is a list of its movie credits. This is a feature of much of the Moroccan south, where landscapes are routinely fantastic and cheap, exotic-looking extras in ready supply but even so the Benhaddou kasbahs have a definite edge. *Lawrence* was here, of course, and with *Jesus of Nazareth* the whole lower part of the village was rebuilt.

If this puts you off – and Ait Benhaddou is not really the place to catch a glimpse of fading kasbah life – don't, however, dismiss it too easily. Piled upon a dark shaft of rock above a shallow reed-strewn river, this is one of the most spectacular of Atlas villages and its kasbahs among the most elaborately decorated and best preserved. They are less fortified than usual among the Drâa or Dades, but, towered and crenellated and with high sheer walls of dark red pisé, must have been near inviolable in this remote, hillside site. How old any of them are is impossible to gauge, though there seem to have been kasbahs here at least since the C16. The importance of the site, which commands land for many miles around, was its position on the route from Marrakesh through Telouet to Ouazarzate and the south: a significance which disappeared with the creation of the new French road over the Tishka pass, and has led to severe depopulation over the last thirty years. There are now only half a dozen families living in the kasbahs, earning a sparse living from the valley agriculture and from the steady trickle of tourists.

When you reach the village the road gives out at a newly-built cafe, where you'll be adopted by the village **guide** and led up through the incredibly confusing web of streets. If you ask, it's usually possible to see the interior of one or two of the **kasbahs**. At the top of the hill, above, are ruins of a vast and imposing **agadir**, within whose keep the village must once have been able to retreat. **To get to Ait Benhaddou** is simple enough by car. Leaving Ouazarzate on the P31 (Tishka: Marrakesh) road, you turn right after 22km – along a good, signposted 9km track. Without a car you're dependent on hitching the track (which isn't easy) and later picking up one of the buses going back into Ouazarzate (not all of which are inclined to stop). As often in the south, the best solution is probably to negotiate a lift with other tourists: if you ask around in the evening at Ouazarzate's campsite (or at *La Gazelle*), someone can usually be persuaded to go. If you're into walking, the track beyond Ait Benhaddou continues to TAMDAGHT, and there are mulepaths on from here along the old pass to TELOUET.

Much easier of access than Ait Benhaddou – and a more rewarding day's trip if you don't have transport – are the kasbahs and ksour of SKOURA, the first place of any size along the Dades and a beautiful and rambling oasis (see p. 262). 42km from Ouazarzate, you can get there on any of the BOUMALNE/TINERHIR/ER RACHIDIA buses and catch another back (or on) without great difficulty.

SOUTH TO ZAGORA: THE DRÂA OASES

The route from OUAZARZATE to ZAGORA begins unpromisingly: the course of the Drâa is some way to the east, and the road laid across bleak, stony flatlands of semi-desert. At AIT SAOUN, however, one of the few roadside hamlets, there is dramatic change. Leaving the plains below, you begin a really monumental ascent into the **Djebel Sarhro** – the steepest of all the Anti Atlas ranges, with a tremendous grandeur and desolation in its brown-grey, heat-hazed ridge of peaks. It's a good road – wide and well conditioned – though it does seem to claim a lot of tyres. As throughout the south, if you're driving make sure you've a good spare and the tools to change it: traffic is regular but you can easily go half an hour or an hour without seeing or passing a thing.

The main pass along this road, the 1,660m **Tizi n'Tinififft**, comes just 4km beyond Ait Saoun but it is not for another 20km or so that you emerge from the mountains to catch a first, extraordinary glimpse of the valley and the oases – a thick line of palms reaching out into the haze, and the first sign of the Drâa kasbahs, rising as if from the land where the green gives way to desert. You descend to the valley at **AGDZ** (68km from Ouazarzate), a stopping point for many of the buses and a minor administrative centre for the region. It is not itself an especially interesting village – the best Drâa *ksour* are a few kilometres beyond – but if you're interested in the valley's rugs and carpets this is about the best place to see them: carpet shops line the road, and over the few minutes before a bus leaves prices can drop to a surprising level.

The **ksour** of the Drâa line the route more or less continuously to Zagora: most of the larger and older ones grouped a little way from the road, up above the terraces of date palms. Few that are in use can be more than a hundred years old, though you frequently see the ruins and walls of earlier ksour abandoned just a short way from their modern counterparts. Most are populated by Berbers, but there are also Arab villages here, and even a few scattered communities of Jews, still living in their Mellahs. All of the southern valleys, too, have groups of Haratin: blacks descended from the Sudanese slaves brought into Morocco along these caravan routes. Inevitably these populations have to some extent mixed – and the Jews here are almost certainly converted Berbers – though it is interesting quite how distinct many of the ksour still appear, both in their architecture and custom. There is, for example, a great difference from village to village in the women's costume, and above all in the wearing and extent of veils.

Although Zagora is the ostensible target of this journey along the Drâa, the valley is the real attraction. If you've a car, try to resist the impulse to burn down to the desert, and take the opportunity of walking out to one or other of the ksour or kasbahs. Among the most dramatic and extravagant is **TAMNOUGALT** – off to the left of the road, about 4km beyond Agdz. A collection of ksour, each fabulously decorated with pock-marked walls and tapering towers, this was once a capital of the region and its assembly of families (the *djemaa*) administered what was virtually an independent republic. Another striking group of ksour, dominated by a beautiful and imposing caidal kasbah, is at **TINZOULINE**, 30km before Zagora. There is a Monday souk held here and if you're travelling by bus it is one of the more realistic places to break the journey for a while. Bear in mind, however, that all of the Drâa ksour and kasbahs tend to be further from the road than they look: it's quite possible to walk for a couple of hours without reaching the edge of the oasis and the upper terraced levels.

ZAGORA AND BEYOND

ZAGORA at first sight seems a re-run of Ouazarzate: the same grouping of modern administrative buildings and hotels, the same single street and highway. Two things, however, set it apart. The first is its location: for this is the most productive stretch of the Drâa (indeed of all the southern valleys) and you've only to walk a mile or so out of town to find yourself amid the palms and oasis cultivation. The second is a distinct air of unreality. Directly behind the town rises a bizarre Hollywood-sunset mountain, at the end of the main street is a mock serious sign to Timbuctou ('52 jours': by camel), and in summer the heat and the dryness of the air is totally staggering.

The details are easily enough set down. There are three cheap **hotels** (and one very expensive), all of them along the main drag Avenue Mohammed V. Cheapest of the lot is the *Hôtel-Café-Restaurant des Amis*, on the left of the road in the centre, which in summer lets out (slightly cooler) space on its terrace. Immediately next door is the 1*A *Café-Hôtel Vallée du Drâa*, whilst at the far end of the street, marginally preferable, is the *Hôtel de la Palmeraie* (1*B). Both the *Drâa* and *Palmeraie* have **bars**, as does the *Tamegroute Restaurant* on Blvd Allal Ben Abdallah, the other main street in the centre. If you've the money, Zagora's big hotel, *La Tinsouline*, is the grandest of a chain of 'grand hotels' scattered about the south. Invariably empty through the summer – in the winter/spring 'season' it's a stagey, archaic resort with guests dressing for dinner – it is usually possible to negotiate use of the **swimming pool**, either for a daily fee or, not much more expensive, by having a meal.

Camping, for once, is also a promising option though the town's two sites are each some way out and a long hike without your own transport. To get to either, follow the Av. Mohammed V down to the roundabout and leave the town by the left fork. This road crosses to the left bank of the river and leads to another intersection – left for the Zagora mountain, right for the ksour of Amazrou. Take the right – briefly – and, now nearly 3km from Zagora, you'll come to signs for the two campsites on either side of the road. To the right, at the edge of the Amazrou oasis, is *Camping d'Amazrou:* reached along a slim 600m track by the side of a water channel. Left, after nearly 2km of dusty track, you finally come to *Camping Montagne* – a really beautiful site in the shadow of the mountain, with water, cold drinks (sometimes food) and very friendly people in charge.

Though both of these sites seem ridiculously far from the centre of town they are actually where you want to be to explore the Zagora oasis. **Amazrou** – the closest village – is at the heart of the palmery and a wonderful place to spend the afternoon, wandering amid the shade of its gardens and ksour. It is, inevitably, wise to tourism (the kids try to drag you in for mint tea), but the oasis life and cultivation are still pretty unaffected. The dates here are some of the best in Morocco and if you meet up with a guide he'll probably explain a few of the infinite varieties: the sweet *boufeggou* which last for up to four years if stored correctly; the small, black *bousthami;* and the light, olive-coloured *bouzekri.* The local sight, which any of the kids will lead you towards, is the old Jewish kasbah (*la kasbah des Juifs*). If you have the energy or can find transport the other sight of Zagora, and the real focus of the oasis, is the mountain, or **Djebel**. There is a narrow, somewhat hair-raising track to the summit (2½km after you leave the Tamegroute road). Up there, if you can make it in the early morning or the last few hours before sunset, the views are fairly startling – looking out across the palmery to further ksour and even a stretch of sand dunes to the south. On the spur itself there are ruins of two enclosures built by the Almoravides in the C11 as a fortress outpost against the powerful rulers of Tafilalt.

M'hamid and Tamegroute

The Zagora oasis reaches some 30km south of the town, when the Drâa disappears for a while, to resurface in a last fertile belt before the desert – the **M'hamid el Ghouzlane**, 'Plain of the Gazelles'. You can follow this route all the way down – the road was metalled as far as **M'HAMID** in 1982 – and, with a car, it's an enticing option. It is necessary to get authorisation from the *Supercaid* in Zagora before setting out, though this is really a formality: M'hamid is in a military zone but it is five years since the Polisario were active anywhere in this region.* Permission is normally granted without any charge, but you are required to hire a local guide for the half-day – a regulation that is probably as much an employment device as to keep any serious watch over tourists. If you don't have access to a car (and it should be possible to share a trip with someone if you ask around the campsites and hotels), you could get to

---

*M'hamid actually marks the northernmost attack launched by the Polisario – in October 1980. There was a symbolic importance to this raid, as it was in the market-place at M'hamid, on 25 February 1958, that Mohammed V first publicly laid claim to the Western Sahara as part of the Moroccan kingdom 'by the evidence of history and the will of its inhabitants'.

M'hamid by negotiating a guide and *grand taxi;* this, though, is really more effort and expense than it's worth. The ride down is spectacular, and there are some ksour at M'hamid and Tagounite that may date from the C17, but the town itself is little more than a small administrative village, and the Monday **camel market** touted by the tourist board hasn't seen a dromedary or blue man in years.

Although there is less drama in the journey or on the map, the village of **TAMEGROUTE**, just 20km from Zagora, is an interesting alternative. Here too, you get to see the desert – a stretch of dunes begins 3km to the south – and the village itself is highly unusual. It is essentially a group of ksour and kasbahs, wedged tight together and separated by low covered passageways, but at its heart is a very ancient and once highly prestigious **zaouia**. This, the base of the Naciri brotherhood, exercised great influence over the Drâaoui tribes from the C17 through to the last few decades. Its sheikhs, the saint-leaders, were known as the 'peace-makers of the desert' and it was they who settled disputes among the ksour and among the caravan traders converging on Zagora from the Sudan. They were missionaries too, and even as late as the C17-18, sent envoys to preach and convert the wilder tribes of the Rif, Middle and Anti Atlas. When you arrive at the village (which is reached by a straight-forward road down the left bank of the Drâa) you'll be adopted by a guide and taken off to see the zaouia's **outer sanctuary**, even today a refuge of the sick and mad, and its **library** – once the richest in Morocco and still preserving a number of very early korans printed on gazelle hide. The village also has a small souk of **potters' workshops**. To get out there, leave Zagora on the left fork and carry straight on past the turning up to the Djebel; Tamegroute lies about 3km back from the edge of the oasis belt, on the left bank of the Drâa. Hitching would be possible – though not too much fun in the summer months and once again best negotiated before setting out.

On from Zagora: the pistes
Almost all travellers return from Zagora to Ouazarzate: the only route possible by bus and in some ways the most interesting – allowing you to continue along the Dades to reach Tinerhir and the Todhra gorge. With your own transport, however, and with a fair amount of confidence for desert driving, there are two (and perhaps three) alternatives; possibilities that are open too, to hardened hitchers. These are outlined below to give an idea of what's involved though they are not routes we've personally done: the information comes from a driver for *Guerba*, an English tour company who run small groups along the pistes in their converted four-wheel-drive trucks.

Most accessible – and probably most exciting – is the long route east from **Zagora to Rissani** in the Tafilalt. This is taken by some cars as well as trucks, though unless you've a really good sense of direction (and comprehensive spares and supplies) it is wise to drive back up the Drâa to TANSIKHT for the first section to TAZZARINE: the unmetalled road marked on the *Kummerley & Frey* map direct from Zagora to Tazzarine has partially disappeared and you have to negotiate a tricky (and difficult to follow) track round by AIT MENAD and AJMOU N'AIT ALI OU HASSO. **TAZZARINE**, which sees an occasional bus or *grand taxi* from Tansikht, has a fairly large **cafe-hotel** with cold drinks. People tend either to stop here for a night or at **ALNIF** (67km further), a very small oasis with a cafe where you can **camp** and change water. RISSANI is 100km beyond Alnif, along a fair track over flattish valleys framed by the mountains of the Djebel Ougnat. This whole route is said to be covered 'daily' by local lorries (*camions*) and it should be possible to find (and pay for) a lift if you ask about in Zagora.

West from Zagora the maps indicate a road direct to **FOUM ZGUID**: a route which extends beyond to TATA (see p. 291) and from there on towards TIZNIT or TAROUDANNT. At the present, however, the Zagora-Foum Zguid section is closed, or at least open only with specially granted permits from the Zagora *gendarmerie*. Ask there for further details if you are interested. Lorries apparently cover the route every Sunday and Wednesday.

Lastly, and again to the west, there is a piste from **AGDZ to TAZENAKHT**, on the road to TALIOUINE. This is a dirt track, quite practicable for cars but at times very difficult to follow — at least until you reach the bitumened section from the cobalt mines at ARHBAR. It *may* be possible to approach Foum Zguid from this direction — but, again, ask.

THE DADES AND TODRHA

The Dades, east from Ouazarzate, is the harshest and most desolate of the southern valleys. Along much of its length the river is barely visible above the ground, and the road and plain hemmed in between the parallel ranges of the High and Anti Atlas — broken black-red volcanic rocks and dismal limestone peaks. This makes the oases, when they appear, still more astonishing, and there are two here — **Skoura** and **Tinerhir** — that are among the richest and most beautiful in the country. Each lies along the main bus route from Ouazarzate to Er Rachidia, offering an easy and excellent opportunity for a close look at a working oasis and at Skoura a startling range of kasbahs.

Impressive though this is, however, it is the two **gorges** which cut out from the valley into the High Atlas that are the highpoints of this route. The **Dades** itself is one, carving a final, fertile strip of land up behind Boumalne. The other – a classic, narrowing gorge of high walls of rock – is the **Todrha**, which you can follow by car or transit truck from Tinerhir right into the heart of the Atlas. If you're happy with the isolation and uncertainties of the **pistes beyond**, it is possible, too, to continue across the mountains – emerging finally near Beni Mellal on the road from Marrakesh to Fes. This needs a good four or five days if you're relying on local Berber trucks, and a certain craziness of travel lust, but it's about as exciting and rewarding a journey as you can make this side of the Sahara.

SKOURA, BOUMALNE AND THE DADES GORGE

The **SKOURA OASIS** begins, quite suddenly, a little over 30km out from Ouazarzate. It is an extraordinary sight even from the road, which for the most part follows its edge – very extensive, very dense, and with an incredibly confusing network of tracks winding across fords and through the palms to scattered groups of ksour and kasbahs.

If you have a car, the best point to stop and explore is some 4km before you arrive at the village proper (38km from Ouazarzate). Here, 600m to the left of the road, is the kasbah of **Amerhidl**, grandest and most extravagantly decorated in the oasis. As soon as you stop you'll be surrounded by any number of boys, and you've really no option but to pay one to watch your car and another to take you on as a guide. Arriving by bus at **SKOURA** village – a market square and cluster of administrative buildings – you'll also probably want to accept a guide (and, if you plan to stay, negotiate a *room*). Among the other main kasbahs you can ask to be shown are those of the **Dar Ait Sidi el Mati**, **Dar Ait Haddou**, and two former Glaoui residences – the **Dar Toundout** and **Dar Lahsoune**. Most of these are at least in part C19, though the majority of the Skoura and Dades kasbahs are much more modern. Dozens of the older fortifications were destroyed in a very severe tribal war in 1893 and many more of those that survived were pulled down in the French 'pacification' of the 1930s. The kasbah walls in the Dades – higher and flatter than in the Drâa – often seem unscaleable, but in the course of siege and war there were always other methods of conquest. A favourite means of attack in the 1890s, according to Walter Harris who journeyed through the region in disguise, was to divert the water channels of the oasis around a kasbah and simply wait for its foundations to dissolve.

Travelling this route in spring, you'll find Skoura's fields covered in the bloom of thousands of pink Persian roses. At **EL KELAA DES MGOUNA**, 50km on across another shaft of semi-desert plateau, there are still more, along with an immense kasbah-like rosewater factory where the *attar* is distilled. Here in late May (or sometimes early June) a **rose festival** is held to celebrate the new year's crops: a good time to be here by all accounts with villagers coming down from the mountains for the market, music and dancing. The rest of the year El Kelaa's single, shambling street is less impressive. There's a **Wednesday souk**, worth a break in the bus ride, but little else of interest beyond the site – above and back from the river – and the locked and deserted ruins of a **Glaoui kasbah**, on a spur above. The only **hotel** of any kind is the luxury 4*A *Les Roses du Dades*, next to the kasbah: if you've a car and money for a drink it should be possible to stop here and use their pool.

Better, though, to press on to Boumalne and the Dades gorge – or if you're pushed for time straight to Tinerhir. **BOUMALNE**, once again, is nothing much in itself: a garrison town with a long market square (**cafe** with a few *rooms* at the end of this), a 'Grând Hotel du Sud' (the 4*B *El Madayeq*, with pool and bar) and tyre-repair shop. But it is here that you can get a landrover-taxi up the Dades gorge, the approach road to which veers off to the left a couple of kilometres before you reach the town. The trip as far as MSEMRIR (47km; 2hrs) is a fairly standard local transport route and you should be able to get a *place* for around 7-8dhs. With your own transport you will probably want to venture only to the bridge over the Dades at AIT OUDINAR (24km).

The Dades gorge

The **DADES GORGES** – high cliffs of limestone and weirdly shaped erosions – begin almost as soon as you leave the main road behind Boumalne. For the first 15-20km they are quite wide and the valley carved out between them green and well populated. There are ksour and kasbahs clustered all about this stretch, many of them flanked now by more modern-looking houses but retaining the decorative imagination of the traditional architecture. Just 2km in, you pass an old **Glaoui kasbah** – strategically sited as ever to control all passage through. 3km further, as the road is turning more and more into a hairpin corniche, there is another dramatic group, the **ksour of the Ait Arbi**, hung against a fabulous volcanic twist of the rocks. These, like all the kasbahs of the Dades and Todrha, seem natural extensions of their settings: coloured with the colour of the earth and so fabulously varied, ranging through bleak lime-white to dark reds and greenish blacks.

The **bridge over the Dades**, where the road gives out to a very poor and difficult track, is about ¾hr's drive from Boumalne. There is a **cafe** here, where you can eat, rent a room and if you're driving ask about the state of the road beyond. Within walking distance of the cafe is one of the most spectacular sections of the gorge, but it is possible to get a car to MSEMRIR, and from there to IMILCHIL, or across to TAMTA-

TOUCHTE or AIT HANI (see the plan overleaf) where you can loop round to TINERHIR through the Todrha. It must be stressed, though, that these are really routes for trucks or landrovers. Renault 4's *can* make it round to Todhra between mid-June and late-September but you'll need to be a confident driver (hairpins are routine) and an even more confident mechanic: hire cars are uninsured for trips like this and not usually in good enough condition. Also if you're really intent on crossing from the Dades to Todrha, you'll find it considerably easier in the other direction: this way it's a long uphill haul and the hundred or so kilometres of piste can quite easily take a full day. The approach to AGOUDAZ and IMILCHIL, too, is easier from the Todrha – both for drivers or if you're waiting for trucks.

TINERHIR, THE TODRHA GORGE AND ACROSS THE ATLAS

Whilst **TINERHIR** is again pre-eminently a base – this time for the trip up into the **Todrha gorge** – it is also a much more interesting town than the other administrative centres along this route. Only a couple of kilometres east of the modern section is the beginning of its oasis, a world quite apart with its groups of tribal ksour built at intervals in the rocky hills above. When you're passing through don't be in a hurry to catch the first truck out to Todhra or the next bus on: this itself makes a rewarding day's exploration and is completely ignored by most of the tourists.

Arriving, things are again pretty straightforward. The buses stop at the arcaded Place Principal, and here too you'll find all the other facilities – three cheap hotels, a couple of cafes, a post office and *Banque Populaire*. Best value of the hotels is the unclassified *Salam*, a good place to eat as well, and with cooler rooms than the *Oasis*, over on the far side of the square. The other option, the *Hôtel Todgha*, is officially 2*A, though apart from its spectacularly kitsch decor it doesn't seem a lot different. It does, however, have a **bar**. If you want to **camp**, you'll have to press on some 8km up the Todrha: this is the site signposted in the town, be warned. Once more the only **swimming pool** belongs to the big luxury hotel (4*B *Hôtel Sargho*): this is to the left of the main road as you come in from Skoura/Ouazarzate. Nearby, dominating the town and with a tremendous view over towards the Todhra is yet another **Glaoui kasbah** – one of the grandest and most ornamental after Telouet and Ouazarzate, though now substantially in ruins.

To reach the **oasis** walk out – or hitch a lift – along one of the tracks behind the town. When you arrive it is possible to hire a mule (and guide) in the main village, the old Jewish quarter, now essentially Berber but still known as the Mellah. The finest of the kasbahs is that of the Ait

Amitane, with extraordinarily complex patterns incised on its walls. This is just one of many ksour and kasbah here, however, and it's as satisfying to wander at will. The oasis follows the usual pattern in these valleys: date palms at the edge, further in terraces of olive, pomegranate, almond and fruit trees, with grain and vegetable crops planted beneath them. The ksour each originally controlled one section of the oasis, and there were frequent disputes over territory and above all over access to the mountain streams for each ksour's network of water channels. Even in this century the fortifications were built for real, and, as Walter Harris wrote (melodramatically but probably without exaggeration): 'the whole life was one of warfare and gloom. Every tribe had its enemies, every family had its blood-feuds, and every man his would-be murderer'.

The Todhra gorge and a route over the Atlas

Whatever else you do in the south, at least spend a night at the **TODRHA GORGE**. You don't need your own transport, nor any great expeditionary zeal, to get up there, and yet it seems totally remote from the routes through the main valleys – very still, very quiet and really magnificent in the fading evening light. The highest, narrowest and most spectacular part is only 15km from Tinerhir, and there are three small hotels at its mouth where you can get a room or sleep out on the roof. Beyond, the road becomes *piste* and you're into real isolation: a route which you can take all the way over the Atlas if you've time to fit in with the Berber trucks, or considerable confidence and a very reliable, sturdy car.

From Tinerhir the beginning of the gorge (the *Hôtel el Mansour*) can be reached either by Peugeot **grand taxi** or, considerably cheaper, by **Berber truck**: both leave regularly through the day from the Place Principal. En route to the gorge proper, the road climbs along a last, fertile shaft of land – narrowing at points to a ribbon-like line of palms between the cliffs. There are villages more or less continuously along this part, all of them the pink-grey colour of the local rock and with the ruins of kasbahs and ksour up above or behind. To the right of the road, 9km from Tinerhir, there is a freshwater pool, rather fancifully named '**The Source of the Sacred Fish**' and flanking a particularly luxuriant palmery. It is a beautiful spot, with a small *café-hôtel* opposite and a couple of *campsites* in the clearing. Anywhere else this would be a major recommendation, though here it seems almost churlish not to continue to the beginning of the gorge. If it's not amazingly hot, however, there's a lot to be said for getting the truck to set you down here and walking the last 6km on.

The really enclosed section of **the gorge**, where the cliffwalls rise sheer to 100ft on either side, runs for only a short while – an hour or so's walk from the hotels at its entrance. The main pull of this site, though, is lost unless you stay a night: the evening skies here are like something out of *Local Hero*, and if you're remotely interested in birdlife this is one of the best locations I came upon. The first hotel here, *El Mansour*, is generally the cheapest: a very easy-going place with a pair of palm trees growing out through the roof, reasonable food, and a choice of sleeping on the roof (easily the best option) or on couches downstairs. If you feel you want a room walk on round the corner to either the *Hôtel des Roches* or the *Yasmina:* slightly more expensive and upmarket and with restaurants which cater for the one or two tourgroups who come up during the day. The Yasmina has the best food; the Roches, like El Mansour, allows you to sleep on its terrace.

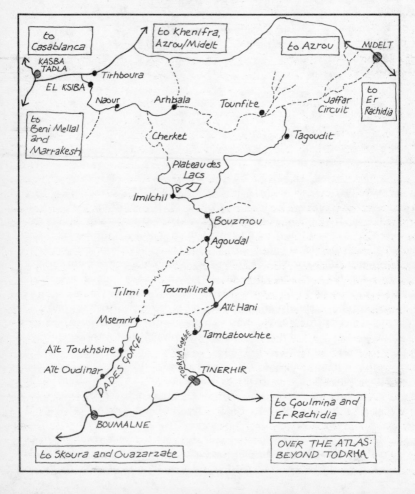

during the day. The Yasmina has the best food; the Roches, like El Mansour, allows you to sleep on its terrace.

If you want to continue beyond the gorge to TAMTATOUCHTE, and from there **across the High Atlas** to IMILCHIL and ARHBALA, it is possible to do so by catching a succession of **Berber trucks.** These inevitably are difficult to predict, though the people at the hotels usually have some idea of when there'll next be a lift as far as AIT HANI. Beyond there you just have to fit in with the pattern of the local souks, or – and this is perhaps the best approach – be prepared to do some walking over one or more of the stages. If you rely wholly on trucks (*camions,* as they're known) you will almost certainly find yourself stuck in a village for a day or two – and quite possibly for three or four. Eventually, however, everyone seems to get across to ARHBALA or NAOUR, where there is an asphalt road again and regular buses down to EL KSIBA and KASBA TADLA or KHENIFRA.

Since travelling across the Atlas on this route is so different from standard Moroccan travel, and since you can't do other than be flexible about your route, it seems worth while to include here more than just the facts about the villages en route and the roads. Below, then, with no apologies for the shift in style (and typeface), is **a personal account** by Dan Richardson and Jill Denton. Neither spoke Arabic – though they could both speak French and travelled with someone they met at Todrha who had a useful spattering of phrases. This, they felt, made some difference in the way they were received.

Bouzmou and beyond

As we clambered into the back of the truck the hotel owner tried to dissuade us. 'You don't want to go there . . . this truck's only going to Ait Hani, a horrible place . . .', but after 14 hours waiting on the porch for a lift we weren't to be deterred. Whatever was up there in the dry wastes of the High Atlas – the maps were enticingly vague – we meant to find out. The truck bumped and strained along the unsurfaced track, swathed in choking dust, and climbed steadily up out of the Gorge of Todrha. As the sun fell the stars gradually emerged until the bowl of the sky sparkled with dozens of constellations and shooting stars. After 4 hours we reached a vast plateau and the gates of **Ait Hani**, incongruously manned by an armed soldier. Inside the village – a jumbled blur of mud huts and towers – there was a lengthy discussion on what to do with the *Nazarenes* (Christians). Finally a man offered us his stable, outside the village. Despite our misgivings he did us proud, bringing rugs for the floor and re-appearing the next morning with mint tea, bread and his wife, who was entranced by our foreign appearance. We found *her* looks fascinating too – a tattooed chin, luminous eyes and a bizarre dress resembling a huge tinfoil doily shot with pale blue threads.

It was only in the daylight that we understood the previous day's warnings. The mountain, plateau and buildings were uniformly barren and colourless, except for a few tiny plots of withered vegetables. People peered at us from courtyards and from behind grilled windows, ignoring our tentative greetings, and our host of the night before led us to a low mud building bearing (in English) the name of 'The Modern Coffee House'. This title, we later learned, had been bestowed by a lone Englishman who had been marooned for four days in the village. I suppose we were luckier – we only had to wait for two.

Once the sun was up swarms of flies would lift off from piles of dung and come to crawl all over us. There was virtually nothing to see – the heat kept everyone indoors – and little to do but drink mint tea and gaze glumly at the decor of the coffee house; sooty mud walls, pastel colours and a collage of sardine cans, postcards and Koranic inscriptions. The proprietor was a diminutive, dessicated ancient who vastly enjoyed our plight and told us that the next truck out wasn't due 'for some time, if Allah wills it', and in the meantime wouldn't we like some food, which he could procure with great difficulty? Naturally the price was astronomical, while the eggs smelt sulphurous and their yolks were flecked with blood. We couldn't really blame him though, for in a village where there had been no rain for four *years*, where agriculture had almost collapsed and most of the young men fled, we represented a veritable goldmine.

When we eventually left it was in a subdued state – obvious enough to the truck driver, too, for he demanded an enormous price (25dhs each to Imilchil) which, stupidly, we paid. A cardinal rule of this kind of travel is to pay only on arrival at one's destination, as the Berbers do themselves, and it was all too predictable when, five hours later, the driver pulled into a village some 50km short of our destination and announced he was going no further. Our protests were useless – the man shrugged, pretended to speak no French, and smirked at the other passengers. Then, inspired, the Belgian we were travelling with quoted a Koranic phrase equivalent to 'by their deeds shall thee know them',* adding for good measure that the driver's behaviour was 'not beautiful' (*hryba*) in the sight of Allah. The effect was miraculous. The driver shrivelled with humiliation, and returned half the money to us. In a more cheerful mood we surveyed the village of Bouzmou, found an excellent teahouse on the roadside, and a chirpy lad to show us around.

Bouzmou was delightful: domed, honey-coloured houses, lofty trees, a gushing spring, and a football match

*The phrase, which means literally 'you can tell by the traces on his forehead how a man prays', can be rendered phonetically as: *Si-ma-HOM-fi-hiJOO-hi-HEEM.*

with fifty participants stirring up the dust in the *place*. Enchanting little girls with hennaed hair and huge earrings, torn between fear and the desire to touch us, scurried back and forth, clinging to each other and shrieking with laughter. The women were straightforward and curious to talk with us, a rarity in Morocco – even in the more 'open' communities of Berber villages. Jill was swiftly adopted, lent a shawl and her eyebrows and cheeks hennaed. It was proposed that the women tattoo her, as well, though the needle was like a cobbler's awl and caked with grime. Later we were all directed to a small square where a rain dance was just beginning. Villagers formed circles around the dancers, beating tom-toms and uttering shrill cries. Once we were discovered they demanded that we join in. Despite the clouds of dust, the noise and the heat, we gave a good ten-minute performance, hoping foolishly that the rain would fall and make us village heroes (it didn't).

Next morning – a Monday – nomads came in for the souk with their sheep herds roped neck to neck, to buy clothing, salt and tinware. Among the curiosities on sale were white rocks, which if burned 'would reveal in the fire the face of your secret enemy', and smooth, sweet-smelling stones to be used as an 'after-shave'.

We had to leave Bouzmou that afternoon, for our money was low and all the trucks were departing, laden with sheep and people. Our own – and I counted – held some 30 sheep on the upper deck, an unknown number on the lower, and 28 Berbers balanced on the rails and luggage racks. In the scorching heat, at an average speed of 20km an hour, we spent the next six hours ascending tortuous roads, circumventing precipices, and seemed to *accelerate* as we approached blind corners. At every bend, the sheep bleated with fear and pissed and crapped over everyone's feet and luggage, while above them a Berber periodically unwrapped from the folds of his *djellabah* a hunk of fresh mutton which he prodded appreciatively.

At some point in the journey we passed through **Imilchil**, and skirted one of the azure, salt-rimmed lakes on the **Plateau des Lacs**. We saw black nomad tents pegged in the wilderness, the occasional camel, and dozens of donkeys laden with firewood from the distant forests. At a crossroads, around 15km from Arhbala, we got down from the sheep truck and picked up another – this time comparatively luxurious with its freight of rough-cut stones.

Arhbala, a small town surrounded by soft mountains and oak and cedar forests, seemed almost metropolitan with its semi-paved streets, electric lighting, and double row of shops and cafes. There was no bus to Khenifra, where we hoped to change money, until 3am but, as is common in Morocco, we were 'adopted' and taken home to eat. The meal – couscous specially prepared in our honour – was delicious and our host and two older, male companions hospitable. It left a sour taste, though,

as the lightbulb in the kitchen was brought out to give us extra light, leaving the man's wife and daughters (who had prepared the meal but not appeared) to crouch over the remains of the meal in the dark.

Around one, we left for the bus, crawled onto the seats and tried to sleep. Arguments – always so intense that you imagine they are about to escalate to killing – blew around us but the journey was straightforward, and, after the mountains, dull, routine and enormously anticlimactic. At **Khenifra** we were back on the main road to Fes and could sample all that civilisation had to offer: croissants, squat toilets and banks.

To this only a few specifics need to be added.

IMILCHIL is for most people the main target of the route: a beautiful village, with a fine kaidal kasbah, where in September Morocco's most famous moussem – the *Marriage-market of the Ait Haddidou* – takes place. The moussem, once a genuine tribal function, is now considerably corrupted by tourism (landrover parties are shuttled up from Marrakesh for the day), but it's a lively, extravagant occasion all the same. Imilchil has no hotel but you can get rooms here, or camp beside one or other of the twin lakes – Isli and Tislit.

If you're **driving**, the worst part of the route is the first section, from the beginning of the gorge to TAMTATOUCHTE (17km; cafe with rooms/camping); here the track is little more than the stones of the riverpath. Beyond it improves considerably, though it is still slow, difficult mountain driving – and practicable for cars only from June until September.

There is of course no **bank** between Tinerhir and Khenifra/Kasba Tadla. Don't underestimate the expense of buying **food** in the mountains (30-100% over normal rates), nor the prices charged for lifts in the **Berber trucks;** as a very general guide, the standard rate for the journey from Ait Hani to Imilchil (66km) is around 8-10dhs. **Presents** – clothing, cigarettes, basic medicines and plasters, and for kids, sweets, pens and pencils – are everywhere appreciated.

TOWARDS TAFILALT: FROM TINERHIR TO ER RACHIDIA AND ERFOUD

East by bus from Tinerhir you have no choice but to make for ER RACHIDIA: a straightforward and largely barren route, broken only by the oases of TINEJDAD and GOULMINA. GOULMINA, a long straggling palmery, is made up of some twenty or so scattered ksour, whose towers, so it is said, are unusual in their height and fortification. Without transport, though, and without the time to work out the complex network of tracks, you'll see little of it. The modern, one-road town beside the highway is about as drab as any in Morocco – the only sign of life in the sentryboxes set down by its 'triumphal' entrance and exit arches. (These arches, which you find all over the south, were introduced by the French – presumably as a kind of militaristic flourish; it's a tradition that's been carried on by the Moroccans since Independence.)

The alternative route – **direct to Erfoud** – is more interesting, and in parts eerily impressive. It is not, however, covered by bus, and any kind of transport along it is sparse: if you're driving stock up well with water since any breakdown could let you in for a long (quite probably half-day) wait. The road cuts off from the main route to Rachidia at **TINEJDAD** and follows much of the course of this oasis – a mightily lush strip populated by the Ait Atta tribe, traditional warriors of the south who used to control land and exact tribute as far afield as the Drâa. Once you leave the oasis, at MELLAB, there is desert *hammada* more or less continuously until the beginning of the DJORF PALMERY outside ERFOUD. Beside the road, over much of this distance, the land is pock-marked by strange volcanic looking humps – actually man-made repair points for the underground **irrigation channels** which brought water to the Tafilalt almost 100km from the Todrha and Ferkla rivers. Another curiosity which you notice here, and elsewhere along the oasis routes, are the bizarre Berber **cemeteries** walled off from the desert at the edge of the ksour. These consist of long fields of pointed stones, thrust into the ground but otherwise unidentified – a wholly practical measure to prevent Jackals from unearthing the bodies (and in so doing, blocking their entrance to Paradise).

Although tarmacked all the way to Erfoud, sections of this latter road are sometimes covered over with sand: the result of small, spiralling sandstorms which can suddenly blow across the region and for 20 or 30 seconds block out all visibility. It's a simple road to drive, however, and shouldn't be a problem to follow.

ER RACHIDIA AND THE TAFILALT

The great date-palm growing regions of **the Tafilalt** come as near as anywhere in Morocco to fulfilling all the Western fantasies about the

Sahara. They do so by occupying the last, desert, stretches of the Ziz river valley: a route shot through with lush and amazingly filmic scenes, from its beginnings at the *source bleu* and oasis meeting-point of **Meski** to an eventual climax amid the rolling sand dunes of **Merzouga**. Along the way, once again, are an impressive succession of ksour, and an extraordinarily rich palmery – traditionally the most important territory this side of the Atlas.

As a terminus of the strategic caravan routes across the desert, Tafilalt has often given rise to religious dissent and separatist movements. It formed an independent kingdom in the C8-9, and was at the centre of the Kharijisite heresy (a movement which used a Berber version of the Koran – orthodox Islam forbids any translation of God's direct Arabic revelation to Muhammad); later it was to become a stronghold of Shi'ite Muslims; and in the C15 again emerged as a source of trouble, fostering the Marabout uprising that toppled the Saadian dynasty. It is with the rise of Moulay er Rachid, and the establishment of the **Alaouite** (or, after their birthplace, *Filali*) dynasty that the region is most closely associated. Launched from a zaouia at Rissani, this is the dynasty which still holds power in Morocco – through Hassan II, 14th sultan in the line. The Alaouites are also the secret of the wealth and influence behind many of the old kasbahs and ksour; from the time of Moulay Ismail, right through to this century, the sultans exiled princes and disenchanted relatives out here in the desert.

ER RACHIDIA AND THE SOURCE BLEU AT MESKI

ER RACHIDIA, established by the French as a regional capital, represents more than anywhere else the new face of the Moroccan south: a shift away from the old desert markets and trading routes, and, alongside it, increasing militarisation. During the Protectorate this was directed against the tribal uncertainty of the region; since Independence, the perceived threat has turned to the Polisario and to vague territorial claims from Algeria. Neither of these, however, have any direct bearing on the town – which is basically an administrative centre and a garrison for troops who may be needed elsewhere.

Unless you need to use the town's facilities – or await an early morning bus out – you're unlikely to want to stay. The *Source Bleu* at Meski, a near perfect place to rest up (and meet other travellers), lies just 22km to the south, accessible by shared *grand taxi* or on any of the buses to Figuig or Erfoud. Rachidia itself is like a slightly larger version of Ouazarzate: a functional sprawl of buildings which line the highway for some 3-4km before climaxing, inevitably, in a pretentious ceremonial arch. The only sight – worth the walk if you really have time to kill – is a large C19 **ksar**, visible from the bridge leading out to Erfoud.

From the **bus station** just about everything you might want to make use of is off along the main street/highway (**Av. Mohammed V**) to your right. About 250m down is a **tourist office**, and opposite it the *Banque Populaire* (the only **bank** that operates substantially in the south). The **post office** is down a sideroad behind the bank – turn left just before you reach it. Note that Er Rachidia and Erfoud have the only banks in the Tafilalt – there's nowhere official to change money at either Meski or Rissani, and if you're going on to Figuig and Algeria (see p. 278) you'll need to change travellers cheques here. Er Rachidia is useful, too, if you want **car repairs** or spares: the *Elf* garage in the main square carries a large supply of standard parts and will order others efficiently from Fes. For **cheap hotels**, cut up to the left of Mohammed V after you pass the municipal market and you'll find yourself – in the square with the garage – facing a choice of three; best of these, though there's not a lot between them, is the *Hôtel Saada*. Alternatives, if you can afford 2*A prices, are the *Hôtel Oasis* (Rue Abou Abdellah) and the *Hôtel Meski* (Av. Moulay Ali Cherif), both of which have pools and bars. Or lastly there is a **campsite** – 2km from the bus station, beside the road to Erfoud; this too has a pool, though it doesn't match Meski in style. **Eating** is cheapest at the foodstalls around the bus station; otherwise there are quite a number of restaurants along Av. Mohammed V.

Buses leave Er Rachidia at least four times a day for Erfoud/Rissani, and a similar number north to Midelt and Fes or Meknes. If you miss out on these it is usually no problem to get a place in a **grand taxi** to Erfoud, or, if you rustle together a group of people, to Meski. All of these leave from opposite the bus station. NB that the only bus to **Figuig** currently leaves at 5am, passing the turning to Meski 25mins or so later.

Meski: the source bleu

As near perfect a camping ground as could be imagined, the small palm grove of **MESKI** centres on a natural springwater pool – the famous *source bleu*. Nearby, along the riverside, spread a line of wheat and barley fields, across the bank an ancient ruined ksar (Old Meski) and its more modern farming village successor (New Meski). To say that the whole tends towards the over-romantic is an understatement. You need to be very puritan about Morocco to resist stopping off here at least for a night on the way south – or on the way back from Merzouga and the desert.

The oasis is rather insignificantly signposted, to the right of the Erfoud road, 22km south of Er Rachidia. You will need to ask the bus to put you down by the turning: from here it's only a 400m walk down to the palms and the entrance to the **campsite**. This can be distinctly over-crowded around Easter and in midsummer – and the *Club Med* ambience that develops around the cafe in the evenings a little overpowering – but it's nevertheless an extraordinarily relaxed and welcoming place. Prices both for tents and for meals and drinks are a little above usual odds, though not drastically so considering the captive market, and if you're a hardened camper you can always bring your own food from Er Rachidia or Erfoud or buy basic supplies up at the village. In the summer months a sleeping bag is all that's needed, and you could get away with just a blanket (which, conveniently, are sold by the site). The one warning rumour that has to be repeated is that there are bilharzia worms in the pool: some guides advise against swimming, though nobody who stays here takes any notice, and I for one survived.

Going on to Erfoud or back to Er Rachidia can be a slight problem, since some of the buses pass by full and don't stop. However, this is one of the easiest places around to hitch lifts and you should never be stranded for long.

SOUTH TO ERFOUD, RISSANI AND MERZOUGA

Make sure you travel this last section of the Ziz in daylight. It's one of the most pleasing of all the southern routes: a dry red belt of desert just beyond Meski and then suddenly a drop into the valley and the great palmery and grain fields of central Tafilalt. Away from the road, **ksour** are almost continuous – glimpsed through the trees and the high walls enclosing gardens and plots of farming land. If you want to stop and take a closer look, AOUFOUSS, midway to Erfoud and the site of a Thursday market, is perhaps the most accessible. MAADID, too, off to the left of the road as you approach Erfoud, is interesting – a really massive ksour and, like many in the Tafilalt (but few elsewhere in the south), with an entirely Arabic population.

ERFOUD, once again, is a disappointing modern administrative centre – though saved from complete drabness by its desultory frontier town atmosphere. Arriving from Er Rachidia you get a first, powerful sense of closeness to the desert, with frequent sand-blasts ripping through the streets. If you have the energy, climb up to the Borj Est, the military hill fort 3km across the river (leave by the back of the main square), and you can glimpse the sands to the south – if things are clear you can look back, too, right across the Tafilalt oasis to the beginnings of the Atlas.

This apart, though, for most travellers Erfoud functions very much as a staging post for going on to Rissani and the sand dunes near Merzouga. It has the last **bank** and **post office** (both in the centre of town, by the intersection of the two main roads – Mohammed V and Moulay Ismail), and unless you have to wait over for these there is no great reason to stay – four buses a day go on to Rissani and innumerable *grands taxis* (about 5dhs a place). If you do need a bed, there are three cheap **hotels** around Mohammed V/Moulay Ismail (walk down to the right as you come out of the bus station); again there's nothing much to choose between them, and nothing much to be said for any of them either. The town's **campsite** is also fairly basic but on the whole slightly more congenial: if you don't have a tent you can rent a small, very cheap cabin for the night. Don't, however, expect its swimming pool to be full – water is heavily rationed in Erfoud. To get there it's a ten-minute walk, signposted from Av. Mohammed V.

Getting to Merzouga by local transport, the usual route is to go down first to RISSANI, from where – on market days only (Sun, Tues, Thurs) – there are Berber trucks along the desert piste. If you are driving, however, it is quite possible to take the road direct from Erfoud: this is not asphalted but it is well marked (whatever the Erfoud hustlers tell you), no problem for Renault 4s, and takes little over 45 minutes. There is even a small **cafe** with a gesture of a swimming pool, about two-thirds of the way along. Hitching, you may be able to find someone driving this way at the Meski or Erfoud campsites. Otherwise, if you feel like paying their prices, trips out to watch the sunset over the Merzouga dunes (and maybe a little beyond) are touted by landrover-guides in Erfoud. Ordinary *grands taxis* won't be persuaded to take you along this route.

Rissani and Merzouga

RISSANI stands at the last visible point of the Ziz river: beyond, steadily encroaching on the village and its ancient ruined ksour, begins the desert. The former capital of Tafilalt, this was for eleven centuries the final stop on the great caravan routes south. Here, around 707, was founded the first Arab kingdom of the south – the semi-legendary Sijilmassa, and it was at the zaouia here (still an important national shrine) that the Alaouite dynasty launched their bid for power, conquering first the oases of the south, later the vital Taza gap, and finally Fes and Marrakesh.

The **modern village** musters scarcely enough houses to merit the name. Most of the people live in a single, large and decaying **ksar**, and in addition to this there is just a single administrative street with a couple of **cafes** and a waterless, shamelessly overpriced **hotel**. If you plan to stay here, rather than go on to Merzouga, the best place to sleep – and the cheapest point to negotiate – is up on the roof. The only life of any kind comes with the three-times-weekly **market**, though even then it's a quiet place compared to the old times when the caravan trade passed through. This was still active into the 1890s, when the English journalist Walter Harris reported thriving gold and slave auctions. Predictably enough, today's money-spinning goods are all touristic, and prices average fairly high. However, there's often a good selection of local Berber jewellery – including the crude, almost iconographic designs of the desert Touaregs – and some of the basic products (dried fruits, farming materials and so on) are interestingly distinct from those of the richer north. Don't expect camels, though: apart from the caravans these were never very common in Tafilalt, the Berbers preferring (as they still do) more economical donkeys.

Rissani's older monuments are well into the process of erosion – both through crumbling materials and by the slow progress of the sands. Sijilmassa, whose ruins were clearly visible at the beginning of this century, has more or less vanished, though at a stretch you can make out a few remains along by the course of the river west of the village. The various kasbahs and reminders of the Alaouites, too, are mostly in some degree of ruin, but there is enough remaining to reward a morning's battle with the heat. The ksar still occupied by the market square is itself C17 in origin, though much restored since, and from here you can cut across diagonally from the bus terminal towards another collection of ksour. First in order, about 2½km to the south-east, is the Zaouia of Moulay Ali Shereef, the original Alaouite stronghold and the mausoleum of their founder. Many times rebuilt – the last after floods in 1955 – the shrine is forbidden to non-Muslims, though you are allowed to look in from the outside. Beside it, dominating this group of buildings, is the Ksar d'Abbar, an awesomely grandiose ruin which was once a kind of palace exile, housing the unwanted members of the Alaouite family and the wives of the dead sultans. Most of the structure, which still bears considerable traces of its former decoration, dates from the beginning of the C19. A third royal ksar, the Oulad Abd el-Halim, stands about 1km further on. Notable for its huge ramparts and the elaborate decorative effects of its blind arches and unplastered brick patterning, this is one of the few really impressive imperial buildings completed in this century. It was constructed around 1900 for the Sultan Moulay Hassan's elder brother, appointed governor of the Tafilalt.

MERZOUGA, 2hrs by truck from Rissani, is not the only, nor the least commercial, way to see the sun rise or set over the desert sands – but it must certainly be the most impressive. Above the hamlet, and stretching from some fifteen or so kilometres into the haze, is the Erg Chebbi: 'the small erg', Morocco's largest sand dune. It is now very much part of the tourist circuit, though this should in no way put you off. Just getting out from Rissani is an adventure in itself – and this piste is really a more appropriate approach than the road from Erfoud – and the isolation and silence of the desert is a bizarre experience, particularly if you stay the night here at the very basic cafe-hotel below the dunes.

The market-day trucks from Rissani charge around 12dhs for the trip. Getting back after the morning's sunrise is usually quite easy, since there are nearly always car-driving tourists with a little spare capacity (and it's hard for them to refuse with temperatures climbing over 120°F within a couple of hours). If you stay the night, or even if you just come down for a glimpse, bring your own bottled water as there is none sold here.

The track south from Merzouga to TAOUZ is currently closed to non-Moroccans, though for a glimpse further into the desert, the **landrover guides** sometimes drive out to nomadic encampments (not always genuinely so!) or to vantage points for witnessing the heat and desert's (authentic) mirage effects.

OUT EAST TO FIGUIG AND THE ALGERIAN BORDER

The ten-hour desert journey from **Er Rachidia to Figuig** is one of the most exhilarating and spectacular that you can make – certainly among those accessible to travellers without landrovers and proper expeditionary planning. It is startlingly isolated – almost over the entire 393km length – and physically quite extraordinary, the real outlands of Morocco, dominated by huge empty landscapes and blank red mountains.

What you have by way of a human presence is a series of struggling mining villages and military outposts, ranging from the desolate little mud hut type constructions of MENGOUB to the prosperous administrative and garrison centre of BOUARFA (where you'll probably have to change buses). The real focus of the region though, is **Figuig** itself – a great medieval date-palm oasis, hemmed within a bowl of mountains and right on the borders with Algeria. If you want to go through **into Algeria**, the frontier point here is almost always open – and for independent, non car-driving travellers is usually more straightforward than Oujda (see the details that follow, and p. 85). Staying in Morocco, you can head north from Figuig to OUJDA (7hrs by bus) and the Mediterranean coast.

THE FIGUIG OASIS

The southern oases are traditionally measured by the number of their palms, rather than in terms of area or population. FIGUIG, with something over 200,000 trees, has always been one of the largest – an importance further enhanced by its strategic border position. Twice at least it has been lost – in the C17 wars, and again at the end of Moulay Ismail's reign – and as recently as 1963 there was fighting in the streets between Moroccan and Algerian troops.

The oasis has even less of an administrative town than usual, still basically consisting of seven distinct ksour villages – which in the past were themselves often at dispute. Getting your orientation is relatively simple. The road up from the **bus station** leads up to an open *place* and

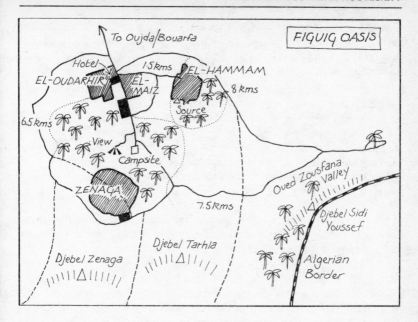

the **administrative buildings**, passing on the way the town's single (and pretty rudimentary) **hotel**, the *Sahara*. There is another, with a pool and modern facilities, in construction up at the administrative centre, though whether this will ever be finished (Figuig doesn't see many tourists) is a little doubtful.

From the 'centre' of Figuig, **the ksour** spread out about the base of the hill – each enclosing its own palmery within high, turreted walls. Although normally organised into a loose confederacy, they were until this century fiercely independent – and their relations with each other punctuated by long and bitter blood feuds and, above all, disputes over the limited water supplies. Their extraordinarily archaic shape – with watchtowers positioned above the snaking *feggaguir* (or irrigation channels) – evolved as much from this internal tension as from any need to protect themselves from the nomadic tribes of the desert. Likewise, within each of the ksour, the elaborate tunnel-like networks of alleys are deliberate (and successful) attempts to prevent any sudden or easy progress.

Your best chance of getting an overview of all this is to make for the **platforme**, close by the campsite and poised above the ksar of Zenaga. The view from here spans a large part of the palmery and its pink-tinged ksour, and you can gaze round at the weird, multi-coloured layers of the enclosing mountains. If you can muster the energy – Figuig in summer feels a little like sitting inside a fan-heater – plunge down from here into Zenaga, the largest of the seven villages. Heading in a leftward direction you should reach its centre, a grander metropolis than most with a couple of cubicle shops and a cafe in addition to its mosque.

Of the other ksour, it is possible to loop round to the right of the main administrative road, past El-Maiz to El-Hammam el Foukanni. El Maiz is the prettiest of the ksour, with small vaulted lanes and houses with broad verandahs pointing out to the south. At El Hammam, as the name suggests, there is a hot spring, used by the people for their ablutions. Anyone who offers to guide you will show this off. Back on the other side of the administrative road is the Ksar El-Oudarhir, which too has natural springs (one hot, one salty), and similar terraces to those of El Maiz. All of the ksour have exclusively Berber populations, though up until the 1950s/60s there was also a considerable Jewish population. Through to the early years of this century Figuig was the last Moroccan staging post on the overland journey to Mecca.

Into Algeria: the frontier

There are two overland crossing points between Morocco and Algeria: this one (FIGUIG-BENI OUNIL) and OUJDA-MAGHNIA, 329km up to the north. The traditional advantage for travellers in Figuig is that the Moroccans make no fuss about you crossing on foot. At Oujda they often enforce a bizarre system of bureaucracy that demands you cross in a car – and that your date of entry into Morocco corresponds with that of the vehicle. It is all pretty silly but there's no point whatever in kicking against the rules – if you run into problems just hang back, stay patient and try later on in the day with a new set of officials.

Getting to the actual frontier from Figuig you will probably need to hitch: it's only 8km but at present there's no bus and the one local taxi can be difficult to get hold of. You will also need at least **£130 in French francs** (*not* dirhams) to change at the border into Algerian currency: a stipulation that is waived only if you can produce a full and valid International Student Card. Here there may well be a problem, as the Figuig bank doesn't usually take travellers cheques or credit cards, and it doesn't always have a supply of francs. To be safe, change in advance either at Oujda or Er Rachidia. On the Algerian side of the border it is easy enough to get a lift into BENI OUNIL and from there you can continue by bus or train.

For details of the Oujda crossing see p. 85.

On towards Oujda and other small towns in the East

Unless you've an urgent fascination with (very) small town life, there is really nowhere else on this eastern plateau which offers very much temptation. **TENDRARA** (Tuesday market) and **AIT BENIMATHAR**, on the road to Oujda, both have basic cafe-hotels but you'd be hard pushed to find a reason to stay the night. Ait Benimather does, however, have a quiet little **hot water oasis**, full of tortoises and snakes, and it's not a bad place to break the journey and spend the middle of the afternoon. You can do this by taking the early morning bus from Figuig, and catching one of the later ones for the last 50km on to Oujda.

To the west of **BOUARFA** – where a mainly freight carrying (and extremely slow) railway begins the haul north to Oujda – the towns are all fairly bleak. If you're into piste driving, there are said to be troglodyte (cave) dwellings up in the hills behind BOUDENIB, towards GOUMARRA.

TRAVEL DETAILS

Buses
From Ouazarzate Marrakesh (4 daily; 6hrs); Zagora (3; 5½hrs); Tailiouine/Taroudannt (2; 3½hrs/5hrs); Tinerhir (3; 5hrs).
From Zagora,Only to Ouazarzate (3 daily; 5½hrs).
From Tinerhir Er Rachidia (2 daily; 3hrs); Ouazarzate (3; 5hrs).
From Er Rachidia Erfoud/Rissani (4 daily; 2½hrs/5hrs); Tinerhir (2; 3hrs); Figuig (1 daily via BOUARFA, currently at 5am; 10hrs); Midelt (5; 3½hrs); Fes (3; 8½hrs); Meknes (1; 8hrs).
From Erfoud Rissani (4 daily; 2hrs); Er Rachidia (4; 2½hrs).
From Figuig Oujda (4 daily; 7hrs); Er Rachidia (via Bouarfa; 1 daily; 10hrs).

Grands Taxis
From Ouazarzate Regularly to Zagora (4hrs). Negotiable for Skoura (1hr) and Ait Benhaddou (1¾hrs but costly private run).
From Boumalne Landrover taxi at least daily to Msemrir (3hrs). Regular run to Tinerhir (50mins).
From Tinerhir Regular runs to Boumalne (50mins) and Tinejdad (1hr: thence to Er Rachidia).
From Er Rachidia Fairly frequent runs to Erfoud (along which route you can negotiate a *place* to Meski), and to Tinejdad 2hrs).
From Erfoud Fairly frequent runs to Rissani (1½hrs) and Erfoud (2hrs). Landrover trips direct to Merzouga (1hr; relatively expensive).

Train
There is a line **from Bouarfa to Oujda** (8hrs) but this is a night train, carries mainly freight and is a distinctly eccentric alternative to the bus from Figuig.

Chapter seven
AGADIR, THE ANTI ATLAS AND THE DEEP SOUTH

If you fly to Morocco, it will probably be to **Agadir** – purpose built as a resort after an earthquake in 1960, and something of a showpiece for the 'New Nation'. It is unlikely though that you'll want to stay for long. Agadir has been very carefully developed – its image and winter holidays definitely upmarket – and beyond the beach and package hotels there is not a great deal of life to be found. There is certainly nothing at all Moroccan: this is tourism at its most bland and irrelevant, straining to avoid contact.

Fortunately, little of this applies to the rest of **the coast.** Just north of Agadir are a series of small fishing villages and beaches, yet to see electricity or running water. Of these, the best known, and the most attractive, is **Tarhazoute**, a popular hippy centre in the early 1970s though today fairly quiet. Inland from here, and part of the same mythology, is 'Paradise Valley', a beautiful and exotic palm gorge which culminates in the spring/winter waterfalls of **Immouzer des Ida Outanane**. To the south the beaches are almost totally deserted in summer, ranging from the solitary campsites at **Sidi Rbat** and **Sidi Moussa d'Aglou** down to the old Spanish port of **Sidi Ifni** – only relinquished to Morocco in 1969 and full of bizarrely grandiose deco colonial architecture.

Inland, the two main towns of the **Anti Atlas** – and for outsiders, the highlights – are Taroudannt and Tafraoute, provincial and rather genteel centres whose populations share the unusual distinction of having cornered the country's grocery trade. *Tafraoutis*, in particular, can be found throughout Morocco (and also in Paris and Marseilles), running the small local 'corner shops', before eventually returning home to retire. Physically, though, the two towns could hardly be more distinct. **Taroudannt**, massively walled, is the modern and traditional capital of the fertile Souss plain; not a town with any particular 'sights', but an animated and natural place to stay en route to Marrakesh or Ouazarzate. Further south, and reached by bus via Tiznit, **Tafraoute** is essentially a collection of villages – stone-housed and absurdly picturesque in a startling natural landscape of pink granite and strange, vast formations of rocks. If you've time only to get to one place in the south-west, it should be here.

The **Deep South** at the moment is in a mess, with its trans-Saharan

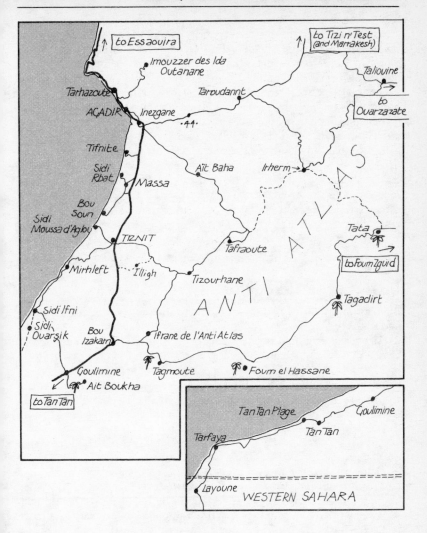

routes closed, and all territory beyond Goulimine essentially under military control. The war here, in the former colonial territory of the Spanish Sahara, has been going on since 1973 when the nationalist Polisario Front launched attacks against the Spanish authorities. When Spain withdrew in 1975, the Polisario declared an independent state, the *Sahrawi Arab Democratic Republic*, but this has never been recognised by Morocco, who claim the territory, tribally and historically, as their own and have effectively annexed the northern section. An end to the war doesn't seem immediately likely: meanwhile its maintenance puts an increasing strain on Moroccan resources and on its relations with the Algerian government, Polisario's principal support.

For travellers, there's not a lot going for this part of the desert. **Goulimine**, the famous camel market and meeting place of the 'Blue Men' (Touareg tribesmen, whose faces are tinged blue by their veil and robes), is now more frequented by tourists than anything else – and its few camels brought in mainly for their benefit. **Tan Tan,** 35km further south, marks the beginning of the military zone and the end of practical tourist travel. You can go down there – and can fly from Agadir to **Layoune,** too – though unless you're making for the Canary Islands it's a fairly futile gesture. Better, if you want an exciting route in this region, to cut east before Goulimine along the string of oases leading towards **Tata:** from here it is possible to complete a long (and little travelled) loop to Taroudannt.

AGADIR AND INEZGANE

Built up in organised sectors – one for tourist hotels, one for the port, and a third, some way out, for industry and local people – **AGADIR** doesn't really lend itself to excitement or spontaneity. It does, admittedly, have a magnificent swathe of beach, and it has avoided the tower block architecture of Spanish costa counterparts, but this is about as far as being positive will stretch. Unless you actually want a day or two's suspension from ordinary Moroccan life, best pass straight through. Rooms, in any case, can be quite a problem to find in midsummer or in the winter/spring season.

The basic layout of Agadir is pretty straightforward. The **beach** and the **commercial zone** (centred on Place and Avenue Hassan II) are marked on the map; the **port area** is to the north, below the old kasbah; and the **industrial zone** spreads back to the south towards the town of **Inezgane,** now almost a suburb. If you're coming in by bus from the south, you may actually arrive at Inezgane: and if you don't plan to stay in Agadir there are buses out from here to most destinations, and a handful of cheapish hotels. To get into Agadir from Inezgane, any number of local 'city' buses will drop you at the **Place Salam terminal** (bottom right-hand corner on our plan). All other coaches – both CTM and private – use the **main bus station** behind the Place Lahcen Tamri (top of plan, centre right). The **airport** is 4km out of town on the Inezgane road: there's a bus from here to the Place Salam every hour, or you can share one of the *grands taxis* always available (about 30 dhs for the whole taxi).

Most of the large hotels are spread back from the seafront along the boulevards 20 Août and Mohammed V. They tend to be block booked in August, and again around Christmas, but if you have the money to blow it can be worth trying the 4*A *Hôtel Salam* (Blvd Mohammed V – see the plan; Tel. 221-20), friendly and quite modestly priced for the luxury going. Other, cheaper options around the centre and seafront include the *Hôtel Cinq Partis du Monde* (keyed 12) and 1*A *Hôtel Petit Suède* (keyed 13), or the 2*A *Atlantic* (just off Blvd Hassan II, behind the Post Office) and *Palmiers* (Av. Sidi Mohammed). Most travellers,

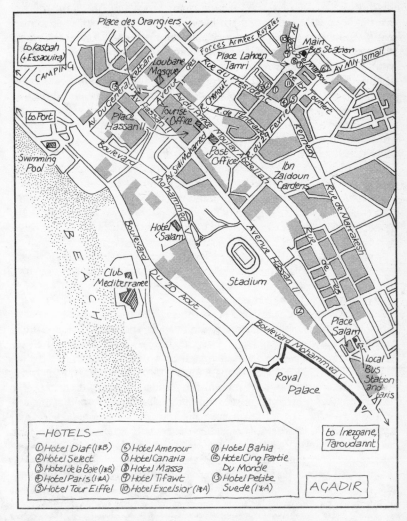

—HOTELS—

① Hotel Diaf (1*B)   ⑥ Hotel Amenour   ⑪ Hotel Bahia
② Hotel Select   ⑦ Hotel Canaria   ⑫ Hotel Cinq Partie
③ Hotel de la Baie (1*B) ⑧ Hotel Massa   Du Monde
④ Hotel Paris (1*A)   ⑨ Hotel Tifawt   ⑬ Hotel Petite
⑤ Hotel Tour Eiffel   ⑩ Hotel Excelsior (1*A)   Suede (1*A)

to Inezgane,
Taroudannt

AGADIR

however, make straight for the places around the **Place Lahcen Tamri**, just below the main bus station: an area that is something of an 'alternative Agadir', and frequented to an extent by young Moroccans on holiday. All of these hotels are keyed and marked on our plan. Best, if they have room, are the *Bahia* (not the cheapest but unusually clean, tasteful and good value), followed, some way behind, by the *de la Baie* (1*B) and *Paris* (1*A) on Av. President Kennedy. The **campsite**, quite a walk along Blvd Mohammed V, is one of the more expensive in Morocco, though reasonably secure and with a snack-bar and other facilities.

What **nightlife** there is tends to be in the big hotels or (less so) along the small strip of 'seafront' restaurants and 'English Bars' on Blvd du 20 Août. Among the former you might try the *Tan Tan Disco* in the Hôtel Salam, though don't expect too much. The cheaper **cafes and restaurants** – most of them not selling alcohol – again concentrate around the Place Lahcen Tamri, and this is where a lot of travellers end up whiling away the evenings. Eating, elsewhere in the town, takes a surprisingly low profile, with many of the package hotels offering full board. Two good, non rip-off places can be found on the Place des Orangiers (off Av. Hassan II): the *Restaurant Daffy*, which has an excellent set menu with fish or chicken tajine, and, around the corner and a little more basic, the *Le Tanalt*. If you want to buy your own food try the market just off Place Lahcen Tamri; for cheap wine and beer (and fixed price craft goods) there's a large *Co-op* store at the corner of Av. Hassan II/Av. Sidi Mohammed.

Agadir's only 'sight' – the **old kasbah** on the top of the hill to the north – deserves a mention, though not perhaps a visit unless you have a car for the 8km trip. Primarily what you see when you get up there is a marvellous view back over Agadir and the beach. The kasbah, the main quarter of the old pre-earthquake town, is itself little more than the bare outlines of walls, and an entrance arch with an inscription in Dutch recording that they began trading here in 1746 – capitalising on the rich sugar plantations of the Souss plain. It's not much but it is one of the few reminders that Agadir has any past at all, so completely did the 1960 earthquake wreak its destruction. In fact, Agadir's history closely parallels that of the other Atlantic ports: first being colonised by the Portuguese in the C15, then recaptured by the Saadians in the C16 and thereafter trading with intermittent prosperity – overshadowed, more often than not, by the activities of Mogador-Essaouira. In 1911, then relatively insignificant, Agadir was the scene of a protest by the Germans against French and British plans to carve up North Africa. A German gunboat, the *Panther*, loosed off a few rounds across the bay – an event, like the Fashoda crisis in Egypt, that very nearly started the First World War.

Some details

If you're heading for the **Anti Atlas,** or cutting across to the **South,** Agadir offers the last substantial facilities. It is also one of the cheapest (because competitive) places in the country to **hire a car** – which many of the rental firms will allow you to return to Marrakesh, Casablanca or Fes.

AIRLINES *Royal Air Maroc* fly from Agadir to Layoune and the Canary Islands, and (via Casa) to Tangier. Their office is on Av. du General Kettani (Tel. 231-45).

AMERICAN EXPRESS c/o *Voyages Schwarz*, Blvd Hassan II; open Mon-Fri 9-12 & 3-6, Weekends closed.

BANKS *SGMB, Crédit du Maroc* and others can be found in the centre, mainly along the Av. des F.A.R. The *Hôtel Sahara* (Av. Mohammed V) offer currency exchange at normal bank rates.

BARGAINING If you do buy anything in Agadir – rugs, carpets, babouches, etc. are all sold – you may need to offer as little as a tenth of the asking price. For once, fixed price shops are often a better deal.

BOOKS English paperbacks at the *Débit Pilote* bookshop on Av. Hassan II. **Newspapers** also available on the Av. Hassan II and from some big hotels.

BUSES Local ones to the airport, Inezgane and Tarhazoute run from the Place Salam; all others from the main terminal (book early in summer).

CAR HIRE Again, *Leasing Cars* (107 Av. Hassan II, Tel. 209-81; and at the airport) are among the cheapest and most reliable. *L.V.S.*, with branches in Marrakesh and Casablanca, are also worth asking: here they're at 52 Av. Hassan II. Others, including *Hertz, Avis* and *InterRent*, are grouped along Av. Hassan II and towards the campsite on Blvd Mohammed V.

CAR REPAIRS For Renaults try *Castano* (Av. El Moukouama; Tel. 238-21); Citroens, *Garage Citroën* (angle of Rue Bertholet/Rue Ampere); Fiats, *Auto-Hall* (Rue de la Foire; Tel. 224-86). Many others.

GRANDS TAXIS Routine runs to Inezgane and the airport from Place Salam. At Inezgane you can get another grand taxi (or rather a succession of two with a connection midway at Ouled Teima, or *Quarant-Quatre*, '44', as locals call it) to Taroudannt, or to Tiznit.

HOSPITAL *Hospital Hassan II*, Route de Marrakesh (Tel. 224-77). Most of the big hotels can provide addresses for English-speaking doctors.

MOPED RENTALS A couple of outlets back from the beach along the Blvd du 20 Août. Only intended for local use, they'll at least get you to Banana Village and Tarhazoute (see the following section).

POST OFFICE Main *PTT* is right in the middle of town at the end of Av. Sidi Mohammed: oddly enough it's touted in various guides for having won an 'architectural prize' (far more impressive are the colonial delights of the post offices at Sidi Ifni and Rabat, or even the solid ugliness of the one at Tafraoute). Hours are Mon-Fri 9-12 & 3-6, Sats 9-12 only; the telephones section stays open 24hrs a day (and works well!).

SWIMMING POOL   Municipal pool at the north end of the beach if you don't fancy the sea.

TOURIST OFFICES   *ONMT* (Block A, Av. Sidi Mohammed: along the raised walk opposite the post office). *Syndicat d'Initiative* (Av. Mohammed V; Tel. 226-95). One or other may be able to give you a date for the Goulimine moussem (see p. 296).

AROUND AGADIR: TARHAZOUTE, IMMOUZER AND THE BEACHES

If you feel a certain pull towards Agadir's long white-sand beach but can't stand the city itself, don't despair. Tourist development is quite amazingly limited in this area, and you need only take a local 18km bus ride to enter a totally different environment. This is **TARHAZOUTE** (or **TAGHAGANT**), a cluster of compact, colour-washed houses which resemble nothing so much as a Greek island fishing village. To either side – indeed all the way north to Cap Rhir and south back to Agadir – is a great swathe of beach, broken intermittently by headlands and for the most part completely deserted. What strikes you most about Tarhazoute, however, is just how close the hippy past is around here. There must be more hash (kif, chocolate, dope) smoked in the village than anywhere else outside the Rif, and only Bob Marley has penetrated the general Crossby, Stills, Nash and Young sounds that come out of the cafes in winter. In summer – when the hippies traditionally migrate north for seasonal work in Spain – things are altogether quieter and more subdued.

True to style, you'll find no official hotels, electricity or running water in the village – though there's no shortage of people to offer you a basic **room** in a house (cheap, and cheaper the longer you stay), with a bucket to fetch water from the spring beside the mosque. Alternatively, if this way of life seems altogether retrogressive, make your way down to the beach itself, a kilometre back towards Agadir, where there's a **campsite** with a cafe and cold showers, and more Moroccans than tourists – a good opportunity to meet and talk with people who are on holiday, and don't need to make money from you. Eating, everyone seems to graduate either to the street of cafes at the edge of the village, or to the excellent *Taoui-Fik* restaurant on the beach.

On the way to Tarhazoute, 6km or so back, you'll have passed through what the Tarhazoute people – and most of the locals – refer to as **'BANANA VILLAGE'**. This, naturally enough, is at the edge of a thriving banana grove, and all along the roadside are stalls selling the great yellow fruit. If you stop in a car you'll need to bargain hard and not a little outrageously. If you're on the coastal bus (which runs hourly between

Tarhazoute and Agadir's Place Salam terminal), get down here and you should be able to hitch a lift up the neatly named 'PARADISE VALLEY': a deep and fabulous palm-lined gorge, which must have seemed to the hippies who named it a kind of spiritual counterpart to Tarhazoute. It still gets a community of campers in the spring – with just enough room to set up a tent beside the well-stocked river snaking along the base of the valley – though by June it is almost completely empty, and a compelling place to go walking for a day, and ideally to spend the night.

The road up the valley heads off pretty much at the centre of 'Banana Village' (signposted to IMMOUZER DES IDA OUTANANE) where it gives out to a rough and very remote mountain piste. There are two buses daily from Agadir (main station) to Immouzer but if you're not in too much of a hurry you might just as easily settle for a combination of walking and lifts: locals themselves often rely on tourists going up to see the waterfalls just outside Immouzer. Waiting around at Banana Village, there are a couple of good cafe-restaurants to sustain you, and there is another, makeshift and not always open, a little way into the gorge itself. With a little time to spare, you can camp here, and if you go up to one of the villages off to the side of the road it is possible to hire mules for a more leisurely exploration.

For most people, though, it is IMMOUZER that is the target, a small village right at the top of the mountains and a minor regional and market centre (of the Ida Outanane, as its full name suggests; souk every Thursday). The falls, which anyone will point you towards, are 4km below the village: down through the market square and off to the left. Spectacular in spring – when the waters are in flood and the almonds in blossom all about – they are virtually dried up in midsummer, trickling down the eroded sides of the cliffs. However, it is the overall feel of things up here that is really appealing. There's a small hamlet just across the stream from the falls, and a cafe where you could eat and maybe get a room, or camp. If you can afford it, though, try to stay at the Auberge des Cascades, on the edge of Immouzer (and signposted from its main square). Designated 3*B, but only a little more expensive than the most basic places in Agadir, this must be one of the most beautiful and beautifully sited hotels in Morocco – enclosed by gardens of vines, apple and olive trees and hollyhocks, and with a huge and peaceful panorama of the mountains rolling down to the coast. Its food, too, is spectacular.

South of Agadir, towards Tiznit, there is almost no development at all beyond the 3-4km sprawl at the edge of the town. Even the villages on the map tend to be no more than fishing hamlets: TIFNITE, for instance, is a grim little straggle of huts, for all its proximity to 'International' Agadir. If you want isolation, though, and some interesting birdlife, you could do a lot worse than make for SIDI RBAT: a small Dutch-run camping-rooms compound, out on its own beside the sea, and reached along a track beside the lagoon of the river Massa (itself a restricted nature reserve). It is possible, though time-consuming, to get to Sidi Rbat with a combination of buses and walking – there's never a bus the whole way since there's no village, only a marabout's tomb at the end of the track. From Agadir or Inezgane, take a bus to MASSA, just off the Tiznit road: here, ask directions for the river (Oued) and start walking – you may well get a lift along the way. There is a tearoom and evening restaurant, and cabins to rent, at the *camping;* these are all more expensive than usual, though also quite pleasant. The beach here is as good as anywhere, but it can be surprisingly misty and overcast even when Agadir's in the sun.

TAROUDANNT

With its majestic, ochre-red circuit of walls, **TAROUDANNT** is one of the more elegant towns in Morocco. Sited at the head of the fertile Sous valley and plain, it has always been an important commercial and urban centre, and often the first target and base of new Imperial dynasties. It never became a 'great city' however – even the Saadians (who made this their capital in the C16) moved on to Marrakesh – and its present status, a bustling but rather mundane market town of 30,000 or so population, is probably much as it has always been. The usual historical pattern of Moroccan towns and cities is of a rise to power and a period of great wealth and building, followed, conclusively, by total destruction and obscurity. Taroudannt chanced this fate only once, at the end of its Saadian golden age, with a disastrous rebellion against Moulay Ismail; Ismail, though, contented himself with a massacre, and repopulated the town with equally troublesome Berbers from the Rif.

The walls, the souks, and the stark, sometimes heat-hazed backdrop of the High Atlas to the north, are the town's chief attraction: none of them quite packageable enough to pull in the Agadir tour-groups in any great numbers. Staying here, consequently, is worthwhile; if only in passing, or for the privilege of being able to get up at 5am for the bus over the Tizi n'Test to Marrakesh – arguably the country's most beautiful and terrifying journey (see p. 228).

Arriving, the town can seem confusing, with ramparts heading off for miles in each direction and large areas of open space and walled gardens. In fact, once you've got initial bearings, it is all very straightforward. There are two main squares – the **Place Tamoklate** (where the *CTM* buses stop) and the **Place Assarag** (where *SATAS* buses and *grands taxis* arrive) – and between them is the principal town street, lined with shops, stalls and an astonishing number of dentists, whose lurid false teeth signs are for me at least the enduring feature. The **cheap hotels** are almost all gathered around the Place Assarag, which with its low arcaded front and cafes is very much the centre of life; coming out of the *CTM* station in Pl. Tamoklate you'll need to follow the main street from the opposite (ie far right hand) corner. All of the basic, unclassified places here are extremely cheap, and cheapest of all, with a working shower, is the *Hôtel de la Place*. If this is full there's not a lot to choose between the others alongside, or the two on the main street (though here the *Hôtel Saada* is probably preferable). On the other hand, if you're happy to pay 1*A prices, then make straight for the *Hôtel Taroudannt* (also on the Pl. Assarag), well worth the extra for its patio garden, coolness, bar, and, not least, the eccentricities of its proprietress. Going well upmarket, Taroudannt also offers the opportunity to stay in a **palace** – albeit a fairly recent one – in the old kasbah quarter just outside the main walls of the town. This, the *Hôtel Palais Salam* (4*A), is really beautiful, with its rooms spread about towers and pavilions in the garden, and with a small swimming pool (which in summer, if you ask, may be open to non-residents). To get to the Salam you might as well blow the additional money on a *petit taxi* from the square; walking, follow the main street past the Pl. Tamoklate and out to the ramparts (10mins) where you'll see the kasbah quarter ahead and signs to direct you to the hotel.

Taroudannt's **souks** are not large by city standards but they are varied: there's a strong local craft tradition, and much of the work you find here is of outstanding quality. Go in by the road next to the Bank Marocaine in the Place Assarag (you'll probably come out by the other square: it's that small an area), and look out especially for the 'antique' jewellery and for the unusual limestone sculptures. The sculptures, similar to those you find in the north at Chaouen, are an obvious oddity, often figurative in design and much more African than Islamic; the jewellery is mainly of the bold, traditional Berber variety, though there are influences too from the south (the town played its part in trans-Saharan trade) and from the Jewish artesans who flourished here into the 1960s. In April the town is still host to an *artesania and folklore* fair.

The leather **tanneries**, as ever, are some distance from the main souks: placed outside the town walls on account of their smell (leather is cured in cattle urine) and for proximity to a ready water supply. In comparison to Marrakesh, or particularly Fes, the ones here are again small but, if you're interested, there are a great number of skins on sale – not just the ubiquitous sheep and cows but silver foxes, racoons and mountain cats. To get out there, follow the continuation of the main street past the Hotel Taroudannt to the ramparts: there, turn left for 100m and then take the first right – they're on your right, and smell strong enough to be impossible to miss.

The other feature of the town you can't avoid are the **walls and bastions** – best explored, if you have the energy, by hiring a bike from either the *Hôtel Salam* or from one of the shops on the main street. On your way round, take a good look at the old kasbah quarter around the Salam. Today a kind of ramshackle village within the town, this was once a winter palace complex for the Saadians and boasts remains, too, of a fortress built by Moulay Ismail. Going forward a few hundred years, you might also be curious enough to follow the signs to the *Hôtel Gazelle d'Or*, renowned as the most exclusive in the country and set within its own park. This was where the French colonials came to winter, and to an extent still do.

Finally, a few **practical details**. The two **bus companies**, *SATAS* and *CTM*, both run services to Agadir but share most of the other routes. *SATAS* has the 5am run over the Tizi n'Test (arriving at Marrakesh around 1.30-2.00pm), and the thrice weekly departures for Tata (leaving at 4am on Weds, Thurs & Fris) detailed in the following section. *CTM* has an express to Casa, and four buses daily to Ouazarzate via Taliouine – a route again outlined below. There are several **banks** and a **post office** in the Place Assarag. **Eating**, you'll find a terrific one-table-hole-in-the-wall *tajine stall* at no. 164 on the main street between the two squares, or French cooking at the *Hôtel Taroudannt;* for breakfast, the *Café des Arcades* in Place Assarag squeezes fresh orange juice.

OUT FROM TAROUDANNT: TALIOUINE AND THE TATA CIRCUIT

Looking at the map – and the possible routes out from Taroudannt – it becomes obvious just how important the town must have been in the past, both as a trading centre and for the control of the south. The epic TIZI N'TEST pass, the S501 to Marrakesh, has already been described (in reverse: see p. 228). The other main route, **east to TALIOUINE** and **OUAZARZATE**, is considerably less spectacular, passing as it does through a long initial stretch of drab, scrublike *hammada*. It is an efficient approach to the southern oases, though, and livens up beyond Taliouine as the landscape changes to semi-desert and views open up onto the beautiful, weirdly-shaped mountains of the Anti Atlas. **TALIOUINE** itself lies at a pass, its land gathered into a bowl, and is dominated by a huge and magnificent **Glaoui kasbah**. This is now largely in ruins, and much of it used for farmyard animals, but the part best preserved is still inhabited (as the TV aerial proclaims). Its decoration is different to the kasbahs further south: the walls beautifully patterned, the windows moulded by palm-fronds which in places are still painted, and the towers (some of which, though derelict, you can ascend) built about squat down-ward tapering pillars. If you arrive here on one of the morning buses it is quite possible to look around for a few hours and pick up another to get to Ouazarzate for the evening. But unless you're in a hurry, you might as well come here later in the day and spend the night. Few tourists do, despite two **hotels**: a 'Grand Hôtel du Sud' (the *Ibn Toumert*) and, much recommended, the small *Auberge Souktana*. The latter is right next to the kasbah, does tremendous meals and has candles rather than electricity: it is also reasonably cheap.

The third possible route from Taroudannt is more exacting – taking you **south across the Anti Atlas** to the oases of TATA and FOUM EL HASSANE. In all, three buses make this trip a week, all departing from the *SATAS* terminal in Taroudannt (currently at 4am; Weds, Fris and Suns) and arriving at Tata around 8 or 9pm. Apart from this bare information, though, it's difficult to give any solid advice. I set out on a Monday, taking a shared taxi to **IRHERM** where I assumed it would be no problem to find a truck going on to TATA. By midday on Tuesday nothing had shown up, and it needs a lot of endurance to stay in Irherm any longer than that: there are rooms of a kind at the *Café de Jeunesse* but the place itself, a low scrabble of an administrative street, is even more desolate than the rocky scrub of the surrounding countryside, and staggeringly hot. For anyone hoping for better luck, the buses from Taroudannt seem to be straightforward – despite a very bad stretch of piste between Irherm and Tata. The best day to travel is undoubtedly Wednesday, when Irherm (so it is said) comes alive with a major regional souk, and there is regular traffic on to Tata, the bus stopping here for a couple of hours on its way. The **TATA OASIS** is reckoned one of the largest and most beautiful in the south, with its pink clay ksour and a rush of spring water from the three streams which converge there; it has several basic hotels. From TATA there are routine daily buses (and a good road) through to BOU IZAKARN and TIZNIT.

If you've a car, and no time or inclination for the Tata circuit, you might still take the **IRHERM** road for 4-5km to the small oasis and ruined kasbah of **FRIEJA**. This is an easy excursion from Taroudannt and only a brief detour from the roads to Tizi n'Test or Taliouine. You can extend it, with increasing drama and isolation, by carrying on down the road to Irherm and then bearing right, over a piste, to the larger oasis of **TIOUTE**, the last this side of the Anti Atlas.

TIZNIT

Founded as late as 1882 when the Sultan Moulay Hassan was undertaking a *harka* – a subjugation, or (literally) 'burning raid' – in the Sous and Anti Atlas, **TIZNIT** still seems to signal a shift towards a desert frontier town mentality. To the west in the Anti Atlas the Chleuh Berbers suffered their first true occupation only with the bitter French 'pacification' of the 1930s. To the south – admittedly quite some way to the south – the Moroccan government continues its traditional struggle to bring the Reguibat Touaregs into the control and administration of the state. The town bears the stamp of all this – huge pisé walls (over 5km in total), neat administrative streets, and a considerable garrison – but it's not such a bad staging post if (as is likely) you arrive here too late in the day to move on to Tafraoute, Sidi Ifni or Tata. There are, too, exhilarating beaches nearby at SIDI MOUSSA, where the surf and the fierce Atlantic currents have staved off all but the most limited development.

Arriving, buses or *grands taxis* will drop you in the **Mechouar** – the old parade ground, and now the main square – just inside the town walls. It's here that you'll find most of the facilities (bank, post office, bus offices) and all of the **cheap hotels**. Best of these is the *Hôtel d'Atlas*, with a roof terrace from which you can look out over the town; if it doesn't appeal, the *Hôtel Minzah* (115 Rue de Tafoukt) is a slightly upmarket – 2*A – alternative, and has a small pool. There are any number of **cafes** in and around the Mechouar, though things are slightly more animated (which isn't saying a great deal) out of the main gates on Av. Mohammed V.

Tiznit is an important market centre and holds a large **Thursday souk** (out on the road to Tafraoute), but this apart the promise of its walls turns out a little empty. There is, though, a certain fascination in just how recent it all is – a traditional walled town built only a century ago – and it's interesting to see how the builders simply enclosed a number of existing ksour within their new grid of streets. Taking a brief loop through the town, start out at the **jewellery souks** (*souk des bijoutiers*), still an active craft industry here despite the loss to Israel of the town's once considerable Jewish artesan population. These are at the end of the main souk area: leaving the Mechouar in the direction of the main gates, turn right one block before you reach the walls.

In the other direction from the Mechouar – to the right at the far end of the square – Rue de Hopital winds round (past the hospital, over a stream and up beside a cemetery) to the **Grand Mosque** and, beside it, the *Source Bleu de Lalla Tiznit*. The mosque has an unusual minaret, punctuated by a series of waterspouts, or perches, said to be an aid to the dead in climbing up to Paradise. The **source**, resplendent on postcards of the town, is dedicated to the town's patroness, a saint and former prostitute martyred on this spot (whereby a spring miraculously appeared). In summer, at least, it is now profoundly unflattering to her. Following the street on from here you reach the north gate, **Bab Targua**, and the walls: take a right here and you can get up on them, a rather mournful vantage point looking out over decaying olive groves and an abandoned palmery.

To get out to **the beach** at SIDI MOUSSA D'AGLOU you'll need to negotiate a *grand taxi* from just outside the Mechouar (towards Mohammed V). There is said to be a bus too, though I wouldn't depend on it. The beach, 14km out from Tiznit along a barren scrub-lined road, is, however, worth the effort: an isolated haze of sand with a wild, body-busting Atlantic surf (and with a dangerous undertow, too – take care). There's no village at the beach itself, but walking round the headland to the right (as you face the sea) you come to a tiny **troglodyte fishing hamlet**, its huts dug right back into the rocks and quite surreal in their primitive austerity. On a more practical level, there are a dozen or so ramshackle **cabins** just to the left of the road as you come down to the beach, and, 1500m or so further on (along a track back from the beach), a **campsite** with a **cafe** and a handful of rooms. To the right of the road, still in construction, is a new, larger campsite, though this seems a wildly optimistic gesture. Except at midsummer, and around Christmas (when Moroccan families and migrant workers back from France come out here to camp), you're quite likely to be the only people about. Hitching back into Tiznit, however, is not usually a problem.

A few details about **Tiznit's transport**. All the private line **buses** (twice daily to Tafraoute and to Sidi Ifni, four or five down towards Goulimine) leave from the Mechouar. *CTM* generally run from a gate called Bab Oulad Jarrar – 200m back from the Mechouar along the Agadir road (and just back from the roundabout and junction of the roads to Goulimine, Tafraoute and Mirhleft/Sidi Ifni). **Grands taxis** towards Goulimine can be negotiated from outside the Mechouar, or by the road out past the roundabout. For Tafroute there are **landrover taxis** (not always possible to get a place, and the last leaves at 4pm) from between the new *Hôtel Tiznit* and the Thursday marketplace on the Tafraoute road (again 50m or so past the roundabout).

TAFRAOUTE

Reached (from Tiznit) over a beautiful road and a succession of gorges through the Anti Atlas, **TAFRAOUTE** is worth all the effort and time it takes to get out there. The town and its circle of stone-built villages are set about the strange, wind-eroded slopes of the Ameln valley, shot through with bulbous, pink and mauve tinged fingers of granite, and enclosed by a jagged panorama of mountains – 'like the badlands of South Dakota', as Paul Bowles put it, 'writ on a grand scale'.

The rich and organised come to Tafraoute in mid-February in order to catch the almond trees here in full blossom and the festival that follows. At any time of the year, though, a couple of days spent wandering about the Ameln is rewarding: both in the extraordinary physical features of the land, and in the interest of its unique social set-up. Among the Tafraouti villages, work emigration to the successful grocery trade is a controlling aspect of life. The men always return to retire, building European-looking villas amid the rocks, and most manage to come back for a month's holiday each year – whether from Casa, Tangier, Paris or

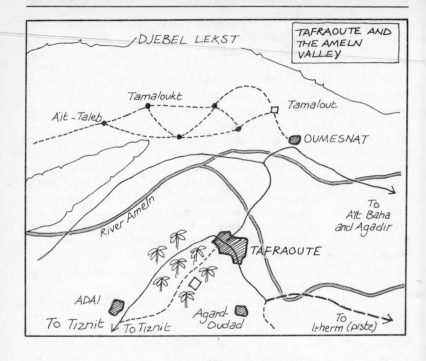

Belgium. But for much of the year, it is the women who run life in the valley, and only the old, affluent or family-supported who remain. It is a system which seems to work well enough: enormously industrious, and very community-minded, the Tafraoutis have managed to retain their villages in the face of any standard economic criteria, importing all foodstuffs except for a little barley, the famed Tafraouti almonds and bitter Argan tree oil. Oddly, this way of life has exact parallels in Tunisia with the people of Djerba; less surprisingly, both developed through crisis and necessity. Between 1880 and 1882 this whole region was devastated by famine.

The town of Tafraoute, at the edge of a rambling and quite unexpected palmery, is largely a French administrative creation. Most Tafraoutis have kept to their villages – the largest of which, Agard-Oudad, rears up behind the town to the south. Nevertheless, it's in the town that you'll almost certainly be staying. All four of its **hotels** are grouped about the bus station, and once again there's not a lot to choose between them: the *Tanger* is marginally the cheapest, the *Salam* has the best rooms, the *Redouane* and *Tafraoute* come somewhere in between. Eating, the *Salam* also offers substantial meals, or, somewhat pricier, you could try the restaurant *l'Etoile du Sud*. The only **bar** is at the 'Grand Hôtel', *Les Amandiers*, a drab mock kasbah 10mins walk above the town; this is a bad choice if you're thinking of blowing money on a night of luxury, though it does have a **pool** (usually dry in summer – but worth asking) and can be a useful source of information on the villages and festivals around. In the main market square of the town there is a **bank, post office** and **chemist**. The big **souk** here is held on Wednesdays; others take place in and around the valley most other days of the week – back up the Tiznit road at SOUK EL HAD DE TAHALA (7km) on a Sunday, for example, or 5km further, on a Monday, at SOUK EL TNINE.

The obvious and most enjoyable excursion, however, is over to the villages strung out along the rocky north face of the **Ameln valley**. OUMESNAT, 7½km from the town, is the best place to start: you can usually get a lift out here (it's just above the road out to Ait Baha and Agadir) and occasionally there's a bus. Like most of the twenty-seven Ameln villages, Oumesnat emerges from a startling green and purple background, set right up amid the rocks of the valley wall and accessible from the main road only after crossing an intricate network of irrigation channels and tiny, cultivated plots. The village houses, perched above, have from a distance a kind of bourgeois solidity about them – sensible blocks of stone, often three storeys high with parallel series of windows, and all quite unlike anything else in Morocco. Closer in they become even more bizarre, many of them supported on older houses which have simply been deserted when they became too small or decayed; some, too, with rooms jutting out over the cliffs, are held up by great stilts, and have raised doorways entered by short (and retractable) ladders.

From OUMESNAT it is possible to walk, through and above the villages, all the way to AIT TALEB: a good 3-4hr ramble, and enough really in the summer heat. You could do a longer circuit, returning to Tafraoute via the small palmery of ADAI, but it's much easier to hitch back along the road to the town and go on if you want from there.

AGARD OUDAD, 3km south of the town, is a shorter but still rewarding walk – a dramatic looking village, set below a particularly bizarre outcrop of granite. Like many of the rocks in this region it has been given a name. Most of the others are animals, and people will point out their shapes to you; this one's known as *le chapeau de Napoleon* – Morocco was, after all, a French colony. If you decide to stay some time at Tafraoute you might try, too, to get to AHEMUR: in summer, at least, this is said to be especially beautiful, with a *source bleu*, (and a daily bus, currently at 8am).

Going on from Tafraoute (or perhaps, more particularly, coming here) it might seem logical to take the 'direct' road **to Agadir** via **AIT BAHA**. This, however, is an unusually drab route and not an easy one without your own car since the twice-weekly bus had an accident and went out of commission (in 1983). If you're determined, the only solution is to try and hitch as far as AIT BAHA – a bleak roadside village with a small hotel, two cafes and little shade; from here at least two buses (one at about 4pm) run daily to Inezgane. Much more exciting though, by all accounts, is the route over the mountains to Taroudannt via IRHERM. This is a very rough piste – difficult for ordinary cars – but there is reputedly a weekly bus, leaving Tafraoute every Saturday.

Returning to the TIZNIT-GOULIMINE road, there are cafes with rooms in most of the larger villages, and if you want to walk, stopping off along this route could be a tempting option. With a car, you might also want to consider making a brief loop towards the end of the road: cutting across via ILLIGH and the ZAOUIA OF SIDI AHMED OU MOUSSA. This is now a much neglected area but until Sultan Moulay Hassan led his *harka* here in 1882 Illigh was capital of an independent kingdom – the Tazeroualt, established by a marabout in the C16 and at times encompassing all of the Sous and even the Drâa valley. The marabout, Sidi Ahmed, is still the patron saint of the Sous – and of Moroccan acrobats, almost all of whom come from the villages of this area.

SOUTH TO GOULIMINE: SIDI IFNI AND IFRANE DE L'ANTI ATLAS

Goulimine sounds tremendous in the tourist brochures (and indeed in most other guides): the 'gateway to the Sahara', with its nomadic 'Blue Men' and traditional camel market. In truth, though, it is all rather mundane. The scenery is impressively bleak (there are liberal doses of it in both *Lawrence of Arabia* and *Mohammed, Messenger of God*) but the camel market is a sham, you're still far short of the Saharan dunes, and there are so many tourists coached down from Agadir that locals have set up amateur theatric cons, taking people out to see 'genuine hommes bleus' in their tents outside the town.

Two things, however, might tip the balance in favour of continuing down to the 'Deep South'. The first is if you can coincide with one of Goulimine's annual **moussems** – the only time you are at all likely to see any real Touareg nomads in town, or indeed anything that is not put on purely for the benefit of tourists. It's impossibly difficult to get any exact information about the dates of these moussems – they vary considerably from year to year – but by general agreement there is usually one held in June at Asrir, 10km to the south-east of Goulimine; another, according to the locals, takes place in August, though the tourist board in Agadir deny this completely. The second factor is **the route down,** or rather two possible detours off it. Along the coast (and easily accessible by bus) is the former Spanish enclave of **Sidi Ifni** – a unique memorial to colonialism and surely the only Art Deco military town ever built. And to the east, off the inland road from Tiznit, there is the region around **Ifrane de l'Anti Atlas**, less easy to explore without a car but with fabulous conglomerations of ksour and kasbahs. From Tiznit, if you've time and energy for a real desert experience, you could also go by bus to the **oases of Tata and Foum el Hassane** (see p. 291).

Sidi Ifni and the coast

In summer, at least, **SIDI IFNI** is not the most obvious of tourist spots — empty, prone to lingering sea mists and, all in all, extraordinarily wistful and melancholic. The town itself, relinquished only in 1969* to Moroccan rule, has a distinct air of dissolution. Its harbour, once thriving as a duty-free zone, is now more or less disused, many of the old Spanish houses locked and left to slow decay. However, if the mood takes you (as it did me), it's rather wonderful: built in 1934 on a grand clifftop site, and full of sweeping Deco lines, elaborate ironwork and architectural jokes. Nearby, too, and at the roadside village of MIRHLEFT (midway on the bus route: basic hotel and cafes), there are some fine, totally deserted beaches.

Coming in from Tiznit, the **buses** pass first through an extended Moroccan village, built across the valley from Ifni as a kind of rival and garrison post. The Spanish town begins at the base of the hill beyond: to the right a road leads down to the sea and a reasonable **beach**; straight on you wind round to the two main streets and the **Place Hassan II**, only partially relabelled from its previous incarnation as the Plaza de España. This, really, is the centre and main attraction of the town, with its Andalusian garden and tiled fountain for the evening paseo. It remains, in the absence of any effort or inclination to change, totally and lethargically Spanish. At one side of the square a Spanish consulate (a building straight out of a Marquez novel) remains open for business, and on the other, manically confused in its mix of ideology and architecture, is a Moorish-Deco style church.

Below the Plaza, monumental steps lead down to the beach and the main classified **hotel**, the 1*A *Hôtel Ait Ba Hamram;* on the way, near the bottom of the steps, is the cheaper and steadily decaying *Hôtel Suerta*, every bit a Spanish small-town fonda with its bodega-bar (no drinks though) and table football. The best places to stay, however, must be either the *Hôtel Beau Rivage* (on the hill above – follow the signs) or the *Hôtel Bellevue* (1*A), just off Place Hassan II. This last was closed when I was there but it's an amazing building with great slabs of 1930s fluorescence on its walls. The Beau Rivage, friendly and cheap, is about

---

*Spain moved out only after the Moroccan government closed all landward entrance to the enclave in 1966. Their claim to Ifni stemmed from the Treaty of Tetouan (1860): the culmination of Morocco's first military defeat by a European power in 200 years, and the beginning of the carving up of the country by the major colonial powers.

the only place you'll find a meal, and it has a bar, too, which is pretty much the climax of Ifni nightlife.

Ifrane de l'Anti Atlas

The small region centred on **IFRANE DE L'ANTI ATLAS** is one of the longest settled in Morocco and among the last to convert to Islam – there were still Jewish and Christian Berber communities here in the C12. Much to our discredit, it's an area we failed to cover so information here is necessarily a bit sketchy; other travellers, though, say it is rewarding – if difficult and frustrating without your own car. Ifrane itself is connected by bus to **BOU IZARKEN** on the Tiznit-Goulimine road, and it has a basic hotel. Unless you're walking, however, the villages and ksour round about are not really feasible.

Unsubstantiable history suggests that Ifrane was originally settled by Jews fleeing the C6BC persecutions of the Babylonian and Biblical King Nebuchadnezzar, and that they converted groups of the indigenous (Pagan) Berbers. By way of support for this theory there is said to be a C4BC tomb in the old Jewish graveyard, though this apart there is nothing else to evoke such a past. Ifrane's present attraction is in its site overlooking the plain and in the dramatic grouping of some thirty ksour which make up the oasis. Further along the road to Tata and Foum el Hassane (Ifrane itself lies 10km north of this) you come to **TARHJIJT** and **TAGMOUT**. The former is a great C12 kasbah, and once a Christian settlement. From here you can get up to the village of **AMTOUDI**, which commands a tremendous view over all possible southern approaches to this section of the Anti Atlas, and to the river valley behind.

GOULIMINE, TAN TAN AND BEYOND

There's an obvious fascination in reaching the end of a road – or at least as far as the state of the desert war will allow – and coming out to **GOULIMINE** you might as well accept this as your motivation and goal. You might as well, too, travel down to coincide with Goulimine's **Saturday 'Camel' Market**. Although it's difficult to recommend this in any positive way there is absolutely nothing happening the rest of the week and you'll probably leave with a sneaking admiration for the lengths to which people have gone to hide the fact that there's been no real market here for some years – what few camels there are have been brought in either for show or for sale as meat. The market is held about a kilometre outside the town on the road out to Tan Tan; it starts around 6am and a couple of hours later the first tourist coaches arrive from Agadir, which to be honest makes the whole thing considerably more interesting.

The camel market aside, Goulimine is a fairly standard administrative town – stretched out and somewhat shapeless, though with a distinctly desert feel about it and a couple of animated little souks. The main street, **Av. Mohammed V**, is flanked at its top end by **Place Bir Nazarene**, where there is a **bank, post office** and (tucked in between this and the Grand Mosque) an excellent **hammam**. A five minute walk down the hill takes you to the other – and livelier – square, **Place Hassan II**, the main commercial centre of the town and the best place to eat. If you arrive by bus you'll be dropped just below this square; by *grand taxi* you will probably find yourself in the Nazarene.

Accommodation is limited in Goulimine and prices inflated on a Friday night. For this reason – and since the most basic hotels are all too small and crowded to cope with the summer heat – it's probably worth paying the 5-6dhs extra for a room at the *Hôtel Salam*, 2*B and Goulimine's grandest. This is near the Place Nazare on the Route de Tan Tan. Among the others, all on this street or around the Nazarene, the *L'Ere Nouvelle* and *de la Jeunesse* are preferable. Alternatively, for terrace-space, without water, you could try the *Cafe Alag* in Place Hassan II, or at a last gasp the **campsite** – stoney, exposed and about 1200m walk from Place Hassan II (follow the signs: the site is just below the military garrison).

There is little enough to do in Goulimine but, if you're here on a Friday evening, performances of the traditionally erotic (and frequently suppressed) **Guedra dance** are put on at the *Hôtel Mauretania* and at the *Rendezvous des Hommes Bleu Café*. The dance, performed kneeling down, relies entirely on the movement of hips and arms for its effect, and like most Berber and Arabic entertainment it takes a good few hours to get going. The tourist shows don't rise to such dizzy heights, though they do have a certain curiosity value. With an afternoon to fill, you might take a trip out to one of the oases dotted to the south-east of the town. The largest and most spectacular of these is at AIT BOUKHA, seventeen kilometres from Goulimine – the last seven along a piste from Asrir (from where the oasis is visible). An opulent-looking palmery, Boukha is an active agricultural community, little bothered by tourists or anything else (although it's a recommended *Michelin* guide excursion and if you see any French with cars you might try to get a lift!). Its 'sight' is a lush strip of canal, irrigated from the old riverbed and emerging from a flat expanse of sand; to reach this, head for the thicket of palms 2km or so behind the oasis (or pick up a guide on the way). There are much smaller oases, closer to Goulimine, at ABBAYNOU and IGUISSEL, but these are both very much hustlers' territory (someone is bound to offer to take you out on their moped), and full of imitation blue men selling paste jewellery to tourists. At Abbaynou there is a hot spring, where you can swim, and a small *hotel-camping*, but unless you've no chance of seeing the desert elsewhere you would probably be better off lazing about in the Goulimine *hammam*. If you do decide to try any excursions from Goulimine, *grands taxis* can be negotiated (after intensive bargaining) in the Place Bir Nazarene.

On to Tan Tan and Layoune

In many ways **TAN TAN** is even more disappointing than Goulimine as there is really nothing there for the traveller at all – except perhaps the chance to pick up some strange military anecdotes. Ours revolve around an abortive attempt to go for a swim at TAN TAN PLAGE (25km out from the town). Having failed miserably to get a bus or taxi, we were suddenly whisked off there with a group of soldiers and a coachload of children – on their way to spontaneously applaud the opening of a new harbour complex and what everyone said was the beginning of a 'tourist village'. The beach, incidentally, was too dangerous to swim from due to thickets of floating seaweed, though we did get filmed by Moroccan television.

This apart – and you may not be so lucky – the most impressive thing about Tan Tan is undoubtedly the drive down: 125km of straight desert road across a totally bleak shaft of stone and scrub. Coming from Goulimine it is best to do this by **grand taxi** (they leave out on the Tan Tan road – towards the camel market site) since the buses are slow and erratic and you have to stop along the way at numerous military checkpoints. At the last of these, just before entering the town, you will probably be hauled out of the taxi altogether and taken down to the *gendarmerie* to fill in more forms and state the intention of your visit. If you're planning to continue to Layoune this is the moment to sort out how you're going to travel. Usually the road is closed to tourists and you'll have to fly, but it's always worth asking if you can join a jeep: recently the Layoune military have been allowing this from their direction.

Once these procedures are completed (and they have a drama) you will be let loose on the town, which turns out to be very odd but, apart from the political fact of its existence and development, quite without interest. Once the frontier post with the Spanish Western Sahara, it now survives on the strength of the war in the desert, with more or less duty-free shops full of razors, radios and bags, and several small hotels for families of troops on leave. Nothing of this seems exactly thriving, though the town did have a brief moment of glory in 1975 as one of the major departure points for the famous *Marche Verte* ('Green March'), when 350,000 unarmed Moroccans set out into the desert to reclaim their birthright. There is still propaganda mileage made out of this – postcards of the action are sold throughout the south – but it is only fair to say that the Spanish had by this stage agreed to leave the Sahara and the Polisario had not yet taken off as a military or political force.

If you want to stay in Tan Tan – or you have to, waiting for a flight out to Layoune – there are five or six **hotels** and several cafe-restaurants around the main square, **Place Layoune**, and several others nearby. The **bus station** is 200m or so along the main street, just off to the right. There is no swimming pool, so far as anyone knew, though there is a small cinema for Saturday night action. LAYOUNE (or AL AYOUN) is pretty much a carbon copy of Tan Tan, if perhaps slightly less animated. LAYOUNE PLAGE, its port and beach, is 20km distant but no longer has passenger ferries to the Canary Islands – you have to fly from the main town.

TRAVEL DETAILS

Buses
From Agadir Marrakesh (10 daily; 3½hrs); Essaouira (6; 3½hrs); Taroudannt (6; 2½hrs); Tiznit (4; 2hrs); Goulimine (2; 4½hrs).
From Inezgane Marrakesh (4 daily; 2hrs40); Goulimine (5; 4½hrs); Taroudannt (4; 2hrs); Taliouine/Ouzarzate (4; 3½hrs/5hrs).
From Taroudannt Marrakesh (Tizn n'Test, via Idni & Asni; daily at 5am; 8½hrs); Taliouine/Ouazarzate (5 daily; 1½hrs/3hrs); Tata (3 a week; 16hrs).
From Tiznit Tafraoute (4 daily; 3½hrs); Goulimine (6; 2½hrs); Sidi Ifni (2; 2½hrs); Tata (1; 9hrs).
From Goulimine Tan Tan (3 daily; 3hrs).

Grands Taxis
From Agadir Regularly to Inezgane (15mins).
From Inezgane Regularly to Taroudannt (2hrs: with a connection at '44', *Quarante-Quatre*, or Oulad Teima as it's also known) and Tiznit (1½hrs).
From Tiznit Landrover taxi to Tafraoute (regular run but not always easy to get on and stops at around 4pm; 2½hrs). Regularly to Goulimine (2hrs: sometimes with a connection at Bou Izarkan).
From Goulimine Regularly to Tan Tan (2¼hrs).

Flights
From Agadir Daily to Casablanca (and thence Tangier etc); several times a week to Tan Tan, Layoune and Las Palmas (Canary Islands). International flights to London etc, though not especially cheap bought from this end.
From Tan Tan Most days to Layoune.
From Layoune Most days to Las Palmas (Canary Islands).

Part three
CONTEXTS

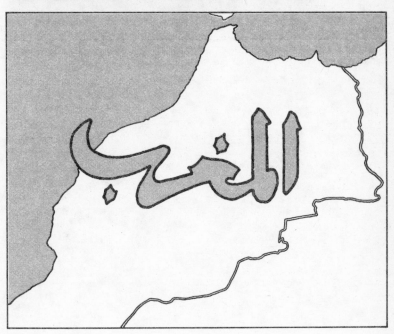

HISTORICAL FRAMEWORK

Morocco's emergence as a 'modern' nation state is astonishingly recent, dating as it does from the French and Spanish occupation of the country at the beginning of this century and its subsequent independence in 1956. Prior to this, it is best seen as a kind of patchwork of tribes, whose shifting alliances and sporadic bids for power defined both the government and its extent. With a handful of exceptions, the country's ruling sultans only ever controlled the plains, the coastal ports and the regions around the Imperial Capitals of Fes, Marrakesh, Rabat and Meknes. These were known as the **Bled el Makhzen** – the governed lands, literally 'lands of the storehouse'. The rest of the Moroccan territories – the Rif, the three Atlas ranges and the deserts beyond – comprised the **Bled es Siba**, 'the lands of the dissidents'; they were populated almost exclusively by Berbers, the original (pre-Arab) inhabitants, and rarely recognised anything more than local tribal authority.

The balance between government control and tribal independence is one of the two enduring themes of Moroccan history. The other is the emergence, expansion and eventual replacement of the various **sultanate dynasties**. These at first seem dauntingly complicated – a succession of short-lived tribal movements and confusingly similar-named sultans – but there are actually just six main groups. The first, the **Idrissids**, set the model, founding towards the end of the C8 the city of Fes, and bringing a coalition of Berber and Arab forces under a central *Makhzen* authority. The last, the **Alaouites**, emerged in the mid C17 from the great palm oasis of Tafilalt, and through the current king, Hassan II, continue to hold constitutional power. It is around these – and the medieval dynasties of the **Almoravids, Almohads, Merenids** and **Saadians** – that the bulk of the following sections are organised.

Prehistory, Carthaginian and Roman rule

The first inhabitants of the **Maghreb** – the Arab term for the northern African countries – probably occupied the **Sahara**, which was for millennia a great savannah plain, fertile enough to support elephants, zebra and a whole range of game and wildlife. Little is known about them, though it seems probable that there were groups of hunter-gatherer hominids as early as 1,000,000BC. Around 15,000BC there seem to have been **Palaeolithic** settlements, and before the Sahara went into decline (from 3,000BC) primitive pastoral and agricultural systems had begun to develop. It is possible, too, to trace the arrival of two independent civilisations in the Maghreb: the Neolithic **Capsian man** (c.10,000-5,000BC), probably emerging from Egypt, and slightly later, the **Mouillian**. To these cultures, fair-skinned and speaking a remote 'Libyan' language, belong the cave and rock drawings of the pre-Sahara and High Atlas, the earliest archaeological sites in Morocco.

Recorded history, however, begins about 1100BC with a series of trading settlements established by the **Phoenicians**. These were small isolated colonies, usually built on defensible headlands around the coast, and there was probably little initial contact between them and the inhabitants of the interior, whom they knew as Libyans and Ethiopians – or collectively as *Barbaroi*, or **Berbers**. As the emphasis shifted away from the Phoenicians themselves, though, and their African trading routes taken over by the former colony of **Carthage** (modern Tunis), some of the ports grew into considerable cities, exporting corn and grapes, and minting their own coinage. On the 'Moroccan' coast, the most important colonies were at Lixus (near Larache), Tingis (Tangier) and Chellah (near Rabat), but they spread as far East as Melilla and in the south a flourishing dye-factory was maintained on the island off Essaouira.

Officially the Carthaginian Empire collapsed with its defeat in the **Punic Wars** (196BC) against Rome, but in these provincial outposts life seems to have been little affected. If anything the colonies grew in stature and prosperity, absorbing hundreds of Punic refugees from the Roman sacking of Carthage. It was a first sign of Morocco's intrinsic historical and geographical isolation in what was to become known as the *Maghreb el-Aksa*, 'the land of the furthest West'. Even after the Romans had annexed, and left, the country, Punic was said to be still widely spoken along the coast.

Before full Roman annexation, and the imposition of direct Imperial rule in 24AD, the 'civilised' Moroccan territories formed for a while the **Berber kingdom** of **Mauritania**. This was probably little more than a confederation of local tribes, centred on Volubilis (near Meknes) and Tangier, but it gained a certain influence through alliance and occasional joint rule with the adjoining Berber state of Numidia – essentially modern Algeria. The most important of these Berber rulers, and the only ones we have any substantial record of, were **Juba II** (25BC-AD23) and his son **Ptolemy** (AD23-24). Both were heavily Romanised, Juba, an Algerian Berber by birth, having been brought up and educated at Rome, where he married the daughter of Antony and Cleopatra. His reign, if limited in its extent, seems to have been ordered and prosperous, and under his son the pattern might well have continued. In AD23, however, the Emperor Caligula summoned Ptolemy to an audience at Lyons and had him assassinated – so the story goes – for appearing in a more brilliant cloak than his own. Whatever the truth, and it may just have been that Rome was eager for direct rule, it proved an inauspicious

beginning. The early years of the new Imperial Province were taken up with near constant rebellions – the first alone needing three years and over twenty thousand troops to subdue.

Perhaps discouraged by this unexpected resistance, the **Romans** never attempted to colonise Morocco-Mauritania beyond its old limits. The Rif and Atlas mountains were left unpenetrated, and of the interior it was only Volubilis – already a city of sorts, and at the heart of the fertile northern vineyards and grain fields – that was in any way exploited. In this the Romans were establishing an enduring precedent: not just in the failure to subdue the *Bled es Siba*, which defied the later sultans, but in the treatment of Morocco as a useful 'corridor' to the greater agricultural wealth of Algeria, Tunisia and Spain. When the legions were withdrawn in 253 and the **Vandals** took power in southern Spain, they were interested only in taking Tangier and Ceuta as staging posts en route to northern Tunisia. Similarly, the **Byzantine** general Count Belisarius, who defeated the Vandals and laid claim to the Maghreb for Justinian's Eastern Empire, did little more than to replace the Ceuta garrison. It was understandable, of course. Any attempt to control Morocco would need manpower far in excess of these armies, and the only overland route through the country – across the Taza gap – was scarcely practicable even in peace time. Not until the C10 and the great northward expansions of the desert nomads was Morocco to become a land worth substantial exploitation in its own right, and even then only through the unifying and evangelising impetus of Islam.

The Coming of Islam and the Idrissids, C7-C10

The irruption of **Islam** into the world began in AD622 when the Prophet Muhammad moved with his followers from Mecca to Medina. Within 30 years they had reached the borders of India to the east; were threatening Byzantine Constantinople to the north; and had established themselves in the Maghreb at Kairouan in present-day Tunisia. After this initial thrust, however, sweeping across the old provinces of the Roman world, the progress of the new religion was temporarily slowed. The Berbers of

Algeria – mainly pagan but including communities of Christians and Jews – put up strong and unusually unified resistance to Arab control. It was only in 680 that the governor of Kairouan, **Oqba Ibn Nafi**, made an initial foray into Morocco, taking in the process the last Byzantine stronghold at Ceuta. What happened subsequently is uncertain. There is a story, perhaps apocryphal, that Oqba embarked on a 5,000km march through Morocco, raiding and subjugating all in his path, and preaching Islam to the limits of the west – the Atlantic ocean. But whether this expedition had any real Islamicising influence on the Moroccan Berbers is unlikely. Oqba left no garrison forces, and was himself killed in Algeria on his return to Kairouan.

It was at least a precedent, and the memory of Oqba's mission and the message of Islam may have taken root among some of the tribes. In the first years of the C8 the new Arab governor of the West, **Moussa ibn Nasr**, returned to Morocco, and managed to establish Arab control (and carry out mass conversions) in both the northern plains and the pre-Sahara. Like the Romans and Byzantines before him, though, his main thrust was towards **Spain**. In 711 the first Muslim force crossed over from Tangier to Tarifa and defeated in a single battle the Visigoths; within a decade they had taken control of all but the remote Spanish mountains in northern Asturias; and their advance was only halted at the Pyrenees by the victory of Charles Martel at Poitiers in 732.

The bulk of this invasionary and occupying force were almost certainly Berber converts to Islam, and the sheer scale of their military success must have had enormous influence in turning Morocco itself into a largely Muslim nation. It was not at this stage, however, in any way an Arab one. The extent of the Islamic Empire – from Persia to Morocco, and Ghana to Spain – was simply too great for Arab numbers. Early attempts to impose taxes on the Moroccan Berbers led to a rebellion and, once again outside the political mainstream, the Maghreb fragmented into a series of small independent **principalities**.

This drift found an echo in the wider events of the Muslim world, which was undergoing its first – and most drastic – dissension with the split into **Sunni** and **Shia** sects. At Damascus the Sunni Abbasid dynasty took power, the Shiites dispersing and seeking refuge both to the east and west. One such, who arrived in Morocco around 787, was **Moulay Idriss**, an evidently charismatic leader and a direct descendant (great-grandson, in fact) of the Prophet Muhammad. He seems to have been adopted almost at once by the citizens of Volubilis – then still a vaguely Romanised city – and by the local Berber Aouraba tribe. He was to survive

for just three years, before being poisoned by order of the Sunni Caliph, but in this time managed to set up the infrastructure of an essentially Arab court and kingdom – the basis of what was to become the Moroccan nation. The most important feature of this, which endures to the present with Hassan II, was his recognition as Imam. To the Moroccans this meant that he was both spiritual and political leader, 'Commander of the Faithful' in every aspect of their lives.

Despite the brevity of Moulay Idriss's reign, and his sudden death in 791 or 792, his successors, the **Idrissids**, were to become the first recognisable Moroccan dynasty. He left a son, born posthumously to a Berber woman, and in 807, after a period of apparently ordered regency, **Moulay Idriss II** was declared Sultan and Imam. He ruled for a little over twenty years – something of a golden age for the emerging Moroccan state, with the extension of a central Arabised authority throughout the north and even to the oases beyond the Atlas. Idriss's most important achievement, however, was the establishment (if perhaps not the foundation) of the city of **Fes**. Here he set up the apparatus of court government, and here too welcomed large contingents of Shiite **refugees**. Most prominent among these were groups from Cordoba and Kairouan, then the two great cities of Western Islam. In their incorporation Fes, and by extension Morocco, became increasingly Arabised, and suddenly projected into a major centre in its own right. The Kairaouine university was established, becoming one of the three most important in Islam (and far ahead of those in Europe); a strong craft tradition took root; and Fes became a vital link in the trade between Spain and the East, and between the Maghreb and Africa south of the Sahara.

Fes was to remain the major Moroccan city, and the country's Arab spiritual heart, right up until the present century. The Idrissid state, however, fragmented again into **principalities**, most of which returned to their old isolation, until at the turn of the C10 the context began to change. In al-Andalus, the Muslim territories of Spain, the Western Caliphate collapsed and itself splintered into small rival states. In Tunisia, the well-established Fatimid dynasty moved their capital to Egypt, clashed with their nominated governors, the Zirids, and unleashed upon them the hostile nomadic tribe of the **Banu Hilal**. It was a move which had devastating effects on the Maghreb's whole lifestyle and ecological balance, as the nomads swept westwards, destroying all in their path, bringing to ruin the irrigation systems, and devastating the agricultural lands with their goats and flocks. The medieval Maghrebi historian Ibn Khaldun described their progress as like a swarm of locusts: 'the very earth seems to have changed its nature', he wrote, 'all the lands that the Arabs have conquered in the last few centuries, civilisation and population have departed from them.'

The Berber Empires: Almoravids and Almohads, 1062-1248

Morocco was to some extent cushioned from the Hilalians, and by the time they reached its southern oases (where they settled) the worst was probably over. But with the shattered social order of the Maghreb, and shifting power struggles in Spain, came an obvious vacuum of power. It was this which created the opportunity for the two great Berber dynasties of the Middle Ages – the **Almoravids** and **Almohads**. Both were to emerge from the south, and in each case their motivating force was religious, a purifying zeal to reform or destroy the decadent ways which had reached Morocco from the wealthy Andalusian Muslims of Spain. The two dynasties, together, lasted only a century and a half but for this period Morocco was preeminent in all of Western Islam, maintaining an Empire which at its peak stretched right across the Maghreb to Libya, south to Senegal and Ghana, and north into Spain. Subsequent history and achievements never matched up to this Imperial dream, though even today its memories are part of the Moroccan concept of nation: **'Greater Morocco'**, the nationalist goal of the late 1950s, sketched out areas taking in Mauritania, Algeria, Tunisia and Libya, while even the present war in the Sahara looks back to the reality of the medieval empires.

The **Almoravids**, the first of these dynasties, began as a reforming movement amongst the Sanhaja Berbers in what is now Mauritania. A nomadic desert tribe – similar to the Touaregs who occupy the area today – they had been converted to Islam in the C9, but perhaps only to nominal effect. The founders of the movement, a local sheikh who had returned from the pilgrimage to Mecca and a *fakir* from the Souss, found widespread abuse of Orthodox practice. In particular they preached against the use of palm wine, of licentious music, and of taking in excess of four wives. It seems an unlikely message to have captivated an already ascetic, tent-living people, but, founding a *ribat* – a kind of warrior-monastery similar to the European Templar castles, and from which the movement takes its name – they soon gained a following and considerable military force. In 1054 they set out from the ribat to spread the message through *jihad*, holy war, and within four years had gained control of Ghana to the south. Turning towards Morocco, they were established at Marrakesh by 1062 and, now under the leadership of **Youssef bin Tachfine**, went on to extend their rule through the north of Morocco and, to the East, as far as Algiers.

At no time did any leader have such strong control over these territories, their tribes united for the first time under a single religious doctrine – a simple, rigorous and puritanical form of Sunni orthodoxy. And so it remained, at least as long as the impetus of jihad was sustained. In 1085 Youssef had made a first, possibly reluctant expedition to Spain, invited by the Muslim princes of **al-Andalus** after the fall of Toledo to the Christians. He crossed over again in 1090, this time to take control of Spain himself. In this he was successful, and before his death in 1107 had restored Muslim control to Valencia and other territories lost in the first wave of the Christian Reconquest.

The new Spanish territories had two decisive effects. The first was to re-orientate Moroccan culture towards the far more sophisticated and affluent Andalusian civilisation, the second to over-stretch Almoravid numbers. Both were to contribute to the dynasty's decline. Youssef, disgusted by Andalusian decadence, had ruled largely from Marrakesh, leaving governors in Seville and other cities. After his death they proved disinclined to accept these foreign overlords, whilst the Moroccans themselves became vulnerable to charges of corruption and departure from their puritan ideals. Youssef's son, **Ali**, was in fact extraordinarily pious but, unprepared for (and disinterested in) ceaseless military activity, was forced to use Christian mercenaries to maintain control. His reign, and that of the Almoravids, was effectively finished by the early 1140s, as a new movement, the Almohads, steadily seized control of the main Moroccan cities.

Ironically, the **Almohads** shared much in common with their predecessors. Again they were forged from the Berber tribes – this time in the High Atlas – and again based their thrust for power on an intense puritanism. Their founder **Ibn Toumert** attacked the Almoravids for allowing their women to ride (a tradition in the desert), for wearing extravagant clothes and for what may have been Andalusian corruptions – the revived use of music and wine. He also provoked a theological crisis, claiming that they did not recognise the essential unitary and unknowable nature of God: the basis of Almohad belief, and the source of their name – the 'unitarians'. Banished from Marrakesh by Ali, Ibn Toumert set up a *ribat* in the Atlas at Tin Mal. Here he waged war on local tribes until they would accept his authority, and eventually revealed himself to them as the Mahdi – 'the chosen one' and final Prophet promised in the Koran.

Charismatic, and brutal in his methods, Toumert was aided by a shrewd assistant and brilliant military leader, **Abd el Moumen**, who took over the movement after his death and extended the radius of their raids. In 1145 he was strong enough to displace the Almoravids from Fes, and two years later from their stronghold at Marrakesh. With the two cities subdued he was effectively Sultan, resistance fell away and once again a Moroccan dynasty moved towards Spain – finally secured by the third Almohad sultan, **Yacoub el Mansour** ('the Victorious'), who in 1195 defeated the Christians at Alarcos. El Mansour also pushed the frontiers of the Empire east to Tripoli, and for the first time there was a single rule across the entire Maghreb. With the ensuing wealth and prestige he launched a new building programme – the first and most ambitious in Moroccan history – which included a new capital at Rabat and the magnificent gateways and minarets of Marrakesh and Seville.

Once more, however, Imperial expansion precipitated disintegration. In 1212 Yacoub's successor, **Mohammed en Nasr** attempted to drive the Spanish Christians back as far as the Pyrenees and met with decisive defeat at the battle of **Las Navas de Tolosa**. The balance was changing, and within four decades only the kingdom of Granada remained in Spanish Muslim hands. In the Maghreb, meanwhile, the Eastern provinces had declared independence from Almohad rule and Morocco itself was returning to the authority of local tribes. In 1248 one of these, the Merenids (or Beni Merin), took the northern capital of Fes and turned towards Marrakesh.

Merenids and Wattasids: the last Berber dynasties. 1248-1554

This last, 300-year, period of Berber rule in Morocco is very much a tailpiece to the Almoravid and Almohad Empires – marked by increasing domestic **instability** and economic stagnation, and signalling too the beginning of Morocco's **isolation** from both European and Muslim worlds. The Spanish territories were not regained, and the last,

Granada, fell to Ferdinand and Isabella in 1492; Portuguese seapower saw foreign seaports established on the Atlantic and Mediterranean coasts; and to the East, the rest of the Maghreb fell under Turkish domination, as part of the Ottoman Empire. In Morocco itself the main development was of a centralised administrative system – the **Makhzen** –

which was maintained without tribal support by standing armies of Arab and Christian mercenaries. It is to this age that the real distinction of *Bled el Makhzen* and *Bled es Siba* belongs – the latter coming to mean everything outside the immediate vicinities of the Imperial cities.

Perhaps with this background it is not surprising that few of the twenty-one **Merenid sultans** – or their cousins and successors, the Wattasids – made any great impression. The early sultans were occupied mainly with Spain, at first in trying to regain a foothold on the coast, later with shoring up the kingdom of Granada. There were minor successes in the C14 under the 'Black Sultan' **Abou el Hassan**, who for a time occupied Tunis, but he was to die before being able to launch a planned major invasion of al-Andalus and his son, **Abou Inan**, himself fell victim to the power struggles within the mercenary army. The C13 and C14, however, did leave a considerable legacy of building, perhaps in defiance

of the lack of political progress (and certainly a product of the move towards government by forced taxation). In 1279 the garrison city of Fes el Jdid was established, and it was followed by a series of brilliantly endowed colleges, or *medressas*, which are among the finest surviving Moorish monuments. Culture, too, saw a final flourishing. The historians Ibn Khaldun and Leo Africanus, and the traveller Ibn Battuta, all studied at Fes under Merenid patronage.

The **Wattasids**, who usurped Merenid power in 1465, had ruled in effect for 45 years previously as a line of hereditary viziers. They maintained a semblance of control for a little under a century, though the extent of the Makhzen lands was by now minimal. The Portuguese had annexed and colonised the seaports of Tetouan, Ceuta, Tangier, Asilah, Agadir and Safi, whilst large tracts of the interior lay in the hands of religious factions, or **marabouts**, on whose alliances the sultans had increasingly to depend.

The Saadians and Civil War, 1554-1669

The rise and fall of the **Saadians** was in some respects a foreshortened version of all of the dynasties that had come before. They were the most powerful of the marabouts to emerge in the early years of the C16, rising to power on the basis of their religious power (they were *Shereefs* – descendants of the Prophet), climaxing in a single, particularly brilliant reign, and declining amidst a chaos of political assassinations, bitter factional strife and eventually civil war. As the first Arab dynasty since the Idrissids, they mark the end (to date) of Moroccan Berber rule, though this was probably less significant at the time than the fact that theirs was a government with no tribal basis. The Makhzen had to be even further extended than under the Merenids and Turkish guards – a new point of intrigue – added to the Imperial armies.

Slower to establish themselves than preceding dynasties, the Saadians began by setting up a small principality in the Souss, where they held a first capital at Taroudannt. This was normally a regular part of the *Bled el Makhzen* but the absence of government in the south allowed them to extend their

power to Marrakesh around 1520, the Wattasids for a time retaining Fes and ruling the north. In the following decades, however, the Saadians made breakthroughs along the coast, capturing Agadir in 1540 and driving the Portuguese from Safi and Essaouira, and when the Wattasids fell into bankruptcy and invited the Turks into Fes they were ready to consolidate their power. This proved harder, and more confusing, than anyone might have expected. **Mohammed esh Sheikh**, the first Saadian sultan to control both southern and northern kingdoms, was himself soon using Turkish troops and was assassinated by a group of them in 1557. His death unleashed an incredibly convoluted sequence of factional murder and power politics, which was only resolved, quite fortuitously, by a battle with the Portuguese twenty years later.

This event, **'The Battle of the Three Kings'**, was essentially a Portuguese crusade, led by the youthful King Sebastian on the nominal behalf of a deposed Saadian king against his uncle and rival. At the day's end all three were to perish on the battlefield, the Portuguese having been crushingly defeated, and a little-known Saadian prince emerged as sole acknowledged ruler of Morocco. This was **Ahmed 'el Mansour'**, so titled after this momentous victory, and easily the most impressive sultan of the dynasty. He began his reign not only clear of the intrigue and rivalry that had dogged his predecessors but fantastically wealthy. Portuguese ransoms for the remnants of their nobility were immense, bankrupting the country – which, with its remaining Moroccan enclaves, passed into the control of Habsburg Spain. Breaking with tradition, Ahmed actively involved himself in European politics, generally supporting the Protestant north against the Spanish and encouraging Dutch and British trade. Within Morocco he was able to maintain a reasonable level of order and peace, and diverted criticism of his use of Turkish troops (and his own Turkish educated ways) by embarking on an invasion of Timbuctou and the South. This secured control of the Saharan salt mines and the gold and slave routes from Senegal, each sources of phenomenal wealth, which won him the additional epithet of *Ed Dhahabi* ('the

Golden'). It also reduced his need to tax Moroccans, which made him a popular man.

Ahmed's death in 1603 inevitably caused abrupt and lasting chaos. He left three sons, none of whom could gain real authority, and the country, split by **civil war**, again broke into principalities. A succession of **Saadian rulers** retained power in the Souss and at Marrakesh (where their tombs remain testimony to the opulence and turbulence of the age); another Maraboutic force, the **Djila**, gained control of Fes; while around Salé and Rabat arose the bizarre **Republic of the Bou Regreg**. This last depended almost entirely on piracy, a unique development in Morocco though common enough along the Mediterranean coasts of Algeria and Tunisia. Its members were essentially the last Moors expelled from Spain – mainly from Granada and Badajoz – and conducted a looting war primarily against Spanish shipping. For a time they met with astounding success, raiding as far afield as the Irish coast, dealing in arms with the British and French, and even accepting foreign consuls.

Moulay Ismail and the early Alaouites, 1660s-1870s

Like the Saadians, the **Alaouites** were *shereefs* and first established themselves as religious leaders – this time at Rissani in the Tafilalt. Their struggle to establish power, too, followed a similar pattern, spreading first to Taza and Fes and finally, under the sultan **Moulay Rashid**, reaching Marrakesh in 1669. Rashid, however, was unable to enjoy the fruits of his work, being assassinated in a particularly bloody palace revolution in 1672, and it was only with Moulay Ismail, the ablest of his rival sons, that an Alaouite leader gained real control over the country.

Moulay Ismail's reign, perhaps the most notorious in all of Morocco's history, stretched over 55 years (1672-1727) and was to be the country's last stab at Imperial glory. In Morocco, where his shrine at Meknes is still an object of pilgrimage, he is remembered as a great and just, if unusually ruthless, ruler; to contemporary Europeans – and in subsequent histories – it was for his

extravagant cruelty. This certainly was tyrannical, with arbitrary killings, and appalling treatment of slaves, though perhaps it was little worse than the European nations of the day. The C17 was the age of the witch trials in Protestant Europe, and of the Catholic Inquisition.

Whatever, Moulay Ismail stands out among the Alaouites through the grandness of the scale on which he acted. At Meknes, which he made a new Imperial capital, he garrisoned a permanent army of some 140,000 negro troops, a legendary guard which he built up personally through enslaving expeditions in Mauritania and the south, and by starting a human breeding programme. The army kept order throughout the kingdom – Morocco is still today littered with its kasbahs – and were able to raise taxes as required. The Bou Regreg pirates, too, the so-called Sallee Rovers, were brought under the control of the state along with their increasingly lucrative revenues.

With all this, Ismail was able to build a palace at Meknes the rival of contemporary Versailles, and to negotiate on equal terms with the Europeans. Indeed, it was probably the reputation he established for Morocco that allowed the country another century and a half before the European colonial powers began their carve-up of the country.

The record of his immediate **Alaouite successors** was at all events uninspiring. Like all the great, long-reigning Moroccan sultans he left innumerable sons and a terminal dispute for the throne, which the powerful standing army supported and dropped at will. Remarkably, a capable ruler did quite soon emerge – the sultan **Sidi Mohammed** – and for a while it appeared that the Shereefian Empire

was moving back into the mainstream of European and world events. Mohammed regained El Jadida from the Portuguese, founded the port of Essaouira, traded and conducted treaties with the Europeans, and even recognised the United States of America – one of the first rulers to do so. At his death in 1790, however, the state collapsed into civil war, the two capitals of Fes and Marrakesh in turn promoting claimants. When this period drew to some kind of end, with **Moulay Suleiman** (1792-1822) asserting authority in both cities, there was little left to govern. The army had dispersed; the *Bled es Siba* reasserted its old limits; and in Europe, with the ending of the Napoleonic wars, Britain, France, Spain and Germany were all looking to establish themselves in Africa.

The last Sultans and European domination

Once started, the European domination of Moroccan affairs took on an inevitable air – with an outdated medieval form of government, virtual bankruptcy and armies scratched up from the tribes to secure taxes, there was little that could be done to resist it. The first pressures came from the **French**, who in 1830 defeated the Ottomans to occupy Algiers. Called to defend his fellow Muslims, the Sultan **Abd er Rahman** (1822-59) mustered a force but was severely defeated at Isly. In the following reign, that of **Mohammed III** (1859-73), **Spanish** aspirations too were established with the occupation of Tetouan – only regained by the Moroccans by the offer of massive indemnities and an Atlantic port (which Spain later claimed in Sidi Ifni).

Outright occupation, and colonisation, was by the end of the C19 proving more difficult to justify, but both the French and the Spanish had learnt to use every opportunity to step in and 'protect' their own nationals. Complaints by **Moulay Hassan** (1873-94), the last sultan with real power, actually led to a debate on this at the 1880 **Madrid Conference**, but its effect was only to regularise the practice on a wider scale, including the beginning of 'International Administration' in Tangier. After this failure to gain diplomatic support, Moulay Hassan was condemned to the old ways of raising money in Morocco by a series of

harkas or burning raids. In this he was more effective than usual, setting up a new town at Tiznit to garrison the south, but it eventually cost him his life, in 1893, as he returned with his armies across the Atlas from Tafilalt.

An account of Moulay Hassan's death by the *Times* journalist Walter Harris is reprinted on p. 332. 'A pitiful period and one best forgotten' is how Harris described the last years of independent rule under the sultan's successors, **Moulay Abd el Aziz** (1894-1907) and **Moulay Hafid** (1907-1912). The reign of Abd el Aziz, in particular, reads as a ghastly parody of Morocco's situation: the sultan, a boy of ten on his accession, indulging in a series of expensive toys and entertainments and surrounded by a motley court of Europeans – including a lion-tamer, a German dentist and a bagpipe player. He was eventually deposed by his brother, Hafid, who claimed that he had sold out to the French – ironically what he himself quite literally ended up doing, delaying the signing of the Protectorate treaty whilst he negotiated his terms for abdication and exile.

The **European manipulations** over this period were remorselessly cynical. In 1904 the French negotiated agreements on 'spheres of influence' with the British (who were to hold Egypt and Cyprus), and with the Italians (who got Tripolitana, or Libya). The following year saw the German Kaiser Wilhelm visiting Tangier and swearing to protect Morocco's integrity but he was later bought off with the chance to 'develop' the Congo. France and Spain meanwhile had reached a secret arrangement on how they were going to divide Morocco and were simply waiting for the critical moment. In 1907 the French moved troops into Oujda, on the Algerian border, and, after a mob attack on French construction workers, into Casablanca. Two years later the Spanish brought over a 90,000 strong force to garrison their established port at Melilla, again ostensibly to protect nationals – this time in the mineral mines of the Rif.

Finally, in 1910, the two strands came together. Moulay Hafid was driven into the hands of the French by the appearance of a new pretender at Meknes – one of a whole series in these decades – and, with Berber tribesmen under the walls of his capital at Fes, was forced to accept their terms. These were ratified and signed as the **Treaty of Fes** in 1912, giving the French the right to defend Morocco, represent it abroad and conquer the *Bled es Siba*. A similar document was also signed by the Spanish, who were to take control of a strip of territory along the northern coast with its capital at Tetouan and another thinner strip of land in the south, running eastwards from Tarfaya. In between, with the exception of a small Spanish enclave at Sidi Ifni, was French Morocco. A separate agreement gave Spain colonial rights to the Sahara, stretching south from Tarfaya to the borders of French Mauritania. The arbitrary way in which these boundaries were drawn was to have a profound effect on modern Moroccan history. When Moroccan nationalists laid claim to the Sahara in the 1950s – and to large stretches of Mauritania, Algeria and even Mali – they based their case on the obvious artificiality of colonial divisions.

The French and Spanish 'Protectorates', 1912-56

The fate of Spanish and French Morocco under colonial rule was to be very distinct. When France signed its Protectorate agreement with the Sultan in 1912, the sense of its **colonial mission** was running high. The colonial lobby in France argued that the colonies were vital as markets for French goods and as symbols of France's greatness, but also because of France's *'mission civilisatrice'* – bringing the benefits of French culture and language to all corners of the globe.

There may have been Spaniards with the same conception of their role in North Africa, but the reality was different. They showed no interest in developing the Sahara until the 1960s; in the north the Spanish saw themselves as conquerors, more than colonists. The government there, described by one contemporary as a mixture of 'battlefield, tavern and brothel', did much to provoke the Rif rebellions of the 1920s.

France's first Resident General in Morocco was **General Hubert Lyautey**, often held up as the ideal of French colonialism. 'Do not offend a single tradition, do not change a single habit.' Thus Lyautey recommended respect for the terms of the protectorate agreement, which placed strict limits on French interference in Moroccan affairs. He recognised the existence of a functioning Moroccan bureaucracy based on the Sultan's court with which the French could co-operate – a hierarchy of officials, with diplomatic representation abroad, and with its own social institutions.'

But there were other forces at work, French soldiers were busy unifying the country, ending tribal rebellion; in their wake came a system of roads and railways opening the country to colonial exploitation. For the first time in Moroccan history, the central government exerted permanent control over the mountain regions. The '**pacification**' of the country brought a flood of French settlers and administrators.

In France these developments were presented as an echo of the history of the opening up of the 'Wild West' in America. 'Innumerable articles celebrated the transformation taking place, the stupendous development of Casablanca port, the birth of new towns, the construction of roads and dams. . . . The image of the virgin lands in Morocco is contrasted often with metropolitan France, wrapped up in its history and its routines. . . .'

Naturally the interests of the natives were submerged in this rapid economic development, and the restrictions of the protectorate agreement were increasingly ignored.

The early history of the **Spanish zone** was strikingly different. Before 1920 Spanish influence outside the main towns of Ceuta, Melilla and Tetouan was minimal. When the Spanish tried to extend their control into the Rif mountains of the interior they ran into the fiercely independent Berber tribes of the region.

Normally the various tribes are divided, but faced with the Spanish troops they united under the leadership of **Abd el-Krim**, later to become a hero of the Moroccan nationalists. In the summer of 1921 he inflicted a series of crushing defeats on the Spanish army, culminating in the massacre of at least 13,000 soldiers at Anual. The scale of the defeat, at the hands of tribal fighters armed only with rifles, outraged the Spanish public and worried the French, who had their own Berber tribes to deal with in the Atlas mountains. As the war began to spread into the French zone, the two colonial powers combined to crush the rebellion. It took a combined force of around 360,000 colonial troops to do so.

It was the last of the great tribal rebellions. Abd el-Krim had fought for an independent **Riffian state** – an educated man, he had realised the potential wealth that could result from exploitation of the mineral deposits of the Rif. After the rebellion was crushed, the route to Moroccan independence changed from armed revolt to the evolving middle-class resistance to the colonial rulers.

Nationalism

The French had hoped that by educating a middle-class elite they would find native allies in the task of binding Morocco permanently to France. It had the opposite effect. The educated classes of Rabat and Fes were the first to demand reforms from the French to give greater rights to Moroccans. When the government failed to respond, the demand for reforms escalated into demands for total independence.

Religion also played an important part in the development of a nationalist movement. France's first inkling of the depth of nationalist feeling came in 1930, when the colonial government tried to bring in a **Berber dahir** – a law setting up a separate system of justice for the Berber areas. This was an obvious breach of the protectorate agreement, which prevented the French from changing the Islamic nature of government. Popular agitation forced the French to back down.

It was a classic attempt to 'divide and rule', and as the nationalists gained strength the French were to resort more and more to the threat of 'unleashing' the Berber hill tribes against the Arab town-dwellers. They hoped that by spreading Christianity and setting up French schools in Berber areas, the tribes would become more 'European' and thus useful allies against the Muslim Arabs.

Before the 1939-45 war, the nationalists were weak and their demands were for reform of the existing system, not independence. After riots in 1937 the government was able to round up the entire executive committee of the small nationalist party.

In 1943 the party took the name of **Istiqlal** (independence); the call for complete separation from France became more insistent. The loyal performance of Moroccan troops during the world war had raised hopes of a fairer treatment for nationalist demands, but France continued to ignore Istiqlal, exiling its leaders and banning its publications. But during these years it was developing at last into a mass party – from 10,000 members in 1947 to 100,000 by 1951.

The developments of the 1950s, leading to Moroccan independence in 1956, bear striking resemblance to the events in Algeria and Tunisia. The French under-estimated the strength of independence movements, resisted and finally conceded defeat. However, in Algeria and Tunisia the independence parties gained power and consolidated their positions once the French had left. In Morocco, in contrast, Istiqlal was never uncontested after 1956 and the party soon began to fragment – by the 1970s it had become a marginal force in politics.

The decline and fall of Istiqlal was due mainly to the astute way in which the

Sultan, later King, **Mohammed V** associated himself with the independence movement. Despite the threats of the French government, Mohammed became more and more outspoken in his support for independence, paralysing government operations by refusing to sign legislation. Serious rioting in 1951 persuaded the French to act – after a period of house arrest, the Sultan was sent into exile in 1953.

This only increased his popularity.

After a brief attempt to rule in alliance with **Thami el-Glaoui**, the Berber pasha of Marrakesh, who saw the Sultan's absence as an opportunity to expand his power base in the south, the French capitulated in 1955, allowing the Sultan to return. The government in Paris could see no way out of the spiralling violence of nationalist guerillas, and counter-violence from the French settlers; in 1956 Morocco was given full **Independence** by France and Spain.

Independence – Morocco from 1956

The years since 1956 have seen a progressive strengthening in the position of the king – on the death of Mohammed V in 1961 he was succeeded by the present head of state, Hassan II. Unlike his ancestors, the Sultans, **Mohammed V** inherited a united country with a well-developed industrial sector, an extensive system of irrigation and a network of roads and railways. But years of French administration had robbed the king of a pliant bureaucracy enjoyed by the Sultans. For the monarchy, the task ahead in 1956 was to develop a network of power at all levels of government, offsetting one source of power in society against another.

In 1956 the king's principal rival was Istiqlal. Party members held the key posts in the first government. The king bided his time, building links with the army – with the help of Crown Prince Hassan as commander-in-chief – and with the police. He also lent his support to the Mouvement Populaire (MP), a moderate party set up to represent the Berbers, and for the king a useful counterweight to Istiqlal.

In 1959 the king's strategy paid its first dividend. Istiqlal was seriously weakened by a split which hived off the more left-wing members into a separate party, the Union Nationale des Forces Populaires (UNFP) under Mehdi Ben Barka. There had always been a certain tension within Istiqlal between the moderates and those who favoured a more radical policy, in alliance with the unions.

Even before independence, in a speech of 1955, Mohammed V had promised to set up 'democratic institutions resulting from the holding of free elections'. The country's first **Constitution** was not ready until after his death

and was put to a popular referendum in 1962 by his son, **Hassan II**. The constitution was drafted in such a way as to favour the pro-monarchy parties of the centre – a special alliance, the Front pour la Défense des Institutions Constitutionelles (FDIC) was formed to contest the parliamentary **elections** that followed in 1963 on a ticket that gave total support to the king's policy.

The king soon felt the forces of the left were running out of control, however, as their criticism of the monarchy became more and more strident. In 1963 a plot against Hassan's life was 'discovered', leading to the arrest of UNFP leaders and the exile of Ben Barka. The king was also tiring of the 1962 constitution, which failed to give him the power he wanted over parliamentary institutions – the main candidates of the FDIC had failed to get elected in the 1963 elections. Finally after student riots in Casablanca in 1965, Hassan declared a **state of emergency** and took over the government directly.

The relative ease with which Hassan was able to rule without democratic institutions underlined the weakness of the parties. Istiqlal was never able to recover from the split of 1959 and as an opposition party its power dwindled further. UNFP and the unions were weakened by the arrests of their leaders and by internal divisions on policy. Despite the increasingly strident attacks on the 'feudal' and 'paternalistic' regime, the UNFP never managed to develop a coherent platform to oppose the king and build real popular support.

The weakness of the parties was further revealed in 1970 when Hassan announced a **new Constitution**, to bring an end to emergency rule. Its terms gave the king even greater control over parliament than in 1962. As a sign more of their weakness in the face of royal power than of any new-found unity, UNFP and Istiqlal came together in a 'national front' to oppose it.

The events of 1971-2, however, were to show the real nature of the threat to the monarchy. In July 1971 a group of soldiers led by an army general broke into the royal palace at Skhirat in an attempt to mount a **coup**; more than 100 people were killed, but in the confusion Hassan escaped. The following year another attempt was launched, as the king's private jet was attacked by fighters of the Moroccan airforce. Again he escaped by a hairsbreadth – his pilot was able to convince the attacking aircraft by radio that the king was already dead. But having successfully dominated the political parties, the king now had to deal with a much simpler but more dramatic threat to his power. His former interior minister, General Oufkir, seems to have been behind the 1972 coup attempt and it was followed by a major shake-up in the armed forces.

The king's real problem was to give a sense of destiny to the country, especially to the increasingly disillusioned Moroccan youth. The game of the political parties had proved sterile. What Hassan needed was a cause similar to the struggle for independence that had brought such prestige for his father.

That cause was provided in 1975, when the Spanish finally decided to pull out of their colony in the **Western Sahara**. In the 1950s Istiqlal had laid claim to the Sahara, as well as tracts of Mauritania, Algeria and Mali as part of their quest for the 'greater Morocco'. By 1975 Hassan had patched up the border dispute with Algeria and recognised the independent government in Mauritania; it turned out that this was only a prelude to a more realistic design – Moroccan control of the western Sahara.

The discovery of vast phosphate reserves in the Sahara during the 1960s brought about Spain's first real attempt to develop its Sahara colony. Before then it had been content merely to garrison the small coastal forts at Dakhla and La Guera, with occasional forays into the interior to pacify the tribes. With increased investment in the region during the 1960s, the nomads began to settle in the newly created towns along the coast, particularly the new capital at Layoune. As education spread, the Spanish were confronted with the same problem the French had faced in Morocco thirty years before – the rise of nationalism.

Pressure began to mount on General Franco's government to decolonise one of the last colonies in Africa. In 1966 he promised the UN that Spain would hold a referendum 'as soon as the country was ready for it'. Economic interests kept Spain from fulfilling the promise, and in 1969 work began on opening the phosphate mines at Bou Craa. Meanwhile the Saharans began to press the case for independence themselves. In 1973 they formed the Frente Popular para la Liberacion de Saguia el-Hamra y Rio de Oro, or *Polisario*, which began guerilla operations against the Spanish. Polisario gained in strength as Spain began to signal it would pull out of the Sahara and as the threat to Saharan independence from Morocco and Mauritania grew more obvious.

Spanish withdrawal in 1975 coincided with General Franco's last illness. King Hassan timed his move perfectly, despatching 350,000 Moroccan civilians southwards on the '**Green March**' to the Sahara. Spain could either go to war with Morocco by attacking the advancing Moroccans or take the easy way out and withdraw without holding the promised referendum. Hassan's bluff worked – in November 1975 a secret agreement was reached in Madrid to split the Spanish Sahara between Morocco and Mauritania as soon as the Spanish troops withdrew.

The coup attempts of 1971-2 and the popular unrest of the 1960s was forgotten in a wave of patriotism. Without shedding blood, Morocco had 'recaptured' part of its former empire. However, the king had underestimated Algeria's interest in the conflict as well as the determination of Polisario to fight for an independent Sahara. Some 40,000 Saharans fled the Moroccan advance to settle near the Algerian oasis of Tindouf. From here guerilla activities against Morocco and Mauritania were organised.

After a shaky start, Morocco now seems to have consolidated its position – with the help of massive military support from France and the US. Mauritania was forced to make peace with

Polisario in 1979 and pull out of the southern part of the Sahara, after guerilla attacks had all but bankrupted the country. Since 1979 Morocco has built a system of defensive sand walls in the desert, protecting the inhabited areas of the Sahara from guerilla attacks. Although this has kept out Polisario, it has also pinned down around 100,000 Moroccan troops in the desert to defend the walls.

The war has put an increasing strain on the economy, forcing Morocco to turn to the IMF for assistance. Failure to hold a referendum, although initially promised, has also isolated Morocco diplomatically.

In November 1984 Morocco withdrew from the OAU (Organisation of African Unity) over the Western Sahara issue, having earlier in the same year signed a 'Union Treaty' with the maverick regime of Libya's Colonel Qaddafi – both counyries had got bogged down in dessert wars, Libya in Chad, Morocco in the Sahara, and it was perhaps not so surprising that they should come together for political support.

What happens now in Morocco is difficult to predict. Hassan has basically staked his reputation on the Sahara war – and any forced pull-out would be unacceptable. The war meanwhile dominates the political and economic life of the country, and will inevitably continue to do so unless Algeria withdraws support from the Polisario. It is not an issue that seems open to any negotiation: criticism of the Sahara policy is rare, and all of the political parties who fought the low-key 1984 election were in agreement that Morocco should continue to fight for the 'Saharan provinces'. With support from France and the US the government at present appears stable. There were, however, brief explosions of violence in Casablanca in 1981 over food price increases, and again in January 1984, and with critical levels of unemployment (around 60%), a population overweighted towards youth, and an exodus from the drought-ridden rural areas, the government's domestic situation is unenviable.

ARCHITECTURAL CHRONOLOGY

10,000–5,000BC	**Capsian** and **Mouillian** man spread across the Maghreb Neolithic cultures	**Rock-drawings** at Oukaimeden, Foum el Hassan, and other inaccessible sites Bronze Age. First trading port at **Lixus** (nr Larache)
110BC	**Phoenician** settlements	
500BC	**Carthaginians** take over Phoenician settlements and greatly expand them	Remains at Lixus, and in Rabat Archaeological museum
146BC	Fall of Carthage at end of the Third Punic War; **Roman** influence spreads into Berber kingdoms of Mauritania-Numidia	Bust of Juba II (Rabat) **Volubilis** developed as provincial capital; other minor sites at Lixus and Tangier, Mosaics at Tetouan and Rabat museums
27BC	Direct Roman rule under Emperor Caligula	
253AD	Roman legions withdrawn	
429	**Vandals** pass through	
535	**Byzantines** occupy Ceuta	

ISLAM		
622	Muhammad and followers move from Mecca to Medina and start spread of Islam	
682	Oqba ben Nafi leads first Islamic raid into Morocco	
c705	**Moussa Ibn Nasr** establishes Arab rule in north and pre-Sahara, and in 711 leads Berber invasion of Spain	

Idrissid dynasty (788–923)		
788	**Moulay Idriss** establishes first Moroccan Arab dynasty	Foundation of Moulay Idriss and Fes
807	Moulay Idriss II (807–836)	**Fes** developed with Kairouan and Andalusian refugee quarters, and establishment of Kairnovine mosque
c10–11	Hilali tribes wreak havoc on Maghrebi infrastructure	

Almoravid dynasty (1062–1147)		
1062	**Youssef bin Tachfine** establishes capital at Marrakesh: first great Berber dynasty	**Koubba** at Marrakesh only surviving monument, except for walls and possibly a minaret at Tit (nr El Jadida)
1090	Almoravid invasion of **Spain**	

Almohad dynasty (1147–1248)		
1120s	**Ibn Toumert** sets up a ribat at Tin Mal in the High Atlas	Ruined mosque of Tin Mal
1145, 1147	**Abd el Moumen** takes first Fes and then Marrakesh	Extensive building of walls, gates and **minarets**, including the Koutoubia in Marrakesh
1195	**Yacoub el Mansour** (1184–99) extends Almohad rule to Spain, and east as far as Tripoli	New capital begun at **Rabat**: Hassan tower, Oudaia gate
1212	Almohad defeat in Spain at Las Navas de Tolosa	

Merenid dynasty (1248–1465)

1250s	**Abou Youssef Yacoub** (1258–86) establishes effective power	Zaouia and mausoleum at **Chellah** (Rabat); new city (el Jdid) built at **Fes**
1330s–50s	**Abou el Hassan** (1331–51) and **Abou Inan** (1351–8), two of the most successful Merenids, extend rule briefly to Tunis	**Medressas** at Fes (Bou Inania, Attarin, etc.), Meknes and Salé
1415	**Portuguese** begin attacks on Moroccan coast, taking Ceuta and later other towns	

Wattasid dynasty (1465–1554)

1465	Wattasids – Merenid viziers – usurp power	**Portuguese** cistern at El Jadida; walls and remains at Azzemour, Asilah and Safi
1492	Fall of **Granada**, last Muslim kingdom in Spain; Jewish and Muslim refugees settle in Morocco over next 100 yrs or so	**Chaouen** built and **Tetouan** refounded by refugees
c15–c16	**Marabouts** establish zaouias, controlling parts of the country	

Saadian dynasty (1554–1669)

1550s	**Mohammed esh Sheikh** (d. 1557) founds dynasty at Marrakesh	**Saadian tombs** and Ben Youssef medressa (Marrakesh); pavilion extensions to Kairaouine mosque (Fes)
1578	Battle of Three Kings leads to accession of **Ahmed el Mansour** (1578–1603), who goes on to conquer Timbuctou and the gold and slave routes to the south	**El Badi** palace (Marrakesh)
1627	Pirate **Republic of Bou Regreg** set up by Andalusian refugees	**Rabat** medina

Alaouite dynasty (1669–   )

1690s–1727	**Rashid** (1669–72) establishes power base but it is **Moulay Ismail** (1672–1727) who most firmly imprints the Alaouite dynasty on Morocco	New Imperial Capital at **Meknes** (Ismail's mausoleum, etc.); **kasbahs** and **forts** built throughout the country; **palaces** at Tangier and Rabat
c18	**Sidi Mohammed** (1757–90) refounds Essaouira **Moulay Suleiman** (1792–1822)	Ismail and his successors rebuild **Great Mosques**, etc. especially in **Marrakesh** where many later Alaouites make their capital – many of the city's **pavilions** and **gardens** date from the early c18
1860–2	**Spanish** occupy Tetouan	
1880	**Madrid Conference**	Europeans control **Tangier**
1894	Death of **Moulay Hassan**, last effective sultan of 'Old Morocco'	Final burst of **palace** building – El Badi (Marrakesh), Dar and Palais Jamai (Meknes and Fes)
1912	**Treaty of Fes** brings into being French and Spanish '**Protectorates**'	European **Villes Nouvelles** built outside the Moroccan

1921–7	Under the leadership of Abd el Krim the Riffian tribesmen set up an independent state; it takes over 350,000 French and Spanish troops to finally put down	Medinas in all large towns: the policy of France's first Resident General, Lyautey; '**Mauresque**' architecture developed for administrative buildings (best at Casa, Rabat, Tetouan and Sidi Ifni)
1920s–56	**T'Hami el Glaoui** becomes Pasha of Marrakesh and rules south for French	**Glaoui palaces** at Telouet and Marrakesh; **kasbah** fortresses throughout the south
1943	Nationalist **Istiqlal** party formed at Fes	
1953–6	**Mohammed V** in exile while French rule collapses	
1956	**Independence**	
1961	Accession of **Hassan II**	New royal **palaces** in all major towns – most recently and spectacularly at Agadir

ISLAM IN MOROCCO

It's difficult to get any grasp of Morocco, and even more so of Moroccan history, without first knowing something of Islam. What follows is a very basic background: some theory, some history and an idea of Morocco's place in the modern Islamic world. For more depth on each of these subjects see the book listings in the section that follows.

The beginnings: Islamic practice and belief

Islam was a new religion born from the wreckage of the Graeco-Roman world around the South of the Mediterranean. Its founder, a merchant called **Muhammad*** from the wealthy city of Mecca (now in Saudi Arabia), had been chosen as God's Prophet: in about 609AD he began to hear divine messages which he transcribed directly into the **Koran**, Islam's Bible. This was the same God worshipped by Judaism and Christianity – Jesus is just one of the minor prophets in Islam – but claiming to have been misunderstood by both earlier religions.

The distinctive feature of this new faith was directness – a reaction to the increasing complexity of established religions and an obvious attraction. In Islam there is no intermediary between man and God in the form of an institutionalised priesthood or complicated liturgy; and worship, in the form of prayer, is a direct and personal communication with God. Believers face just five essential requirements, the so-called '**Pillars of faith**': prayer five times daily; the pilgrimage (*hadj*) to Mecca; the Ramadan fast; a religious levy; and, most fundamental of all, the acceptance that 'There is no God but God and Muhammad is His Prophet.'

The pillars of faith are still central to Muslim life, articulating and informing daily existence. Ritual **prayers** are the most visible. Bearing in mind that the Islamic day begins at sunset, the five daily times are: sunset; after dark; dawn; noon; afternoon. Prayers can be performed anywhere, but for preference in a mosque, or in Arabic *djemaa*. In the past, and even today in some places, a *muezzin* would climb his minaret each time and summon the faithful. Nowadays the call is likely to be less frequent, and pre-recorded; even so, this most distinctive of Islamic sounds has a beauty all its own, especially when neighbouring muezzins are audible simultaneously. Their message is simplicity itself: 'God is most great (*Allah Akhbar*). I testify that there is no God but Allah. I testify that Muhammad is His Prophet. Come to prayer, come to security. God is great.' Another phrase is added in the morning, 'prayer is better than sleep'.

Prayers are preceded by ritual washing, and are spoken with the feet bare. Facing towards Mecca (the direction indicated in a mosque by the *Mihrab*), the worshipper recites the Fatina, the first chapter of the Koran: 'Praise be to God, Lord of the worlds, the Compassionate, the Merciful, King of the Day of Judgement, Thee do we worship and Thine aid we seek. Guide us on the straight path, the path of those on whom thou hast bestowed thy Grace, not the path of those who incur Thine anger nor of those who go astray.' The same words are then repeated twice in the prostrate position, with some interjections of *Allah Akhbar*. It is a highly ritualised procedure, the prostrate position symbolic of the worshipper's role as servant (Islam literally means 'obedience'), and the sight of thousands of people going through the same motions simultaneously in a mosque is a powerful one. On Islam's holy day, Friday, all believers are expected to attend prayers in their local Great Mosque. Here the whole community comes together in worship led by an Imam, who may also deliver the *Khutba*, or sermon.

Ramadan is the name of the ninth month in the lunar Islamic calendar, the month in which the Koran was revealed to Muhammad. For the whole of the month believers must obey a rigorous fast (the custom was originally modelled

---

* 'Muhammad' is today the standard spelling of the Prophet's name – and a more accurate transcription from the Arabic. In Morocco there is some confusion as the former sultan, *Mohammed* V, is still so spelt on maps and streetsigns and in most Western histories.

on Jewish and Christian practice), forgoing all forms of consumption between sunrise and sundown; this includes food, drink, cigarettes and any form of sexual contact. Only a few categories of people are exempted: travellers, children, pregnant women and warriors engaged in a *jihad*, or holy war. Given the climates in which many Muslims live, the fast is a formidable undertaking, but in practice it becomes a time of some intense celebration (see p.19).

The pilgrimage, or **hadj**, to Mecca is an annual event, millions flocking from all over the world to Muhammad's birthplace at Mecca. Here they go through several days of rituals, the central one a sevenfold circumambulation of the Kaba, before kissing a black stone set in its wall. Islam requires that all believers go on hadj as often as is practically possible, but for the poor it may well be a once-in-a-lifetime occasion, and is sometimes replaced by a series of visits to lesser, local shrines – in Morocco, for instance, to Fes and Moulay Idriss.

Based on these central articles the new Islamic faith proved inspirational. Muhammad's own Arab nation was soon converted, and proceeded to carry their religion far and wide in an extraordinarily rapid territorial expansion. Many peoples of the Middle East and North Africa, who had for centuries only grudgingly accepted Roman paganism or Christianity, embraced Islam almost immediately.

Development in Morocco

Islam made a particularly spectacular arrival in Morocco. **Oqba Ibn Nafi**, the crusading general who had already expelled the Byzantines from Tunisia, marked his subjugation of the far West by riding fully armed into the waves of the Atlantic. 'O God,' he is said to have exclaimed, 'I call you to witness that there is no ford here. If there was I would cross it.'

This compulsory appreciation of Morocco's remoteness was prophetic in a way, because over the succeeding centuries Moroccan Islam was to acquire and retain a highly distinctive character. Where mainstream Islamic history is concerned, its development has been relatively straightforward – it was virtually untouched for instance by

the Sunni-Shia conflict which split the Muslim world – but the country's unusual geographical and social circumstances have conspired to tip the balance away from official orthodoxy.

Orthodoxy, by its very nature, has to be an urban-based tradition. Learned men – lawyers, Koranic scholars and others – could only congregate in the cities where, gathered together and known collectively as the *Ulama*, they regulated the faith. In Islam this included both law and education. Teaching was at first based entirely in mosques, later around a system of colleges, *medressas*, in which students would live while studying at the often adjoining mosque. In most parts of the Islamic world, this very learned and sophisticated urban hierarchy was dominant but Morocco also developed a powerful tradition of **popular religion**, first manifested in the C8 Kharijite rebellion – which effectively divided the country into separate Berber kingdoms – and enduring to this day in the mountains and countryside.

There are three main strands to this popular religion, all of them deriving from the worship of saints. Everywhere in Morocco, as well as elsewhere in North Africa, the countryside is dotted with small domed **marabouts:** the tombs of holy men, which become centres of worship and pilgrimage. This elevation of individuals goes against strict Islamic teaching, but probably derives from the Berbers' pre-Islamic tendency to focus worship around individual holy men. At the simplest, local level these saint-cults attracted the loyalty of the Moroccan villages and the more remote regions. More prosperous cults would also endow educational institutions attached to the marabout, known as **zaouias**, which provided an alternative to the official education given in urban medressas. These inevitably posed a threat to the authority of the urban hierarchy, and as rural cults extended their influence some became so popular that they endowed their saints with genealogies traced back to the Prophet. The title accorded to these men and their descendents was *shereef*, and many grew into strong political forces. The classic example in Morocco is the tomb of Moulay Idris, in the C8 just a local marabout but eventually, as the base of the Idrisid clan, a centre of enormous influence which reached far beyond its rural origins.

Loyalty to a particular family – religiously sanctified, but essentially political – was at the centre of the shereefian movements. In the third strand of popular devotion, the focus was more narrowly religious. Again, the origins lay in small localised cults of individuals, but these were individuals worshipped for their magical and mystical powers. Taken up and developed by subsequent followers, their rituals became the focal point of **brotherhoods** of initiates. Perhaps the most famous Moroccan example is that of Sidi Mohammed Bin Aissa. Born in Sus in the C15, he travelled in northern Morocco before settling as a teacher in Meknes and founding a *zaouia*. There, his powers of mystical healing became famous, and he provoked enough official suspicion to be exiled briefly to the desert – where he again revealed his exceptional powers by proving himself immune to scorpions, snakes, live flames and other hostile manifestations. His followers tried to achieve the same state of grace. Six hundred were said to have attained perfection – and during the saint's lifetime *zaouias* devoted to his teachings were founded in Figuig and elsewhere in the Maghreb. Bound by its practice of a common fund of ritual, the Aissaoua brotherhood made itself notorious with displays of scorpion-eating, charcoal-walking and other ecstatic customs designed to bring union with God. It was perhaps the most flamboyant of these brotherhoods, but most used some kind of dancing or music, and indeed continued to do so well into this century. The more extreme and fanatical of these rites are now outlawed, though the attainment of trance is still an important part of the *moussems* or festivals of the various confraternities.

Towards crisis

With all its different forms, Islam permeated every aspect of the country's pre-C20 life. Unlike Christianity, at least Protestant Christianity, which has to some extent accepted the separation of Church and State, Islam sees no such distinction. **Civil law** was provided by the *Sharia*, the religious law contained in the Koran; **Intellectual life** by the *msids* (Koranic primary schools where the

6200 verses were learnt by heart) and by the great medieval mosque universities, of which the Kairaouine at Fes was (with those of Tunis's Zitoura and Cairo's Al Azhar) the most important in the Arab world.

The religious basis of Arab study and intellectual life did not prevent its scholars and scientists from producing work that was hundreds of years ahead of contemporary 'Dark Age' Europe. The remains of a monumental water-clock at Fes, and the work of the historian Ibn Khaldoun, are just two Moroccan examples. Arab work in developing and transmitting Graeco-Roman culture was vital, too, to the whole development of the European Renaissance. By this time, however, the Islamic world – and isolated Morocco in particular – was beginning to move apart from the west. The crusades had been one enduring influence towards division. Another were the Islamic authorities themselves, increasingly suspicious (like the Western church) of any challenge, and actively discouraging of innovation. At first it did not matter in political terms that Islamic culture became static. But by the end of the C18, Europe was ready to take advantage. Napoleon's expedition to Egypt in 1798 marked the beginning of a century in which virtually every Islamic country came under the control of a **European power**.

Islam cannot, of course, be held solely responsible for the Muslim world's material decline. But because it influences every part of its believers' lives, and because East-West rivalry had always been viewed in primarily religious terms, the C19 and C20 saw something of a **crisis in religious confidence**. Why had Islam's former power now passed to infidel foreigners?

Reactions and answers veered between two extremes. There were those who felt that Islam should try to incorporate some of the West's materialism; and, on the other side, movements which held that Islam should turn its back on the West, purify itself of all corrupt additions, and thus rediscover its former power. While they were colonies of European powers, however, Muslim nations had little chance of putting any such ideas into effective practice. They could only emerge in the form of cooperation with, or rebellion against, the ruling power. But the post-war era of **decolonisation**, and the simultaneous acquisition through oil of relative economic independence, brought the Islamic world suddenly face to face with the question of its own spiritual identity. How should it deal with Western values and influence, now that it could afford – both politically and economically – almost total rejection.

A return to the totality of Islam – **fundamentalism** – is a conscious choice of one consistent spiritual identity, one that is deeply embedded in the consciousness of a culture already unusually aware of tradition. It is too a rejection of the West – and of its colonial and exploitative values. Traditional Islam, at least on some interpretations, offers a positivist brand of freedom which is clearly opposed to the negative freedoms of Western materialism. The most vehement Islamic fundamentalists are not passive reactionaries thinking of the past, but young radicals – often students – keen to assert newfound independence. Islam has in a sense become the 'anti-imperialist' religion – hence for example the Black Muslim movement in America – and there is frequent confusion and even conflict between secular, left-wing ideals, and more purely religious ones.

Modern Morocco

There are two basic reasons why only a few Islamic countries have embraced a rigidly traditional or fundamentalist stance. The first is an ethical one: however undesirable Western materialism may appear, the rejection of all Western values involves rejecting also what the West sees as 'benefits' of development. Perhaps it is begging the question in strictly Islamic terms to say that the emancipation of women, say, is a 'benefit'. But many countries' leaders feel that such steps are both desirable and reconcilable with a more liberal brand of Islam, which will retain its place in the national identity. The other argument against militant Islam is a more

pragmatic, economic one. Morocco is only one of many countries which would suffer severe economic hardship if they cut themselves off from the West: they have to tread a narrow line which allows them to maintain good relations both with the West and with the Islamic world.

In Morocco today, Islam is the official state religion, and King Hassan's secular status interwoven with the role as Commander of the Faithful. Internationally, too, he plays a leading role. Meetings of the Islamic Conference Organisation are frequently held in Morocco and, in one most unlikely exchange, students from Tashkent in the USSR have come to study at Fes University. For all these indications of Islamic solidarity though, **State policy** remains distinctly moderate – sometimes in the face of extremist pressure.

Not surprisingly, all of this has had more effect on urban life than on rural – a difference accentuated by the gap between them which has always existed in Morocco. Polarisation in religious attitudes is far greater in the **cities**, where there is inevitably tension between those for and against secularisation. Islamic fundamentalism offers a convenient scapegoat to many Western-oriented governments in the Muslim world, but if its actual strength is sometimes open to doubt, its existence is probably not.

Away from the cities, religious attitudes have changed less over the past two generations. Religious brotherhoods such as the Aissaoua have declined since the beginning of the century, when they were still very powerful, and the influence of mystics generally has fallen. As the official histories put it, popular credulity in Morocco provided an ideal setting for charlatans as well as saviours, and much of this has now passed. All the same, the rhythms of **rural life** are still based around local marabouts and the annual *moussems*, or festivals-cum-pilgrimages, are still vital and impressive displays.

Peter Morris

BOOKS AND MUSIC

Travel

Walter Harris, *Morocco that Was* (Eland Books, £4.95) Harris, *Times* correspondent in Tangier from the 1890s until his death in 1933, saw the country at probably the strangest stage ever in its history – the last years of 'Old Morocco' in its feudal isolation and the first of French occupation. This book, originally published in 1921, is brilliant: alternately sharp, melodramatic and extremely funny. *Land of an African Sultan* (1889) and *Tafilet* (1895), Harris's earlier travel books, are both incorporated to some extent in 'Morocco that Was'

Gavin Maxwell, *Lords of the Atlas* (Century, £4.95) Drawing heavily on Harris's accounts of the Moorish court, this is the story of the extraordinary Glaoui family – literally the 'Lords' of the High Atlas, where they exercised almost complete control from the turn of the C19 right through to Moroccan Independence in 1956. Not an attractive tale but a compelling one, again superbly written, and enormously recommended if you're going anywhere near Marrakesh, the south or the Atlas.

Elias Canetti, *The Voices of Marrakesh* (Marion Boyars, £3.50) More of a conventional travel book, though in its own way nothing like one – as you can see from the excerpt printed in the following section.

Peter Mayne, *A Year in Marrakesh* (Eland Books, £4.95) Mayne went to Marrakesh in the early 1950s, found a house in an ordinary district of the Medina, and tried to live like a Moroccan. He couldn't, but wrote an unusually perceptive account explaining why.

Wyndham Lewis, *Journey into Barbary* (Black Sparrow Press, Santa Barbara, $12.50) Terrific drawings, an obscure, eccentric and very rambling text.

Edith Wharton *In Morocco* (Century, £4.95) Why this was reprinted is difficult to work out -- it's a dull account and ploddingly pro-French.

Shirley Kay, *Morocco* (Quartet, £7.50) Glossy picture book introduction to the country and pretty good as such.

Paul Bowles, *Points in Time* (Peter Owen, £6.95), *Their Heads are Green* (Peter Owen, o/p) Novelist, poet and composer, Paul Bowles has lived in Tangier most of his life and more or less singlehandedly brought translations of local writers (see below) to Western attention. These, loosely, are travel books. *Points* is a remarkable series of tales and short pieces inspired by episodes and sources from earliest times to the present day – one is excerpted in the following section. *Heads* includes travel essays on Algeria and Sri Lanka as well as a couple on Morocco and a terrific piece on the psychology of desert travel.

Nina Epton, *Saints and Sorcerers* (Cassell, o/p) Readable travelogue concentrating on folk customs and religious sects and confraternities.

Rom Landau, *Morocco: Marrakesh, Fez, Rabat* (Elek, o/p), *Kasbahs of Southern Morocco* (Faber, o/p). Landau has written numerous books on Morocco, none of them very inspiring. These two have redeeming features: the first an excellent series of photos (including mosque interiors) by Wim Swaan; *Kasbahs* by the fact that, Gavin Maxwell aside, there's not a lot else on the subject.

Budgett Meakin, *The Land of the Moors* (1901), *The Moors: A Comprehensive Description* (1902) Wonderful encyclopaedic volumes, long out of print, these were the first really detailed books on Morocco and Moroccan life and have been plundered by virtually every travel writer, historian and travel guide since. Understandably, too, for many of Meakin's descriptions remain accurate, and the sheer breadth of his knowledge (from 'Berber Feuds' to 'Specimen Recipes' and musical notations of 'Calls to Prayer') make these marvellous books to browse through – if you can find them in a library.

Leo Africanus, *History and Description of Africa* Written in the mid C16, this was the book Meakin himself followed, 'astounded at the confirmation [of its accuracy] received from natives of remote and almost inaccessible districts'. Leo, Moroccan by birth, was captured as a young man by Christian pirates, subsequently converting and living in Italy; the book was suggested to him by the Pope, so there's more than a hint of propaganda about some of the accounts. Again well worth a browse – there's no recent edition but most libraries have a translation.

Ibn Battuta, *Travels in Asia and Africa, 1325-1354* (RKP, £5.95) Ibn Battuta, too, was a Moroccan – a native of Tangier and scholar at Fes. Morocco is mentioned only incidentally in these accounts of his travels throughout the Muslim World, on the Pilgrimage to Mecca, to India and Ceylon, China and Niger.

History

Neville Barbour, *Morocco* (Thames & Hudson, o/p) The standard book – a lucid, straightforward account of Morocco from the Phoenicians to 'the present day' (1965).

David Woolman, *Rebels in the Rif* (OUP, o/p) Excellent, very readable study of the Riffian war in the 1920s and of the tribes' uprising against the Moroccan government in 1956.

Walter Harris, *France, Spain and the Rif* (1921, o/p) Harris's contemporary account – and one of Woolman's best sources.

Wilfrid Blunt, *Black Sunrise* (Methuen, o/p) Popularly written and highly intriguing history of the tyrannical C17 sultan Moulay Ismail.

Roger Le Tourneau, *The Almohad Movement* (Princeton UP, o/p) Short, interesting study of Morocco's most powerful medieval dynasty.

J.M. Abun-Nasr, *History of the Maghreb* (CUP, £8.95) Not the easiest book to read, but a useful one, placing Morocco in the wider historical context of N.W. Africa. Abun-Nasr is a distinguished Arab historian.

Bernard Lewis, *The Jews of Islam* (RKP, £18.95) Morocco had over 300,000 Jews until the mass emigrations to Israel in the 1940s and 1950s. Lewis discusses their position (which was perhaps the most oppressive within the Arab world) and their political and cultural contributions. In this it's an excellent book, though disppointingly he doesn't attempt to cover the period of emigration itself.

Peter Mansfield, *The Arabs* (Penguin, £3.50) Far and away the best general introduction to the Arab world, from its beginnings through to the 1970s. Short final sections deal with each individual country.

R. Oliver and **J.D. Fage**, *A Short History of Africa* (Penguin African Library, £2.50) Morocco within the context of its continent.

E.W. Bovill, *The Golden Trade of the Moors* (OUP, £2.95). Wide-ranging book about the trans-Saharan trade, including the old routes down from Morocco to Timbuctou and Niger.

Ibn Khaldun, *The Muqaddimah: An Introduction to History* (RKP, £6.95). Edited translation of the greatest work of the C14 Moorish scholar – a fascinating mix of history, sociology and anthropology, centuries ahead of its time.

Politics and society

Tony Hodges, *Western Sahara: the Roots of a Desert War* (Croom Helm, £16.95) The former Spanish colony of Western Sahara-Rio d'Oro is the most contentious issue of modern Moroccan politics: this is the latest, fullest and most interesting book on the subject.

Minority Rights Group Report, *The Sahrawis* (MRG, £1.25) Shorter pamphlet on the origins of the dispute, and sympathetic to the claims for autonomy. Not an advisable piece to carry around Morocco.

Fatima Mernissi, *Beyond the Veil: the Sexual Ideology of Islam* (Schenkman,

US, 1975) Seminal book by Moroccan sociologist from the Mohammed V University in Rabat.

Elizabeth Fernea, *A Street in Marrakesh, Middle Eastern Women Speak Out* (University of Texas, US, 1977) Straightforward and accessible social anthropology. *M.E. Women* includes some interesting transcriptions of Berber women's songs from the High Atlas.

Lois Beck and **Nicki Keddie**, *Women in the Muslim World* (Harvard UP). Includes essays on women in Moroccan Islam, and recent social change.

Ernest Gellner and **Charles Micaud** (eds.), *Arabs and Berbers* (Duckworth, 1973) A serious collection of anthropological articles on Berbers and tribalism in Morocco. Interesting, if on a rather selective basis.

Ernest Gellner, *Saints of the Atlas* (Weidenfeld & Nicolson, 1969) The bulk of this book is an in-depth study of a group of zaouia-villages in the High Atlas, but there are excellent introductory chapters on Morocco's recent past and the concept and origins of Berbers.

Kevin Dwyer, *Moroccan Dialogues* (Johns Hopkins UP, 1982) Fascinating series of recorded conversations with a farmer from a village near Taroudannt, ranging through attitudes to women, religion and village life to popular Moroccan perceptions of the Jews, the French, and even the hippies. Well worth a look.

South, Afric-Asia, Arabia and **Africa Now** are all magazines that include regular coverage of Moroccan politics and issues. **Amnesty International** (10 Southampton St, London WC2), too, have found need for regular Moroccan coverage and detail human rights violations in each of their recent annual reports.

Islam

The Koran (OUP £1.95; Penguin £6.95) The Word of God as handed down to the Prophet is the basis of all Islam, so essential reading for anyone interested. The cheaper OUP edition is better translated.

S.H. Nasr, *Ideas and Realities of Islam* (Allen & Unwin, £2.25) Probably the clearest and most useful general introduction.

Maxime Rodinson, *Mohammed* (Penguin, £2.95) New, challenging account of the Prophet's life and the immediate impact of his ideology.

Art and architecture

Richard Parker, *A Practical Guide to Islamic Monuments in Morocco* (Baraka Press, Charlottesville, Virginia) Exactly what it claims to be – very helpful and well informed, with introductory sections on architectural forms and motifs, and craft traditions. Available in Rabat.

Titus Burckhardt, *Fes: City of Islam* (Islamic Texts Society), *Moorish Art in Spain* (Allen & Unwin, o/p) Burckhardt's *Spain* is a superb study of architecture, history, Islamic city-design and the mystical significance of its art – as such it's entirely relevant to medieval Morocco. *Fes* is in part equally good, though at times its conceptual approach and respect for tradition can be a bit hard going.

Michael Brett, *The Moors* (Orbis, £10) If you've got the money this is worth acquiring – a beautifully illustrated survey of the Moorish Empire, extremely well thought out and with an outstanding text.

David Talbot Rice, *Islamic Art* (Thames & Hudson, £3.95) Clear, interesting survey – and with hundreds of photos excellent value – though only two chapters directly concern Morocco.

Andre Paccard, *Traditional Islamic Craft in Moroccan Architecture* (Editions Atelier, France, 2 vols, £130!) Coffee table tome beyond all possible rival, and not a book anyone's going to sit down and read (it weighs about 2 stone and much of the text is very crass). However, the illustrations – uniquely – include photographs of Moroccan Royal Palaces currently in use: this alone makes it worth a look.

Moroccan fiction

Five Eyes, Stories by **Abdeslam Boulaich, Mohammed Choukri, Larbi Layachi, Mohammed Mrabet** and **Ahmed Yacoubi** (Black Sparrow Press, Santa Barbara, $5.00).

Mohammed Mrabet, *Love with a Few Hairs* (Peter Owen, £6.95), *The Lemon* (Peter Owen, £6.95), *M'Hashish* (City Lights, San Francisco $1.50), *The Boy Who Set The Fire* (Black Sparrow, o/p), *Harmless Poisons, Blameless Sins* (Black Sparrow, $10), *Look and Move On: An Autobiography* (Black Sparrow, o/p), *The Big Mirror* (Black Sparrow,

$4.00), *The Beach Cafe & The Voice* (Black Sparrow, $4.00), *The Chest* (Tombouctou Press, Bolinas, California, $7.50).

Mohammed Choukri, *For Bread Alone: An Autobiography* (Peter Owen, £6.95).

Driss ben Hamed Charhadi (Larbi Layachi), *A Life Full of Holes: An Autobiography* (Grove Press, New York o/p). All of the above are taped and translated from the Moghrebi, sometimes edited too, by **Paul Bowles**. It is hard to generalise about them, except to say that they are for the most part 'tales' (even the autobiographies, which seem little different from the fiction), share a common fixation with intrigue and unexpected twists in the narrative, and are often punctuated by episodes of extreme violence. None have particular characterisation, though this hardly seems relevant since they have such a strong, vigorous narrative style – brilliantly matched by Bowles's sharp, economic language. The Mrabet stories – *The Beach Cafe* is perhaps his best – are often kif-inspired, and this gives them a slightly paranoid quality, as Mrabet himself explained: 'Give me twenty or thirty pipes . . . and an empty room can fill up with wonderful things, or terrible things. And the stories come from these things.'

Other Moroccan fiction currently available in English is:

Abdelhake Serhane, *Messaouda* (Carcanet, £6.95) Adventurous, semi-autobiographical novel about growing up in Azrou during the 1950s. The narrator's development parallels that of his country, with his attempts to free himself from the patriarchy and authoritarianism of his father used as an allegory for the struggle against French colonialism and its aftermath.

Driss Chraibi, *Heirs to the Past* (Heinemann African Writers, £1.50) Again concerned with the crisis of Moroccans' post-Colonial identity, and again semi-autobiographical as the author-narrator (who has lived in France since the war) returns to Morocco for the funeral of his father.

Morocco in fiction

Paul Bowles, NOVELS: *The Sheltering Sky* (Granada, £1.95), *Let it Come Down* (Peter Owen £6.95/Black Sparrow $7.50), *The Spider's House* (Black Sparrow, $9.00). STORIES: Most are included in either *Collected Stories 1939-76* (Black Sparrow, $9.00) or the later *Midnight Mass* (Black Sparrow, $7.50). A group of nine stories from the 1950s and 1960s have been published in Britain as *Pages from Cold Point* (Zenith, £1.95).

As with Moroccan literature, **Bowles** stands out as the most interesting (and the most prolific) writer using North African themes. Many of his stories are in fact quite close to Mrabet's – with the same sparse forms, bizarre twists and interjections of violence. The novels are something different, exploring both Morocco (or, in *The Sheltering Sky*, Algeria) and the ways in which Europeans and Americans react to and are affected by it. If you read nothing else on the country, at least get hold of *The Spider's House* – one of the best political novels ever written, its backdrop the traditional daily life of Fes, its theme the conflicts and transformation at the last stages of the French occupation of the country.

Other novels which take Morocco as their setting include:

Arturo Barea, *The Forging of a Rebel* (Flamingo; 3 vols, £2.95 each). Translation of a Spanish autobiographical novel of the 1930s. The second volume, *The Track*, concerns the war and colonisation of the Rif, the Spanish entry into Chaouen and life in Tetouan. Highly recommended.

Richard Hughes, *In the Lap of Atlas* (Chatto, £4.95) Traditional Moroccan stories – cunning, humorous and ironical – reworked by the author of *A High Wind in Jamaica*. Also includes a narrative of Hughes's visit to Telouet and the Atlas in 1928.

Anthony Burgess, *Earthly Powers*, *The Enderby novels* (Penguin) Sporadic scenes in 1950s - decadent Tangier.

Music: records

Morocco has a strong musical culture, most active and most obvious in Marrakesh and in the High Atlas, at *moussems* and other festivals (see Basics) and during the month of Ramadan. If you're intrigued, there are rough recorded cassettes on sale in most Moroccan cities, or there are several outstanding French and American **records**. These include:

Rais Lhaj Aomar Ouahrouch, *Maroc/1: Musique Tachelhit* (Ocora, Paris); **The Rwais**, *Moroccan Berber Musicians from the High Atlas* (Lyrichord, New York) Probably the two most accessible – in a musical sense – of Moroccan records available. Ouahrouch's compositions are also widely availabe on Moroccan-produced tapes – ask to hear some.

Berberes du Maroc, *Ahwach* (Le Chant du Monde, Paris) Ritual music from near Ouazarzate – haunting and brilliantly recorded.

Kwaku Baah & Ganoua, *Trance* (Island, London) Former Traffic percussionist Reebop with a group of the black Moroccan trance-musicians.

Brian Jones presents the Pan-Pipers of Jajouka (Rolling Stone, London) Cult record of the 1960s recorded and produced by former Stones guitarist; now hard to find, except on very expensive Japanese import. The Jajouka musicians come from a village near Tangier and still sometimes play in the city and at their summer Boujeloud (or Pan) *moussem*.

Festival de Marrakesh, *Folklore National du Maroc, 2 Vols* (Barclay, Paris) Also features the Jajouka musicians, along with groups from all parts of the country performing in the annual Marrakesh festival.

Music of Morocco (Ethnic Folkways Library, New York) Authentic, though rather primitive, recordings made in the early 1960s.

Also: *Moroccan Street Music, Music of Morocco: the Pan Islamic Tradition, Moroccan Sufi Music, Moroccan Folk Music, Morocco* (all on Lyrichord, 141 Perry St, New York, NY10014) *Ballads and Songs of the Sephardic Jews of Tetouan and Tangier* (Ethnic Folkways).

Sources

Best all round **bookshops** in Morocco are the *Librairie de L'Oasis* in Fes (68 Av. Hassan II) and the *American Bookstore* in Rabat (Rue Tanja). In London, for out-of-print travel books and for most of the Paul Bowles novels and translations, try *The Travel Bookshop* (13 Blenheim Crescent, W11; 01-229 5260). *Collets International Bookshop* (129 Charing Cross Rd, London W1; 01-734 0782) are useful for all ethnic **records**, as are *Discovery Records* (Broad St, Beechingstoke, Wiltshire; 067-285 406).

WRITERS ON MOROCCO

As any glimpse at the preceding pages will show, there's a long tradition of British and American writing on Morocco. The pieces that follow from **Budgett Meakin, Walter Harris, Elias Canetti** and **Paul Bowles** – represent the best of this and much of its range. Apart from Meakin, whose books are encyclopaedic in size as well as scope, all are currently available in reasonably priced editions; thanks to John Hatt, Marion Boyars and Peter Owen for allowing us to excerpt and reprint.

In Moorish guise

To those who have not themselves experienced what the attempt to see an eastern country in native guise entails, a few stray notes of what it has been my lot to encounter in seeking for knowledge in this style, will no doubt be of interest. Such an undertaking, like every other style of adventure, has both its advantages and disadvantages. To the student of the people the former are immense, and if he can put up with whatever comes, he will be well repaid for all the trials by the way. In no other manner can a European mix with any freedom with the natives of this country. When once he has discarded the outward distinguishing features of what they consider a hostile infidelity, and has as far as possible adopted their dress and their mode of life, he has spanned one of the great gulfs which have hitherto yawned between them.

Squatted on the floor, one of a circle round a low table on which is a steaming dish into which each plunges his fist in search of dainty morsels, the once distant Moor thaws to an astonishing extent, becoming really friendly and communicative, in a manner totally impossible towards the starchy European who sits uneasily on a chair, conversing with his host at ease on the floor. And when the third cup of tea syrup comes, and each lolls contentedly on the cushions, there is manifested a brotherly feeling not unnoted in western circles under analagous circumstances, here fortunately without a suggestion of anything stronger than 'gunpowder.'

Yes, this style of thing decidedly has its delights – of which the above must not be taken as the most elevating specimen – and many are the pleasant memories which come before me as I mentally review my life 'as a Moor.' In doing so I seem to be again transported to another world, to live another life, as was my continual feeling at the time. Everything around me was so different, my very actions and thoughts so complete a change from what they were under civilization, that when the courier brought the periodical budget of letters and papers I felt as one in a dream, even my mother tongue sounding strange after not having heard it so long.

Often I have had to 'put up' in strange quarters; sometimes without any quarters at all. I have slept in the mansions of Moorish merchants, and rolled up in my cloak in the street. I have occupied the guest chambers of country governors and sheikhs, and I have passed the night on the wheat in a granary, wondering whether fleas or grains were more numerous. I have been accommodated in the house of a Jewish Rabbi, making a somewhat similar observation and I have been the guest of a Jewish Consular Agent of a Foreign Power, where the awful stench from the drains was not exceeded by that of the worst hovel I ever entered. I have even succeeded in wooing Morpheus out on the sea-shore, under the lea of a rock, and I have found the debris by the side of a straw rick an excellent couch till it came on to rain. Yet again, I have been one of half a dozen on the floor of a windowless and doorless summer-house in the middle of the rainy season. The tent of the wandering Arab has afforded me shelter, along with calves and chickens and legions of fleas, and I have actually passed the night in a village mosque.

When I set out on my travels in Moorish guise, it was with no thought of penetrating spots so venerated by the Moors that all non-Muslims are excluded, but the idea grew upon me as I journeyed, and the Moors themselves were the cause. This is how it came about. Having become acquainted to some extent with the language and customs of the people during a residence of several years among them as a European, when I travelled – with the view of rendering myself less conspicuous, and mixing more easily with the natives – I adopted their dress and followed their style of life, making, however, no attempt to conceal my nationality. After a while I found that when I went where I was not known, all took me for a Moor till they heard my speech, and recognised the foreign accent and the blunders which no native could make. My Moorish friends would often remark that were it not for this I could enter mosques and saint-houses with impunity.

For convenience' sake I had instructed the one faithful attendant who accompanied me to call me by a Muslim name resembling my own, and I afterwards added a corruption of my surname which sounded well, and soon began to seem quite natural. This prevented the attention of the bystanders being arrested when I was addressed by my man, who was careful also always to refer to me as 'Seyyid,' Master, a term which is never applied to Europeans or Jews.

Having got so far, a plan occurred to me to account for my way of speaking. I had seen a lad from Manchester, born there of an English mother, but the son of a Moor, who knew not a word of Arabic when sent to Morocco by his father. Why could I not pass as such an one, who had not yet perfected himself in the Arabic tongue? Happy thought! Was I not born in Europe, and educated there? Of course I was, and here was the whole affair complete. I remember, too, that on one or two occasions I had had quite a difficulty to persuade natives that I was *not* similarly situated to this lad. On the first occasion I was taken by surprise, as one among a party of English people, the only one dressed in Moorish costume, which I thought under those circumstances would deceive no one. When asked whence I came, I replied 'England,' and was then asked 'Is there a mosque there?' I answered that I was not aware that there was one, but that I knew a project had been set on foot to build one near London. Other questions followed, as to my family and what my father's occupation was, till I was astonished at the enquiry, 'Has your father been to Mekka yet?'

'Why, no,' I answered, as it dawned upon me what had been my interrogator's idea – 'he's not a Muslim!'

'Don't say that!' said the man.

'But we are not,' I reiterated, 'we are Christians.'

It was as difficult to persuade him that I was not at least a convert to Christianity from Islam, as I should have thought it would have been to persuade him that I was a Muslim. Bearing this in mind. I had no doubt that by simply telling the strict truth about myself, and allowing them to draw their own conclusions, I should generally pass for the son of a Moorish merchant settled in England, and thus it proved. Once, during a day's ride in Moorish dress, I counted the number of people saluted by the way, and was gratified to find that although on a European saddle suggested to the thoughtful that my mother must have been a European, and I heard one or two ask my man whether she was a legal wife or a slave! In conversation, however, I was proud and grateful to proclaim myself a Christian and an Englishman. My native dress meant after all no more than European dress does on an Oriental in England: it brought me in touch with the Moors, and it enabled me to pass among them unobserved.

Another striking instance of this occurred in Fez, where, before entering any house, I paid an unintentional visit to the very shrine I wished to see. Outside the gates I had stopped to change my costume, and passing in apart from my faithful Mohammed, after a stroll to about the centre of the city, I asked at a shop the way to a certain house. The owner called a lad who knew the neighbourhood, to whom I explained what I wanted, and off we started. In a few minutes I paused on the threshold of a finely ornamented building, different from any other I had seen. All unsuspicious, I inquired what it was, and learned that we were in a street as sacred as a mosque, and that my guide was taking me a short cut through the sanctuary of Mulai Idrees!

Some days later, lantern and slippers in one hand, and rosary in the other, I entered with the crowd for sunset prayers. Perspiring freely within, but outwardly with the calmest appearance I could muster, I spread my prayer-cloth and went through the motions prescribed by law, making my observations in the pauses, and concluding by a guarded survey of the place. I need hardly say that I breathed with a feeling of relief when I found myself in the pure air again, and felt better after I had had my supper and sat down to commit my notes to paper. In the Karûeeïn I once caught a suspicious stare at my glasses, so, pausing, I returned the stare with a contemptuous indignation that made my critic slink off abashed. There was nothing to do but to 'face it out.'

From *The Land of the Moors: a Comprehensive Description* by Budgett Meakin (publ. London, 1901).

The Death of a Sultan

In 1893 Mulai Hassen determined to visit the desert regions of Morocco, including far-off Tafilet, the great oasis from which his dynasty had originally sprung, and where, before becoming the ruling branch of the royal family, they had resided ever since their founder, the great-grandson of the Prophet, had settled there, an exile from the East.

Leaving Fez in the summer, the Sultan proceeded south, crossing the Atlas above Kasba-el-Maghzen, and descended to the upper waters of the Wad Ziz. An expedition such as this would have required a system of organisation far in excess of the capabilities of the Moors, great though their resources were. Food was lacking; the desert regions could provide little. The water was bad, the heat very great. Every kind of delay, including rebellion and the consequent punishment of the tribes, hampered the Sultan's movements; and it was only toward winter that he arrived in Tafilet with a fever-stricken army and greatly diminished transport.

Mulai Hassen returned from Tafilet a dying man. The internal complaint from which he was suffering had become acute from the hardships he had undergone, and he was unable to obtain the rest that his state of health required, nor would he place himself under a régime. For a few months he remained in the southern capital, and in the late spring 1894 set out to suppress a rebellion that had broken out in the Tadla region.

While camping in the enemy country he died. Now, the death of the Sultan under such circumstances was fraught with danger to the State. He was an absolute monarch, and with his disappearance all authority and government lapsed until his successor should have taken up the reins. Again, the expedition was in hostile country, and any inkling of the Sultan's death would have brought the tribes down to pillage and loot the Imperial camp. As long as the Sultan lived, and was present with his expedition, his prestige was sufficient to prevent an attack of the tribes, though even this was not unknown on one or two occasions, and to hold his forces together as a sort of concrete body. But his death, if known, would have meant speedy disorganisation, nor could the troops themselves be trusted not to seize this opportunity to murder and loot.

It was therefore necessary that the Sultan's demise should be kept an absolute secret. He had died in the recesses of his tents, themselves enclosed in a great canvas wall, inside which, except on very special occasions, no one was permitted to penetrate. The knowledge of his death was therefore limited to the personal slaves and to his Chamberlain, Bou Ahmed.

Orders were given that the Sultan would start on his journey at down, and before daylight the State palanquin was carried into the Imperial enclosure, the corpse laid within it, and its doors closed and the curtains drawn. At the first pale break of dawn the palanquin was brought out, supported by sturdy mules. Bugles were blown, the band played, and the bowing courtiers and officials poured forth their stentorian cry, 'May God protect the life of our Lord.' The procession formed up, and, led by flying banners, the dead Sultan set out on his march.

A great distance was covered that

day. Only once did the procession stop, when the Palanquin was carried into a tent by the roadside, that the Sultan might breakfast. Food was borne in and out; tea, with all the paraphernalia of its brewing, was served: but none but the slaves who knew the secret were permitted to enter. The Chamberlain remained with the corpse, and when a certain time had passed, he emerged to state that His Majesty was rested and had breakfasted, and would proceed on his journey — and once more the procession moved on. Another long march was made to where the great camp was pitched for the night.

The Sultan was tired, the Chamberlain said. He would not come out of his enclosure to transact business as usual in the 'Diwan' tent, where he granted audiences. Documents were taken in to the royal quarters by the Chamberlain himself, and, when necessary, they emerged bearing the seal of State, and verbal replies were given to a host of questions.

Then another day of forced marches, for the expedition was still in dangerous country; but Mulai Hassen's death could no longer be concealed. It was summer, and the state of the Sultan's body told its own secret.

Bou Ahmed announced that His Majesty had died two days before, and that by this time his young son, Mulai Abdul Aziz, chosen and nominated by his father, had been proclaimed at Rabat, whither the fleetest of runners had been sent with the news immediately after the death had occurred.

It was a *fait accompli*. The army was now free of the danger of being attacked by the tribes; and the knowledge that the new Sultan was already reigning, and that tranquillity existed elsewhere, deterred the troops from any excesses. Many took the occasion of a certain disorganisation to desert, but so customary was this practice that it attracted little or no attention.

Two days later the body of the dead Sultan, now in a terrible state of decomposition, arrived at Rabat. It must have been a gruesome procession from the description his son Mulai Abdul Aziz gave me: the hurried arrival of the swaying palanquin bearing its terrible burden, five days dead in the great heat of summer; the escort, who had bound scarves over their faces — but even this precaution could not keep them from constant sickness — and even the mules that bore the palanquin seemed affected by the horrible atmosphere, and tried from time to time to break loose.

No corpse is, by tradition, allowed to enter through the gates into a Moorish city, and even in the case of the Sovereign no exception was made. A hole was excavated in the town wall, through which the procession passed direct into the precincts of the palace, where the burial took place. Immediately after, the wall was restored.

From *Morocco that Was* by Walter Harris (1921). Reprinted in a paperback edition by Eland Press.

The unseen

At twilight I went to the great square in the middle of the city, and what I sought there were not its colour and bustle, those I was familiar with, I sought a small, brown bundle on the ground consisting not even of a voice but of a single sound. This was a deep, long-drawn-out, buzz-ing 'e-e-e-e-e-e-e-e-'. It did not diminish, it did not increase, it just went on and on; beneath all the thousands of calls and cries in the square it was always audible. It was the most unchanging sound in the Djema el Fna, remaining the same all evening and from evening to evening.

While still a long way off I was already listening for it. A restlessness drove me there that I cannot satisfactorily explain. I would have gone to the square in any case, there was so much there to attract me; nor did I ever doubt I would find it each time, with all that went with it. Only for this voice, reduced to a single sound, did I feel something akin to fear. It was at the very edge of the living; the life that engendered it consisted of nothing but that sound. Listening greedily, anxiously, I invariably reached a point in my walk, in exactly the same place, where I suddenly became aware of it like the buzzing of an insect: 'e-e-e-e-e-e-e-'

I felt a mysterious calm spread through my body, and whereas my steps had been hesitant and uncertain hitherto I now, all of a sudden, made determinedly for the sound. I knew where it came from. I knew the small, brown bundle on the ground, of which I had never seen anything more than a piece of dark, coarse cloth. I had never seen the mouth from which the 'e-e-e-e-' issued; nor the eye; nor the cheek; nor any part of the face. I could not have said whether it was the face of a blind man or whether it could see. The brown, soiled cloth was pulled right down over the head like a hood, concealing everything. The creature – as it must have been – squatted on the ground, its back arched under the material. There was not much of the creature there, it seemed slight and feeble, that was all one could conjecture. I had no idea how tall it was because I had never seen it standing. What there was of it on the ground kept so low that one would have stumbled over it quite unsuspectingly, had the sound ever stopped. I never saw it come, I never saw it go; I do not know whether it was brought and put down there or whether it walked there by itself.

The place it had chosen was by no means sheltered. It was the most open part of the square and there was an incessant coming and going on all sides of the little brown heap. On busy evenings it disappeared completely behind people's legs, and although I knew exactly where it was and could always hear the voice I had difficulty in finding it. But then the people dispersed, and it was still in its place when all around it, far and wide, the square was empty. Then it lay there in the darkness like an old and very dirty garment that someone had wanted to get rid of and had surreptitiously dropped in the midst of all the people where no one would notice. Now, however, the people had dispersed and only the bundle lay there. I never waited until it got up or was

fetched. I slunk away in the darkness with a choking feeling of helplessness and pride.

The helplessness was in regard to myself. I sensed that I would never do anything to discover the bundle's secret. I had a dread of its shape; and since I could give it no other I left it lying there on the ground. When I was getting close I took care not to bump into it, as if I might hurt or endanger it. It was there every evening, and every evening my heart stood still when I first distinguished the sound, and it stood still again when I caught sight of the bundle. How it got there and how it got away again were matters more sacred to me than my own movements. I never spied on it and I do not know where it disappeared to for the rest of the night and the following day. It was something apart, and perhaps it saw itself as such. I was sometimes tempted to touch the brown hood very lightly with one finger – the creature was bound to notice, and perhaps it had a second sound with which it would have responded. But this temptation always succumbed swiftly to my helplessness.

I have said that another feeling choked me as I slunk away: pride. I was proud of the bundle because it was alive. What it thought to itself as it breathed down there, far below other people, I shall never know. The meaning of its call remained as obscure to me as its whole existence: but it was alive, and every day at the same time, there it was. I never saw it pick up the coins that people threw it; they did not throw many, there were never more than two or three coins lying there. Perhaps it had no arms with which to reach for the coins. Perhaps it had no tongue with which to form the 'l' of 'Allah' and to it the name of God was abbreviated to 'e-e-e-e-'. But it was alive, and with a diligence and persistence that were unparalleled it uttered its one sound, uttered it hour after hour, until it was the only sound in the whole enormous square, the sound that outlived all others.

From *The Voices of Marrakesh* by Elias Canetti (Marion Boyars, London, 1978); first published in German in 1967.

Points in Time, X

The country of the Anjra is almost devoid of paved roads. It is a region of high jagged mountains and wooded valleys, and does not contain a town of any size. During the rainy season there are landslides. Then, until the government sends men to repair the damage, the roads cannot be used. All this is very much on the minds of the people who live in the Anjra, particularly when they are waiting for the highways to be rebuilt so that trucks can move again between the villages. Four or five soldiers had been sent several months earlier to repair the potholes along the road between Ksar es Seghir and Melloussa. Their tent was beside the road, near a curve in the river.

A peasant named Hattash, whose village lay a few miles up the valley, constantly passed by the place on his way to and from Ksar es Seghir. Hattash had no fixed work of any sort, but he kept very busy looking for a chance to pick up a little money one way or another in the market and the cafés. He was the kind of man who prided himself on his cleverness in swindling foreigners, by which he meant men from outside the Anjra. Since his friends shared his dislike of outsiders, they found his exploits amusing, although they were careful to have no dealings with him.

Over the months Hattash had become friendly with the soldiers living in the tent, often stopping to smoke a pipe of kif with them, perhaps squatting down to play a few games of ronda. Thus when one day the soldiers decided to give a party, it was natural that they should mention it to Hattash, who knew everyone for miles around, and therefore might be able to help them. The soldiers came from the south, and their isolation there by the river kept them from meeting anyone who did not regularly pass their tent.

I can get you whatever you want, Hattash told them. The hens, the vegetables, oil, spices, salad, whatever.

Fine. And we want some girls or boys, they added.

Don't worry about that. You'll have plenty to choose from. What you don't want you can send back.

They discussed the cost of the party for an hour or so, after which the soldiers handed Hattash twenty-five thousand francs. He set off, ostensibly for the market.

Instead of going there, he went to the house of a nearby farmer and bought five of his best hens, with the understanding that if the person for whom he was buying them should not want them, he could return the hens and get his money back.

Soon Hattash was outside the soldiers' tent with the hens. How are they? he said. The men squeezed them and examined them, and pronounced them excellent. Good, said Hattash. I'll take them home now and cook them.

He went back to the farmer with the hens and told him that the buyer had refused them. The farmer shrugged and gave Hattash his money.

This seemed to be the moment to leave Ksar es Seghir, Hattash decided. He stopped at a café and invited everyone there to the soldiers' tent that evening, telling them there would be food, wine and girls. Then he bought bread, cheese and fruit, and began to walk along the trails that would lead him over the mountains to Khemiss dl Anjra.

With the twenty-five thousand francs he was able to live for several weeks there in Khemmiss dl Anjra. When he had come to the end of them, he began to think of leaving.

In the market one morning he met Hadj Abdallah, a rich farmer from Farsioua, which was a village only a few miles from his own. Hadj Abdallah, a burly, truculent man, always had eyed Hattash with distrust.

Ah, Hattash! What are you doing up here? It's a while since I've seen you.

And you? said Hattash.

Me? I'm on my way to Tetuan. I'm leaving my mule here and taking the bus.

That's where I'm going, said Hattash.

Well, see you in Tetuan, said Hadj Abdallah, and he turned, unhitched his mule, and rode off.

Khemiss dl Anjra is a very small town, so that it was not difficult for Hattash to follow along at some distance, and see the house where Hadj Abdallah tethered his mule and into which he then disappeared. He walked to the bus station and sat under a tree.

An hour or so later, when the bus was filling up with people, Hadj Abdallah arrived and bought his ticket. Hattash approached him.

Can you lend me a thousand francs? I haven't got enough to buy the ticket.

Hadj Abdallah looked at him. No. I can't, he said. Why don't you stay here? And he went and got into the bus.

Hattash, his eyes very narrow, sat down again under the tree. When the bus had left, and the cloud of smoke and dust had drifted off over the meadows, he walked back to the house where the Hadj had left his mule. She still stood there, so he quietly unhitched her, got astride her, and rode her in the direction of Mgas Tleta. He was still smarting under Hadj Abdallah's insult, and he vowed to give him as much trouble as he could.

Mgas Tleta was a small tchar. He took the mule to the fondaq and left it in charge of the guardian. Being ravenously hungry, he searched in his clothing for a coin or two to buy a piece of bread, and found nothing.

In the road outside the fondaq he caught sight of a peasant carrying a loaf in the hood of his djellaba. Unable to take his eyes from the bread, he walked towards the man and greeted him. Then he asked him if he had work, and was not surprised when the man answered no. He went on, still looking at the bread: If you want to earn a thousand francs, you can take my mule to Mdiq. My father's waiting for her and he'll pay you. Just ask for Si Mohammed Tsuli. Everybody in Mdiq knows him. He always has a lot of men working for him. He'll give you work there too if you want it.

The peasant's eyes lit up. He agreed immediately.

Hattash sighed. It's a long time since I've seen good country bread like that, he said, pointing at the loaf that emerged from the hood of the djellaba. The man took it out and handed it to him. Here. Take it.

In return Hattash presented him with the receipt for the mule. You'll have to pay a hundred francs to get her out of the fondaq, he told him. My father will give it back to you.

That's all right. The man was eager to start out for Mdiq.

Si Mohammed Tsuli. Don't forget.

No, no! Bslemah.

Hattash, well satisfied, watched the man ride off. Then he sat down on a rock and ate the whole loaf of bread. He had no intention of returning home to risk meeting the soldiers or Hadj Abdallah, so he decided to hide himself for a while in Tetuan, where he had friends.

When the peasant arrived at Mdiq the following day, he found that no one could tell him where Si Mohammed Tsuli lived. He wandered back and forth through every street in the town, searching and inquiring. When evening came, he went to the gendarmerie and asked if he might leave the mule there. But they questioned him and accused him of having stolen the animal. His story was ridiculous, they said, and they locked him into a cell.

Not many days later Hadj Abdallah, having finished his business in Tetuan, went back to Khemiss dl Anjra to get his mule and ride her home. When he heard that she had disappeared directly after he had taken the bus, he remembered Hattash, and was certain that he was the culprit. The theft had to be reported in Tetuan, and much against his will he returned there.

Your mule is in Mdiq, the police told him.

Hadj Abdallah took another bus up to Mdiq.

Papers, said the gendarmes. Proof of ownership.

The Hadj had no documents of that sort. They told him to go to Tetuan and apply for the forms.

During the days while he waited for the papers to be drawn up, signed and stamped, Hadj Abdallah grew constantly angrier. He went twice a day to talk with the police. I know who took her! he would shout. I know the son of a whore.

If you ever catch sight of him, hold on to him, they told him. We'll take care of him.

Although Tetuan is a big place with many crowded quarters, the unlikely occurred. In a narrow passageway near the Souq el Fouqi late one evening Hadj Abdallah and Hattash came face to face.

The surprise was so great that Hattash remained frozen to the spot, merely staring into Hadj Abdallah's eyes. Then he heard a grunt of rage, and felt himself seized by the other man's strong arm.

Police! Police! roared Hadj Abdallah. Hattash squirmed, but was unable to free himself.

One policeman arrived, and then another. Hadj Abdallah did not release his grip of Hattash for an instant while he delivered his denunciation. Then with an oath he struck his prisoner, knocking him flat on the sidewalk. Hattash lay there in the dark without moving.

Why did you do that? the policemen cried. Now you're the one who's going to be in trouble.

Hadj Abdallah was already frightened. I know. I ought not to have hit him.

It's very bad, said one policeman, bending over Hattash, who lay completely still. You see, there's blood coming out of his head.

A small crowd was collecting in the passageway.

There were only a few drops of blood, but the policeman had seen Hattash open one eye and had heard him whisper: Listen.

He bent over still farther, so that his ear was close to Hattash's lips.

He's got money, Hattash whispered.

The policeman rose and went over to Hadj Abdallah. We'll have to call an ambulance, he said, and you'll have to come to the police station. You had no right to hit him.

At that moment Hattash began to groan.

He's alive, at least! cried Hadj Abdallah. Hamdul'lah!

Then the policemen began to speak with him in low tones, advising him to settle the affair immediately by paying cash to the injured man.

Hadj Abdallah was willing. How much do you think? he whispered.

It's a bad cut he has on his head, the same policeman said, going back to Hattash. Come and look.

Hadj Abdallah remained where he was, and Hattash groaned as the man bent over him again. Then he murmured: Twenty thousand. Five for each of you.

When the policeman rejoined Hadj Abdallah, he told him the amount. You're lucky to be out of it.

Hadj Abdallah gave the money to the policeman, who took it over to Hattash and prodded him. Can you hear me? he shouted.

Ouakha, groaned Hattash.

Here. Take this. He held out the banknotes in such a way that Hadj Abdallah and the crowd watching could see them clearly. Hattash stretched up his hand and took them, slipping them into his pocket.

Hadj Abdallah glared at the crowd and pushed his way through, eager to get away from the spot.

After he had gone, Hattash slowly sat up and rubbed his head. The onlookers still stood there watching. This bothered the two policemen, who were intent on getting their share of the money. The recent disclosures of corruption, however, had made the public all too attentive at such moments. The crowd was waiting to see them speak to Hattash or, if he should move, follow him.

Hattash saw the situation and understood. He rose to his feet and quickly walked up the alley.

The policemen looked at each other, waited for a few seconds, and then began to saunter casually in the same direction. Once they were out of sight of the group of onlookers they hurried along, flashing their lights up each alley in their search. But Hattash knew the quarter as well as they, and got safely to the house of his friends.

He decided, however, that with the two policemen on the lookout for him, Tetuan was no longer the right place for him, and that his own tchar in rhe Anjra would be preferable.

Once he was back there, he made discreet inquiries about the state of the road to Ksar es Seghir. The repairs were finished, his neighbours told him, and the soldiers had been sent to some other part of the country.

From *Points in Time* by Paul Bowles (Peter Owen, London, 1982).

ONWARDS: ALGERIA, TUNISIA AND THE MAGHREB CIRCUIT

Going on from Morocco there are two basic options. The most obvious is to take in something of **SPAIN**, and if you've developed any interest in Moorish art to visit the three great Andalusian cities of the south – Granada, Cordoba and Sevilla. Each of these boast superb Islamic monuments, which to be honest are more spectacular than any in Morocco. Granada has the fabulous C15 Alhambra palace, home of the last Moorish rulers in al-Andalus; Cordoba, a C10 mosque, now the city's cathedral; and Sevilla, one of Yacoub el Mansour's magnificent Almohad towers, again adapted to Christian use as the local belltower or 'Giralda'. For all of this – and a great deal more – the new edition of *The Rough Guide to Spain* (RKP, £3.95) is helpful.

The second option, Considerably more ambitious, is to travel '**The MAGHREB CIRCUIT**': east from Morocco into Algeria and Tunisia, where, if you've still time and energy, you can cross over by ferry to Italy and either loop back to Northern Europe (Italian trains are cheap) or take another ferry on from Bari or Brindisi to Greece. Don't be put off by the distances involved in any of this, nor by travellers' tales of Algerian bureaucracy at the frontiers (though these are true enough); it's an exciting, feasible and immensely satisfying circuit, and there's an added fascination in that all of this region – from Spain and Morocco up as far as Sicily – comprised the Western Arab Empire in the early Middle Ages.

ALGERIA considerably less well known than either Morocco or Tunisia has always been the most adventurous part of North Africa to travel. This it remains – a vast expanse of often quite extraordinary routes. Algerians have a popular image of hostility towards westerners, largely undeserved although there *is* still widespread and intense resentment of the French colonial past, Ironically the French language endures even more strongly here than in Morocco and all European travellers are initially assumed to be French. Once you get over this it can be a very open and hospitable country. Not so for women,

however. The veil is still widespread and, outside Algiers, women have no public presence in society. **Harassment** for foreign travellers, unless within a group of men, is frequent and sometimes dangerous. Even travelling as a couple you have problems: not least in that the cheapest categories of hotels (including rooms at local *hammams*) are limited to men.

Entry requirements for Algeria vary from time to time, but visas are essential for all except British or European nationals. These can be fairly routinely acquired at the Algerian consulate in Oujda (see p. 85), though you'll need a day to hang around (along with 30dhs and 4 passport-sized photos). At the border you are required to change around £140 cash – which should ideally be in French francs – into Algerian currency. This restriction is no longer waived for students, as in the past, and money cannot be re-exchanged

There are usually two **frontiers** open between Morocco and Algeria – at OUJDA and, 300 km to the south, at the desert oasis of FIGUIG. Details on both of these are given in the relevant sections of the guide (see p. 85, 276) and you should read these before deciding which to head for.

The frontiers are a sensitive issue at the best of times, and one particularly absurd result of this is that the Moroccans do not usually allow non car-drivers to cross at Oujda. You can usually get around this by hitching – the train stops for some 15km or so on either side of the border – but don't count on it. Be warned, too, that Algeria can be a frustrating and uncomfortable country to treat as a 'transit': the **Trans-Maghreb Express** (officially from Rabat to Tunis) is not quite what its name suggests, invariably crowded and excruciatingly slow. Once in Algeria you are really much better off on the buses.

The fastest route through Algeria cuts across the big **northern cities** of ORAN, ALGIERS and CONSTANTINE. This is not in itself the most interesting part of the country though the mountain scenery is often spectacular. Making relatively short detours the rewards are greater.

TIMGAD, almost completely preserved, is one of the most extraordinary Roman towns anywhere; any one of the roads between BATNA and the immense oasis of BISKRA will take you through dramatic canyons; the *TURQUOISE COAST*, west of Algiers, is a long series of mountainous and isolated coves; and in the mountains by the Moroccan border, TLEMCEN's Islamic architecture is among the most important and beautiful in North Africa. Mosques, incidentally, may be visited freely in Algeria and to an extent in Tunisia.

If you have time to spare, though, even as little as a week, try to take in at least something of **the south**. The sheer size of the desert regions here is hard to grasp: TAMANRASSET, near the Niger border, for instance, is further from Algiers than is London. Closer, and easily accessible from the north, there are too some of the most spectacular Saharan dunes – stretching between EL OUED, so-called 'City of a thousand domes', and the fantastic architecture of GHARDAIA.

Movement in the Deep South really does feel more like travel than tourism and it needs time and energy to explore the desert *pistes*. The two really compelling attractions are both mountain ranges: the HOGGAR, rising over 10,000ft to the north of Tamanrasset, and the TASSILI, some way to the east with its exceptional prehistoric cave paintings. If you're spending any time down here – and above all if you are driving down to AGADES (Niger) or GAO (Mali) – Simon and Jan Glen's *Sahara Handbook* (Lascelles, £9.95) is useful.

Crossing from Algeria to **TUNISIA** is normally straightforward, though the number of border posts that are open vary according to the state of relations between the two countries. The most regular are in the north at ANNABA-BABOUCH and SOUK AHRAS-GHAR-DIMAO (the train crossing), but at the time of writing you can cross in the south, too, at EL OUED-HAZOUA.

Much more Westernised than either Morocco or Algeria, Tunisia is recognisably Mediterranean in character – a relaxed place to end up after a week or so of desert travelling. Its best-known attraction are the long white-sand **beaches** and easygoing resorts, and in a North African context these are perhaps its great novelty. But there is considerably more to the country than this – not least its highly individual **desert architecture**, and the Maghreb's most important **Roman sites** – and the accessibility of everything (you can comfortably travel its length in a couple of days) makes it a satisfying place to get to grips with. For a full treatment *The Rough Guide to Tunisia* (RKP, £3.95) seems again an obvious choice; it's available at the main Tunis bookshops.

Continuing from Tunisia there are daily, year-round **ferries** to the Sicilian ports of PALERMO and TRAPANI, and links beyond to Naples, Genoa, Sardinia and Malta. Apart from the last two weeks of August (when all ferries from Tunis are packed out with returning migrant workers) it is usually possible to get tickets on these; if you've a car, however, it's essential to book in advance for travel between July and September. Tunis, incidentally, is also a major link on international airline routes and you can often pick up **bargain flights** to Cairo, Nairobi, Casablanca and Algiers, as well as to Madrid, Rome, Athens and most points in Europe.

A last alternative, onwards from Morocco, is to make for the **CANARY ISLANDS**, which are actually just a few miles offshore from the disputed territory of the Western Sahara. There are no passenger ferries across but you can fly from the desert town of LAYOUNE (see p. 301) or from AGADIR.

LANGUAGE

Very few people who come to Morocco learn to speak a word of Arabic, let alone anything of the country's three individual Berber dialects. This is a pity – you're treated in a very different way if you make even a small effort to master basic phrases – though it is not really surprising. Moroccans are superb linguists, much of the country is bilingual in French, and anyone who has significant dealings with tourists will probably know English and maybe half a dozen other languages too.

If you can speak **French** you'll certainly be able to get by almost anywhere you care to go; **Spanish** is also useful, and widely understood in the old Spanish Colonial Zone around Tetouan and the Rif. For those with no French, a few essentials are listed at the end of this section but the bulk of words and phrases below are in **Moroccan Arabic**. This is substantially different from 'Classical' Arabic, or from the modern Arabic spoken in Egypt and the Gulf States, but it is taught in the schools and except in the most remote country areas is generally understood.

Arabic: words and phrases
Pronunciation. There are no 'silent' letters – you pronounce everything that's written. Letters and syllables in *italics* should be stressed.

BASICS

Yes, No	*Wa*ha, *La*	(Very) good	Mue*zyen* (bu*zef*)
Please	Min*fad*lik	Bad	Mushee mue*zyen*
Thankyou	*Shok*ran	Today	L'*youm*
Thankyou (Berber)	Barra*kla*fik	Tomorrow	*Ghed*da

GREETINGS

Hello, alright?	*La*bass	My name is . . .	Ana *is*mee . . .
Hello (formal)	O sa*lam* o-a*lay*koom	See you later . . . perhaps	N'shoof'k *min*bad *Im*ken
(literally 'peace be with you', to which the response is 'O-a*lay*koom salam')		. . . Godwilling	Insh'*Al*lah
		Thanks to God!	L'*ham*dullah!
Goodnight	*Lee*la sa*yee*da	Okay	*Wa*ha
Goodbye	B'*sle*mah	Fine	Mue*zyen*
What's your name . . .	*Shnoo smeed*'k	Watch out!	Ba*lek*!

DIRECTIONS, BUSES AND HOTELS

Where is . . . ?	*Feen* . . . ?	When is the bus?	K'*tesh* lekar?
. . . a (good) hotel	*Ou*tel (mue*zyena*)	First/Last/Next	*Le*wel/L'*harr*/ *Le*minbad
. . . a campsite	. . . mouk *hay*yem	Write it (please)	(Min*fad*lik) k'*tib*'h
. . . a restaurant	. . . restaurant	Have you a room?	Wush *l*'bit?
. . . the bank	. . . banque	Can I see it?	Wush *yim*ken n'*shuf*?
. . . the bus station	. . . *ma*tat d'l *ke*run	Is there . . . ?	Wush . . . ?
. . . the train station	. . . *ma*tat l'*qi*tar	. . . a (hot) shower	. . . *Doosh* (s'*hoon*)
. . . the toilet	. . . l'*mer*had	. . . a window	. . . B'*shu*razem
Left, Right	Lech*mal*, *Li*min	. . . a key	. . . *Muf*ta/Sa*rout*
Near, Far	*Qrib*, *Ba*'id	Can we camp here?	. . . Wush *yim*ken n'*hay*na

BUYING AND NUMBERS

How much (is that)?	Ish'hal (Hedi)?	I want something . . .	Wush Breet shihaza . . .
Write it please	Minfadlik k'tib'h	. . . different	. . . hurra
It's no good	Mushee muezyen	. . . better	. . . khyer
It's too expensive (for me)	Ghali bezzaf (aliya)	. . . larger/smaller	. . . k'burr/s'burr
		. . . cheaper	. . . marhess
Still too expensive!	Mazal ghali bezzaf!	. . . like that	. . . bhal hadi
Do you have anything . . .	Wush ghendek . . .	Okay!	Waha!

1	Wahid	9	T'saoud	30	T'lat-teen
2	Joosh	10	Ashra	50	Ham-seen
3	T'latla	11	Hadash	100	Meeya
4	Arba	12	T'nash	500	Hams meeya
5	Hamsa	13	Teltash	1000	Alf
6	S'ta	15	Hamstash	Kilo	Kilo
7	S'baa	20	Ashreen	½	Noos
8	T'minya	21	Wahid ou ashreen	¼	Arba

REACTIONS

I've seen it already!	Shuftaa	Help!	Ownee!
I don't want any	Mabreech	I've lost my . . .	Dee-aat . . .
I don't understand	Maf hemsh	. . . passport	. . . passeport
Do you understand?	Wush Fempteee?	. . . ticket	. . . teedkeera
		. . . key	. . . mufta/sarout
Get lost!	Imshee!	. . . baggage	. . . l'atat
Everything's great!	Koolshee muezyen	How do you say	
Let's go!	Yalla!	. . . ?	Keef t'koolaou

French essentials

BASICS AND GREETINGS

Yes/No	Oui/Non	Could you?	Voulez-vous?
Hello, good day	Bonjour	Why?	Porquoi!
Sorry, excuse me	Pardon	What	Quoi
How are you?	Ça va?	Open	Ouvert
Goodbye	Au revoir	Closed	Fermé
Please	S'il vous plait	Go away!	Va-t-en!
Thank you	Merci	Stop messing me about!	Arrête de m'emmerder!
I/You	Je/tu	No confidence!	Pas de confidence

DIRECTIONS

Where is the road for . . . ?	Quelle est la route de . . . ?	When?	Quand?
Where is . . . ?	Où est . . . ?	At what time	A quelle heure?
Do you have . . . ?	Avez vous . . . ?	Write it down, please	L'écrivez, s'il vous plait
. . . a room?	. . . une chambre?	Now	Maintenant
Here, There	Ici, La	Later	Plus tard
Right	Droite	Never	Jamais
Left	Gauche	Today	Aujourd'hui
Straight on	En avant	Tomorrow	Demain
Near	Proche	Yesterday	Hier
Far	Loin		

THINGS

Bus	Car, autobus	Key	Clef
Bus station	Gare routière	Roof	Terrasse
Railway	Chemin de fer	Passport	Passeport
Airport	Aeroport	Exchange	Change
Rail station	Gare	Post office	Poste
Ferry	Ferry	Stamps	Timbres
Lorry	Camion	Left Luggage	Consigne
Ticket (return)	Billet (de retour)	Visa	Visa
Bank	Banque	Money	Argent

BUYING

How much?	Combien?	Like this/that	Comme ceci/cela
How much does that cost?	Combien ça coute?	What is it?	Qu'est-ce que c'est?
Too expensive	Trop cher	How much, many?	Combien?
More/less	Plus/mois	Enough	Assez
Cheap	Bon marché	Big, little	Grand, petit

Phrasebooks and courses

Moroccan Arabic is so different to Classical/Gulf Arabic that all the standard, available English-Arabic **phrasebooks** are next to useless. There is in fact no English-Moroccan Arabic phrasebook, other than a small duplicated pamphlet available at the *Pension Castellana* in Chaouen, while the only popularly available French-Moroccan Arabic phrasebook – *Lamzoudi's Guide de Conversation* (Editions el-Atlassi, Casablanca) – is not particularly functional. If you're serious about learning it's possible to arrange **lessons** through the British or American cultural centres (see Rabat for addresses), or you could try to get hold of Ernest T. Abdel Massin's *An Introduction to Moroccan Arabic* (Univ. of Michigan, 1973) or Richard S. Harris and Mohammed Abn Tald's *Basic Course in Moroccan Arabic* (Georgetown Univ., 1980). Both of these books, along with introductory primers to the Berber dialects, are usually on sale at the **American Bookstore** in Rue Tanja, Rabat.

If you know no **French**, the most useful introductory phrasebook is the *French Travelmate* (Drew, £1. 25).

INDEX

UPDATE 1987

A number of changes, openings/closures and additions. Thanks to all readers who contributed accounts and information.

Basics

p5 Creative Leisure have moved. New address: 4a William St (2nd floor), London SW1 (Tel. 01-235 2210).

Moroccan Travel Bureau, 304 Coleherne Rd, London SW5 (Tel. 01-373 4411) are also worth a ring for flights/packages.

Encounter Overland (267 Old Brompton Rd, London SW5; Tel. 01-370 6845), an experienced overland tour operator, have started running 14-day trips down to Meski and the Todhra gorge.

p7 The **Gibraltar-Tangier hydrofoil** now runs daily, year-round. There is also a summer-only hydro service between **Gibraltar and Mdiq** (see p61).

p9 Costs. Prices for accommodation and food have risen by around 20-25% since publication. In 1986, however, the **dirham** was devalued by 40% against other currencies, so most costs have actually dropped in £/$ terms. Current rate for the dirham is 14 to the £1 sterling

p11 Maps. An excellent new 1:900,000 map of the country has appeared – **Hildebrand's Travel Map: 20. Morocco**: clear, up-to-date and highly recommended.

A limited selection of Moroccan **survey sheet maps** can be obtained in Rabat at the cartographic office in rue d'Annaba.

p12 Coaches. The train company, ONCF, now operate fast and very comfortable **express coach services** connecting Agadir, Tetouan and Nador to the express trains running from Marrakesh, Tangier and Taourirt (Oujda) respectively. Prices run about double those of local buses and compete with the grands taxis.

p13 Expedition routes. Another interesting source of information on hikes and hiking in the Atlas is *La Grande Traversée de l'Atlas Marocain* by Michael Peyron. It is written in French but there are summaries of several sections in English and a lot of the actual routing can be followed with an elementary level of French. It is available in larger book-

shops in Rabat and Casa and sometimes in the "Shopping Centre" in Imlil.

p15 Camping out in the winter months you'll need a warm sleeping bag even in the South – desert nights are cool. In the desert, strong tent pegs are also useful since winds can be surprisingly fierce.

p19 Official admission charges, with government tickets, have been introduced at major monuments.

p23 Harassment/hustling. Considerable measures have been taken against "unofficial guides" throughout Morocco and particularly in Marrakesh and Tangier. They've had some effect. On the negative side, however, laws brought in by the government to solve the problems can make ordinary, friendly relationships with Moroccans problematic. In theory at least, one of the laws allows arrest and imprisonment of any Moroccan (without a guide's permit) seen with a tourist; another, with a theoretical 15 year sentence, imprisonment of any Moroccan man found in a hotel room with a woman tourist. How long (or widely) these laws are likely to be enforced is impossible to predict. But if you do have a relationship with a Moroccan you may need to be discreet – particularly in Agadir and other 'tourist towns'. Or alternatively, be open – reporting in to the police to explain your relationship (eg as a family friend).

p25 Time. Morocco has a summer time-change (usually mid-June), GMT + 1hr. The remainder of the year is GMT.

Chapter one

p32 Airport taxis now charge a standard 70dh for the trip into Tangier.

Train services from Tangier have been greatly improved. There is a new, twice-daily express to Casablanca (currently at 7am and 7pm) that takes just 5)hrs: leaving on the early morning train allows ample time to catch the evening express **from Casa to Marrakesh** (which arrives about 9.30pm). Similar modern express connections have cut down the time of the **Tangier-Fes** journey, dispensing with long waits at Sidi Kacem.

p47 Asilah. *Hotel Oasis* has gone downhill – no longer recommended.

It is possible to get a taxi from **Asilah to Tangier airport** for around 30dhs, making the town a useful alternative to Tangier as a first/last stop. Standard fare for taxis **from the airport into Tangier** now seems to be 70dh.

p53 Ceuta border. The exchange office at the frontier accepts cash only. Don't be stuck with cheques or you'll be at everyone's mercy.

p61 Tetouan beaches. For a Mediterranean beach stay, *Camping Al Fraja* at **Restinga-Smir** is worth considering: a friendly, well-equipped place, which lets out secure (padlocked) tents. It's a couple of kilometres along the coast from the Club Med complex.

There is a more or less daily bus between Chaouen and **Oued Laou** (see below).

p63 Chaouen. *Pension Castellana* has changed hands and not everyone finds it that relaxed anymore. *Hotel Rif* has had positive reports, largely due to the manager, Mustapha; marked slightly wrongly on the map, it's in fact on the same road as the Salam (just above the 'B' of Bab Hammar). *Pension Ibn Batouta*, quieter than most, is also worth considering: it's signposted down an alley to the left about 30m into the medina.

The **hammam** next to the Pension Castellana now operates exclusively for women; westerners may be asked to hire it separately, in the evening, rather than paying to join locals.

The best **restaurant** in Chaouen is undisputably the *Zouar*, outside the medina. From the main square walk towards the walls of the medina then just before the gate head up the steep hill on your left – the restaurant is about 50m up on your right.

Daily **buses from Chaouen** run to **the Ceuta border** (11am; 2hrs) and also to **Oued Laou** (5pm; 1)hrs).

Chapter two

p73 El Jebha does have an occasional bus to/from Tetouan (6hrs) but it's becoming arguable whether you'd want to make use of it. The village's beach and sea have become polluted.

p82 Oujda. A good new hotel, with 1* prices and very reasonable meals, is the *Marrakech* (101 Rue de Marrakech).

p84 Algerian border. French francs are available for travellers' cheques at the border post. Two readers report being allowed to ride across the border on bicycles, despite warnings that this was impossible from the Algerian consulate

and the tourist office in Oujda.

Beware of 500 dinar notes – withdrawn from use in Algeria – which you may well be offered in Oujda at promising rates.

Chapter three

p100 Rabat. Greatly recommended new French-Moroccan **restaurant**: *Les Fouquets*, 285 Ave Mohammed V.

The *Oasis* **bookshop** has been closed as it was a 'front' for Christian missionary activities.

p111-116 Casablanca. Arriving by train at the **Gare des Voyageurs**, you can catch bus 30 into the centre from the square in front.

Airlines: British Caledonian have ceased operations in Morocco; British Airways have taken over and have an office at 57 Place Zellaqa.

The **British Consulate**, contrary to reports of its demise, continues – at 60 Blvd d'Anfa (Tel. 22.16.53 or 22.17.41).

p117 Travel Details. There are now some 3 trains a day from Rabat to Casa (Gare du Port) and another 5 to Casa (Gare des Voyageurs). See the update note for p32 for details of the new express connections with Tangier and Marrakesh.

Chapter four

p121 Meknes map. The main **train station** is just east of the Hotel Majestic – not as indicated.

There is an accessible **hammam** in the Medina close by the Maroc Hotel, just off Rue Roumazin.

p130 The Volubilis campsite has been closed down (for selling alcohol to Moroccans).

p136-169 Fes. Reasonable inexpensive **hotels** remain elusive: *Hotel du Parc* has been de-recommended by a lice-bitten reader. One good additional choice in the New Town is the 1*A *Hotel Kairaouine* on Ave Mohammed el Korri (off Ave Hassan II).

There is an excellent **hammam** (admission by ticket from booth outside) opposite the CTM bus station in the New Town; it's down an alley beside a fruit juice shop and newsagent.

Best place for **changing money/cheques** in the New Town is *Watabank*, across the road from the Credit du Maroc on Blvd Mohammed V.

Beware of **unofficial taxi drivers** who

wait at the train station and charge very unofficial rates for the trip into town; standard fare for this should be around 3dh50.

p177 Midelt. Good food and coffee at the *Brasserie Chez Aziz*, just before the *Roi de la Biere*. The *Hotel Excelsior* no longer lets out rooms and its restaurant too seems to have hit hard times – now distinctly unenticing.

p179 Around El Ksiba. Above the town, along the road towards Arhbala, is a long stretch of campsites, hidden away in the wooded Atlas slopes. Fabulous walking – and you could spend days going from one site to another.

p180 Cascades d'Ouzoud. Buses run fairly regularly from Beni Mellal to Azilal (and most days from Marrakesh to Azilal). Ouzoud is 12dh by collective taxi from Azilal.

Near the cascades is the so-called **Mexican Village**, a fascinating place with quarters interconnected by semi-underground passages. To get there, follow the path down to the bottom pools and then take the path climbing up to the west (left), past a farmhouse and up to the top of the plain.

Chapter five

p190-216 Marrakesh. Various **hotel changes**: the *Hotel de France* has new ownership and is now one of the best of the cheapies; the *Chellah* has become rather hustley; the *Central* is best avoided (beds by the hour); the *Gallia* is semi-exclusively gay; the *Hotel Minaret* (good value 2*; 10 Rue du Dispensaire) has recently opened in the street behind the Grand Hotel Tazi. The **youth hostel** manager has an annoying habit of not letting anyone wait until 7am – despite the fact that a lot of buses run at 5am!

Restaurants: the *Cafe el Fath* on the Djemaa el Fna has had very mixed reports. Much better is the *Restaurant Argana*, opposite the Banque du Maroc/Hotel CTM.

Bikes can be rented from various hotels in the New Town. Phone 439-06 or 453-20 for details.

Changing money at weekends, the *BMCE* on Place Foucauld (about 50m past the side entrance to the PTT) stays open till 8pm every day.

See the update note for p32 for details of the new **express train** links to Casa and Tangier – and see the update note for p12 on the new ONCF **express**

coaches to Agadir. See also the note for p221 (below) on buses from Marrakesh to **Asni**.

p218 Setti Fatma/Ourika. The *Hotel Chaumiere* has become a lot less luxurious; the *Atlas* no longer has rooms (though it lets roofspace); both now close for the winter months.

It is possible to walk, in a not too strenous two days, from **Setti Fatma to Oukaimeden** – staying at rooms overnight at the village of Timichi, reached by a path up the Ourika. This has been very highly recommended. So too has the hike from **Oukaimeden to Imlil** via Amsacrou and Ikiss – again very pleasant and fairly easygoing walking at altitudes of around 9,000-10,000ft.

NB. Boufraden Mohammed Bella is *not* a hiking guide. If you want information on routes ask at the first café you come to in the village: the people here are reliable.

p219 Oukaimeden. The CAF hut is not available to non-members though the guardian may let you stay one night. Even if you're not skiing, a ride up the teleski is worthwhile for the panoramic views, especially in winter.

p221 Getting to Asni. Buses for Asni now leave from the main bus station at Bab Doukkala – about every hour. They still stop at Bab Robb to pick up passengers but are usually pretty full by this stage.

p221/222 Atlas hiking Season. Depending on snow conditions, this can extend from April to November/December.

p223 Asni. There is now a fairly regular **taxi** service to Imlil (10dhs). If you're not in a hurry to leave, however, an enjoyable 2km walk from Asni will take you to **Moulay Brahim**, a very religious town perched on the mountainside; there is a fine hammam here and interesting sorcery stalls.

p224 Imlil. "1740km" (!) should read 1740m. Besides the CAF hut in the village there is a **cafe-hotel**, *Shems*, with cheaper (and dirtier) rooms. A couple of other small hotels are being built as well. **Guide/porter rates** displayed on the CAF hut are long out of date: reckon on around 65-75dh per day for a guide, 45dh a day (or 25dh to Aremd) for mules. The latter are arranged through the "chef", who will soon appear if you express interest. Guides – official or otherwise – are best negotiated with over a tea or three at the cafe.

p225 Aremd. The description on how to get to Aremd from Imlil is a bit misleading. The west side of the river is the Imlil side if you consider the CAF hut and "Shopping Centre" to be Imlil. On that side is the well-defined mule-track which climbs up above the river, levels out for a bit and then drops to the river again where it can be crossed to reach Aremd. There is now also a rough dirt road that more or less follows this track.

p227 Tachedirrt. The daily Berber truck from Imlil no longer operates. However, it supposedly runs on Saturday when the villagers travel to and from the souk in Asni.

p229-230 The Hotel Alpina at Idni has closed. Alas, following the death of Madame Gipolou the hotel and cafe are abandoned – the buses no longer stop there. If you find yourself stranded, the Berber cafe opposite does its best, offering bedmats and whatever food is available.

Ijoukak now makes a much better base for this area. There are no longer CAF facilities in the village but simple **rooms** can be found at either of the cafes. Walking out, you can quite easily explore the River Nifis, Tin Mal, Talat n'Yacoub (where an interesting mountain souk takes place on Wednesdays), the Goundafi Kasbah and the Agoundis Valley.

p239 Essaouira. The *Remparts* bar has closed but the **hotel** remains the nicest in town. If it's full, a good cheap fallback is the *Hotel Majestic* in Rue Lallaj Oud (right, off the top end of Rue Sidi Mohammed Ben Abdallah). *Hotel Atlantique* has closed.

There is an excellent value **hammam** (with robust massaging and body scouring) just behind the bus station.

Recently opened, the **Museum of Sidi Mohammed Ben Abdallah** (8.30-12 & 2.30-6, cl. Tues) is worth searching out: featuring exhibitions of marquetry and hennaing, as well as standard artesan collections, it is housed in a 19th century mansion in the road running down from the ramparts to Avenue d'Istiqlal. Next door is an **Ensemble Artisanal** which displays, without pressure, the best of modern local crafts.

The **islands** can apparently be visited. Small boats will take you across for around 200dh – ask around near *Chez Sam* at the port – and pay when they come to take you back in the evening!

Chapter six

p254 Ouazarzate. You can now **hire cars** in the town – and also at **Tinerhir** – for a trip up the Todrha gorge.

Hotels: the *Royal* is being modernised – excellent value; the *Saada* has closed. **Eating**, try the *Cafe-Restaurant Essalan* on Rue Marche.

p258 Zagora. Camping, beware of kids telling you that the *Montagne* **campsite** has closed and directing you to the *Amazrou*. The *Montagne* is still going strong and still far superior!

The *Hotel Tinsouline* has dropped a star (now 3*A), becoming a very tempting option. In addition, the hotel's head waiter organises **tours to Amazrou and the dunes south of Tamegroute**, where an overnight stop is made at a hotel in **Tinfou**, a place with an impressive air of unreality. The Tinfou hotel (3* prices) is run by a family of artists and even boasts a ramshackle pool; it is sited at the junction where the track to the dunes joins the main road.

p262 Skoura hotel. A *Hotel de la Palmerie* has appeared: pretty basic but the oasis is a much nicer place to stay than Ouazarzate.

p263 Boumalne du Dades. A new **auberge** has just opened, close by the big hotel.

p263 Dades gorge: Msemrir. At Msemrir there is a small cafe with a very basic room (floorspace and a mattress) to let.

p264 Tinerhir. The *Oasis* **hotel** is now a lot better than the *Salem*.

Exploring the **oasis** don't underestimate its size: the Ait Amitane kasbah is a 7km walk from town.

p267 Todrha Gorge/crossing the Atlas. The best days for getting lorries across to Imilchil/Arhbala are Thursdays and Sundays: if you turn up a day or two in advance, the manager of the *El Mansour Hotel* can usually fix you a ride. **Arhbala** is a 12hr run, including an hour's stop at Imilchil. From there you can pick up the daily (2pm) bus to Beni Mellal.

p269 Goulmina-Erfoud. An occasional bus does cover this route, running via Tinejdad in a little over 3hrs.

p272 Er Rachidia hotels. *Hotel Saada* is now defunct. *Hotel Renaissance* (19 Rue Moulay Youssef – the road opposite the bus station) is clean and good value for both rooms and food.

p274 Rissani. The **Sunday market** is worth trying to co-incide with.

Transport: in addition to the Berber

trucks there are also local landrovers (their park is almost opposite the cafes where buses arriving in town stop) offering rides to Merzouga. Getting *back* to Rissani from Merzouga can be harder so if possible try to arrange a return lift.

p276 Merzouga. The *Maison Berbere* (411 Souk de Rissan) has one of the best collections of **carpets/rugs** in the country: a must for anyone seriously interested in buying.

The **cafe-hotel** is about 1km walk from the 'main' village – well-run and with good evenimg meals. For other meals it's best to come with your own food as the village is so small there's little in the food line to buy. Sidi Harazem, however, is now usually available.

Merzouga's lake is well worth seeing. It is about a 3km walk from the cafe: across the 'Black Desert' (the sand here is specked with black cobalt rock) in the Rissani direction. The lake is home to a large flock of pink flamingos – a spectacular if somewhat bizarre sight – and a Berber tea tent.

p276 Figuig hotels. There is now an alternative to the *Sahara*. This is the newly built *Hotel Elmeliasse*, located above a petrol station on the right of the main road as you come into town from Bouarfa. Clean double rooms with shower and toilet en-suite for 50dh.

p278 Algerian frontier crossing. You now need to change £140 but this doesn't have to be cash – British/American travellers cheques are acceptable. The important thing is to have the money and the willingness to change it (which may well involve you in a 5km walk to the nearest bank).

Even more important is to have your **passport stamped in Figuig** before setting out for the border. If you haven't done so, you'll be sent back – no joke if you did the 8km on foot. The police station in Figuig, incidentally, doesn't open for passport business until 9.30am.

Chapter seven
p282-285 Agadir. First, an additional sight: the **Royal Palace** nears completion on the outskirts of town and looks spectacular – even from outside its vast encircling wall. Best vantage point is from the river estuary, 3km walk along the beach. If you're into **birdwatching**, the estuary itself is a sight, too – covered in flocks of sea birds.

A scattering of **practicalities**. The **airport bus** into the Place Salam has

become irregular: to save a potentially long wait, walk the 1km down to the Agadir-Inezgane road and catch one of the regular city buses. Some of the Agadir **banks** charge a 5dh commission for exchange of cheques: the one across from the Post Office does not and it opens for a couple of hours on Saturday mornings. A new **English bookshop**, *Crown Books*, has opened, right by the ONMT office on Ave Sidi Mohammed.
Car hire: *Afric Cars* (Blvd Mohammed V) are one of the least expensive agencies.
Motorbikes: the *Moto-Rent* (see p285) now offers Yamaha 125s at about 130dh a day (considerably less by the week) in addition to mopeds – well worth considering, though if you want helmets you'll have to bring them with you!
Hiking tours in the High Atlas and Anti-Atlas can be booked through the *Marocorama* tour agency on Blvd. Mohammed V: they are run by Dan and Christine Eitzen, Americans who speak good Moroccan Arabic and some Berber, and take in unusual and very well-planned routes. **Cheapest store**, for drink and much else, is the *Uni Prix* on the corner of Ave Sidi Mohammed/Ave Hassan II.

Moving on. Getting to **Taroudannt**, you can usually pick up a grand taxi direct from Agadir to 44 (which is also known as "Hoowara"). For most **buses**, however, it's still necessary to get to Inezgane and change. The proposed bus station move to Agadir didn't materialise and only *two* buses daily run direct to Marrakesh.

p286 Tarhazoute. The renting of rooms is officially illegal, as no tax is paid; the police make occasional raids, searching travellers at the same time for drugs.

p287 Immouzer. The *Auberge des Cascades* remains wonderful, though prices (at least initially quoted ones) are up to around 100dh double a night.

p290 Taroudannt-Marrakesh bus. Try to buy tickets the evening before: the bus often leaves full.

p291 Tata circuit. The two main **approaches to Tata** are from Taroudannt (*SATAS* bus 4 times weekly; 8-9hrs via Irherm) or Tiznit ("daily" at 5am). The road is being surfaced between Irherm and Tata and was completed as far as Tleta n'Tagmoute as of mid-1986.

The best part of the circuit is the road **between Tata and Bou Izakarn**. With your own transport the many oases along the way could easily be visited – even without, buses are rarely full so it should be no problem to stop off for a night. **Tisgui el Haratine** and **Oua Belli** are both beautiful, densely palmed oases. The kasbahs at **Aguerd**, **Ait Herbil** and especially at **Foum el Hassane** are worth visiting. Don't be put off by the apparent lack of accomodation in the area. The people here have a tradition of hospitality and asking at the cafes should always elicit a room.

At **Tata**, the largest of these oasis towns, there are three **hotels**: best of them, and with a restaurant, is the comfortable 1*A *Hotel Renaissance* overlooking the river at the bottom end of town. There is a **bank** and **post office** in the town.

Moving on from Tata, there are buses to Taroudannt on alternate days (early morning departure) and twice daily to Agadir via Tiznit at 4am and 7am. The latter, on weekdays, goes via Ifrane de Anti Atlas to collect the post.

A more adventurous possibility is to **head along the piste to Zagora**. This is a road for 4-wheel drive vehicles only but it is covered fairly regularly by truck. Lorries always leave Tata for Foum Zguid for the Thursday souk: you could stay at the cafe here and hitch a (supposedly quite frequent) truck on to Zagora.

p293 Tiznit and beyond. A very laid-back beach-resort, with similarities to Tarhazoute near Agadir, is **Mirleft**, reachable by bus or grand taxi from Tiznit. The town is set 1km back from a beautiful sweep of sand. There are several basic hotels, including the *Atlas*.

The **Tata bus** is supposed to leave Tiznit daily at 5am – though it doesn't always show up (see the note for Tata – p290, above).

p293 Tafraoute hotels. The *Salam* has burnt down. For cheap rooms try the *Redouane*, run by a friendly family who also serve very adequate meals.

There's a **hammam** at the opposite end of town (turn left rather than right where the bus stops).

On the sightseeing front, **Tafraoute's rocks** have become stranger still after a crazy Belgian artist painted several groups in bold primary colours. The effect as you round the corner on this ensemble is startling. Walk out to the Chapeau de Napoleon and follow the flat piste out of Agard Oudad for about 1500m: the art-rocks, pretty much unmissable (and unweathered), are over to the left.

At **Tazagha**, about 2km past the *Grand Hotel* there are some pre-historic paintings of gazelles – proving the theory that the desert was once a fertile plain-home to many animals now disappeared.

p297 Sidi Ifni. There's a huge **Sunday Souk** with storytellers, musicians, hundreds of donkeys and not a tourist in sight...

Hotel Bellevue has reopened. **Grands taxis** run to Goulimine.

p298 Ifrane de l'Anti Atlas can be reached by the Tata-Tiznit bus but you are safest getting a grand taxi from Bou Izakarn (5dh a person: a regular run). Ifrane is undoubtedly one of the most beautiful oases in the south, a really out of the way place that sees very few visitors. Be prepared for curiosity. Its pleasure lies in walking. The settlement consists of three kasbahs, endless walls and a large old fort. Outside are a series of Berber *douar*, surrounded by shadey, water channeled fields and springs. Get there and explore!

There is a clean but rather drab **hotel** on the road as you enter Ifrane, with a cafe that does meals. A more attractive base is the *Cafe de la Paix*, which has a few very nice rooms on the roof, with a balcony view looking out onto the valley and oases beyond. This is also the best place to eat.

If you are unfortunate enough to be stuck in **Bou Izakarn** the *Hotel Anti Atlas* is perhaps the best of a group around the main square.

Amtoudi – see the main text – is actually reached by a track 15km beyond Tagmoute and Tarhjijt on the Tata road; it is then another 25-35km of piste to Amtoudi (Id Aissa). The trip is a surprisingly popular one with tourists shuttled up from Agadir by landrover almost every day to climb up to the *agadir* and walk through the palm groves to a waterfall.

Special thanks on this update to Andrew Gilchrist, Pat Yale and Dan Eitzen. Also, for invaluable suggestions and revisions, to Elaine Webb and Mike Travers, Carolyn Hill, Steven Le Poole, Richard Marriott, Julie Lockwood, Lyn Williams and James Salmon.

HELP US UPDATE

We've added an interim **1987 update** to this first edition of *The Rough Guide to Morocco*. Next time round we will be re-setting the main text to make more extensive revisions – and will hopefully be adding further places, possibilities and accounts.

To do this, and to keep sharp all the basic information on hotels, places to eat, opening hours, transport etc, it helps enormously to get feedback from travellers using the guide. A couple of lines on a postcard can be invaluable; a detailed hiking route or a new *piste* description, still more so.

All **letters** that we include or make use of will be acknowledged and for the best ones we'll send a **free copy** of the next edition (or, if you prefer, any one of the other *Rough Guides*).

Please write to:

Mark Ellingham & Shaun McVeigh
The Rough Guides
Routledge & Kegan Paul
11 New Fetter Lane
London EC4P 4EE

The essentials of independent travel...

If you want to travel at your own pace, seeing what you want to see and keeping to a budget, the Rough Guide series and the services of STA Travel are invaluable.

STA Travel works exclusively for the independent traveller. We offer the greatest selection of low-cost fares worldwide, including over 40 different destinations across Africa. We can follow these up with onward flights around the continent, comprehensive insurance and a range of selected tours lasting anything from 1 week to 1 year for those who want more than the usual package.

So when you've read the book and want to go travelling, make sure your first call is at STA Travel.

TRAVEL OFFICES:
74 Old Brompton Road, SW7
117 Euston Road, NW1
25 Queens Road, Bristol
ULU, Malet Street, WC1
Queen Mary College, E1
Imperial College, SW7
London School of Economics, WC2
Ealing College, W5
Goldsmiths College, SE14
Kent University

Enquiries and Bookings
01-581-8233
STA Travel Africa Desk
01-388-2266

Government Bonded under ATOL 822 in Association with SATAC Charterers Ltd.